SAINTS AND FESTIVALS

OF THE

CHRISTIAN CHURCH

SAINTS AND FESTIVALS

of the

CHRISTIAN CHURCH

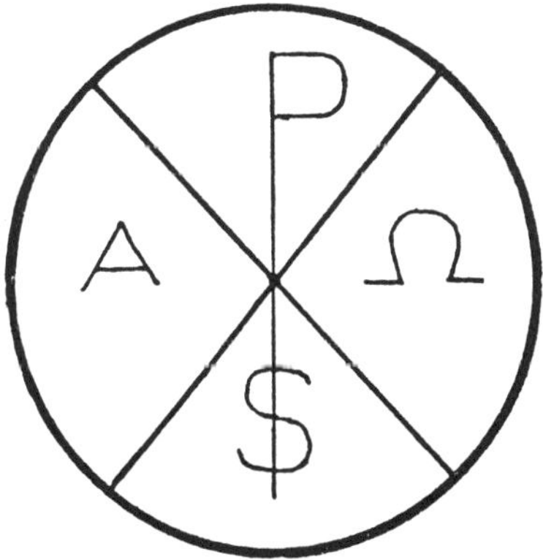

BY

H. POMEROY BREWSTER

Author of "The Cross in Iconography, Archæology, Architecture and Christian Art," "Christian Symbols," etc.

Illustrated

NEW YORK

FREDERICK A. STOKES COMPANY

PUBLISHERS

Republished by Omnigraphics • Penobscot Building • Detroit • 1990

Library of Congress Cataloging-in-Publication Data

Brewster, H. Pomeroy, d. 1906.
Saints and festivals of the Christian church / by H. Pomeroy Brewster.
p. cm.
Reprint. Originally published: New York : F.A. Stokes, 1904.
ISBN 1-55888-878-0 (lib. bdg. : alk. paper)
1. Christian saints—Calendars. 2. Fasts and feasts.
3. Christian saints—Biography. I. Title.
BR1710.B7 1990
299′.932—dc20 89-43339
CIP

♾ This book is printed on acid-free paper meeting the ANSI Z39.48 Standard. The infinity symbol that appears above indicates that the paper in this book meets that standard.

Printed in the United States of America

TO
THE CHERISHED MEMORY
OF
M. P. B.

PUBLISHER'S NOTE

A considerable part of the matter presented in the following pages was printed a series of articles in the *Union and Advertiser* of Rochester, N. Y.

The absolute truthfulness of these articles from both archæological and historic standpoints as well as their entire freedom from all denominational bias, with the knowledge of profane and ecclesiastical history and canon law shown in them, at once attracted a wide circle of readers and won the hearty approval of the clergy and laity of both the Protestant and Roman branches of the Christian Church.

On their completion, at the request of many eminent divines, the author has carefully revised the entire work, adding to the original MSS. much valuable material, and he has thus produced what is practically a Church Year Book in which is told the origin, history and present status of each of the chief festivals of the entire Christian Church as well as of a number of local feasts and festivals which obtain in certain parts of Europe. While it is beyond the scope of the present work to attempt to tell the story of every one of the numerous canonized saints whom the Church has chosen to honour, the author has each day throughout the year selected a few of the most noted among them and made brief sketches of the lives of those who are remembered on that day. But in the Alphabetical Index are given the name and "saint-day" of a far more comprehensive list; while in the general index will be found the names of those especially mentioned.

As the largest number of the feasts, fasts, and festivals of the Church occur on dates dependant upon the date of Easter, these are spoken of at approximate dates to be found in the general index; while others, like Christmas, whose dates are fixed are treated of on their proper days.

In conclusion we may say that this book is the only one published—except those huge tomes extending into from twelve to twenty volumes—wherein may be found such complete and tersely told hagiology.

CONTENTS

INTRODUCTORY.

KALENDARS—THEIR ORIGIN—WHEN FIRST USED—CLOG ALMANACS.

It was the custom in ancient Rome for an official to post in some public place upon the first day of each month a notice to apprise the people what religious ceremonies would occur during that current month. Thus the first day of every month came to be known as the Kalendae, from the Greek word "kaleo" (I call, or I proclaim) and so in turn our word "kalendar" or "calendar" (a book referring to days) was derived therefrom and by custom its original meaning broadened.

A similar custom to that of the Romans just mentioned also prevailed in Greece, but there the original Kalendar was not made public, an excerpt only of such portions of it being given out as the priests deemed best, and usually confined to notices of the feasts and festivals in prospect. The Kalendar in its entirety, with its astronomical calculations and astrological deductions, was preserved as a part of the esoteric learning of the priests, and to advise them when proper legal proceedings might be instituted.

About 300 B. C. one Encius Flavius, secretary of Claudius (Appius Cæcus the Blind), a consul of Rome and the builder of the first aqueduct through the Pontine marshes, exhibited these "fasti calendares," as the monthly proclamations came to be termed, upon marble tablets, which he placed in the Forum at Rome.

It has been said, but upon what, or how good authority I am unable to learn, that the Greeks of Alexandria during the time (or very soon after) of Ptolemy, the famous Egyptian astronomer, mathematician and geographer of the II. century, constructed written almanacs. In a similar way, and far from being proven, it has been claimed that there were Christian almanacs made in the IV. century. Whether these assertions are true or not, the first written almanacs of which we have any fairly authentic record date nearly a thousand years after those claimed for the Greeks of Alexandria. These were prepared by a learned Jew, a rabbi and an author, whose name is given by different writers as Ben Solomon Jarchi, or Raschi, and as Solomon Jarchus, the last being the one by which he is most widely known. He was born in 1104 and died in 1180, his almanac being dated in 1150.

Without doubt the most famous of these older almanacs is the manuscript almanacs preserved in the Savilian Library, Oxford, England, and was prepared by Petrus de Dacia and is dated "A. D. 1300." This almanac comments on the influence of the planets and the author has the credit of formulating the "Homo Signorum" (the Man of Signs) so commonly seen in our almanacs to-day.

The first printed almanac was published in Buda, Hungary in 1475, and the first one in England appeared in 1497, and bore the title of the "Sheapherds' Kalendar."

The first almanac "with predictions" was issued by Michael Nostrandum, which, strange as it sounds, was the man's real name. He was "a doctor of Oxford," a member of the Royal College of Physicians and a voluminous writer; born in 1503 and died in 1566, two years after his almanac appeared. By his contemporaries he was variously regarded. Not a few considered him "as a driveling idiot," while others held him in high esteem. Some of the stories told of him border on the ridiculous for his predictions were not confined to the weather but ranged over every possible subject, and being rather a shrewd guesser, he gained not a little reputation, especially among the more superstitious as "a prophet."

The next class of almanacs, and those which in some ways are the most interesting, since they give us an insight into the religious feelings of the people by "signs," not words, are the famous "Clog Almanacs," of which my readers will see many examples in the series of articles which will follow, for these "Clogs" were the household Kalendar on which the common people relied, to tell them when the feasts, fasts and festivals of the Church would occur and who the especial saint of the day was. There seems to be no date as to when, where or how, they came into existence, but, like the "tally-stick," or Robinson Crusoe's "calendar," were the outcome of necessity by people who could neither read nor write, yet must have some means of recording their daily life, transactions and, above all, their church obligations, until at last these "Clogs" were devoted wholly to the latter purpose. This was the case when we find the first mention of them in England.

In a folio written in 1636 by Dr. Robert Plot, an antiquarian and a somewhat voluminous author, there is a long account of them. Dr. Plot has been often and widely quoted on many subjects, and was a man of whom as noted a writer as Mr. Hargrave Jennings said: "He was both a very painstaking and reliable writer." For this reason I condense the long description of these "Clog Almanacs" for the benefit of my readers, though they have been published many times in more elaborate shape. Already when Dr. Plot wrote (1636) their use in England was widespread.

These Clog Almanacs consisted of a series of sticks, sometimes three or more, frequently four in number, formed of some kind of hard wood, upon which signs or symbols could be engraved. They were from two and a half to three inches square and eight to twelve inches long, with a knob or handle at the top of each. Each stick served, according to their number, for the record of three or four calendar months. When four were used the fourth side was used for miscellaneous emblems. The angle or corner of the stick was notched (see illustrations) each marking one day. Each seventh day was made prominent by a patulous stroke turned upward. Against these notches, as the case might be, a saint's day or some feast, fast or festival of the Church, symbols were engraved to denote the event. These symbols were in a large measure arbitrary creations and thus the Clogs of one locality varied from those of another, save in regard to the fixed church days, as one saint would be especially regarded in one locality, where in another some different saints' emblem would appear.

Occasionally these "Clog sticks" when intended for some public place were made very large and elaborately carved; but as a rule they were rather crude affairs and the engraving, even on the best of them, was seldom clear cut and clean, and in the specimens I shall give I have had them copied as nearly as possible exact, with all their imperfections, just as they appear in the set of Clogs from which they are taken, the original now being in Copenhagen, Denmark.

These Clogs were first introduced into England from Holland, but in these, as in the Danish ones, the symbols used seldom correspond with those used in Christian art and iconography, or even when they attempt this are little more than the rudest possible copies. To give an idea in advance of the character of these symbols the accompanying symbol of the New Year is presented. The perpendicular line being the angle or corner of the "Clog stick" and the one notch marks the first day, while the circle is supposed to represent the complete New Year.

To illustrate the crudeness of these emblems in many cases I copy the Clog Almanac emblem of St. Matthias the Apostle, which appears February 24th and which one would hardly guess is supposed to represent a leg.

These "Clogs" have sometimes been termed "Runic Kalendars," from certain "supposed" Runic characters found upon some of the earliest specimens, more especially those used during the reign of Queen Elizabeth in England. But it was no infrequent case that the owners of these sticks interpolated upon them designs of their own to mark some date or event which they wished still to keep secret, and when we recall the fact that the original meaning of the word

"Runic" is "secret," it is but a fair venture to believe that they received this name from this fact and not from the implied antiquity the name Runic gives.

The following illustration shows two of these Clog sticks, and if examined closely both of the illustrations of the symbol of New Year's and the emblem of St. Matthias will be found.

To turn, however, from these quaint and curious Kalendars, of which a small volume would hardly serve to tell their story, to the subject that will occupy the succeeding articles in this series, the mediæval Church made a marked distinction between the Feasts of Obligation and Days of Devotion. At the time of the Reformation, the Reformed church discarded most or all of the latter, but retained in the church a great number of the former, while the Roman Church still regard them as sacred.

As the articles to follow this are to be of a purely archæological nature and not theological, there will be no difference made in considering all the days recognized by both branches of the Christian Church and none intentionally omitted.

The list of the canonized saints who are recognized by the Roman Church and whose names were retained by the Reformed church and thus found a place in the Kalendar of the English church is a very long one; far too extended to be given in its entirety, much less for comment upon each. In the daily Kalendar prepared will be found the names of the most prominent of these saints, and mention is made of one or more, with a brief sketch of the life and the especial characteristics for which they were honoured by canonization. In so doing I necessarily refer to the popular legends of these saints for in very many cases these traditions are almost the only records left beyond a few bald, dry statistics. Nor shall I attempt to prove or disavow the authenticity or error of any of the legends which will be recorded. I can only repeat them as I find them; but where actual facts regarding the lives and work of the holy men is given it will be taken from undoubted authorities and will be given as fully as my space will admit. The order in which these names will be recorded follows that of the Kalendars and is not arbitrarily chosen.

It is a very curious fact and one seldom noticed, that these

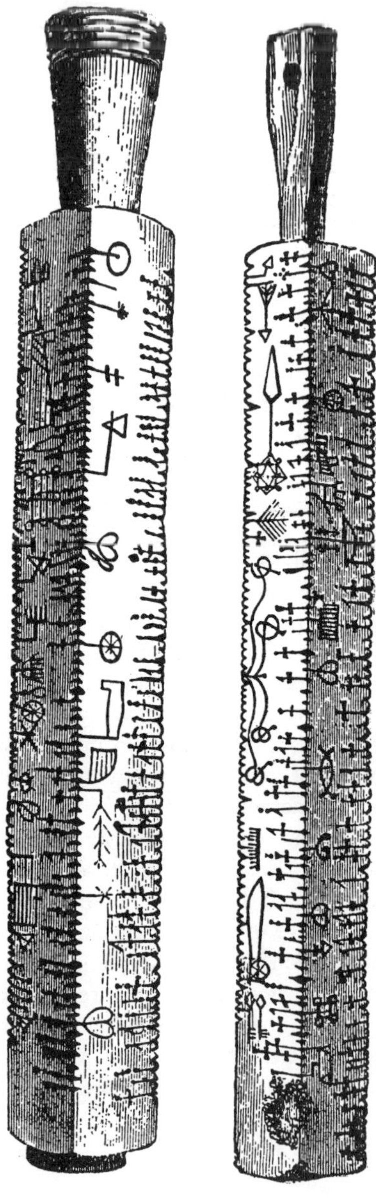

saints' days now only in a limited number of cases observed by the Protestant church were all retained and observed by them after the Reformation in common with their Roman brethren, and appear in all their Kalendars down to the time in 1752 when the change in "style" from the "old to the new style" took place, as everyone may see by examining one of those old quaint "Poor Robin's" Almanacs. Even then a very large number of the names of these holy men remained in the Anglican Kalendar, and thus by some, but utterly without reason, termed "Anglican saints," for there are *no such* saints. It is, however, ample evidence of the reverence in which these holy men were and still are held by the Protestant church to read the list of saints in whose honour so many thousand church edifices have been built and named in England, Germany and our own country and which will for ever keep their "saints' days" sacred.

In the Alphabetical Index

appended will be found the names of many saints not named in the daily Kalendar which includes only the more prominent of these personages.

The dates given are those which the Roman Church has fixed for their festivals.

On only a few especial festivals will the canonical colour for the day be given as every Church Almanac furnishes this information.

THE AUTHOR.

ADVENT

The beginning of the Christian Year has for ages been fixed by every branch of the Christian Church, Greek, Latin, Coptic and Reformed, upon Advent Sunday. This day always occurs upon the *nearest* Sunday to the Feast of St. Andrews, which is November 30th in every year; whether this Sunday falls upon a day before or after St. Andrew's day, and the four weeks thus included are termed the Advent Season. Thus Advent Sunday becomes a moveable feast, dependent upon the day when Christmas falls and therefore cannot come before November 27th in any year or later than upon December 3rd. Added to the universal usage, the Latin Church by ecclesiastical decree, at a very early period also fixed this day and selected the term "Advent" for the four weeks which immediately precede Christmas as a collective title to indicate the approach of the time which had been selected as the date of the Birth of Our Lord and Saviour, Christ.

"The Church has set aside," says an old writer, "the Sundays of Advent and the week days which follow after them as a solemn time of preparation for the great Feast of the Nativity; as Lent is before the Feast of the Resurrection, and therefore this time is called by some 'Altera Quadragesima.'"

It is claimed that this holy season was instituted by St. Peter, and therefore *is* apostolic. Be this as it may, while it is impossible —as is the case with many of the services of the Church—to fix its exact date of adoption, there is no doubt in regard to the extreme antiquity of the custom of observing these days in the most solemn manner. An homily written by Maximus Tauriensis, in 450, upon the observance of this day shows that it was regarded even then as "ancient," but unfortunately it fails to tell of its earlier history.

The canonical colour for the First Sunday in Advent is violet but at Vespers or Even-song the colour changes to red.

For the reason above given, I have selected the date November 27th whereon to begin the record of the Saints and Festivals of the Christian Church.

SAINTS AND FESTIVALS

OF THE

CHRISTIAN CHURCH

NOVEMBER 27th

Is sacred to the memory of one of those holy men who in the early centuries of the Christian Era did not hesitate to lay aside wealth or rank that they might serve the Great Master — St. Maximus, erstwhile bishop of Reiz. To him as a young man the world presented peculiar attractions. He had ample wealth, while his unusual manly beauty, his genial temperament and his wit made him an especial favourite both among men and women. Thus for years after reaching manhood he lived in the world and enjoyed its pleasures. But even during these years he felt there was "yet one thing lacking." His heart and conscience told him what that was, and at last he cast everything aside that he might attain the prize he sought.

Following Christ's teaching, he first distributed his worldly goods to the poor and then sought refuge in the monastery of Lerins. It seems needless to say his life here was in conformity to the great purpose which had led him to seek it, winning for him the love and respect of his brethren. It was this display of earnest purpose which induced St. Honoratus, the founder of the monastery and its first abbot, to select Maximus as his successor in the abbacy, when the saint was made archbishop of Arles in 426.

The chronicles of the day show that the monastery, already in high repute for its sanctity and learning, under the new abbot "seemed to gain new lustre," while the cheerfulness of the abbot made the "monks scarcely to feel the severity of the rules," and drew crowds of eager devotees to it.

True worth in man has in no age of the world allowed its possessor to remain hidden and thus it was that in 433, when the see of Reiz became vacant, Maximus was sought for to fill the episcopate. Much as he loved the peaceful retirement of his monastery, duty at all times took precedence above all else, and he reluctantly accepted the high honour. But with his new dignity he still remained the same humble, self-sacrificing, generous man he ever had been and in him his people found not alone a pastor, but also a physician and a teacher whom they loved and trusted. His ministrations continued during twenty-seven years until his death in 460. He is the patron saint of the diocese of Boulogne in Picardy, and the common people universally called him "Masse."

I must not omit mention of another saint whose festival is held this day, St. James, surnamed "Intercisus," a Persian, though I have not space for details in regard to this distinguished martyr of the time when Theodosius the Younger apostatized to win favour from King Isdegerdes. In many respects it is the old story of refusal by St. James to abjure the Christian faith ; but the manner of his execution was brutal, being literally cut to pieces. When his fingers and toes had been chopped off he calmly said: "Now the boughs are gone, cut down the trunk." But instead of this, one by one, his feet, hands, arms and legs were cut off and at last his head. The high rank borne by St. James as a noble of the first class added to his reputation for probity and justice made this vindictive exhibition of wrath against the Christians a most impressive object lesson for the moment, but it has served also to render the name of the faithful prince an immortal one in the Kalendar of the Church.

NOVEMBER 28th.

In the name of St. Stephen, "The Younger," of St. Auxentius Mount, which is remembered by the Church to-day, is presented one of the most renowned martyrs of the so-called "Persecution of the Iconoclasts."

Born in Constantinople, of a family of immense wealth, he had entered the monastery of St. Auxentius as a novitiate when fifteen years of age, and though we may not take time to follow his monastic life and his attainments, the latter are evident from the fact that at the age of thirty he was chosen abbot of the monastery.

Leo III., Emperor of the East, surnamed "The Isaurian" (718-741), infamous for his plunder of the Christian Churches, had also grievously persecuted the Jews, but at last had been "bought off" and "possibly as a part of the bargain" was prevailed on "to oppose the respect paid by the faithful to holy images."

In another place I shall remark upon these images, which dated even from the time of our Saviour. They included His, as well as many of His followers, but were neither adored nor worshipped; the Christians only holding them in reverence as the representations of holy men. With this as a pretext, Leo instituted a cruel persecution which his son, Constantine V., surnamed Copronunus, carried on for twenty years after he (in 741) became emperor, against these images. He died in 775. In 754 Constantine caused a council composed of 338 bishops known as "Iconoclast bishops" from their coinciding with his decree suppressing the use of images and to compel the "Catholics" (readers should recall the origin of this word) to conform to his decree. To this St. Stephen refused and soldiers were sent to drag him from his cell. At the same time "suborned witnesses," his legend tells us, charged him with "criminal converse with the holy widow Anne." He was examined and condemned to be beheaded, but this decree was changed to one ordering him to be scourged to death in prison. Learning later that St. Stephen still lived in spite of his scourging, the emperor cried out: "Will no one rid me of this pestilential monk?" It was then that certain courtiers went to the prison and dragged him forth through the streets with his feet tied by cords, and at last dashed out his brains with stones and clubs. The date of this deed is placed in 764, and took place under what has been called "Persecution of the Iconoclasts."

NOVEMBER 29th.

The holy man whom the Church honours this day is another of those early martyrs for the faith; St. Saturninus, Bishop of Toulon. The more I study the lives of these early Christians, the more I feel convinced that we in these modern days do not half appreciate the true heroism of these men who went forth of their own volition, under the guidance of their superiors to fulfil Christ's injunction to preach the Gospel to all the world.

It was in 245 that under the direction of the Pope Fabian, Saturninus went into Gaul to preach the faith to the idolatrous people of that nation. As we read the history of those days, we know what risks they ran both from the pagan priests and the neglect of those who should have protected them, as Roman citizens.

St. Saturninus fixed his see at Toulouse in 250, when Decius and Gratus were consuls, but they evidently gave but little aid toward protecting the holy man from the fury of the priests of the heathen gods. Yet for seven years this faithful man worked on until the pagan priests one day were able to secure his person and carried him into their temple and strove to make him worship at their shrines. Failing, they brought into the temple a wild bull, to which Saturninus was firmly bound by cords. Then after the bull was maddened by torture, they turned it loose and it started on its wild race, dragging the holy man by its side till, mangled and with broken bones, at last the cord broke and left the limp, lifeless body without the gates of the city.

NOVEMBER 30th.

This day is the feast of St. Andrew, as the Apostle and Martyr, and both of these festivals are rigidly observed in all branches of the Christian Church. He was a brother of St. Peter, but strangely, after the Ascension his name is not mentioned in the New Testament. His legends tell of his travels in Scythia, Cappadocia and Bythinia, and Russian folk-lore of his labours among the Muscovites in Sarmatia. He also was in Greece and from thence came to Patras, "a city of Achaia." It was here that, having converted

S. ANDREW. From Stained Glass in Winchester Cathedral.

Maximilla, the wife of Ægus the proconsul, he was condemned to be scourged and crucified. The form of the St. Andrew cross reaches almost every angle, from the acute to the right angle. It is said he chose this form of the cross out of his humility, saying he "was not worthy to suffer death as his Master had done."

Fastened to the cross by cords, not nailed there, but allowed to die amid the torment of thirst and starvation, who can realise his unutterable suffering? After four centuries a part of the relics of St. Andrew were brought to Scotland and since then he has been the patron saint of that country. He is also the patron saint of the "Order of the Golden Fleece of Burzmund," and in Russia of the "Order of the Cross of St. Andrew." Connecting St. Andrew with the Feast of the Advent, Wheatly says: "He was the first who found the Messiah (John I., 38) and the first who brought others to Him (idem I., 42) so the Church for his greater honour commemorates him as the first in her anniversary course of holy days and places his festival at the beginning of Advent, as the most proper to bring the news of Our Saviour's coming. St. Andrew is one of the most popular saints in the English Kalendar. An account of the churches in England says: "Every county except Westmoreland has several churches dedicated to St. Andrew."

He has been represented upon a cross shaped like the letter Y, but to speak of this opens an unending discussion I may not enter on here.

DECEMBER

Like the preceding months of October and November, December takes its name from the place it held in the Kalendar when ten months comprised the year. By the ancient Saxons, December was styled Winter-monat, or Winter month; a term which after their conversion to Christianity was changed to Hiligh-monat or Holy month, from the anniversary which occurs in it of the birth of Christ. Among the modern Germans, December is still from this circumstance distinguished as the Christ-monat.

DECEMBER 1st.

On this day the memory of St. Eligius, Bishop of Noyon and Confessor, is commemorated. A man who by his virtue and holy living rose from being the apprentice of a goldsmith to the high dignity of a Bishop. Being a youth of rare genius he soon not only became an adept in his chosen craft but had gained a wide reputation for the beauty and ingenuity of his designs. What, however, was far better, he had won by his unostentatious purity and upright life the confidence and affection of all who knew him. Having been sent to France on some business, Bobo, then Treasurer of Clotaire II., King of Paris (584-628), heard of him and brought him to the notice of the king who gave him an order to design and make him a chair of State, to be decorated with gold and precious stones, placing at his disposal the needed materials. So great was the satisfaction of the king at the manner the young man executed this command that Eligius was retained in the employ of the court. His former master, besides being a goldsmith, held the position of "Master of the Mint" at Limoges, and thus Eligius had also gained a knowledge of coinage, of which the French made use; for coins bearing Eligius' name issued during the reigns of Dagobert and Clovis II. as appears from Le Blanc's "History of Coins," are yet extant. But his chief employment seems to have been the designing and building of shrines for the relics of saints and the tombs of St. Martin of Tours and St. Dionysius (St. Dennis) are named as among those in the exceptionally long list credited to his wonderful skill as a designer and artisan. The favour of the king did not end here for he recognised in Eligius the higher traits of character which every one who came in contact with him did, also his great virtues, the purity of his life and his unbounded charity. Prosperous as he was his wealth was not lavished upon himself. The king often therefore, gave Eligius both clothing and money, which the latter in turn distributed to the poor, while at the same time he daily fed many of these from his own table even though he himself was fasting. He also was zealous in other good works, ransoming captives, providing for the sick and burying the dead of the poor, buying and freeing the slaves — especially the Saxons—who had been taken prisoners, and setting them free. One of these Saxons (afterward known as St. Theau, whose festival occurs on January 7th) Eligius brought up in his own household. But I must cease details, even omitting mention of the religious houses he founded and endowed, until in 640 (some put this date 646) Eligius went to Rouen, abandoning the honours of court life, and with his friend St. Owen received the episcopal office. Very soon after this our saint was chosen Bishop of Noyon, a district then still largely under pagan influence. With his usual zeal he threw his whole soul into his new work, and his success was equalled by few of his contemporaries, until on December 1st, in 658 the good man was called to his reward.

DECEMBER 2d

Is the passion of St. Bibiana, to whom a church in Rome, behind the Trophies of Marius, is dedicated. Her legend says:

In the time of Julian the Apostate there dwelt in Rome a Christian family consisting of Flavian, his wife Dalfrosa and his two daughters, Bibiana and Demetria. All these died for their faith. Flavian was exiled and died of starvation; Dalfrosa was beheaded;

the sisters imprisoned (A. D. 362) and scourged, Demetria dying at once under the torture. Bibiana glorified God by longer sufferings. Apronius, the prefect of the city, astonished by her beauty, conceived a guilty passion for her and placed her under the care of one of his creatures named Rufina, who was gradually to bend her to his will. But Bibiana repelled his proposals with horror and her firmness excited him to such fury that he commanded her to be bound to a column, and scourged to compliance.

I cannot, however, allow myself to describe the brutal manner in which the command was executed as it is too horrible for repetition, beyond saying she died, but retained her virtue.

The column to which St. Bibiana was bound still stands in the old church between the Santa Croce and Porto Maggiore in Rome.

DECEMBER 3d

Is the anniversary of the death of St. Francis Xavier, Apostle of India. This noted Jesuit was born April 7, 1506, and was educated at the University of Paris, where he later lectured and there shared a room with Peter Faber, a Savoyard, to whom he became tenderly attached. In 1528, Loyola arrived at their college a middle-aged man, meanly clad, worn with austerities and burning with zeal. Loyola made friends with Faber, but Xavier could not endure him and repulsed his approaches. Loyola discerning a desirable spirit in Xavier, nevertheless persevered. One day Xavier had been lecturing on philosophy and having met with much applause, was walking about in a high state of elation when Loyola whispered in his ear: "What shall it profit a man if he gain the whole world and lose his own soul?" The question startled Xavier, and changed the current of his feelings towards Loyola. He associated with him and Faber in study and devotion. Three other students joined them — Lainez, Bobadilla, and Rodriguez — and on the 15th of August, 1534, the six met in a subterranean chapel of the church of Montmartre and took vows of perpetual celibacy, poverty, and labour for the conversion of infidels. Such was the humble beginning of the Society of Jesuits. They resolved to place their lives at the service of the pope, and when preaching at Rome in 1540, Xavier was chosen to go as a missionary to India. A voyage to India was a tedious enterprise in the sixteenth century. He sailed from Lisbon on the 7th of April, 1541, wintered in Africa on the coast of Mozambique, and his ship did not reach Goa until the 6th of May, 1542. He found the Portuguese of Goa were leading worse lives than the heathen except that they did not worship idols, and their conversion was his first business. He learned the language of Malabar, and went preaching among the pearl-fishers, of whom it is said he converted 10,000. For seven years he faithfully laboured in those far off lands. At Malacca, then a great centre of trade, he met three Jesuits, whom Loyola had sent to his aid, and with them made a tour through the Moluccas. At Malacca, he had also met a Japanese whose account of his strange and populous country decided Xavier to visit it. He picked up as much of the language as he could, and in August, 1549, landed in Japan and for about two years travelled through the islands making a host of converts. His mission was continued with great vigour by the Jesuits for nearly a century, when for some cause or other the government took fright, massacred the Christians foreign and native, and sealed Japan against Europeans until our own day. He next determined to plant his faith in China, but the Portuguese merchants pleaded with him not to make the attempt, as he would assuredly be the cause of their utter destruction. Xavier was not to be moved by such alarms and persuaded a Chinaman to run him ahsore by night near Canton.

It was here, on December 2, 1552, the holy man died aged only forty-seven and in the twelfth year of his Asiatic ministry. His body was carried to Goa, and his shrine is to Catholics the holiest place in the Far East. In 1662 he was canonized, and by a papal brief in 1747 was pronounced the patron saint of the East Indies. His festival is observed on the 3d of December.

The pathetic story of this noble man is one of continuous labour in the cause of Christ and uncomplaining self-sacrifice on his own part.

DECEMBER 4th

Is the festival of a man who was somewhat noted in history, St. Anno, Archbishop of Cologne. He was a nobleman and an officer in the army when his uncle, a canon of Baneberg, first urged him to abandon the world for a religious life. He had long been a favourite of Henry III., "The Black," Emperor of Germany 1039–56, who made him provost of Goslar in Lower Saxony; later naming him in 1056 Archbishop of Cologne. From the time he entered upon his duties at Cologne the record of his life is one continued story of acts of love and charity to the poor and an earnest but well digested and firmly executed plan for the reformation of the monasteries in his diocese, which he found to be in a sadly demoralized state; lax in their ecclesiastical duties as well as in their habits of life. He added two new monasteries of the Regular Canons at Cologne and also three of the Benedictine Order elsewhere. After the death of Henry III. the Empress Agnes and the States elected him Regent and Prime Minister during the minority of Prince Henry (afterward Henry IV.) and he assumed the high and responsible position fulfilling its grave duties with such conscientious fidelity that he won for himself the love of the noblest and best but the utter hatred of a class of debauchees who had hoped through the Prince to profit by the death of Henry III.

At last, the Prince — now nearing majority — grew restless under Anno's strict rules of life and succeeded in securing his removal as Regent. But the extortions and injustice of these debauchees whom the Prince thus placed in power caused so great an outcry that "the States" were compelled to recall Anno in 1072, again to assume the administration of the kingdom. The burden of his double duties soon told upon his physical system and on December 4, 1075, he died, honoured and loved by all save the men whom he had thwarted in their purposes of public plunder. His name therefore stands to-day in Roman Martyrology as a true patriot and a faithful prelate of the Holy Church.

DECEMBER 5th.

The name of St. Sebas, one of the most renowned patriarchs of the monks of Palestine, is the first that is mentioned in Roman

Martyrology on this day. He was the son of a soldier and was born in 439. His father, being ordered to Alexandria, took his wife with him and left his son and the care of his estates with his brother Hermias whose wife treated Sebas so harshly that the boy fled to another uncle named Gregory for protection. Then quarrels arose between the two uncles, which finally led Sebas to seek a home in a monastery called Flavinia. A reconciliation of the uncles was at last made but in their avarice they wished to retain possession of the estate, and therefore left Sebas in the monastery. At length through fear or perhaps prompted by conscience, the uncles sought to induce Sebas to leave his retreat and to marry; but the young man had already made his election and nothing could bring him to change his mind, his hope and desire being to be allowed to join a band of converts in "a Laura" (retreat) some twelve miles from Jerusalem under the direction of St. Euthymius. But this good man decided that Sebas was too young for such a life and sent him to a monastery under the care of one Theoctistus, the house being a kind of "noviceship" to the Laura. Sebas was again tempted to resign his religious life; this time by his father in Alexandria, but his purpose was already fixed and he soon found a place of retirement far from human habitations, and for years lived a hermit and at last built for himself and a few devoted men cells in an almost inaccessible spot, over which the Patriarch of Jerusalem made him "exaroh," or superior-general, and which grew at length into an extensive monastery with several hospitals attached. Here, until at the extreme old age of ninety-four, the holy man devoted his life to good works and holy living. He died December 5, 532.

DECEMBER 6th

Is the festival of the noted St. Nicholas, Bishop of Myra. His story is a most marvellous one. From his infancy it is said he displayed such devotional tendencies that his legend says: "He refused to suckle on Wednesdays and Fridays, the fast days appointed by the Church." At an early age he entered the monastery of Sion, later becoming its abbot, a position he held until he was made Archbishop of Myra, where he became noted for his

S. NICHOLAS.
From a MS. in the Bodleion Library.

humility and charity. Beyond doubt St. Nicholas is one of the most popular saints of Christendom; he is invoked as the protector of sailors, and as the patron saint of schoolboys. Mr. Warton says that the custom of going *ad montem* at Eton originated in an imitation of some of the ceremonies and processions usual on this day; but there was no similarity in the two festivities. The procession *ad montem* was held about June 25th. Many legends and miracles are related of this saint, the following being among those by which he is best known. He early succeeded to large riches which he devoted to charity; a special instance of which was exhibited in the case of a nobleman in the city where the saint lived, who being reduced to poverty contemplated abandoning his three daughters to a sinful course as the only means of keeping them from starvation; but Nicholas, hearing of this, went to his house secretly three nights in succession, and, by throwing in at the window at each visit a purse of gold, saved them from infamy.

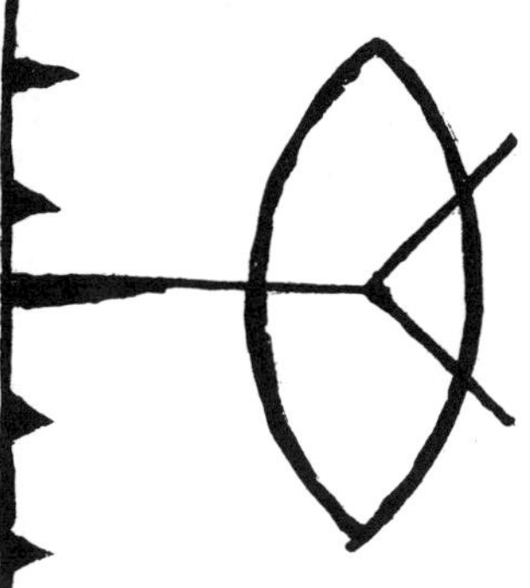

From this incident in his life is derived apparently the practise formerly, if not still, customary in various parts of the continent, of the elder members and friends of a family placing on the eve of St. Nicholas' Day, little presents such as sweetmeats and similar gifts in the shoes or hose of their younger relatives, who on discovering them in the morning are supposed to attribute them to the munificence of St. Nicholas. In convents the young lady-boarders used on the same occasion to place silk-stockings at the door of the apartment of the abbess, with a paper recommending themselves to "Great St. Nicholas of her chamber." The next morning they were summoned together to witness the results of the liberality of the saint who had bountifully filled the stockings with sweetmeats. From the same instance of munificence recorded of St. Nicholas, he is often represented bearing three purses, or three gold balls; the latter emblem forming the well-known pawnbrokers' sign, which with a fair degree of probability has been traced to this origin. It is true indeed that this emblem is proximately derived from the Lombard merchants who settled in England at an early period, and were the first to open establishments for the lending of money. The three golden balls were also the sign of the Medici family of Florence, who, by a successful career of merchandise and money-lending, raised themselves to the supreme power in their native state. But the same origin is traceable in both cases — the emblematic device of the charitable St. Nicholas.

Another legend is told in two different ways. One is that during a famine a certain landlord of an inn was in the habit of stealing children and cutting up their bodies which he pickled as pork, and that St. Nicholas made the horrid discovery of this, and by his making the sign of the cross over the tub where the children lay they were returned to life. It is from this that St. Nicholas is represented almost always as in our illustration with three children in a tub. The other version of the legend makes the victims young men who were travellers.

St. Nicholas as the patron of sailors sometimes has an anchor or ship represented in his pictures.

Perhaps nothing proves more conclusively how popular St. Nicholas is in England than that no less than three hundred and seventy-five churches have been dedicated to him in England alone.

To tell the story of "THE FEAST OF ST. NICHOLAS" would occupy far more space than I have allotted me; but it has become such an "household tale" that mine will hardly be missed.

DECEMBER 7th.

The date of the ordination of St. Ambrose, whose festival occurs on April 4th, is observed this day at Milan. On the above date a short sketch of this eminent man will be given, though in part repeated here:

"The election of Ambrose to the bishopric of Milan is perhaps unequalled in the singularity of all its circumstances. He was carefully educated when young for the civil service, becoming an advocate and practising with such success that at the age of thirty-one he was appointed governor of Liguria. In this capacity he had resided five years at Milan, and was renowned for his prudence and justice when Auxentius, the Arian bishop, died A. D. 374."

It was the opportunity thus offered which roused the Catholics to exert all their power to secure a man of orthodox faith as a successor of the late bishop. So intense was the feeling of both parties that a riot seemed imminent and Ambrose, then prefect of Milan, deemed it his duty to attend the conclave not dreaming of the result. Therefore he hastened to the church where the people had assembled and exhorted them to peace and submission to the laws. His speech was no sooner ended than a child's voice was heard in the crowd, "Ambrose is bishop!" The hint was taken at once and the whole assembly cried out, "Ambrose shall be the man!" The contending factions agreed and thus a layman whose pursuits seemed to exclude him altogether from the notice of either party was chosen by universal consent.

DECEMBER 8th.

THE CONCEPTION OF THE BLESSED VIRGIN.

This Feast which is recognised in the Kalendar of the English church as well as in that of the Roman, is one regarding which a long controversy prevailed.

It is well known that the doctrine of the immaculate conception of the Virgin, of her conception without the taint of original sin, was till recently a theological dogma on which the Church of Rome had pronounced no positive decision. Though accepted by a majority of doctors and strenuously maintained by many theological writers, it was, nevertheless, denied by some, more especially by the Dominicians, and was pronounced by several popes to be an article of faith which was neither to be absolutely enforced nor condemned — a point in short on which the members of the church were free to use their private judgment.

For centuries this question had been the subject of many learned and earnest discourses.

The Feast was instituted by St. Anselm, Archbishop of Canterbury, about the year 1070, to commemorate the escape of the fleet of William the Conqueror from a violent storm. Even from the first the Feast seems to have had those who opposed its recognition, and the discussion went on in England until the Council of Oxford in 1220, when it was decided to leave its observance optional. Indeed it is only within our own day and generation that through the action of Pope Pius IX. in 1854, that the mooted point was settled when he as the head of the Roman Church officially recognised it as a feast of the universal church and named this December 8th as the day for its observance.

In Christian art the conception of the Virgin in most cases shows the Holy Virgin as trampling on the head of a serpent or dragon. Le Clerc represents the Virgin as kneeling in prayer and a bright star appearing to her entranced vision. In the Clog almanacs a plain, unadorned heart is the simple emblem used to mark the day.

Readers must not confound the above Clog symbol with that of the Annunciation of the Virgin, on March 25th, for they are very similar and easily mistaken the one for the other.

In Roman Martyrology we read that to-day at Rome the memory of the Blessed Eulychian, or Eulychianus, Bishop of

Rome and Pope (275–283), is kept sacred: one "who with his own hands buried in diverse places, three hundred and forty-two martyrs. Under the Emperor Numerian, he became their companion, being crowned with martyrdom and buried in the cemetery of Callistus."

This day is also the festival of St. Romaric or Romaricus, abbot of the monastery of Luxeuil, who being the first nobleman at the court of King Theodobert, renounced the world and by his saintly life and the strict observance of the severe monastic discipline has since his death in 653, been held up as a model and example to be followed by all members of monastic orders.

DECEMBER 9th.

When in 297 Emperor Maximian returned victorious from the defeat of the Persian army he celebrated "the quinquennial games" at Samosata, the captial of Syria Comagene, on the banks of the Euphrates; commanding all the inhabitants to assist in the solemn supplication of the gods. The entire populace seemingly responded to the summons, and the air was filled with the noise of trumpets and infected with the odour rising from the burning victims which were being offered in honour of their god. Two men, however, of noble birth and of wealth, had not joined in the general ovation. These were Hipparchus and Philotheus, who had some time prior to this embraced the Christian faith and were then in the house of Hipparchus on the eastern wall engaged in their devotions. With them were five younger men who were seeking instruction from their elders. This was on the third day of Maximian's festival and the emperor had been enquiring in regard to any who had failed to obey his mandate. Then it was that the names of these two nobles came up and messengers were dispatched to bring them into the emperor's presence. Of course the five young men were found with their friends and the whole party was taken into the audience chamber; when the customary form was gone through with and condemnation to the rack and scourge ensued, and after, imprisonment coupled with torture to induce them to do honour to the gods. But each remained true to the faith until at last Maximian, out of patience at their firmness, ordered them to be crucified, — a by no means uncommon mode of inflicting the death penalty both before the time of our Lord's crucifixion and centuries afterward, — without the gates of the city.

These are the Seven Martyrs of Samosata, whom the Church honours this day.

DECEMBER 10th.

St. Melchiades, who succeeded Eusebius in the see of Rome in 311 and filled this high office until his death on December 10, 314, is remembered this day for the persecution he suffered during the reign of Maxentin until the tyrant was vanquished by Constantine.

This day is also the festival of a young virgin and martyr, St. Eulalia of Merida, whose triumphant death is celebrated by the great poet Aurelius Prudentius Clemens. This maid was but twelve years of age when Dioclesian promulgated his fearful decree which caused the martyrdom of so many thousand faithful Christians. On learning of the edict Eulalia went to the prefect of Merida — then the capital city of Lustiania in Spain, now the dilapidated town of Estremadura — and reproached him for his cruelty to the Christians. Indignant at what he declared an insult from "a chit of a girl," the governor at once seized upon her, placing the implements of torture on one side and on the other the offerings for the idols, bidding her choose between them. She cast the offerings on the floor and trampled upon them, and in Roman Martyrology for this day we read: "Finally she was stretched on the rack, torn with iron claws, had her sides burned with lighted torches, and when fire was forced down her throat she expired."

St. Leocadia, a native of Toledo and a friend of Eulalia, when she heard of her death, was already in prison under order of Dacian who had condemned Eulalia, and she kneeled and prayed she might not be separated in death from her loved friend, when as if in answer to her prayer she almost immediately died. The festival of St. Leocadia is fixed for December 9th, a day before that of St. Eulalia.

DECEMBER 11th.

St. Daniel, "the Stylite," whose festival occurs this day, is another of those eccentric holy men who for reasons that seem beyond our comprehension, of their own free will elected to pass their days in the narrow limits afforded by the top of a pillar or column, and who are known as "pillar saints," of whom I shall speak more fully in another place. St. Simon, whose festival occurs on September 3d, was one of these "pillar saints." His column was in Antioch, and it was from seeing him that Daniel was inspired to lead a similar life. For this purpose he chose a spot in the desert mountain bordering on the Euxine sea about seven miles north of Constantinople. Here a friend built for him a pillar, or rather two pillars one above the other, and on the top one surrounded by a balustrade was a vessel like a half barrel in which he dwelt. In 463 the lord of the manor built for Daniel a new (and funny as it sounds) "more commodious pillar." But exposure had its natural result and his limbs were covered with ulcers. Still, he would not leave his chosen home and when he was ordained as a priest Gennadius, Bishop of Constantinople, who performed the ceremony, the ordaining priest, read a portion of the service at the foot of the column, and then climbed to the top to complete it, perhaps the most unique ceremony of its kind in the annals of the Church. A barbarian prince whom Daniel had converted built for the saint a third pillar in part sheltered from storms, and Emperor Leo caused a roof to be placed over his usual standing place — for the saint slept standing — from which he ministered to his disciples. An endless list of miracles and prophecies that were fulfilled are credited to St. Daniel, who thus lived to the ripe age of four

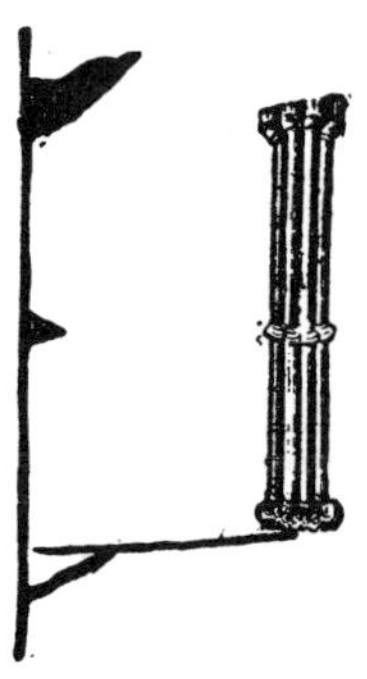

score years, foretelling his own death, which occurred on his pillar December 11, 494.

DECEMBER 12th

Is sacred to one of the most noted as well as most learned men of his age, St. Finian or Finan, Bishop of Cluin-Irard (called Clonard); of whom and of whose celebrated monastic school I shall speak especially in connection with St. Columba, who was one of his pupils, and also the incident of the stolen Psalter and its dénoument, which made St. Columba the first Christian missionary to the Picts and whose monastery at Iona was the beginning of the Christian Church in what is now Scotland.

Next to that of St. Patrick among the primitive teachers in those splendid monastic schools which made Ireland famous during the V., VI. and VII. centuries, stands the name of St. Finan. In his youth he had been taught by the disciples of St. Patrick but like the true student, his thirst for knowledge led him at an early age to seek for this in the famous schools in Wales which had been founded by SS. David and Gildas. After a long residence in Wales St. Finan returned to Ireland in 520, and among other monastic schools which he founded was that of Clonard in Meath, from which came many of the most famous saints, scholars and doctors of Ireland. In the long list of these we read the names of Klaran, "the Younger" Columkille, the two Brendans, Columba, and others equally noted for their piety and learning. Indeed it is not too much to claim that Clonard was in its day the most famous seminary of sacred learning in Ireland, through the wonderful inspiration of its leading spirit. In this school Mr. Skene, in his "Celtic Scotland," says "there were no fewer than three thousand monks." In speaking thus, my readers should remember the full signification of this word "monk" in those earlier days, embracing as it did not only those in holy orders, but the students themselves. I have no space to deal in detail with the influence exerted by this wonderful man; but a single quotation from Dr. Skene's "Monastic Church in Ireland" shows the estimate placed upon St. Finian by this clear-headed discerning Scotch writer. He says: "These expressions all point to an effete, decaying church, restored through the medium of Finian and his monastic school at Clonard and to a great revival and spread of Christianity through a new and living organisation, based upon the monastic institution."

Interesting as the subject is, I cannot enlarge upon it beyond saying that it was by and through the efforts of Finian these monastic schools came to be hardly second to those of Rome. Finian died on December 12, 552.

The St. Columba whose festival is also held this day must not be confounded with St. Columba the "Apostle of the Picts," yet both were pupils of St. Finian.

DECEMBER 13th.

The story of St. Lucy or Lucia, whose name appears in both the Roman and English Church Kalendars, is, even as told in an "English Church Year Book," like some fairy tale; but there is much in her sad life which alas! is only too true. She was born in Sicily, very wealthy, and endowed with almost angelic beauty, a fatal gift which had inspired both the passion and love of a noble (by birth but not as will be seen, character) pagan who against her wishes was betrothed to her. It was in vain that she pleaded with her mother Eutycia, to prevent this betrothal—even when assured that Lucia had taken on herself vows of chastity—until the mother was stricken with what seemed a mortal malady. Persuaded at last by the pleading of her daughter, Eutycia visited Cantania to pay her vows at the shrine of St. Agatha. As the mother and daughter kneeled at the shrine, Lucia had a vision in which St. Agatha assured her that her mother was healed of her infirmity and that she (Lucia) should obtain the favour of Heaven for Syracuse, the city where she then lived. When Eutycia found herself restored she at last yielded to the

S. LUCY.
From a Painting in the Spanish Gallery at Louvre.

importunities of Lucia to annul her betrothal. This did not suit the young pagan, who swore "her beautiful eyes haunted him day and night." With an heroic resolution to end the trying affair Lucia deliberately "cut her eyes out of their sockets and sent them to him; begging that henceforth she might be left in peace." But to quote still from the legend: "God rewarded her for her sacrifice by restoring her eyes, an hundredfold more beautiful than ever before." After this she gave her entire dowry to be distributed to the poor of Syracuse. This last act so enraged her lover that he went to Pascasius, who under the edict of Dioclesian, ordered her to sacrifice to the gods. She refused. Then came the most brutal of the means (not uncommon then used) to secure her consent to sacrifice. She was taken to a brothel, there to be defiled. A fact that is literally true. But she had such strength given her that even the brutes employed at last desisted and she was carried to prison. Once more the Governor ordered her to do sacrifice to the gods or be condemned to death. Again she refused; but when the soldiers attempted to remove her by force for execution she stood as if rooted to the ground, and they could not move her. Even when ropes and pulleys were applied they proved powerless. A fire was kindled on the stone floor around her, but that too, did her no harm; at last one of the servants of the Governor, thinking to pleasure him, stabbed her in the neck with a dagger. Thus in most Clog Almanacs a dagger marks St. Lucy's day. An English Clog has a gridiron for the emblem of St. Lucy, but this would seem far more fitting for St. Laurence. In Christian art St. Lucy is usually represented as in our first illustration, holding a plate in one hand on which are her eyes and a palm branch in the other. Sometimes a pilgrim's shell is substituted for the plate. Again in allusion to her name, Lucia, she sometimes holds a lamp and more rarely still is standing by a flaming cauldron.

DECEMBER 14th.

The study of the lives of the saints of the early Church constantly brings us in contact with the history of the various parts of Europe where the man under consideration lived, and to understand the man and his life we must know of his surroundings. It is for this reason that the scraps of history which I shall record will be introduced. It is thus to-day, when speaking of St. Nicasius and his band of Christians at Rheims, in the beginning of the V. century, then a part of Gaul and in which city a flourishing church had existed for a long time, as St. Nicasius was its ninth bishop, we know in Germany not a few of the Vandals were Arian Christians while the Goths were yet pagans. But both the Goths and Vandals were at enmity at all times with Gaul and it is a mooted point therefore with historians whether the "barbarians" who are said to have besieged and plundered Rheims in 407 were Goths or Arian Vandals. As we have ample evidence of the deadly hatred existing in the hearts of the Arians toward Orthodox Christians, practically it mattered little to the faithful in Rheims which they were who attacked them. Those old worthies of the Church were sturdy men of valour and as such at all times of danger they became leaders not only of their disciples but of others. Thus it was Nicasius appears in the forefront of the battle of the denizens of Rheims for their homes. From the first the Bishop saw defeat was almost certain; but this was no reason why they should not do their duty, and everywhere on that eventful day he was seen going from door to door and from one armed band to another regardless of the personal danger for his own life that he might save others. But the barbarians were too strong and well trained for the peaceful citizens long to resist. Still when they entered the city they met the doughty Bishop fighting them at every step with his Deacon and Lector at his side and thus it happened the holy man was one of the first who fell beneath their sword. Not very far away from this scene of battle, his sister Eutropia watched and waited the outcome for she knew only too well that the defeat of the citizens and capture of herself by their enemies meant the despoiling of her honour though she had done nobly her share and welcomed death rather than to yield to what was worse. These are the saints the Church still keeps in memory by the services held this day in their honour.

DECEMBER 15th

Is the festival of St. Eusebius, Bishop of Vercelli (now in Piedmont) and whose name is especially remembered from the fact that Pope Liberius deputised him with Lucifer of Cagliari to ask the Emperor Constantine to assemble the council which met at Milan in 355, at which time Constantine laid the Nicene creed on the table insisting that all present sign that rule of faith to govern them, before they took up the case of St. Athanasius — the champion of the Orthodox Church — which was then to be considered. The Arians were in the majority of those present but violent as they ever seemed to be, either dared not or would not submit to the demand of the Emperor. Thus, when Dionysius of Milan rose to affix his signature to the paper, Valeus, Bishop of Mursia — one of the most violent of the Arians —" darted forward and snatched the obnoxious document from his (Dionysius) hands, tearing it into fragments which he cast on the floor and then broke the pen into pieces." An adjournment to the palace of the emperor followed and the hasty condemnation of St. Athanasius. To this verdict St. Eusebius objected and refused to sign as did Dionysius and Lucifer of Cagliari, believing St. Athanasius innocent. Whereon the Emperor in rage cried out: " Obey me, or you shall be banished." On a second refusal soldiers entered and tore the holy prelates from the altar, conveying Dionysius into Cappadocia where he died; Lucifer to Syria, and Eusebius to Scythopolis in Palestine to be dealt with by the Arian Bishop Patrophilis. Pope Liberius, powerless to help them, still wrote encouraging letters. The story of Eusebius' sufferings is too long to repeat but on the death of Constantine in 361, Julian gave permission for the banished Bishops to return to their sees. The Bishop seems to have travelled extensively in the East and through Illyricum, preaching and confirming many who had gone astray from the true faith, before his death in 371.

The Roman Missal and Breviary place his office for December 15th. This, however, is supposed to be the date when his relics were translated to Vercelli, as his death is believed to have occurred on August 1st.

DECEMBER 15th.

On this day the first of a series of nine anthems in the Latin service of the English pre-Reformation Church used to be sung in honour of Christ's Advent, taking their place in the ritual, and the anthems were continued to Christmas Eve.

This day is the festival of St. Alice, or as she is often called, Adelaide, whose eventful life might well serve for an historical story of the early part of the X. century as it covers a period full of stirring events in continental history and life in several prominent courts of Europe. I have not the space to tell this story as it should be told ; for abridged as it must be it loses much in historic interest.

The second Burgundy, often called Arles in early days, was erected by Charles II. (The Bold) in 877. In 931 Rudolph or Ralph II. was king of Burgundy when his wife bore him a daughter whom they christened Alice ; though she is often spoken of as Adelaide. Her father died in 937 when she was but six years of age and when sixteen she married Lothaire, king of Italy, and her daughter Emma married Lothaire, king of France. Lothaire, king of Italy and husband of Alice, died in 949, at which time the trials of the young widow began. Berengarius III., the Margrave of Jurea, who by conquests had already possessed himself of Lombardy, and who was an openly declared enemy of Lothaire, succeeded the late king and almost immediately upon some pretext imprisoned Alice the late queen. After some years Queen Alice managed to escape from her prison and fled toward Germany, being met, however, before her arrival by Prince Otho (afterward Otho I.) who at the solicitation of Pope Agapetus II. had raised an army of 50,000 men and was marching to secure her release. Continuing his march he conquered Paris and finally made a treaty with Berengarius, which was soon broken by the latter and a second expedition was sent out which captured the faithless king of Italy, and he was sent a prisoner to Germany where he died. In 963 Otho was crowned Emperor of Germany at Rome, and was married to Alice immediately after his coronation. Otho (the Great) died in 973 and his son Otho II. became emperor, and while under the guidance of his mother, Queen Alice, all went well, but under evil advisors her son at length banished her from court. After nine years, when Otho II. died, Alice was recalled and made regent. Such was the tortuous, trying life of this good woman of whose inner life I have not spoken as it seems so separate and apart from her outer and public life. Except by following her day by day, this hidden life can hardly be told. Neither the pomp and flattery of courts where every kind was beset before her nor the trials adversity brought, ever changed her from being the meek and humble Christian she truly was. Whether wielding the sceptre of state, governing the destinies of her kingdom, or as the imprisoned captive of a tyrant, the same spirit of Christ dominated her every act. As one writer says of her: "Her own household appeared as regular as the most edifying monastery." To do good both by precept and example, was her one aim in life. Her last journey on which she was engaged was as a peacemaker between rebellious subjects of her nephew Ralph in Burgundy and their ruler. Thus it was that while on the road she died at Salces, in Alsace, on December 16, 999.

DECEMBER 17th

Is the festival of another widow, St. Olmypias, whom one venerable writer calls "the glory of the widows in the eastern church." Born of an illustrious family, possessed of immense wealth and of unusual personal beauty, she was early sought for in marriage and in 368 was wedded to Nebridius, treasurer of Emperor Theodosius the Great. But a brief twenty days elapsed after her marriage when death claimed her husband. When the customary term of mourning was ended suitors innumerable asked her hand in marriage, among them men of the most ancient and noble of the patrician families, officials of high rank and gallants from the court, but to one and all she gave the same reply, that during her life she should remain unmarried. Even when the emperor interceded in behalf of one of his nobles she still held to her set purpose. Beset thus on every side she placed her great fortune in the hands of the prefect of Constantinople as her trustee, until she should reach the age of 30. This gave the prefect peculiar authority over her, and to aid one of Olmypias' rejected suitors who thought thus to coerce the widow into compliance, she was interdicted from either going to church or seeing her bishop and spiritual adviser. Complaining to Theodosius, she desired her fortune to be divided between the poor and the church; but the emperor instead directed in 391 the prefect to restore the control of her fortune to the widow herself who thenceforth under the wise counsel of St. Chrysostom began a systematic division of her revenues to both the church and charity until the worthy bishop was so ruthlessly banished in 404. Like other of St. Chrysostom's friends, she suffered in the persecutions which followed and owing to sickness was obliged to leave the city but in 405 she was brought back, heavily fined for refusal to "communicate with Arsocius," her goods sold and the community of nuns she headed scattered. But ever true to her faith no suffering or physical ailment — though she had been for years an invalid — could induce her to waver in her constant conscientious purposes. Thus after many years of trials and sickness this noble specimen of the women of the early church died about 410, the exact year being, like many dates in the early centuries, uncertain. The Greeks honour St. Olmypias on July 25th, but in Roman Martyrology the date is fixed for December 17th.

DECEMBER 18th

Is sacred to St. Winebald, the son of an Anglo-Saxon king, and a family highly honoured in Roman Martyrology as both the father, St. Richard, and our saints' brother, St. Willibald, and their sister, St. Walburga, appear in its Kalendar.

The story has its more especial interest from the evidence it bears of the deep and conscientious purpose of those Anglo-Saxon Christians of whom at best we know very little and must therefore judge them rather from their scantily recorded lives than by the more elaborate records of Churchman of later days.

St. Richard, having determined upon a pilgrimage, also resolved to take his two sons with him. Embarking at Hamble-Haven, they passed through Normandy; but on arriving at Lucca the King sickened and died in 722. After the burial of their father the sons completed their pilgrimage to Rome. Later, Willibald extended his pilgrimage to Palestine but Winebald returned to England. In 738 Winebald and a younger brother accompanied their cousin St. Boniface once more to Rome and from there Winebald, still clinging to his patron St. Boniface, came to Thuringia, where the holy man ordained him as a priest and committed to his care seven of the churches which he (Boniface) had founded, among them being that at Erfust. In 781 St. Willibald, then Bishop of Aychstadt in Franconia, wished to establish one of those double monasteries which were at that time regarded with so much favour by the church, and invited Winebald and their sister, Walburga, to take charge of it as Abbot and Abbess. The neighbourhood was intensely idolatrous, and frequent attempts were made upon the life of Winebald but he was preserved through each, until at last his faithful labours bore fruit among the very men who had endeavoured to harm him. In this effort a grievous malady which for years afflicted him was never allowed to interfere with the task he had set himself and so he is often held up by his biographers as an example of perseverance under trials, thus — to quote from a chronicler — "having been tried and purified * * * as pure gold in the furnace, he went to God, on December 18, 760."

DECEMBER 19th.

St. Nemesion, whom the Church honours this day, was an Egyptian who spent his life labouring among thieves and the lowest classes in striving to bring them back to a right course of living. His life work and character were well enough known to have exempted him from the accusation of being a thief but under the persecution of Decius, for lack of a better reason, this was charged against him. He quickly and easily disproved the false accusation; but once their victim was in their hands these idolators never let loose their deathly grip. Thus it was that when cleared of the false charge he was questioned as to his faith and true as Christ's followers were in those days, Nemesion failed not to testify against himself when he proclaimed he was a Christian, and was at once sent to the "Augustal" Prefect of Egypt to be dealt with. Two questions only were put to the Egyptian Evangelist: "Are you a Christian?" and "Will you repent from your error and do sacrifice to the gods?" Well knowing what awaited his reply, Nemesion without hesitation responded, acknowledging his faith and in burning words then gave his reasons why death was preferable to denying his Lord and Christ. Thus our saint with four Roman soldiers and a civilian who, like Nemesion, held firm to their convictions, were all led forth on the 19th of December to an execution — more merciful than was often the case — for they were beheaded.

DECEMBER 20th

Is the feast of St. Philogonius, Bishop of Antioch, and whose name is especially remembered from the fact that he with the saintly Bishop Alexander and others first began the combat now so famous, against Arius and in support of true Catholicism. He was educated for a lawyer and had won for himself fame as an eloquent speaker, but even more for his keen, clear logic, his wonderful knowledge of the canon law and above all for the purity of his life.

In 318 Arius had broached his heresies at Alexandria and had been condemned by Alexander for them. It was just then the see of Antioch was made vacant and the need felt for a strong man to fill it. The high-toned, true characteristics of Philogonius were well known and fully justified the church in his case dispensing with the canons and placing him as it did, in the bishopric. The condemnation and sentence of Arius by Alexander were conveyed to Philogonius in a synodical letter and the latter's defence of the Catholic faith before the Council of Nice, has most justly made his name famous, even without the added lustre gained by his earnest, effective labours during the storms raised against the Church by Maximian II. and afterward by Licinius, which made our saint deserving of the noble title of confessor. He died in 322, but it was not until 386 his festival was first celebrated and was the occasion seized upon by St. Chrysostom to pronounce a panegyric on the wonderful character of the noted bishop, though he left to Bishop Flavias the honour of speaking in detail of his great and arduous work for the Catholic Church, an effort on the part of St. John Chrysostom which even in these modern days is regarded as one of the most wonderful displays of eloquence of the many that have made the name of Chrysostom famous. Yet no one who reads the life of St. Philogonius can for an instant doubt how fully deserving he was of the eulogy.

This day is the Vigil of St. Thomas the Apostle, and in both the English and Roman churches is marked by especial and appropriate offices.

DECEMBER 21st.

ST. THOMAS' DAY.

The festival of St. Thomas was instituted in the twelfth century and as an old author alleges was assigned an early place in the ecclesiastical calendar from this apostle having been vouchsafed the most indisputable evidence of the resurrection.

St. Thomas, surnamed Didymus, or The Twin, appears to have been a Jew and probably a Galilean; he is said to have travelled and promulgated Christianity among the Parthians, Medes and Persians, to have been the apostle of the Indies, and to have been martyred at Meliapore on the coast of Caromandel at the instigation of the Brahmins. After being stoned and struck with darts he was finally transfixed with a lance. A Christian church exists to this day on the coast of Malabar which traditionally traces its origin to the preaching of St. Thomas, and names itself after him. Wheatly suggests that the church recommends St. Thomas to our meditation at this season as a fit preparative to our Lord's Nativity, for although he first openly doubted the truth of our Lord's Resurrection all doubts fled when he saw his Divine Master.

S. THOMAS.
From Mural Painting in S. Alban's Abbey.

St. Thomas as the patron of architects and builders has for his symbol a builder's or carpenter's square and in Danish clogs his day is marked by one, but upon the English clogs it has, as shown in the second illustration, a purely Runic sign. The square was assigned to St. Thomas about the IX. century from a quaint legend, but too long for repetition here except very much abridged. When the Apostle was in Cæsarea, the Lord appeared to him and said: "Gondoforus, king of the Indies, wishes a palace built for himself which shall exceed in splendour that of the emperor at Rome. Behold, now I will send thee to build it." Gondoforus received the Apostle graciously, gave into his hands immense treasures of gold and silver with which to build the palace; then started on a journey to a far country and was absent two years. After the king's departure Thomas, instead of building the palace, distributed to the last farthing all of the treasures given him among the poor, sick and needy. Upon the king's return and when he found his coveted palace unbuilt and learned what had been done with his immense treasure he was full of wrath and ordered the Apostle imprisoned and commanded he should be put to an horrible death. Meanwhile the king's brother died, and Gondoforus resolved to erect for him a magnificent tomb. But on the fourth day after his brother's death, while the king sat beside the catafalco, his brother rose and sat upright in his sarcophagus and said. 'The man whom thou tortured is a servant of God. I have been in Paradise and the angels showed me a wondrous palace, built of silver, gold and precious stones and they said: 'This is the palace the architect Thomas hath built for thy brother Gondoforus.'" When the king heard these words he ran to the prison and liberated the Apostle who said: "Knowest thou not that they who wouldst possess heavenly things care little for the gauds of this world? There are in heaven such places without number which are prepared for those who purchase the possession of them through faith and charity. Thy riches, O king, may prepare for thee such a palace but they cannot follow thee." A representation of this legend is painted on one of the windows of the Cathedral at Bourges; an appropriate offering from the company of builders of that ancient city. For while the most devout regard the legend as a purely religious fiction or an allegory, like some of the parables of our Saviour, as invented for the instruction of the people, the moral lesson it teaches has and will give it a place always in the story of St. Thomas.

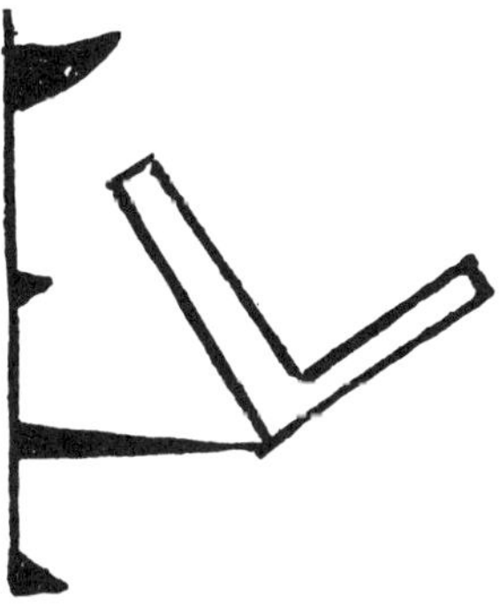

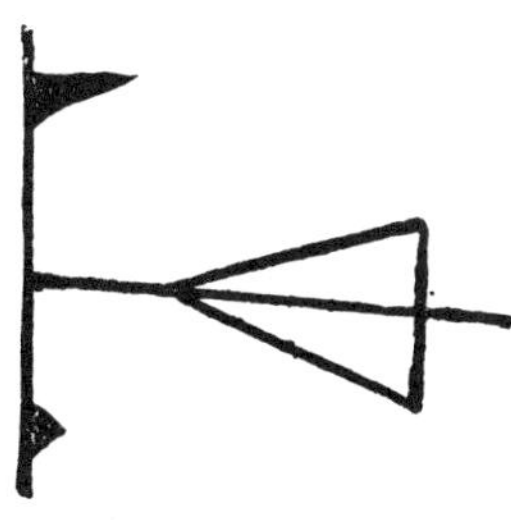

After the dispersion of the Apostles, St. Thomas is said to have preached the gospel to the Medes, Persians, Barbarians, Ethiopians and the Indians: and it was among the latter that he suffered martyrdom at Miliapore. Legends in great number are told of St. Thomas, among them the curious in such matters should read the story told by Sir John Mandeville of St. Thomas' arm, "which yet"— i. e., in Sir John's day — gives judgment between litigants by casting aside the scroll of the unworthy one, when presented "at his fair tomb in the city of Calvary."

St. Thomas' Day falls on the winter solstice, the shortest day in the year, as expressed in the following couplet:

"St. Thomas gray, St. Thomas gray,
The longest night and the shortest day."

DECEMBER 22d.

This day has been selected by the Roman Church to commemorate two missionaries of the IX. century. These two men are sometimes spoken of as "brothers," but this probably came from the fact that they were brethren of the Order of St. Basil. One of these, Cyril, was a philosopher while Methodius was an artist of rare skill as were many monks of the early ages, men who produced those wonderful illuminated missals which are unsurpassed even by the best artists of modern days. Originally Cyril had been named Constantine, but by a very common custom that obtains even now, had changed his name at the time of his consecration. He was born of a Roman "senatorial family," and received every possible advantage which the age afforded; while his bright, analytic mind nature endowed him with and an ardent love for study enabled him to make the most of his resources, so that he early won the rare sobriquet of "The Philosopher." But his piety and virtue were his most shining characteristics, and thus after his ordination to the priesthood his zeal in the service of the Church brought him into notice. His first public recognition came in his defence of St. Ignatius, when in 846 that worthy was advanced to patriarchal dignity and was attacked by Photius as related by Anastasius "the bibliothecarian."

It was about this time when the Chazari, a tribe descended from the ancient Turci, one of the most numerous of the powerful nation of the Huns in European Scythia, had possessed themselves of a territory on the banks of the Danube near Germany, with Moravia on the west, and a tribe of Bulgarians, "the Scrobati," in the mountains on the south, and sent an embassy to Michael III. — the Drunkard — Emperor of the East (died 867), and joined his pious mother in asking that some priest be sent to instruct them in the Christian Faith. The dowager empress at once consulted Ignatius the patriarch and Cyril was selected for the purpose and started on his mission in 848. The selection of Cyril is only an illustration of the care and foresight of those Fathers of the Church in all things. The language of the Chazari was not the Sclavonian then so common among many of the tribal nations, therefore was one to be learned by the missionary. As a student Cyril had learned Greek, Latin and the Sclavonic languages and thus had a solid foundation upon which to build in his study of this new language; his first work was its acquisition which he accomplished in a very short time. Then and not until then, did he attempt to teach; thus avoiding many mistakes that under similar circumstances had retarded if not wholly ruined the efforts of worthy but less critically educated men. Once feeling himself fully equipped for this work he began it, and his success was equalled by the care he had taken in his preparation. I have been thus prolix only to illustrate a fact which will often be seen in the lives of others of the missionaries sent out in those dark ages. For it was through them that the Latin Church, by their arduous labours and missionary work, was laying those broad foundations upon which they later built such a solid structure. When Cyril had completed his work among the Chazari, and arranged for their spiritual welfare in the future, he returned to Constantinople. But he was quickly sent upon his second mission and it was then "his brother Methodius" became his associate in endeavouring to bring the Bulgari under Christian influence. These Bulgari were also a Scythian nation though not of the Huns but of the Sclavi, and their language entirely different from either the Turci or Huns. They were located in ancient Myria and Dacia on both sides of the Danube,— now part of Wallachia, Moldavia, and of modern Hungary. The earliest seeds for the conversion of these barbarians had been sown in the beginning of the reign of Basil II. (The Macedonian), Emperor of the East from 867 to 886—by Grecian captives, but was in Cyril's day nearly dead. The two monks worked each in his own way, but in perfect harmony. Cyril from the pulpit, but Methodius by what we now would call object lessons, through the wonderful power he possessed with his pencil and brush supplementing and illustrating Cyril's burning words. A single instance of their effective work must suffice to show their success. Bogoris (or Boigoris), then king of Bulgaria, a man devoted to the pleasures of the chase and a *bonhomme* (easy-going fellow) as a Frenchman terms him, desired Methodius to paint for him a picture to adorn the wall of his banquet-hall. Instead of selecting a hunting scene, or some other that would please the King but which would carry no lesson with it, the monk chose for his illustration "The Last Judgment," with kings, princes and peasants all standing in a heterogeneous mass without distinction of rank or person before the Great Judge. When completed it was shown the King who demanded an explanation of the meaning of the picture. This Cyril gave in such a realistic manner that the monarch and his courtiers stood awe stricken and terrified. But the result was attained, for in 865 (authorities differ as to this date, some placing it in 861) he was baptised when he took the name of Michael, and in 867 he sent ambassadors to Pope Nicholas I. with presents and a request for instructions as to his future conduct.

But I must refrain from any further comment on these interesting men beyond saying that in Muscovite Kalendars both Cyril and Methodius are termed "Moravian Bishops," and in Roman Martyrology the same title is given them. In the Polish Breviary it is stated Cyril died a monk and that only Methodius was consecrated as an Archbishop sometime after his "brother's" death, by Adrian II.

Stredowski in his "Sacra Moraviæ Historia," styles SS. Cyril and Methodius "Apostles of Moravia, Upper Bohemia, etc., etc., and almost all of the Sclavonian nations."

The Greeks and Muscovites honour St. Cyril on Feburary 14th, and St. Methodius on the 11th of May. The dates of their death are uncertain beyond being between the years 880 and 894.

Roman Martyrology honours these saints on March 9th. This 22d of December, however, is that named by Dr. Butler in his "Lives of the Saints."

DECEMBER 23d.

The story of St. Servulus, whose festival recurs this day, reminds one in its main features of the parable of Dives and Lazarus. From his infancy Servulus had been a paralytic and a beggar. As a baby his mother had carried him to the porch of the historic church of St. Clement's in Rome, and there laid him down to wait for the alms which passers might drop to him. During his whole life he never could sit upright but lay prone at the feet of those who stopped to look at him and thus soon became well known to all about the church. St. Gregory especially became deeply interested in this beggar when by accident he discovered him sharing the alms he had received with his fellow beggars who had been less fortunate than himself reserving only a bare moiety for his own needs. As he lay by the church door he heard and learned to join in the anthems sung within and when he was dying his legend tells: "He suddenly cried out 'Silence! Do you not hear the sweet melody and praises resounding from heaven?'" St. Gregory made this beggar cripple the subject of one of his most noted efforts (Homily 15), drawing from his life and his efforts to aid his fellowmen even amid his own afflictions — a lesson which the prosperous world may well take to heart, though St. Gregory's eulogy was spoken in 590, when Servulus died.

DECEMBER 24th.

This is the Vigil of the Nativity of Our Blessed Lord Jesus Christ, and is a day of fasting and abstination in both the English and Roman churches.

The eves or vigils of the different ecclesiastical festivals of the Christian year are, according to the strict letter of canonical rule, times of fasting and penance, but as in the case of All Saints' Eve and of Christmas Eve, common custom has ignored and incontiently transformed them into seasons of mirth and jollity. Perhaps nothing better can be found to describe this than Sir Walter Scott's "Marmion," and I would advise my gentle readers to take from their shelves that glorious poem and read from where it begins:

"On Christmas Eve the bells were rung;
On Christmas Eve the mass was sung;
That only night, in all the year,
Saw the stoled priest the chalice rear,
The damsel donned her kirtle sheen;
The hall was dressed with holly green;
Forth to the wood did merry-men go,
To gather in the mistletoe."

By far the largest number of the Christmas customs still extant in England and which in a limited way obtain among ourselves are but the survivals of old pagan rites and ceremonies. These, it is needless here to repeat, were extensively retained after the conversion of Britain to Christianity, partly because the Christian teachers found it impossible to wean their converts from their cherished superstitions and observances, and partly because they themselves, as a matter of expediency, ingrafted the rites of the Christian religion on the old heathen ceremonies, believing that thereby the cause of the cross would be rendered more acceptable to the generality of the populace and thus be more effectually promoted. By such an amalgamation, no festival of the Christian year was more thoroughly characterized than Christmas, the festivities of which were originally derived from the Roman Saturnalia, had afterwards been intermingled with the ceremonies observed by the British Druids at the period of the winter solstice, and at a subsequent period became incorporated with the grim mythology of the ancient Saxons. Two popular observances belonging to Christmas are more especially derived from the worship of our pagan ancestors—the hanging up of the mistletoe and the burning of the yule log.

But I must not enter upon any description of these festivities here. Yet I am tempted to quote from the genial pen of Herrick in regard to the yule log:

"Come bring a noise,
My merry, merry boys,
The Christmas log to the firing;

While my good dame she
Bids ye all be free,
  And drink to your heart's desiring.

With the last year's brand
Light the new block, and,
  For good success in his spending,
On your psalteries play
That sweet luck may
  Come while the log is a-teending. *

Drink now the strong beer,
Cut the white loaf here,
  The while the meat is a-shredding;
For the rare mince-pie,
And the plums stand by,
  To fill the paste that's a-kneading."

The allusion in the second verse to the "last year's brand" refers to the old custom of laying aside the charred remains of the yule log of one year and with it to kindle the new log. The same custom prevailed regarding the yule candle from whose remnant the candle which held the central place on the table at the Christmas Eve supper was lighted. While in Germany where, by the way, the Christmas tree first was raised, the candles of the tree are lighted from the last year's yule candle.

At Vespers and Evensong the canonical colour is on this day changed to white.

DECEMBER 25th.

The canonical colour for Christmas Day is white.

THE NATIVITY OF CHRIST.

The birth of Jesus Christ, the deliverer of the human race and the mysterious link connecting the transcendent and incomprehensible attributes of Deity with human sympathies, is and should be regarded as the most glorious event which finds a place in the Ecclesiastical or Civil Kalendars, and as such should be observed with appropriate and solemn religious services.

The question of whether this 25th day of December is really the

* Burning.

anniversary of the birth of Christ was for a long time a mooted one, and the evidence of its truth is at best traditional.

In the earliest periods of which we have any record we find this feast was observed at various periods, the 1st and 6th of January being the dates on which a portion of the Christians celebrated it; others doing so on March 29th, the time of the "Jewish Passover," while yet others selected September 29th, that being "The Feast of the Tabernacles." There were those also who observed it on April 20th, and yet another class who thought it occurred on May 20th, while SS. Epiphanius and Cassian state that in Egypt Christ was believed to have been born on January 6th. For a long time the Greeks celebrated our Lord's birth on the Feast of Epiphany. In a sermon preached by St. Chrysostom at Antioch on December 25, in 386, he says: "It is not ten years since this day (Christmas, December 25th) was clearly known to us; but it has been familiar from the beginning to those who dwell in the West. The Romans have from the earliest days celebrated it (Christmas on December 25th) and thus from ancient tradition transmitted the knowledge to us."

The "Kirchenlexikon" (an accepted and undoubted authority) says that "the special feast in honour of the Saviour's birth was introduced in the year 354 under Pope Liberius, and soon after in Constantinople in 378, but previous to this the feast was celebrated upon Epiphany."

In passing I note Chambers names Pope Julius as having introduced the feast in the church ritual, but if 354, the year named by the Kirchenlexikon is correct, Julius could not have promulgated the office for he died in 352, and Liberius was chosen as his successor.

Be this as it may — for I have no space to argue such a point — it is but reasonable to believe that the Holy Father did not select this day at a random guess, though the reasons or traditions on which he founded his determination are not (as far as I can learn after careful search) upon record; but that he followed what seemed to be the best authoritative traditions in fixing the "Festorum omnium metropolis," as it is styled by Chrysostom.

One curious fact or coincidence yet confronts us, that this date exactly corresponds both in its inception and the length of the festival with the great festival of pagan Rome, the Saturnalia.

Though Christian nations have thus from an early period in the history of the church celebrated Christmas about the period of the winter solstice or the shortest day, it is well known that many and indeed the greater number of the popular festive observances by which it is characterized, are referable to a much more ancient origin. Amid all the pagan nations of antiquity there seems to have been a universal tendency to worship the sun as the giver of life and light and the one visible manifestation of the Deity. Various as were the names bestowed by different peoples on this object of their worship, the sun was still the same divinity. Thus at Rome he appears to have been worshipped under one of the characters attributed to Saturn, the father of the gods; among the Scandinavian nations he was known under the name of Odin or Woden, the father of Thor, who seems afterwards to have shared with his parent the adoration bestowed on the latter as the divinity of which the sun was the visible manifestation; whilst with the ancient Persians the appellation for the god of light was Mithras, apparently the same as the Irish Mithr, and with the Phœnicians or Carthaginians it was Baal or Bel, an epithet familiar to all students of the Bible.

In the early ages of Christianity its ministers frequently experienced the utmost difficulty in inducing the converts to refrain from indulging in the popular amusements which were so largely participated in by their pagan countrymen. Among others the revelry and license which characterized the Saturnalia called for special animadversion. But at last, convinced partly of the inefficacy of such denunciations, and partly influenced by the idea that the spread of Christianity might thereby be advanced, the Church endeavoured to amalgamate as it were the old and new religions, and sought by transferring some of the heathen ceremonies to the solemnities of the Christian festivals to make them subservient to the cause of religion and piety.

Thus it has been suggested, and not without some reason, that in the selection of this day for Christmas, instead of the time-honoured Epiphany, the Holy Father may have been influenced.

The name given by the ancient Goths and Saxons to the festival of the winter solstice was Jul or Yule, the latter term forming to the present day the designation in the Scottish dialect of Christmas, and preserved also in the name of the yule log. Perhaps the etymology of no term has excited any greater discussion among antiquaries. The most probable derivation of the word is from the Gothic gigul or hiul, the origin of the modern word wheel, and bearing the same signification. According to this very probable explanation the yule festival received its name from its being the turning point of the year or the period at which the fiery orb of day made a revolution in its annual circuit and entered his northern journey. A confirmation of this view is afforded by the circumstance that in the old Clog almanacs a wheel is the device employed for marking the season of yule-tide.

Of the interesting subject of Christmas carols I am obliged to limit myself to a brief line or two. The term is believed to be derived from the Latin cantare (to sing) and rola ! an interjection expressive of joy. The practice appears to be as ancient as the celebration of Christmas itself, and we are informed that in the early ages of the Church the bishops were accustomed to sing carols on Christmas Day among their parishioners and clergy, which in time developed into the joyous hymns of our present Christmas carol.

DECEMBER 26th.

This is a day of abstination. The canonical colour is red.

ST. STEPHEN'S DAY.

No more appropriate day could have been selected for the Feast of St. Stephen, the great Proto-Martyr of the Church than this, the first day following Christmas in the Christian Kalendar. Beyond the somewhat terse accounts we have of this Holy

Deacon given in the Acts of the Apostles (vi., 5) and of his arrest, defence and martyrdom in same chapter (8-15) and in vii., and viii., 2, where "devout men carried Stephen to his burial and made great lamentations over him," tradition has added little to the history of the man. He was chosen deacon during the first ministry of Peter. Later, he was falsely accused of speaking blasphemously of the Temple and Jewish law and for this, tried, condemned to death and stoned outside the gate of Jerusalem that now bears his honoured name; and buried by "devout men." Where he was laid there is no record to show and for four hundred years it was a mystery what became of his body. Then his legend tells "that a certain priest of Cariagmala, in Palestine, named Lucian, had a vision in which St. Gamaliel appeared to him." Readers will find this vision told in detail elsewhere and how the relics of St. Stephen were placed side by side those of St. Laurence. St. Stephen is represented in art as a young, handsome, beardless man in the full dress of a deacon. The dalmatica is square and straight at the bottom, with heavy gold tassels hanging from his shoulders. It is always crimson in colour and richly embroidered. The palm branch is often given him and stones in one hand are at all times his attributes while a book is held in the other. He is supposed to have suffered his martyrdom in the year of our Lord 31, but some authorities place the date in 33.

S. STEPHEN.

DECEMBER 27th.

In the Reformed or English church this day is held as especially sacred as St. John the Evangelist's Day.

A special reverence and interest is attached to St. John — "the disciple whom Jesus loved." Through a misapprehension of the Saviour's words, a belief we are informed came to be entertained among the other apostles that this disciple should never die, and the thought was doubtless fostered by the circumstance that John outlived all his brethren and coadjutors in the Christian ministry and he was indeed the only apostle who died a natural death. It is stated he expired peacefully at Ephesus, at the advanced age of 94, in the reign of the Emperor Trajan, and the year of our Lord 100, thus as Brady observes "marking the first century of the Christian era and the apostolic age which terminate together."

S. JOHN EVANGELIST.

Though John thus escaped actual martyrdom he was nevertheless called upon to endure great persecution in the cause of his Friend and Master. Various fathers of the church, among others Tertullian and St. Jerom, relate that in the reign of Domitian the evangelist, having been accused of attempting to subvert the religion of the Roman empire, was transported from Asia to Rome and there in presence of the emperor and senate, before the gate called Porta Latina or the Latin Gate, he was cast into a caldron of boiling oil in which he not only remained for a long time uninjured, but ultimately emerged therefrom with renovated health and vigour. In commemoration of this event the Roman Catholic Church retains in its calendar, on the 6th of May a festival entitled "St. John before the Latin Gate." In my article of April 30th this festival will be especially mentioned.

St. John was a younger brother of St. James the Great, with whom he was brought up in the trade of fishing. Before his coming to Christ he seems for some time to have been disciple to John the

Baptist, being probably that other disciple that was with Andrew when they left the Baptist to follow our Saviour, so particularly does he relate all circumstances of that transaction though modestly (as in other parts of his gospel) concealing his own name. He was at the same time with his brother called by our Lord both to the discipleship and apostolate. He was by far the youngest of all the apostles. He was banished to the Isle of Patmos where he wrote his Revelations, and at the death of Domitian he returned to Ephesus where he ended his days about the year 99. His gospel was written many years after the other three and seems designed to fill up what they had omitted relative to our Lord's Godhead. The last chapter appears to have been subsequently added by him in order to controvert an opinion then current in the church, "that that disciple should not die," but should tarry on the earth until the second coming of his Lord. He outlived all the apostles, and as before spoken of was probably the only one who did not attain to the crown of martyrdom in deed as well as in will.

His gospel was without doubt written by him after his return to Ephesus, and at the earnest entreaty and solicitation of the Asian churches; he first, however, caused them to proclaim a general fast to seek the blessing of Heaven on so great and solemn an undertaking which being done he set about his task. Two causes especially contributed to the writing of it: the one, that he might controvert the early heresies of those times especially of Ebion, Cerinthus, and the rest of that set who began openly to deny Christ's divinity and this was why the Evangelist is so express and copious on that subject. The other was that he might supply those passages of the evangelical history which the rest of the sacred writers had omitted. Collecting therefore the other three evangelists, he first ratified the truth of them with his approbation and consent; and then added his own gospel to the rest, principally insisting upon the acts of Christ from the first commencing of His ministry to the death of John the Baptist, wherein the others are most defective, giving scarce any account of the first year of our Saviour's ministry. He particulary records (as Gregory Nazianzin observes) our Saviour's discourses, but takes little notice of His miracles probably because they are so fully related by the other evangelists.

S. JOHN EVANGELIST.

As an Apostle he is represented with a chalice from which a serpent is issuing (as in illustration) alluding to the legend which tells how St. John, previous to being taken without the Porta Latina had been offered a cup of poison from which the Devil being thus expelled, he drank and remained unhurt. As an Evangelist he is represented as in first illustration writing in a book.

Over two hundred churches are dedicated to St. John in England alone.

The canonical colour for this day is white.

DECEMBER 28th.

INNOCENTS' DAY.

This festival, which is variously styled Innocents' Day, The Holy Innocents' Day, and Childermas Day or Childremas, has been observed from an early period in the history of the church as a commemoration of the barbarous massacre of children in Bethlehem ordered by King Herod, with the view of destroying among them the infant Saviour, as recorded in the Gospel of St. Matthew. It is one of those anniversaries which was retained in the ritual by the English church at the Reformation.

In reference to the three consecutive commemorations, on the 26th, 27th and 28th of December, Wheatly informs us that in these are comprehended three descriptions of martyrdom all of which have their peculiar efficacy though differing in degree. In the death of St. Stephen, an example is furnished of the highest class of martyrdom, that is to say, both in will and deed. St. John the Evangelist who gave practical evidence of his readiness to suffer death for the cause of Christ, though through miraculous interposition he was saved from actually doing so, is an instance of the second description of martyrdom — in will, though not in deed. And the slaughter of the Innocents affords an instance of martyrdom in deed and not in will, these unfortunate children having lost their lives though involuntarily on account of the Saviour, and it being therefore considered "that God supplied the defects of their will by His own acceptance of the sacrifice."

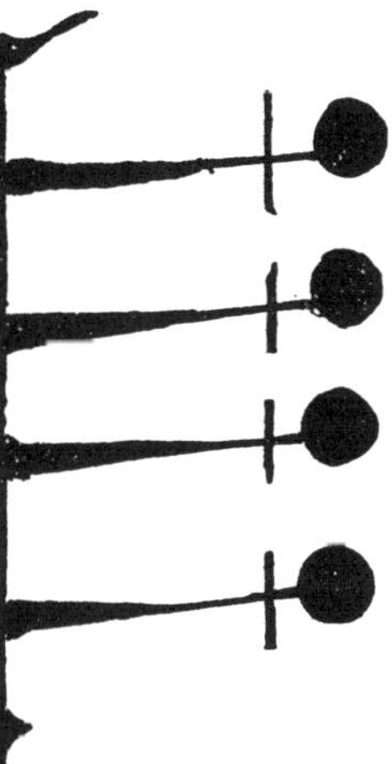

Childermas was ever in the old days regarded with superstitious dread. Even the unprincipled Louis XI. held it in such fear that he would do no work on that day; and when it was discovered that the day set for the coronation of Edward IV. of England was Childermas Day, the ceremony was at once postponed until the following day.

The canonical colour for Innocents' Day is violet.

DECEMBER 29th.

The canonical colour changes this day again to white.

St. Thomas à Becket's name takes precedence in the list of saints who are honoured by a portion of the English and the entire Roman Church on this day. The career and fate of this celebrated ecclesiastic was one of the most remarkable episodes to be found in the history of England during the XII. century. The story has been so often told and widely read that it is a work of superogation seemingly to repeat it. How the merchant's son from a minor clerkship in the office of the Sheriff-of-London attracted the attention of Theobald, Archbishop of Canterbury, by whom he was sent to study civil and ecclesiastical law in Italy and France; of his rapid and merited advancement, due to his wonderful acumen, until he attracted the notice of Henry II., then King of England, who became so much attached to him personally and held his abilities in such high esteem that in 1158, he created him Chancellor of the Realm. Indeed the story of his varied attainments reads like some old romance, of a consummate courtier who in addition to his accomplishments as a clear-headed, sagacious statesman, showed military talents and power of no ordinary character, as proved when he accompanied his royal master into France and at the head of a company of gallant Knights took active part in several sieges, and covered himself with glory and in a single combat "unhorsed" a French Knight of high renown for his bravery and feats of arms, winning if possible, a higher place in the estimation of the King. Then, in 1162, came the change, when it was proposed to make Becket Archbishop of Canterbury, a preferment he sedulously strove to avoid, until his scruples were overborne by the Cardinal of Pisa and Legate from the Holy See at Rome, who cast into the scales both his advice and the weight of his authority.

From the hour of his consecration the gay and worldly chancellor who had joined his sovereign in all his amusements and had indulged himself in every obtainable luxury and splendour, was transformed into the austere and ascetic monk. The silken robes gave place to the "hair-shirt" (now shown in a reliquary, in the English college at Doway) and his sumptuous table which heretofore had rivalled any in the land was reduced to the simplest necessities of life, and his magnificent retinue forever abandoned.

I must not enter on the vexed points which disrupted the affection that had in the old days bound the King and Prelate, nor the cause of his exile, nor of the hollow truce by which Becket was again restored to his see. These, with the events which led up at last to Becket's brutal murder, are all historic, and may be read in a score of places.

From the time of his death, Becket's shrine was one of the most popular places for pilgrims in all England.

The spoilation of Becket's shrine and the burning of his bones by the Cromwell party was one of those episodes of the English Civil War which even the most ardent admirer of the "Great Commoner" have never been able to condone, and it is this — no doubt — that leads the so-called "High Church Party" in the English church to join with their Roman Catholic brethren in commemorating his memory and martyrdom on December 29, 1170.

DECEMBER 30th.

St. Maximus, one of the saints the Church selects for honour on this day was one of those men Providence seems to bring to the front at critical times when peculiar traits of character are needed to meet the emergency. He was born at Constantinople in 580 and educated as befitted his high rank, coming as he did from one of the most ancient and noble families of the city. By nature he was retiring and modest but his rare abilities had by the time he had reached the prime of early manhood attracted the attention of Heraclius (Emperor of the East 612–641), who appointed him his First Secretary of State. The heresy of Monothelism had already made marked progress to the disgust of Maximus who found himself lacking the power to check it, fostered as it was by the Emperor. It was in 608 that Mahomet or Mohammed, had begun to put forth his pretended revelations, though it was not until some time later that he, with the aid of a Jew and a Nestorian monk, compiled the "Alcoran" or "Koran" as it is commonly called. But it was through the indolence and lethargy of Heraclius that the sect of Mahomet was able to establish itself among the Saracens and lay the foundation of their formidable empire. I must not follow the interesting bit of history to the death of Heraclius in 641 and the complications that followed, during which Monothelism had made such dangerous progress that they caused his retirement. From his retreat in the monastery of Chrysopolis, Maximus had regretfully watched all this, but was helpless, until in 645 the patrician Gregory, Governor of Africa, summoned him to hold a conference at Carthage, with Pyrrus, the Patriarch of Constantinople and who favoured the heresy. It was then that Maximus came to the front as a Defender of the Faith, and while I cannot enter upon this remarkable encounter it is enough to say his work in the good cause would have kept his name alive even if he had not suffered the torture unjustly inflicted upon him of being whipped, "having his tongue torn from his mouth and his right hand cut off" by order of a synod of the Monothelites. In spite of his fourscore years the venerable saint lived on fully six months after this inhuman treatment, dying on this day in 662. The Greeks, however, celebrate two feasts in honour of St. Maximus; one on January 21st and the other on August 13th.

DECEMBER 31st.

On this day St. Sylvester — or Silvester as it is sometimes written — is honoured. His name is one of those that were retained in the Kalendar of the Reformed Church and still holds a place in that of the Church of England. He was a native of Rome and had been carefully instructed in the Christian faith by his mother, Justina. He was installed as the head of the Church upon the death of Pope Melchiades in 314. During his incumbency of the pontificate two important events occurred; the great Synod of Arles, and the Œcumenical Council of Nice in 325. Owing to age and infirmities the venerable prelate did not appear at either of these famous meetings but was represented by his legates; when at the latter they did their part against Arianism. It was Sylvester who baptised Constantine the Great and the legend of this event adds that the Emperor, who had been afflicted with leprosy, was instantly cured. St. Sylvester is credited with the conversion of St. Helen and Constantine the Great through having restored to life a dead ox which the Magicians had killed but were unable to resuscitate. He died December 31, 335, and was buried in the cemetery of Priscilla. Pope Gregory IX. in 1227, fixed his festival for this day. The Greeks celebrate it on January 16th.

JANUARY

—— Came old January, wrapped well
In many weeds to keep the cold away;
Yet did he quake and quiver like to quell,
And blowe his nayles to warm them if he may;
For they were numbed with holding all the day
An hatchet keene, with which he felled wood,
And from the trees did lop the needlesse spray.
— *Spenser.*

Numa Pompilius, the second king of Rome, who died in 672 B. C., is credited with promulgating what we now term "The Roman Calendar," which divided the year into twelve months instead of ten which had previously constituted the year, and to have decreed that the year should begin on the first day of January or Januaries, the name he gave the month in honour of the god Janus, the deity supposed to preside over doors (Latin Janua — a door). The ancient Jewish New Year — the 25th of March — however, continued to be held by law in most Christian countries as the initial day of the year until 1752 when January 1st became the legal New Year in England, and the "New Style," as it is popularly termed, came into vogue. In France this change had been made in 1564; in Holland, Protestant Germany and Russia in 1700; while Sweden fell into line in 1753.

The ancient Saxons called January the "Wolf-monat" (Wolf-month), later changing it to "Aefter-Yule." In many parts of Germany even now the month is termed "Jesu-monat." I have a German Kalendar for 1902 lying before me which thus designates January.

JANUARY 1st

Is the festival of "Circumicisio Domini," the circumcision of Jesus Christ, on the Octave of Christmas. The Clog Almanac symbol for the day is as in the illustration, a circle, which was also the symbol universally adopted in early days, as is seen by the paintings on the walls of the Roman Catacombs. Almost as common as the first is the hatchet which appears frequently as a symbol for New Years and no doubt it was this that suggested the lines I quote above from Spenser. In modern art a dove holding a ring in its beak is often used as the symbol of Christ's circumcision.

This day is the festival of St. Odilo or Olon, the sixth abbot of Cluni, and the original founder of All Souls' Day. He was a man of strong convictions and fearless to live up to them. No better evidence perhaps can be given than his act in 1006 during the severe famine when he melted down the rich, sacred vessels and ornaments of his church and sold the gold crown of St. Henry, which had been presented the abbey, that he might by the means thus obtained relieve the necessities of his suffering people. The sanctity in which such utensils are and should be held by every Christian, would from the standpoint of to-day perhaps justify their sacrifice for such an object. But in those early days the superstitious reverence in which they were held required a man of rare courage and firm convictions of his duty, to take upon himself so great a responsibility. Odilo was not only a brilliant pulpit orator but no mean poet, as some of his poems, still extant, show. He died on January 1, 1049.

JANUARY 2d.

St. Adalard, whom the Church honours among others on this day was of a most illustrious birth ; his father being the brother of King Pepin, and therefore Adalard was cousin-german to the Emperor Charlemagne, with whom he was a great favourite and his preferment to high honours only a question of arriving at a suitable age. But from his earliest youth Adalard had determined to lead a monastic life and at the age of twenty in 773, of his own volition, when to most youths the splendour and gaiety of court life would have been so attractive, he abandoned them and took the habit and vows of a monastic life at Corbie in Picardy. For a time later he lived in close retreat at Mount Cassino but returned to Corbie to become its abbot. Charlemagne, however, had not lost sight of his kinsman for in 796 we find him among the "King's Councillors" and the chief minister, and instructor to the young Prince Pepin at Milan where he (Pepin) died in 810. Later, Charlemagne sent him to appear before Leo III. to discuss an important clause in the creed "concerning the procession of the Holy Ghost from the Father and the Son." Charlemagne died January 28, 814, Lewis le Debonnaire succeeding to the throne. Adalard in some way had incurred the displeasure of this king and he was banished to a monastery on the little island of Heri on the coast of Aquitain. Here he spent his days in prayer and study until in 823 he was allowed to resume his Abbacy at Corbie, where he was received with unfeigned love and gratitude and where, in addition to his labours among the people and deeds of charity, he built several hospitals — then greatly needed — and founded the great monastery of "New Corbie," or Corwey, as it is sometimes called, an imperial abbey. He also wrote several books. He died on January 2, 847.

JANUARY 3d.

STE. GENEVIEVE.

Sainte Genevieve, who has occupied from the time of her death to the present day, the distinguished position of Patroness Saint of the City of Paris, lived in the fifth century when Christianity under adverse circumstances was contending with paganism for domination over the minds of rude and warlike races of men. Credible facts of this early period are few, obscure, and not easily separated from the fictions with which they have been combined.

Sainte Genevieve, or Genoveffa, as it is sometimes written, was born in the year 422 at Nanterre, a village about four miles from Paris. At the early age of seven years she was consecrated to the service of religion by St. Germanus, Bishop of Auxerre, who happened to pass through the village and was struck with her devotional manners. At the age of fifteen years she received the veil from the hands of the Archbishop of Paris, in which city she afterwards resided. By strict observance of the services of the Church, and by the practice of those austerities which were then regarded as the surest means of obtaining the blessedness of a future state, she acquired a reputation for sanctity which gave her considerable influence over the rulers and leaders of the people. When the Franks under Clovis had subdued the city of Paris, her solicitations are said to have moved the conqueror to acts of clemency and generosity. The miracles ascribed to Ste. Genevieve must be passed over though they were numerous and very remarkable. The date of her death has been fixed on as January 3, 512, five months after the decease of King Clovis. She was buried near him in the Church of St. Peter and St. Paul, since named the Church of Ste. Genevieve. The present handsome structure was completed in 1764. During the revolutionary period it was withdrawn from the services of religion and named the Pantheon, but has since been restored to ecclesiastical uses and to its former name of Sainte Genevieve. Details of her life are given in Bollandus's "Acta Sanctorum," and in Butler's "Lives of the Saints."

The Clog symbol given above is from an English stick.

JANUARY 4th

Is the Octave of the Holy Innocents. The canonical colour for this day is white.

St. Titus, a disciple of St. Paul, is to-day honoured by the Roman Church the day being named in Martyrology as his "birthday." This disciple was an especial favourite of the Apostle Paul, by whom he was converted. He is many times referred to in St. Paul's Epistles and styled his brother and co-partner in his labours. That the Apostle trusted him to a high degree is evident from many sources. He accompanied the Apostle in 51 to the council held in Jerusalem to consider the Mosaic rites. In 56 Paul sent Titus from Ephesus to Corinth, to remedy the scandals and allay the dissensions then disturbing the church there.

It was while on his return from Rome, after his first imprisonment that Paul stopped at Crete and ordained Titus as Bishop of that island. The confidence reposed in Titus by the great Apostle seems to have been unbounded. Even in 65 when Titus was an old man Paul sent him to Dalmatia to preach. From here Titus returned to Crete and died in the ninety-fourth year of his age at Cardia, a metropolis built by the Saracens and which to-day is under the control of suffragan Bishops of the Greek Church.

JANUARY 5th

Eve of the Epiphany of Our Lord; or Twelfth Night.

St. Simeon Stylites, the saint honoured by the Church this day is so named from being the founder of an order of monks or rather solitary devotees, called pillar-saints. Of all the forms of voluntary self-torture practised by the early Christians this was one of the most extraordinary. Simeon was originally a shepherd in Cilicia; about the year 408 when only thirteen years of age he entered a monastery, later taking Holy Orders. From that time his asceticisms and the austerities of his life became notable for their severity and especially for his almost total abstinence from food or drink during Lent. Owing to a vision Simeon had in or about the year 425, he determined to make his residence on the top of a pillar which was at first nine feet high, but was successfully raised to the somewhat incredible height of sixty feet (forty cubits). The diameter of the top of the pillar was only three feet but it was surrounded by a railing which secured the saint from falling off and afforded him some relief by leaning against it. His clothing consisted of the skins of beasts and he wore an iron collar round his neck. He exhorted the assembled people twice each day and spent the rest of his time in assuming various postures of devotion. Sometimes he prayed kneeling, sometimes in an erect attitude with his arms stretched out in the form of a cross but his most frequent exercise was that of bending his meagre body so as to make his head nearly touch his feet. A spectator once observed him make more than 1,240 such reverential bendings without resting. In this manner he lived on his pillar more than thirty years and there he died in the year 459. His remains were removed to Antioch with great solemnity. His predictions and the miracles ascribed to him are mentioned at large in Theodoretus.

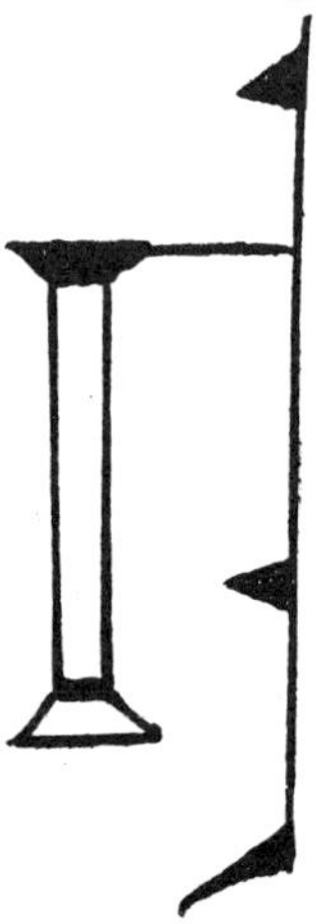

The pillar-saints were never numerous and the propagation of the order was almost exclusively in the warm climates of the East. Among the names recorded is that of another Simeon, styled the younger, who is said to have dwelt sixty years on his pillar.

Twelfth-Day Eve is a rustic festival in England. Persons who are engaged in rural employments or have heretofore been, are accustomed to celebrate it; and the purpose appears to be to secure a blessing for the fruits of the earth.

JANUARY 6th.

THE EPIPHANY OF OUR LORD.

This day called Twelfth-Day as being that number after Christmas is a festival of the Church in commemoration of the Manifestation of Christ to the Gentiles; more expressly to the three Magi or Wise Men of the East who came led by a star to worship Him, immediately after his birth (Matt. ii., 1-12). The Epiphany appears to have been first observed as a separate feast in the year 813. Pope Julius I. is reputed to have taught the Church to distinguish between the Feasts of the Nativity and Epiphany, about the middle of the fourth century. The primitive Christians celebrated the Feast of the Nativity for twelve days observing the first and last with great solemnity; and both were denominated Epiphany, the first the Greater Epiphany, from our Lord having on that day become Incarnate, or made His appearance in "the flesh"; the latter, the Lesser Epiphany, from the three-fold manifestation of His Godhead—the first, by the appearance of the blazing star which conducted Melchior, Jasper and Balthuzar, the three Magi or Wise Men (often styled the three Kings of Cologne), out of the East, to worship the Messiah, and to offer Him presents of "Gold, Frankincense and Myrrh"—Melchoir the Gold in testimony of his royalty as the promised King of the Jews; Jasper the Frankincense in token of his Divinity; and Balthuzar the Myrrh, in allusion to the sorrows which, in the humiliating condition of a man, our Redeemer vouchsafed to take upon him. Again the second of this three-fold manifestation was the descent of the Holy Ghost in the form of a dove, at the Baptism; and the third, of the first miracle of our Lord turning water into wine at the marriage in Cana. While all of these three manifestations of the Divine nature happened on the same day, they did not occur in the same year.

THE ADORATION OF THE MAGI.
From an Ancient Embroidery.

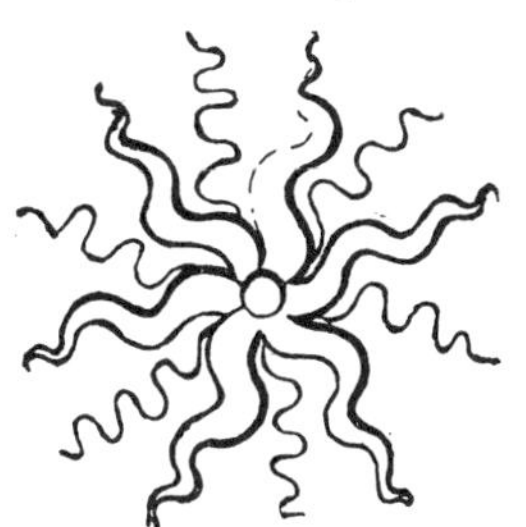

To render due honour to the memory of the ancient Magi who are supposed to have been kings, the monarch of Italy, either personally or through his chamberlain, offers annually at the altar on this day Gold, Frankincense and Myrrh; and the kings of Spain, where the Feast of Epiphany is likewise called the "Feast of Kings," were accustomed to make the like offerings.

The primitive Christians celebrated the Feast of the Nativity during a period of twelve days culminating on Epiphany. The dove on an olive branch with a star was often used in early days as a symbol of Epiphany.

On this day in 1904, Pope Pius X. issued a decree for the beatification of Joan of Arc, "the Maid of Orleans." In passing it should, however, be remembered that the beatification of any one by the Roman Church is but the first step toward canonization and by no means implies that the latter honour will follow. Even when this does occur it is granted, in most cases, only after a lapse of some years.

Nor is this first step of the beatification taken except after long and careful consideration by the prelates of the Church who have the works in charge. By a long established ecclesiastical rite of the Church, there are no less than thirteen or fourteen ceremonies which must be observed in every minute detail.

But before the final "Bull of Canonization" is issued there yet remain certain imperative conditions which must be fulfilled, such as miracles performed by the (prospective) saint in person, or by his or her relics after death, each of which must be proven beyond a possible doubt; the exercise "in a heroic degree" of all theological and cardinal virtues, like "Faith, Hope, Charity, Prudence, Justice and Temperance"; as well as the fulfilment of many other conditions too numerous to be recorded in my brief mention. Then, only, is the Bull issued.

EPIPHANY.

When a decree of beatification has been given, the person thus "beatified" is entitled to the appellation of "Venerable," so frequently found in these pages.

Thus it happens that many who attain to the first degree of beatification fail to reach the supreme honour of sainthood.

There are many of these persons who have been thus "beatified" whose names are yet held in abeyance by the Prelates of the Roman Church during late years. I have before me the names of a number of these but refrain from quoting them.

JANUARY 7th.

In the old days in England this day while not a church festival was widely observed as St. Distaff's Day or "Rock Day," when the women were supposed to resume their work. The word rock from the German "rocken," was applied to the spinning apparatus, and the gathering of the women was called a rocking.

"On Fasten's Eve we had a rocking."

Therefore on not a few old Clog sticks a rude distaff with the wool upon it marks the day.

On this day St. Lucian of Antioch is named both in the Roman and English Kalenders. He was born at Samosata in Syria and was one of the most learned men of his day. He revised the Old Testament translations and by comparing the different editions of the Septuagint and correcting the Hebrew text, as he was a thorough master of that language, produced an edition of the Scriptures which ranked very high and was especially esteemed by St. Jerom. For a time he seems to have been separated from the Catholic communion but later returned to it. He was imprisoned under the Dioclesian edicts and after being almost starved, he was offered as an insult dainty meats and food which had previously been used in sacrifice to idols. After this he suffered on the rack, later dying in prison from famine or, according to St. Chrysostom, "by the sword," in 312.

JANUARY 8th.

Another St. Lucian known as "of Beauvais," in contradistinction from St. Lucian of Antioch, is honoured this day in both the Reformed and Roman churches.

There is a great deal of obscurity about this saint's history; but he is believed to have been the companion of St. Denis in his mission in Gaul and although only a priest his name is among the first mentioned in the Kalendar of the English church, and from their martyrology we learn that he suffered martyrdom at Beauvais in 290 and by this gained the surname "of Beauvais."

This day is also the festival of St. Gudula, the patroness saint of Brussels. She was of noble birth, her mother having been niece to the eldest of the Pepin who was Maire of the Palace to Dagobert I. Her father was Count Witger. She was educated at Nivelle, under the care of her cousin St. Gertrude, after whose death in 664, she returned to her father's castle and dedicated her life to the service of religion. She spent her future years in prayer and abstinence. Her revenues were expended on the poor. She was most devout and constant in attending upon church service, it being her custom to attend midnight Mass at the Church of St. Morgell some two miles distant from her father's mansion, going and returning with no other escort than a female servant, while she herself carried a lighted lantern, to enable them to find their path. "Her devoutness," her legend tells us, "had so enraged the Devil, who was envious of her for the influence her piety gave her among the people, that he constantly endeavoured to entrap her." The pathway to the church was somewhat dangerous, and Satan frequently would by some means extinguish the taper in her lantern, in hopes she would be misled; but by her prayers the taper was always on the instant relighted, and she and her maid went safely on their way. Thus it is that both in art and in the clog almanac her symbol is a lantern.

She died January 8th, 712 and was buried at Ham, near Villevord. Her relics were transferred to Brussels in 978 and deposited in the church at St. Gery, but in 1047 were removed to the collegiate church of Michael, since named after her the Cathedral of St. Gudula. This ancient Gothic structure commenced in 1010 still continues to be one of the architectural ornaments of the city of Brussels. Her life was written by Hubert of Brabant not long after the removal of her relics to the Church of St. Michael.

JANUARY 9th.

St. Fillan or, as he is named in ancient Scottish records, Felan or Foelan, is famous among the Scottish saints from his piety and good works. He spent a considerable part of his holy life at a monastery which he built in Pittenweem of which some remains of the later buildings yet exist in a habitable condition. It is stated that while engaged here in transcribing the Scriptures his left hand sent forth sufficient light to enable him at night to continue his work without a lamp. For the sake of seclusion he finally retired to a wild and lonely vale still called from him Strathfillan in Perthshire, where he died and where his name is still attached to the ruins of a chapel, to a pool, and a bed of rock.

Mr. Skene, in his Celtic Scotland, gives a number of interesting details of this saint saying that Fillan was called "an lobar" (the leper), that according to the Irish Calendars he was of the "Rath Evenn in Albarr" (or the Fort of Earn in Scotland), and that the parish of St. Fillans at the east end of Loch Earn derived its name from him. And again in speaking of Scotch monasteries refers to that of Fillan in Strathfillan, where in ancient days there was a holy pool called St. Fillan's pool in which insane people were dipped and healed. Of the crocier of St. Fillan, called the "Quigrich," and which it is said is now preserved somewhere in Canada — I am not able to learn where which "is of silver gilt elegantly carved and with a jewel in front," Mr. Skene gives some interesting details but too long for quotation here, showing not alone the authenticity of the relic but how the hereditary privilege of bearing it was preserved from the days of King Robert Bruce, and quoting from a letter of King James in 1487 in regard to "ane relik of Saint Fulane called the quigrith * * * * since the tyme of Kyng Robert the Bruys, and before."

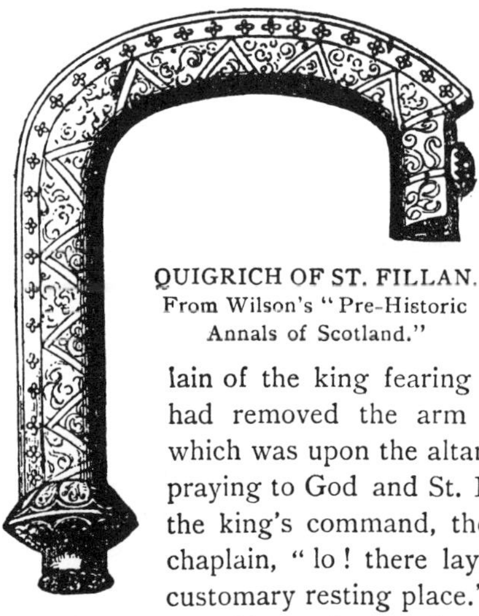

QUIGRICH OF ST. FILLAN.
From Wilson's "Pre-Historic Annals of Scotland."

Hector Boece, the never over-veracious historian, relates a miracle connected with St. Fillan. King Robert Bruce when going to the battle of Bannockburn, had directed the silver case which contained the arm of the saint to be brought along as a talisman. The chaplain of the king fearing to trust the fortunes of war had removed the arm and brought the case only, which was upon the altar before which the king was praying to God and St. Fillan for succor. When, at the king's command, the case was opened by the chaplain, "lo! there lay the arm of the saint in its customary resting place."

The number of miracles credited to St. Fillan would fill a good sized volume, therefore I must not try to repeat any of them. His death is supposed to have taken place about 690.

This is also the festival of SS. Julian martyr, and Basilissa his virgin wife who ended her days in peace. Their story cannot be better told than to quote verbatim from Roman Martyrology in its terse completeness. "But Julian after the death by fire of a multitude of priests and ministers of the Church of Christ, who, driven by the atrocity of the persecution, had fled to them, was by the command of the President Marcian tormented in many ways and executed. With him suffered Antony, a priest, and Anastasius, raised from the dead and made a partaker of the grace of Christ by Julian! also Celsus, a boy, and his mother Marciannilla, seven brothers and many others." This Anastasius and Marciannilla had been converted by Julian, hence the expression "raised from the dead." Their martyrdom was in the year 313 and took place at Antinopolis in Egypt.

JANUARY 10th.

St. William, Archbishop of Bourges, was one of the noted characters in monastic life during the closing years of the twelfth century and the first decade of the thirteenth. He was educated by Peter the Hermit, archdeacon of Soissons, who was his uncle. He took the habit at the Abbey of Pontigny ultimately becoming its prior. On the death of Henry de Sully, the Archbishop of Bourges, the clergy requested his brother, Eudo, Bishop of Paris, to assist them in selecting some abbot of the Cistercian order for his successor. The method adopted by the reverend prelate was at least unusual. Bishop Eudo first wrote three names upon separate slips of paper, laying them upon the altar. After the prayers were over, closing his eyes, he turned and drew the first slip his finger touched and found it to contain the name of William, and by a majority of the votes of the clergy he was chosen to fill the high office on November 23, 1200.

It was far from William's desire to leave Pontigny and the monasteries affiliated with it, but yielded to what he deemed his duty. The sanctity of this man's life is told in the following quotation from Dr. Butler:

"St. William was deemed a model of monastic perfection. The universal mortification of his senses and passions laid in him the foundation of an admirable purity of heart and an extraordinary gift of prayer, in which he received great heavenly lights and tasted of the sweets which God has reserved for those to whom he is pleased to communicate himself. The sweetness and cheerfulness of his countenance testified the uninterrupted joy and peace that overflowed his soul and made virtue appear with the most engaging charms in the midst of austerities. * * * He always wore a hair shirt under his religious habit, and never added or diminished anything in his clothes either winter or summer."

JANUARY 11th

Is the Octave of the Epiphany of Our Lord. The canonical colour for this day is white.

This day is kept in memory of St. Hyginus, who as head of the Church was placed in the chair of St. Peter after the martyrdom of St. Telesphorus in 139. He filled the high office hardly four years, dying in 142. In Roman Martyrology he is styled as "Martyr," but there is no evidence of his having suffered an untimely or cruel death. Dr. Butler concurs in this, suggesting that the persecutions of Christians in those perilous days was of itself martyrdom.

To-day also is held the feast of St. Theodosius who died in 529 at the age of 104. He was a native of Cappadocia but when a young man removed to Jerusalem, in the vicinity of which city he resided during the remainder of his life. He is said to have lived for about thirty years as a hermit in a cave but having been joined by other saintly persons he finally established a monastic community not far from Bethlehem. He was enabled to erect a suitable building to which by degrees he added churches, infirmaries, and houses for the reception of strangers. The monks of Palestine at that period were called Coenobites; and Sallustius, Bishop of Jerusalem, having appointed Theodosius superintendent of the monasteries, he received the name of Coenobiarch. He was banished by the Emperor Anastasius about the year 513, in consequence of his opposition to the Eutychian heresy but was recalled by the Emperor Justinus II., surnamed the Ancient, Emperor of the East (450–527).

The first lesson which he taught his monks was that the continual remembrance of death is the foundation of religious perfection; to imprint this more deeply on their minds, he caused a great grave or pit to be dug which might serve for the common burial-place of the whole community, that by the presence of this memorial of death and by continually meditating on that object, they might more perfectly learn to die daily.

Theodosius died January 11th, 529.

JANUARY 12th.

In old days in England the first Monday after Twelfth Day was called "Plough Monday," as like St. Distaff Day it marked the resumption by the ploughmen and other farm hands of their usual labours, and in the days when the Roman Church was dominant prior to the Reformation, the Ploughmen on the Plough Monday always burned candles at the shrines or before the images of their own especial saint. The Reformation put out the lights but not the frolics that followed on Plough Monday Night, which were maintained in some parts of England even into the earlier years of the eighteenth century.

This day is the festival of St. Benedict (or Bennet) Biscop, one of the most remarkable men of his day. A man who was a thinker, he was far in advance of his day; for he was one who believed in educating the common classes and knowing as he did how impossible under existing circumstances it was to educate the masses to read, sought to teach them — to use his admirable phrase — through "their visual organs," and for this purpose brought to his church from Rome the first paintings and bits of sculpture he could gather to be held up before them that they might carry away some memory of the scenes these pictures taught of the life of Our Lord, and His Holy Followers. I wish I had space to devote to some of his reasons when "brought to book" for his innovation of all previous customs. They are often epigrammatic but most convincing. "They have eyes to see," (he says) "but not minds to understand God's written teachings." So he told the story of (for example) the Crucifixion, and then by exhibiting the painting left on the minds of those simple folk an impression no eloquence of his could have done, by pointing to the picture. The same was true of music. It was Bennet Biscop who first put it to practical use in the service of the Church in England. He was a Northumbrian monk but a man of action; not a sentimentalist to spend his hours in dreaming. Thus he built the two celebrated monasteries at Weremerith (now Wearmouth) and at Girwy (now Jarrow), six miles distant from Weremouth at a point on the Tyne. The first was called St. Peter's and the latter St. Paul's. From these two monasteries his monks went forth, literally scouring the country and teaching the people.

Lambarde, who seems to have been no admirer of ornamental architecture or the fine arts, thus speaks of St. Benedict Biscop: "This man laboured to Rome five several tymes, for what other things I find not save only to procure pope-holye privileges, and curious ornaments for his monasteries Jarrow and Weremouth; for first he gotte for theise houses, wherein he nourished 600 monks, great liberties; then brought he them home from Rome painters, glasiers, free-masons and singers to th' end that his buildings might so shyne with workmanshipe and his churches so sounde with melodye, that simple souls ravished therewithe should fantasie of theim nothinge but heavenly holynes. In this jolitie continued theise houses, and others by theire example embraced the like, till Hinguar and Hubba, the Danish pyrates, A. D. 870, were raised by God to abate their pride, who not only fyred and spoyled them, but also almost all the religious houses on the northeast coast of the island."

In early life Biscop was one of the higher officers at the court of Oswi, king of Northumbria, and possessed of much wealth but at the age of twenty-five he visited Rome and retired from thence to the monastery of Levins where he took the monastic habit. When at last he returned to Northumbria, Egfrid, son of Oswi, sat on the throne and like his father was a true Christian, therefore lent his old friend much aid when he set about building his new monastery. But I may not take further space for this interesting man who passed from his labours on January 12th in 690.

JANUARY 13th

Is the festival of St. Veronica of Milan. Originally, Veronica was only a poor girl employed in the fields near Milan, but her parents though poor were good and pious people and the maid had from infancy been taught to love and reverence sacred things. Thus it was that in her early maidenhood her heart was inspired to become a "religieuse," and she was permitted to enter the nunnery of St. Martha of the Order of St. Austin in Milan where after three years of preparation she took the habit of St. Martha. Her exemplary life was such that in due time she became the Superioress of the nunnery and was looked upon as the model of evangelical perfection. Indeed so highly was she esteemed that after her death, which took place in 1497, Pope Leo X. by a bull issued in 1517 permitted her to be honoured in her monastery in the same manner as if she had been beatified after the usual form.

This name of Veronica brings to mind a very curious legend. It is stated that the Saviour at his passion had his face wiped with a handkerchief by a devout female attendant and that the cloth became miraculously impressed with the image of his countenance. It became Vera Iconica, or a true portrait of those blessed features. The handkerchief, being sent to Abgarus, king of Odessa, passed through a series of adventures but ultimately settled at Rome where it has been kept for many centuries in St. Peter's Church, under the highest veneration. There seems even to be a votive mass, "de Sancta Veronica seu vultu Domini," the idea being thus personified after a manner peculiar to the ancient church. From the term Vera Iconica has come the name Veronica.

This portrait, it is stated in an article in the *London Art Journal* for 1861, has been traced back to the days of the early Catacombs in Rome where it is supposed for a time to have been hidden. Festullian who wrote in A. D. 160, mentions portraits of Christ on sacramental vessels used by the early Christians.

This is also the feast of St. Kentigern, around whom so much mystery has ever clustered.

He appears to have flourished throughout the sixth century and to have died in 601. Through his mother named Thenew, he was connected with the royal family of the Cumbrian Britons — a rude state stretching along the west side of the island between Wales and Argyle. After being educated by Serf at Culross, he returned among his own people and planted a small religious establishment on the banks of a little stream which falls into the Clyde where now the city of Glasgow stands. Upon a tree beside the clearing in the forest he hung his bell to summon the savage neighbours to worship; and the tree with the bell still figures in the arms of Glasgow. Thus was the commencement made of what in time became a seat of population in connection with an episcopal see; and by and by, an industrious town; ultimately what we now see, a magnificent city with half a million of inhabitants. Kentigern, though his amiable character procured him the name of Mungo or the Beloved, had great troubles from the then king of the Strathclyde Britons; and at one time he had to seek refuge in Wales where he employed himself to some purpose as he there founded under the care of a follower, St. Asaph, the religious establishment of that name, now the seat of an English bishopric.

St. Kentigern died at a very advanced age and was buried on the spot where the cathedral bearing his name now stands in Glasgow.

JANUARY 14th.

St. Hilary, whom both the Anglican and Roman churches honour to-day was born at Poictiers in Gaul and was brought up in paganism, but became a convert to Christianity, and in the year 354 was elected Bishop of Poictiers. The first general council, held at Nice (Nicæa) in Bithynia in 325, under the Emperor Constantine, had condemned the doctrine of Arius but had not suppressed it, and Hilarius about thirty years afterwards, when he had made himself acquainted with the arguments, became an opponent of the Arians who were then numerous and were patronized by the Emperor Constantius. The council of Arles held in 353 had condemned Athanasius and others who were opponents of the Arian doctrine, and Hilarius in the council of Beziers held in 356 defended Athanasius in opposition to Saturninus, Bishop of Arles. He was in consequence deposed from his bishopric by the Arians, and banished by Constantius to Phrygia. During his banishment of four years he was a prolific writer and his works are still extant and highly esteemed.

After the death of Constantius in 361 Hilary was restored to his bishopric, where he died in 368.

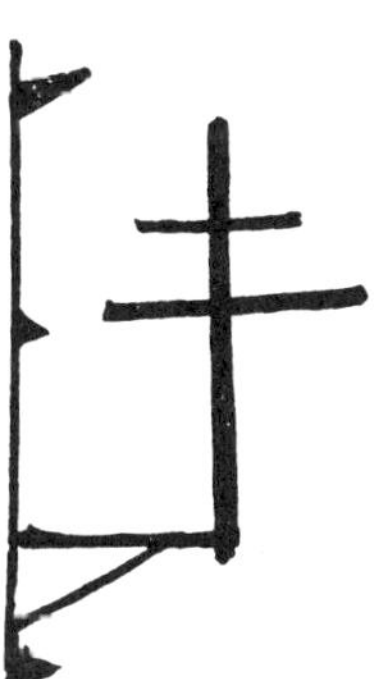

The symbol for St. Hilary given here is from an English Clog stick; but the Danish sticks present nothing to mark the day for this saint.

I notice that in both English church books and American church almanacs the feast of St. Hilary is set for January 13th, but both Chambers' and Roman Martyrology place the date on the 14th.

JANUARY 15th

Is the festival of St. Paul, said to be the first hermit of whom there is mention in church menologies. The account given by Dr. Butler from which this abridged note is made was compiled from the biography written by St. Jerom in 365.

Paul was a native of the Lower Thebias in Egypt. When the bloody persecutions of Decius began in 250, Paul for a time kept himself concealed in the house of his brother-in-law, but convinced of his relative being about to denounce him in order that he might succeed to his estates, he fled to the deserts, where he found shelter in some caverns that in the days of Queen Cleopatra had been used by money coiners. Here, with a spring of water to drink from and palm trees which furnished him both food and raiment, for he clothed himself with garments made from the palm leaf, he remained in security. Paul's legend tells that he was twenty-two years old when he fled to the desert and that for twenty-one years he lived on the fruit he gathered from his palm tree. After that, however, " till his death, he was like Elias of old, miraculously fed with bread brought to him daily by a raven."

Dr. Butler in his account of this hermit says that when St.

Anthony was ninety years old he made a pilgrimage into the desert in search of this noted hermit and after two days found him. Then he says: "While they were discoursing together a raven flew towards them and dropped a loaf of bread before them. Upon which St. Paul said: 'Our good God has sent us a dinner. In this manner have I received half a loaf every day these sixty years past. Now you have come to visit me, Christ has doubled His provision for His servants.'" Dr. Butler adds several other remarkable incidents, among them how Paul foretold his own death and of his burial by St. Anthony and of the trouble he was in as to how he should dig the grave for the hermit. "While he stood thus perplexed, two lions came up quietly and as it were, mourning and tearing up the ground, made a hole large enough to receive the body." St. Paul died in 342 in the 113th year of his age and the ninetieth of his solitary life, and is credited in all places, with being the *first* Christian hermit or recluse.

JANUARY 16th.

This day is kept in memory of St. Marcellus, Pope. He had been a priest under Pope Mercellinus, after whose death the see had remained vacant for three and a half years, when, in 308 he was elected to fill the high office; though "as God willed it for only one year and twenty days," as he died on January 16, 310. Roman Martyrology says he "by command of the tyrant Maxentius was first beaten with clubs, then sent to take care of criminals with a guard to watch him." His trials, however, were of short duration. His body is said to lie in the church which bears his name in Rome.

One of the favourite methods of St. Francis of Assisi — of whom we shall make mention on October 4th, and also of the foundation of the celebrated Order of the Franciscans, — for the advancement of Christianity was by means of missionary labour. It was thus that he sent forth the "Five Friar Minors" whose festival is celebrated in the Roman Church to-day, to preach to the

Mahometans of the West while he in person went to those of the East. These five preached first to the Moors in Seville, suffering many persecutions. Thence they crossed into Morocco but were quickly banished and compelled to return to Seville. The renewal of their preaching at once roused the anger of the infidels who sought to drive them out even as they had been expelled from Morocco. For persevering in their holy labours, they were arrested and brought before an infidel judge.

The antagonism and bitter feeling between the infidel Moors and Christians were intense. Already the impending fate which drove the Moors in 1238 to found the Kingdom of Granada and which was to be their last refuge must have been foreseen. Henry I. was then king, but civil wars were constantly breaking out. Suppressed in one quarter the Friars arose in another; until in 1238, Ferdinand III. (The Holy) ascended the throne. But while this interesting chapter in Spanish history was being enacted our Five Friar Minors were in the hands of an infidel judge, beyond the protection of Henry. These five, Berardus, Peter, Acursius, Adjustus, and Otto, as they are named in Latin Martyrology, were brave, fearless men as Francis must have known them to be when he selected them for this arduous task. Yet, seemingly, they had hardly judged the intense hatred of these infidels or they would not have ventured again into this dangerous region. Be that as it may, for there are no records to show the motives that induced them to do as they did, this judge caused them to be scourged, and added to his cruelty by ordering "boiling oil and vinegar to be poured into their wounds and then that their bodies should be rolled over potsherds." Then their legend continues, "the king caused them to be brought before him and with his own hands with his cimeter he clove their heads asunder to the middle of their foreheads."

It was not until 1481 that these martyrs were canonized by Pope Sixtus IV., though at some earlier date (unrecorded), their relics were ransomed and placed in the monastery of the Holy Cross in Coimbra.

This festival was fixed for January 16th by Pope Sixtus the day he issued his bull of canonization.

JANUARY 17th

Is the festival of St. Antony, or Anthony as the name is sometimes written, or again Antonius. He was born at Coma in Upper Egypt, in 251. His parents were Christians and by them he was most carefully trained. When about twenty years of age, by his parents' death he found himself possessed of a very considerable estate and the care of a sister. Taking Christ's words to a rich young man home to himself, he interpreted them literally. Having first placed his sister " in a house of virgins " (which in passing it is interesting to note is the *first* mention made in Church history of a nunnery) he sold his lands and all his personal effects and saved what was needful to secure his sister from want or bring a burden upon any one — he distributed his wealth among the poor and henceforth led the life of a hermit, and thereby is held in reverence as " The Patriarch of Monks "; as he seems to have been the one who introduced this mode of solitary life into Egypt.

The temptations of St. Antony as related in his legends were almost endless. Satan we are informed first tried by bemuddling his thoughts to divert him from the design of becoming a monk. Then he appeared to him in the forms successively, of a handsome woman and a black boy but without in the least disturbing him. Angry at the defeat, Satan and a multitude of attendant fiends fell upon him during the night and he was found in his cell in the morning lying to all appearances dead. On another occasion these devils expressed their rage by making such a dreadful noise that the walls of his cell shook. They transformed themselves into shapes of all sorts of beasts, lions, bears, leopards, bulls, serpents, asps, scorpions and wolves; but he overcame them all by his prayers and holy life.

I must not, however, attempt to speak of these in detail for they fill a volume. During the persecution under Maximinus about the year 310 some of the solitaries were seized in the wilderness and suffered martyrdom at Alexandria whither Antonius accompained them, but he was not subjected to punishment. After his return he retired farther into the desert but went on one occasion to Alexander in order to preach against the Arians.

The two monastic orders of St. Anthony originated long after the time of the saint — one in Dauphine, in the eleventh century; and the other, a military order in Hainault in the fourteenth century. In Dauphine the people were cured of the erysipelas by the aid, as they thought, of St. Anthony; and the disease from this fact was afterward called St. Anthony's Fire.

It is scarcely necessary to remark that St. Anthony is one of the most notable of all the saints in the Romish Kalendar. One cannot travel anywhere in Europe at the present day and particularly in Italy, without finding in churches, monasteries and familiar conversation of the people, abundant memorials of this early Egyptian anchorite. Even in Scotland, at Leith, a street reveals by its name where a monastery of St. Anthony once stood; while, on the hill of Arthur's Seat overhanging Edinburgh, we still see a fragment of a small church that had been dedicated to him, and a fountain called St. Anton's Well.

St. Anthony reached an extreme old age, dying when one hundred and five years old in 356, in semi-solitude attended only by two of his disciples, Macarius and Amathas, who had for fifteen years remained by him to watch over his needs in his old age.

The Saturday before the second Sunday after Epiphany is one of the "Movable Feasts" of the Roman Church, the "Feast of the Holy Name of Jesus."

JANUARY 18th.

ST. PETER'S CHAIR.

This day at St. Peter's Church in Rome is held a festival with offices and services of an especial character entitled as above. Of this feast Dr. Butler tells us that it is well evidenced to be of great antiquity, being adverted to in a martyrology copied in the time of St. Willibrod in 720. "Christians," he says, "justly celebrate the founding of this mother church, the centre of Catholic communion, in thanksgiving to God for his mercies on his church and to implore his future blessing." The celebration takes place in St. Peter's Church under circumstances of the greatest solemnity and splendour.

This funzioni (function) is not only one of unusual magnificence for even this grand old church, which beyond a doubt has been the scene of a greater number of the most splendid ecclesiastical displays than any other one building now standing in the whole world, but the function itself is also one of great solemnity as befits the occasion.

This chair of the first pope of the church is said to be still preserved in the Church of St. Peter's at Rome.

This day is also the festival of St. Prisca, a virgin martyr under the Emperor Claudius, of whom little is really known. According to her legend she was a Roman virgin of illustrious birth, who, at the age of thirteen was exposed in the amphitheatre because she had confessed she was a Christian. A fierce lion was let loose upon her but her youth and innocence disarmed the fury of the savage beast which, instead of tearing her to pieces, humbly licked her feet, to the great consolation of Christians and the confusion of the idolators. Being led back to prison she was there beheaded. Sometimes she is represented with a lion, sometimes with an eagle, because it is related that an eagle watched by her body till it was laid in the grave. for thus, says the story, was virgin-innocence honoured by kingly bird as well as by kingly beast. A church bearing St. Prisca's name was built by Pope Eutychianus in 280 in Rome and is still standing. According to an old tradition this church stands on the site of the house of Aquila and Priscilla where St. Peter lodged when at Rome and who are the same mentioned by St. Paul as tent-makers, while here is also shown the font from which, according to the same tradition, St. Peter baptised the first Roman converts to Christianity.

S. PRISCA.
From glass in Winchester Cathedral.

St. Prisca's is one of the names that were retained in the Kalendar of the Reformed Church after its division from the Church of Rome, and the day of her festival coincides with that of the Romans. The Clog symbol for this saint is the palm branch of martyrdom.

Another of the names this day honoured is St. Deicolus or St. Deel, an Irish priest who spent his best days in France and whose memory is preserved in Franche-comte where his name Deel is still frequently given in baptism. He appears to have been one of a group of missionaries who in an early but unfortunately unknown period went to Egypt to propagate the faith and became martyrs.

JANUARY 19th

Is given to St. Wulstan who was the last saint of the Anglo-Saxon church and is the connecting link between the old English church and hierarchy and the Norman. He was a monk indeed and an ascetic; still his vocation lay not in the school or cloister but among the people of the market-place and the village, and he rather dwelt on the great broad truths of the gospel than followed them to their dogmatic results. Though a thane's son, a series of unexpected circumstances brought him into the religious profession and he became prior of a monastery at Worcester. Born at Long Itchington in Warwickshire, he was educated at the monasteries of Eversham and Peterborough, the latter one of the richest houses and the most famous schools in England.

Wulstan was one of those blunt outspoken men so easy of access and frank in his conservatism that it made him the idol of the common people though he had little respect for titles and rebuked the high in state as he did his own parishioners. In 1062 two Roman cardinals came to Worcester with Aldred, the late bishop, but who was then Archbishop of York. They spent the whole of Lent at the cathedral monastery where Wulstan was prior, and they were so impressed with his austere and hard working way of life, that partly by their recommendation, as well as the popular voice at Worcester, Wulstan was elected to the vacant bishopric.

It was this prelate who stuck his staff into the tomb of the Confessor which none could remove until they acknowledged Wulstan's sanctity. Anti-slavery men of the old days should have especial reverence for Wulstan, for he was a brave antagonist against the slave trade, which in his day did such a thriving business out from Bristol with the merchants of Ireland. He died on the 19th of January, 1095, in the eighty-seventh year of his age and the thirty-third of his episcopate. Contrary to the usual custom, the body was laid out, arranged in the episcopal vestments and crosier, before the high altar, that the people of Worcester might look once more on their good bishop. His stone coffin is, to this day, shown in the presbytery of the cathedral, the crypt and early Norman portions of which were the work of Wulstan.

In this cathedral there is both a statue of St. Wulstan and the monument of King John. This last is only remarkable from the fact that it is the oldest royal monument now standing in England.

JANUARY 20th.

St. Fabian, Bishop of Rome, whom the Church honours on this day, is yet another in that notable list whose names were retained in the Kalendar of the Reformed Church when the division came, and who still holds its place in the Kalendar of the English as it also does in the Roman Church. His election to succeed Pope Anterus in 236 as told by Eusebius is at least somewhat remarkable. He was a stranger to most of those who had assembled to take a part in the election, when a dove entered the room through an open window. Circling the apartment it hovered over the audience for a moment and then alighted on the head of Fabian, who until then had not been considered as a contestant for the honoured position, as he was but a layman. This omen was regarded by all as a miraculous sign and he was at once chosen. He filled the

S. FABIAN.
From Bodleian MS.
Liturg. 383.

pontifical chair during a period of sixteen years, his most notable act being the sending of Dionysius and other preachers into Gaul as missionaries, and the condemnation of Privatus, who had broached a new heresy in Africa. Under the persecution of Decius, Fabian suffered martyrdom by being beheaded. He is therefore represented as kneeling at the block wearing the triple crown. Often he carries a book and sword, or palm branch, but usually as in our illustration wears the triple crown and bears a cross.

This day too is sacred to St. Sebastian, a noble Roman soldier and the Commander of the First Cohort. His story is a most interesting one but unfortunately too long for repetition here and must be summed up in the brief words of the Roman Martyrology: "For professing Christianity he was tried in the middle of the camp, shot with arrows, and lastly struck with clubs until he expired." This noble man is also honoured in the Kalendar of the English church. His martyrdom took place in 288.

ST. AGNES' EVE.

In the olden days in England when superstitious rites were common, there was no festival more strictly observed by a certain class than St. Agnes' Eve; and if reports are true, even now these customs are not obsolete, by which a maid through divination learned who her future spouse would be. Few of us who ever read Keats' poem "The Eve of St. Agnes," will forget it:

"They told her how, upon St. Agnes' Eve,
Young virgins might have visions of delight,
And soft adorings from their loves receive
Upon the honey'd middle of the night,
If ceremonies due they did aright;
As, supperless to bed they must retire,
And couch supine their beauties lily white;
Nor look behind, nor sideways, but require
Of heaven with upward eyes for all that they desire."

* * * * * * *

JANUARY 21st.

ST. AGNES.

The legend of St. Agnes is not only the oldest, but it is the most authentic of all the stories told of the early saints and martyrs of the Christian Church. She was one of the four "Great Virgins" of the Latin Church, and her story has been sung by poets in every age and tongue, told from the pulpits in every land, in homilies from the lips of venerable and venerated men, until it seems almost like a household word. Even as early as during the IV. century when St. Jerom wrote of her he speaks of others who had already told her story. "So ancient," says Mrs. Jameson, "is the worship paid to St. Agnes, that next to the Evangelists and Apostles there is no saint whose effigy is older."

S. AGNES.
From painted glass.

To abridge the legend of St. Agnes is to rob it of its chief beauties but my readers may find it in Mrs. Jameson's "Legendary and Sacred Art" very fully told though even there somewhat cut. S. Baring-Gould in his "Virgin Saints and Martyrs," also tells the famous story more fully.

Agnes was a maid of but thirteen years yet already a devoted disciple of Christ, when her transcendent beauty of person and the great wealth she was dowered with attracted the son of the prefect of Rome and he fell violently in love. But Agnes repulsed his costly gifts and told him she was the "Bride of Christ." Whereupon the young man fell sick as he confessed "for love," and the father tried his persuasive powers and bribes upon the maiden without effect, then threats, later imprisonment and torments, such as the decrees of Dioclesian permitted against Christians.

"As neither temptation nor the fear of death could prevail with Agnes, Sempronius thought of other means to vanquish her resistance; he ordered her to be carried by force to a place of infamy and exposed to the most degrading outrages. The soldiers who dragged her thither stripped her of her garments and when she saw herself thus exposed she bent down her head in meek shame and prayed; immediately her hair which was already long and abundant became like a veil covering her whole person from head to foot; and those who looked upon her were seized with awe and fear as of something sacred and dared not lift their eyes." So they shut her within a chamber, and there as she prayed an angel bearing a white robe appeared and clothed her. At the last the prefect ordered her to be burned, and when she had been thrown on the pile of fagots they were at once extinguished around her but their heat caused the two soldiers who guarded her to fall dead.

In his anger the prefect ordered her to be stabbed to death and a soldier thus put an end to her trials by mounting the pile of fagots and thrusting her through with a sword. St. Agnes is usually represented in art with a lamb at her feet, possibly from the significance of her name and her spotless purity. She often bears a palm branch and at times a sword is piercing her throat. Her martyrdom occurred in 304. Two churches are dedicated to her in Rome.

JANUARY 22d.

The legend of St. Vincent whose festival occurs this day has, to use Mrs. Jameson's quaint expression, been so "extravagantly embroidered" that one finds difficulty in selecting truth from fiction. He was born in Saragossa in Aragon, a city Prudentius says in his famous hymn which had produced more saints and martyrs than any city in Spain. Dr. Butler says it was "most probably at Osca (now Huesca), in Grenada," where he was educated. The interim until we find Vincent in the clutches of the proconsul, Dacian, infamous even in Spanish annals of cruelty, is so vague I omit it. He then was not more than twenty years of age, but an ordained deacon. When brought before Dacian he defied the tortures threatened him. What follows is but the repetition of the story so often told of torments such as one would think only a devil could invent His body was lacerated by iron hooks, later half broiled over a spiked gridiron from which the Clog Almanacs take the symbol that marks St. Vincent Day. When these torments were ended, he was turned "torn, bleeding and half consumed by fire," into a cell "strewn with potsherds for him to lie upon." But even then his jailor saw his dungeon filled with heavenly light and heard the angel attending him singing songs of triumph. Then Dacian changed his tactics, perfidious as he ever was, gave him a bed of down and allowed his friends to minister to his comfort hoping so to restore him that he might be subjected

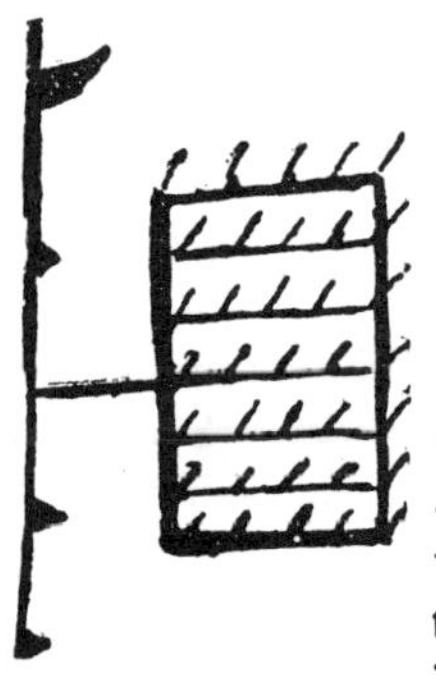

to further torments, but the martyr had already endured all his human body could and he died almost immediately. So furious was Dacian at this that he ordered the body to be thrown out for the wild beasts to devour; but the ravens drove the wolves away. Then the pro-consul ordered the body of the saint to be sewn in an oxhide, as was done to parricides, and cast into the sea, but when the minions who performed the task returned to the shore, the body of the saint lay on the beach where it was left until the waves covered it with sand. This resting place was miraculously revealed many years later and the relics received Christian burial at Valencia. Not, however, to rest in peace, for the Moors carried his relics away. I may not take space to follow their wanderings until these sacred relics found rest in Lisbon. Spanish legends make St. Vincent and St. Laurence brothers but there seems no just grounds to believe this is true.

St. Vincent is also one of those whose names were retained by the Reformed Church and still holds a place in the Kalendar of the Church of England.

JANUARY 23d.

St. Raymund, who is remembered this day, is another Spanish saint of the order of St. Dominic, who by his wonderful exertions restored many of his countrymen who had been led astray by the Moors, to Christianity. He toward the end of his life accompanied King James of Aragon to the island of Majorca, where he converted many pagans. It was now that the immoral life of the king so affected him he wished to return to Spain, but the king forbid him and ordered severe penalties for any who aided him in his efforts to do so. Therefore he walked boldly to the waters, spread his cloak upon them, tied one corner of it to a staff for a sail and having made the sign of the cross, stepped upon the cloak without fear whilst his timorous companion stood trembling and wondering on the shore. On this new kind of vessel the saint was wafted with such rapidity that in six hours he reached the harbour of Barcelona, sixty leagues distant from Majorca, Those who saw him arrive in this manner met him with acclamations. But he, gathering up his cloak which was perfectly dry, put it on, strode through the crowd and entered his monastery.

The above is condensed from the bull of his canonization published by Clement VIII. in 1601. His office was fixed by Clement X. for January 23d. He died in 1275.

JANUARY 24th

Is sacred to St. Timothy, a disciple of St. Paul. When in 51 Paul was preaching in Iconium and Lystra, he heard such accounts of Timothy that he took the young man for his companion and he accompanied him into Philippi and elsewhere — and in 64 Paul made him Bishop of Ephesus with a general supervision over the churches in Asia.

From an account ascribed to Polycrates, Bishop of Ephesus, who died in 196, it is said that: "Under the Emperor Nerva, in the year 97 * * * Timothy was slain with stones and clubs by the heathen while he was endeavouring to oppose their idolatrous ceremonies on one of their festivals called 'Catagogia,' kept on the 22d of January when the idolators called in troops carrying in one hand an idol and in the other a club."

From another source it is said that the relics of St. Timothy were translated in the year 356 from their resting place in Ephesus to Constantinople.

JANUARY 25th.

The festival of the Apostle Paul celebrated to-day is not commemorated by either the Roman or Protestant branches of the Christian Church, as is customary at the date of the birth, death or martyrdom of the saints honoured in their Kalendar; but upon what the Apostle regarded as the most momentous day of his life, his conversion. In like manner the Holy Fathers, in their gratitude for so miraculous and important an instance of the Divine power as well as in recognition of the influence this wonderful event had in the establishment of the Christian Church, instituted the Feast of St. Paul. There was also another and potent reason that moved them to this act, that in St. Paul the world has "a perfect model of true conversion" to which the celebration of this feast will always bring to their attention.

Just when the feast first originated or by whom it was first celebrated is not perfectly clear. Dr. Butler says: "We find mention of it in the Kalendar and Missals of the VIII. and IX. centuries, and also that Pope Innocent III. (1198-1216) commanded it to be observed with solemnity." Mention is made of it as being "a solemn festivalin the records of the Council of Oxford held in 1222 during the reign of Henry III., but so far as the English church chronicles show, it had no official recognition until the Diocesan Synod held at Exeter in 1827 when this feast (with several others) was prescribed and duly ordered to be observed. It had, however, prior to this been long observed by all the churches of the West.

It would be a work of supererogation to recount here the life and work of St. Paul, while the story of his martyrdom will be told on June 29.

The legend that St. Paul visited England has been a hotly contested question among English divines of many faiths; but that he has ever been regarded by Londoners with an especial reverence needs no better evidence than that they have dedicated to him their grandest cathedral and that the Sword of St. Paul holds its place in the dexter quarter of the City Arms, just as the Red Cross refers to St. George, the patron saint of England. The Clog symbol given here is taken from an English stick but I have to confess my inability to make out its import.

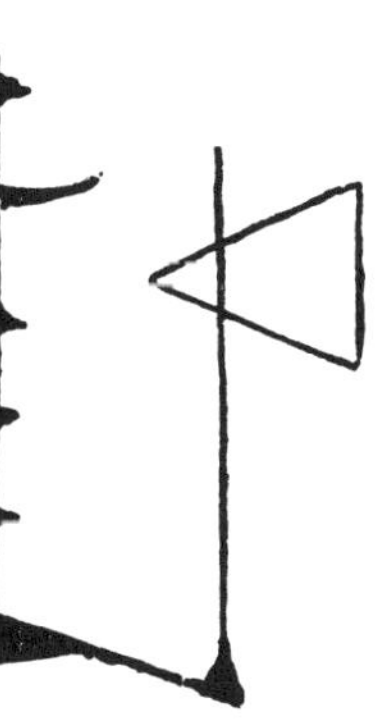

As it is with the Saint Day of most of the noted saints in the Kalendar endless superstitions clustered about St. Paul's Day. One must suffice, a translation of a French belief, though written in old Monkish Latin:

> " If St. Paul's day be fair and clear,
> It does betide a happy year;
> But if it chance to snow or rain,
> Then will be dear all kind of grain;
> If clouds or mists do dark the skie,
> Great store of birds and beasts shall die;
> And if the winds do flie aloft,
> Then war shall vexe the kingdoms oft."

In passing it may not be out of place to say that in 1604, on this day the Hampton Court Conference put forth what is now called the "King James Bible" as an "Authorized version of the Bible," just then translated into English.

JANUARY 26th.

St. Polycarp, who is remembered this day, was one of the earliest " Fathers of the Church" and was a disciple of St. John the Evangelist. He became Bishop of Smyrna before the persecution of Christians which took place in the reign of Marcus Aurelius when Statius Quadratus was pro-consul of Asia. Having incurred the enmity of the infidels, Polycarp was condemned to be burned at the stake. When the fire was lighted his legend tells, " the flames formed themselves into an arch over his head encircling his body but leaving him unharmed. When it was seen that Polycarp was thus miraculously preserved from burning a spearman was ordered to pierce him through his heart which he did, and such a quantity of blood issued from his body that it quenched the fire." But their end had been obtained for the story continues: "At 2 o'clock in the afternoon which these infidels call the eighth hour St. Polycarp received his crown." They also after his death burned his body to ashes. There are two dates given as to when this took place, Tillemont placing it in 166 and Basnage in 169. He was according to the best authorities 120 years old when he suffered and according to his own writing had "served Christ for eighty-six years."

St. Conon another saint honoured this day was a Scotchman and for some time Bishop of Man. His name will long be remembered in the Highlands if for no other reason than the celebrated and still frequently quoted Highland proverb: "Claw for claw, as Conon said to Satan; and the devil take the shortest claw."

JANUARY 27th

Is the festival of St. John Chrysostom or Chrysostomus as some writers make it; a man whose wise words and writings are perhaps more often quoted than those of any of the early fathers, by Christians of every shade of faith — unless it be the words of St. Jerom.

St. John Chrysostomus is also one of the most celebrated fathers of the Eastern, or Greek church. He was born about the year 347 at Antioch. His father was commander of the imperial army in Syria. He was educated for the bar but became a convert to Christianity and as the solitary manner of living then being held in great esteem and very prevalent in Syria, he retired to a mountain not far from Antioch where he lived some years in solitude practising the usual austerities. He returned to the city in 381 and was ordained by Meletius, Bishop of Antioch, to the office of deacon and to that of presbyter in 386. He became one of the most popular preachers of the age; his reputation extending throughout the Christian world; and in 398 on the death of Nectarius he was elected Bishop of Constantinople. He was zealous and resolute in the reform of clerical abuses and two years after his consecration, on his visitation in Asia Minor, he deposed no less than thirteen bishops of Lydia and Phrygia. His denunciations of the licentious manners of the court drew upon him the resentment of the Empress Eudoxia who encouraged Theophilus, Patriarch of Alexandria, to summon a synod at Chalcedon at which a number of accusations were brought against Chrysostom. He was condemned, deposed and banished to Cucusus, a place in the mountain range of Taurus whence after the death of the empress it was determined to remove him to a desert place on the Euxine. He travelled on foot and caught a fever which occasioned his death at Camana in Pontus, September 14, 407, at the age of 60, but his festival is kept on the day of his burial by the Latin Church, the Greeks honouring him on November 13th.

The works of Chrysostom are very numerous consisting of 700 homilies and 242 epistles as well as commentaries, orations and treatises on points of doctrine. His life has been written by Socrates, Sozomen, Theodoret and other early writers and by Neander in more recent times.

The name Chrysostomus or golden-mouthed, on account of his eloquence, was not given to him until some years after his death. Socrates and the other early writers simply call him John, or John of Constantinople.

JANUARY 28th.

St. Cyril, or Cyrillus whom the Church honours this day was the nephew of Theophilus who caused St. Chrysostom to be banished. Upon the death of Theophilus St. Cyril was elected to succeed him as Patriarch of Constantinople. In a later article I will have occasion to refer to Kingsley's celebrated novel, — "Hypatia," where the author refers to the life of St. Cyril. The story of the murder of Hypatia, the daughter of the mathematician Theon of Alexandria, has been related by Socrates, Nicephorus, and other ecclesiastical historians. Hypatia was a lady of such extraordinary ability and learning as to have been chosen to preside over the school of platonic philosophy in Alexandria, and her lectures were attended by a crowd of students from Greece and Asia Minor. She was also greatly esteemed and treated with much respect by Orestes, the governor of Alexandria, who was a decided opponent of the patriarch. Hence the malice of Cyril who is related to have excited a mob of fanatical monks to assault her in the street who dragged her into a church, and there murdered her, actually tearing her body to pieces.

Of St. Cyril's controversy with Nestorius — a monk and priest of Antioch, who was made Bishop of Constantinople in 428 — as to whether Mary was entitled to be termed "the Mother of God," curious and interesting as it is I have not space to enter save to speak of the strange result when Pope Celestine deposed Nestorius and Cyril was called on to execute judgment and summoned a council of sixty at Ephesus and John, Patriarch of Antioch, summoned a counter-council of forty at Antioch who in turn excommunicated Cyril; whereupon the Emperor Theodosius committed both the patriarch and bishop to prison where Cyril remained until through the efforts of Pope Celestine he was in 431 liberated and returned to his see, which he filled until his death in 444.

JANUARY 29th

Is the festival of the noted St. Francis of Sales. We not infrequently hear expressions of surprise at the seeming ease with which the Roman Church regained the influence it had lost in Europe through the Reformation. When, however, we read the story of such a remarkable man as St. Francis the mystery is at once dispelled. The son of pious parents Francis, Count of Sales, had every possible educational advantage as a child at Rocheville and Annecy, later in Paris and afterward in Padua where he went in 1554 to study law under the celebrated preceptor Guy Pancerola. While he was a "past master" in all the polite accomplishments of his day, could ride, dance and hold his own even against experts in the use of the foils, these had not hindered him in the study of the Greek and Hebrew of which he was a perfect master and at Padua he won his degree of doctor of law with the greatest possible eclat. The story of his life has been too often told to need repetition of how he cast fame and fortune behind him for the love of Christ, and was named to the provostship of a church in Geneva where his sermons were of a character to excite even the admiration of modern clerics of every class. But what chiefly won for him the affection of every one who came under his influence was his personal purity and humility. So potent was this that it is said that through his efforts no less than 70,000 Genevese Calvinists were brought back into the communion of the Roman Church. Afterward, in 1594 Francis with a cousin undertook a mission to Chablais on the shores of Lake Geneva where the Catholic religion was already extinct, but within four years he had gained such a power over the hearts of the people that the Protestant form of worship was interdicted by the State. His writings breathe only of divine love and there are extant 520 of these epistles while his "Introduction to a Devout Life" is a model work which cannot be too highly praised and is recognized by many devout clerics of other than the Roman faith. Pope Paul V. erected the Congregation of the Visitation (the Order founded by Francis of Sales) into a religious order. He died at Avignon in 1622. He was canonized in 1665 by Alexander VII. and his feast fixed for January 29th.

This day is also the festival of St. Gildas.

According to his legend he was the son of Can, King of the Britons, of Alclyde (Dumbarton) one of twenty-four brothers who with their father were always at war with King Arthur. But Gildas having shown a disposition for learning was sent to the school of the Welsh saint Iltutus. He afterwards went to study in Gaul whence he returned to Britain and set up a school of his own in South Wales. Subsequently at the invitation of St. Bridget he visited Ireland where he remained a long time and founded several monasteries. He returned to England bringing with him a wonderful bell which he was carrying to the pope; and after having been reconciled with King Arthur who had killed his eldest brother in battle, he proceeded on his journey to Rome.

After his return from Rome he was for a time a hermit in the fastnesses of Wales but later settled in Glastonbury where he died about 570 it is said, though this date is very uncertain.

There were two St. Gildas, both of whom are named on this day. Roman Martyrology gives to one the title of Gildas Badonicus or the Historian, because of the tracts attributed to him. It says that he was born in the year when King Arthur defeated the Saxons in the battle of Mount Badon in Somersetshire; the other they call Gildas the Albanian or Scot, supposing that he was the one who was born at Alclyde. The first has also been called Gildas the Wise. The Gildas spoken of above is known as the author or supposed author, of a book entitled "De Excidio Britanniae," consisting of a short and barren historical sketch of the struggle between the Britons and the Picts and Saxons.

JANUARY 30th.

St. Bathildas or Baldechilde and metamorphosed in French into Bauteur, whose name is to-day honoured by the Church, presents yet another of those romantic stories which we constantly meet in conning the lives of the saints. An English girl by birth she was taken to France and sold as a slave to one Erchinoald, the "Mayor of the palace of Clovis II." when he was a boy. As she matured into womanhood, her beauty and worth attracted the King's attention and in 649 he married her. It is a "far cry" from being a slave, to the throne of France and not without many striking incidents if I had time to tell them.

Bathildas was the mother of three Kings of France, Clotaire III., Childeric II., and Thierry I., all reigning in the above successive order. The death of Clovis II. in 655 when Clotaire was but five years old made her Regent of the kingdom and her power was used with such rare judgment; and the encouragement she gave to the prelates of the Church so great and her own charities so numerous though so unostentatiously bestowed, that her name became a synonym throughout her territory for all that was noble and good. In 665 she resigned her Regency but in those ten years of power she had left many lasting evidences of her devotion to the Church and Christianity. Then she retired to the Royal Nunnery of Chelles founded by St. Clotildes and of which I shall soon speak, and here she died in 680 on January 30th leaving a name which even after these long centuries is held in loving reverence in France.

In the English church this day is kept sacred to the memory of King Charles The Martyr. The only name thus honoured of post-Reformation date in the English church.

FEBRUARY

———Then came old February, sitting
In an old wagon, for he could not ride,
Drawn of two fishes for the season fitting,
Which through the flood before did softly slide
And swim away; yet had he by his side
His plough and harness fit to till the ground.
— *Spenser.*

When Numa Pompilius revised the Roman Kalendar which increased the number of months into which the year was divided from ten to twelve, he named those he then added Januarius and Februare. The last signifies "to expiate or to purify." Numa also gave this month twenty-nine days except in "leap-years" when it was to have twenty-eight. But when Augustus to honour his own month increased the days of August to thirty-one he took the day from Februare leaving that month in ordinary years but twenty-eight days.

Among the Saxons this month was known as "Sproutkale," and later, as the "Sol-monat," while in early days in England it was called "February fill-dyke" as the melting snows filled and overflowed the dykes and rivers.

Brady, the noted antiquarian, says: "The common emblematical representation of February is a man in a sky-coloured dress bearing in his hand the astronomical sign Pices." This, doubtless, Spenser had in mind when he wrote the lines quoted above.

FEBRUARY 1st.

St. Ignatius, the Bishop of Antioch and Martyr, whose name heads the list of saints the Church honours on this day, occupies a most important place in the history of Christianity from his having been a disciple and the immediate successor of the Apostles.

For forty years he filled the important position of Bishop of Antioch; and Christians of every sect and creed unite in testifying to his virtue and pious zeal and his life presents a perfect model of all that goes to make up a true Christian.

In the ninth year of Trajan's reign (107) the emperor set out for the East on an expedition against the Parthians and made a triumphal entry into Antioch on January 7th, and his first order thereafter was for a sacrifice to the gods. Already many Christians had suffered by his orders in and near Antioch. It was therefore only what was to be expected that the refusal of any for this especial sacrifice should suffer. Ignatius' refusal and condemnation to be sent to Rome to be devoured by wild beasts in the ampitheatre is a long but not uncommon story; save that his journey was a continued series of ovations by the Christians in every city through which the noble man and his guard of Roman soldiers passed and that not a few of these loyal Christians later paid severe penalties for their enthusiam. The journey was a long and tedious one, not a small part of it being made on foot which of itself, for a man of his age, was a severe trial but borne with true Christian fortitude and without complaint.

It was therefore not until December 20th of the same year (107) the party arrived in Rome and their victim was at once on reaching the city given to the lions in the Ampitheatre to be devoured. After that, devout brethren gathered up his bones and St. Chrysostom is authority for saying that the casket in which they were placed was "carried in triumph through all the cities from Rome to Antioch." The Greeks keep the feast of St. Ignatius on December 20th but the Latin Church have always held it upon this first day of February.

This day is also the festival of St. Bridget who next to St. Patrick is the one saint above all others dear to the Irish heart. She was the daughter of a prince in Ulster and was born at Fochard. She received the veil from the hands of St. Mel, a nephew of St. Patrick, and has ever been reverenced as the "Mother of Nunneries" in Ireland. She built her first cell under a large oak which had perhaps been the site of pagan worship in earlier times and from whence it was named Kil-dara or the cell of the oak. Round this first Irish nunnery eventually arose the city of Kildare. The date at which St. Bridget founded her cell is said to have been about the year 585. An almost endless number of miracles are credited to her. She died in 523 and was buried at Downpatrick, in the church in which it is said lie the bodies of SS. Patrick and Columba.

St. Bridget — or as in these countries she is called St. Bride — is almost if not equally reverenced in both England and Scotland. In London adjoining St. Bride's Churchyard, Fleet street, is an ancient well dedicated to the saint and commonly called Bride's well. A palace erected near by took the name of Bridewell. This being given by Edward VI. to the city of London as a workhouse for the poor and a house of correction, the name became associated in the popular mind with houses having the same purpose in view. Hence it has arisen that the pure and innocent Bridget — the first of Irish nuns — is now inextricably connected in ordinary English parlance with a class of beings of the most opposite description.

FEBRUARY 2d.

THE PURIFICATION OF THE VIRGIN, COMMONLY CALLED CANDLEMAS DAY.

From a very early, indeed wholly unknown, date in the Christian history the 2d of February has been held as the festival of the Purification of the Virgin, and it is still a holiday of the Church of England, as well as a holy feast of the Latin Church. From the coincidence of the time being the same as that of the Februation or purification of the people in pagan Rome some consider this was a Christian festival engrafted upon a heathen one in order to take advantage of the established habits of the people; but the idea is at least open to a good deal of doubt. The popular name Candlemas is derived from the ceremony which the Church of Rome dictates to be observed on this day; namely, a blessing of candles by the clergy and a distribution of them amongst the people by whom they are afterwards carried lighted in solemn procession. In the Protestant churches this ceremony did not obtain after the Reformation but especial services have always been held in honour of the occasion and are part of the regular ritual of the English church. Down to the end of the XVIII. century in many of the churches in England candles were burned on this day.

At Rome the Pope every year officiates at this festival in the beautiful chapel of the Quirinal. When he has blessed the candles he distributes them with his own hand amongst those in the church each of whom going singly up to him, kneels to receive it. The cardinals go first; then follow the bishops, canons, priors, abbots, priests, etc., down to the sacristans and meanest officers of the church. This candle-bearing has a deeper significance than appears at first as it is intended to refer to what Simeon said when he took the infant Jesus in his arms, and declared that He was "The light to lighten the Gentiles."

THE PURIFICATION.
Painting on Wall, S. Stephen's Chapel, Westminster.

In passing I must allude to a strange custom which prevailed in England in early days and which came from the custom of carrying candles at the Purification of the Virgin ceremonials, which led every woman after child-birth to carry candles with her, occasionally lighting them until her own day for "churching."

What in the old days superstition demanded fashion, now the greater power, commands that the holly used for decorations both in church and house should be taken down on Candlemas Eve or misfortune will come on parish or people. In taking down holly in some parts of England it is thought unlucky to prick the finger if the blood comes, but if a leaf sticks to dress or coat it is a good omen. In old days a branch of holly picked on Christmas Eve was regarded as efficacious as the rowan or mountain ash in protecting from witches and warlocks or evil spells. A twig of holly brought from church might be kept, like the Easter palm, for the same purpose.

FEBRUARY 3d.

St. Wereburg whose festival is kept this day, was one of the earliest and most celebrated of the Anglo-Saxon saints contemporary with the beginning of Christianity in Mercia, and she had a prominent part in establishing the first nunneries known in England. Her father Wulfhere was king of Mercia, and while nominally a Christian was, it is said, kept from paganism only through the influence of his queen and her children and at one time even did apostatise from the Christian faith but was brought back by St. Chad.

Here as is so often the case love and romance enters the life of our saint when a pagan prince named Werbode sued for the hand of Wereburg, and being refused, we are told "he died raving mad." It was after this love passage that Wereburg with no little trouble secured permission from the king her father to enter the monastery of Ely — of whose foundation I shall remark on later — then governed by a cousin, Ethelreda. As a nun of Ely she soon became very famous for her piety and her miracles. Thus when Etheldrod, a brother of Wulfhere, succeeded to the throne in 675 Wereburg was called from Ely and commissioned to found nunneries in Mercia ; of which those at Trentham, Hanbury (now Tutbury) in Staffordshire and Wedon in Northamptonshire were the most noted and of which she was at one and the same time the superior. St. Wereburg died at Trentham on February 3, 699.

This brief sketch only in part tells the story of this saint. For years after her death her relics caused the fire kindled by the Danes to burn the city to be extinguished. It is for this she was made the patroness of Chester.

St. Blasius or Blase is another saint who is honoured to-day, by both the Roman and Reformed Churches and who has a place in the English church Kalendar. He was Bishop of Sebaste in Armenia and was crowned with martyrdom in the persecution of Licinius in 316. From the fact that among the many cruel torments the good man was subjected to his body was torn by iron combs such as the wool-combers used in old days in England, he became their patron saint. In Bradford, Norwich, and many English towns where woolen manufacture is the leading factor St. Blase's Day is even now celebrated with great pomp, when poems are read and processions, in which the Lord Mayor and city officials take part. In early days persons representing the king and queen, the royal family and their guards and attendants, followed. Jason, with his golden fleece and proper attendants, next appeared. Then came Bishop Blase in full canonicals, followed by shepherds and shepherdesses, wool-combers, dyers and other appropriate figures, some wearing wool wigs.

S. BLASIUS.
Glass in Oxford Cathedral.

Many legends tell of Blase in hiding from the minions of Licinius and of wild animals that "waited" upon him. For this in Callot's images and Le Clerc's Almanac, he is surrounded by wild beasts, and the words from Job v., 23.

FEBRUARY 4th.

St. Jane, or Joan, Queen of France, who is this day honoured by the Church is another of those sad romances in real life that constantly come up in studying the lives of the holy men and women.

She was the daughter of Louis XI. and Charlotte of Savoy, born in 1464. Her poor, deformed body made her an object of disgust to her father who was only too glad to be rid of her by marrying her to Louis, Duke of Orleans, her cousin-german, in 1476. It was one of those alliances so often seen among royal kinsfolk. Louis abhorred his wife yet historical students will not forget how Joan repaid his brutal treatment by obtaining for him his life from Charles VIII. which he had forfeited by rebellion; and so we may say in the end, securing for him the crown of France. This of itself should have bound her husband to her even without the quiet Christian patience with which she had borne his tyranny and abuse. But when he as Louis XII. attained this coveted bauble, in 1498, and having in view a marriage with Anne of Brittany (the late king's widow), he made a claim of having been "forced into his marriage with Joan by Louis XI." and for that he sought a divorce which in due course Pope Alexander V. granted. To this decree Joan submitted without a murmur, only too happy to be able at last to follow the bent of her wishes. Thus she retired to Brouges, where wearing always "sackcloth" she consecrated herself and her great revenues to charity. Of this noble work Dr. Butler says: "By the assistance of her confessarius, a virtuous Franciscan friar called Gabriel Maria, she instituted in 1500 the Order of the Nuns of the Annunciation of the Blessed Virgin. It was approved by Julius II., Leo X., Paul V., and Gregory XV." The costume of these nuns is peculiar. They wear black veils, a white cloak, a red scapular, a brown habit with a red cross, and a cord for a girdle. Their superior they call Ancelle (servant). In humility St. Joan took this habit and the vows of the order in 1504 but wore it less than a year as she died on February 4, 1505. The Huguenots "for wanton bigotry and hate" burned her remains in 1562. She was canonized by Clement XII. in 1738.

FEBRUARY 5th.

This day is devoted among others to a most interesting character, St. Agatha, virgin, martyr and patroness of Malta and

Cantania as well as regarded a protectress against dangers from fire.

In her history we can read between the lines how it was that the Emperor Decius who had put to death his predecessor, Philip, on the pretext that he was a Christian, first organized his persecutions against all Christians as a cloak to cover his own ambitions and to attain which he had sacrificed Philip. He then made Quintianius "king of Sicily" where Agatha dwelt in Catania. Her resplendent beauty had excited Quintianius' lusts and he resolved to attain his purpose at all hazards. He knew his danger for she was the daughter of a rich and illustrious house who unfortunately under the decrees of Decius had placed themselves in peril, even had not Agatha's beauty excited Quintianius to do the evil he intended her, who taught as she had been from infancy in the Christian faith rejected every offer and gift of the base "king," who then resorted to the not uncommon tactics of men in power by employing a vile woman to further his interests. But even she at the end of many days told Quintianius how useless were her efforts. It was then that Agatha's torment began. In his wrath the wretched Quintianius ordered her breasts to be cut off "but in the night St. Peter and an angel appeared and healed them with celestial ointment." Then he ordered she should be burned but scarcely had the fires been lighted when an earthquake shook the city and in their terror the citizens begged her release and she was sent back to her prison where she died from her burns. She was embalmed and buried in Catania. Near the city is a volcanic mountain named Mongibello which in 254 burst into action and her legend tells how her veil taken from her tomb stayed the river of fire and lava, and again how in 1551, by her miraculous intervention she saved Malta from invasion by the Turks. She suffered martyrdom in 253 and is one of the early saints who was retained in

S. AGATHA.
Glass in Winchester Cathedral.

the Kalendar by the reformers and still has her place in the English church Kalendar on the same day with that assigned her by the Latin Church. Her name appears in the Kalendar of Carthage as early as 530.

FEBRUARY 6th.

Of the early history of St. Vedast whose festival occurs to-day, nothing reliable seems to be known. His legend tells of his early departure from his home in the west of France, of his life even as a boy, being spent in solitude and holy devotion in the diocese of Toul where he was at last discovered by the bishop, who charmed by his virtues, ordained him to the priesthood. When Clovis I., king of France (481-511, and the son of Childeric, king of the Franks) was returning in 490 from his victory over the Alemanni and was going to Rheims to receive baptism he desired some one to instruct him and Vedast was selected. En route the legend continues Vedast performed a miracle by restoring a blind man to sight, a fact which not only confirmed Clovis in the faith, but won many of his courtiers to embrace Christianity. In 499 he was consecrated Bishop of Arras and it is said that as he entered the city he restored sight to another blind man and cured one who was lame and was thus greatly aided in his holy labours among the infidels. In 510 the great diocese of Cambray which extended beyond Brussels was committed to his care and he jointly governed both of these sees for many years. For nearly forty years without a rest this goodly man had thus devoted himself to the work of his Master when on February 6, 539, his labours came to a peaceful end and he was laid at rest in the cathedral church at Arras which had grown up under his tireless efforts.

FEBRUARY 7th.

In the Roman Church, on the Saturday before Septuagesima Sunday, " the Canticle of the Lord — Alleluia — ceases to be said."

St. Romuald, whose name appears in the Kalendar of the Roman

Church this day presents yet a fresh example of the means God in His Providence uses to lead men to Him. Brought up as he was in luxury he was daily growing more enamoured of the joys and pleasures of worldly life. When about twenty his father, a proud, haughty man, in order to settle a dispute regarding some estate had recourse to a then common custom of a duel with a relative. In spite of protests Romuald was compelled to be present and saw his father kill his opponent. The horror of the scene greatly affected him and in expiation of his share in the affair the young man in penance resolved to seclude himself for a time in the Benedictine monastery of Classis. Before his self-imposed penance was ended the discourse of the pious lay-brother who waited upon him had so impressed his mind that he sought admission as a penitent to the religious habit. This resolution was easier taken than carried out so bitterly was he opposed by his father, but in the end he not only prevailed but by his example led his father himself later to enter the monastery of St. Sevenes as a penitent of St. Benedict's Order.

But I must not take space to follow St. Romuald, until he became Abbot of Classis and later founded the Order of Camaidoll, and a power with the Emperor Otho III., as well as with his successor, St. Henry II.

It is the story of a long, worthy and interesting life of service in the work of a true Christian Knight. His Order is now divided into five, but in each the memory of this remarkable man lives. He died June 19, 1027, on which day I will again speak of him, but his feast was appointed by Clement VIII. for the 7th of February.

FEBRUARY 8th.

SEPTUAGESIMA SUNDAY.

The three Sundays preceding Lent are respectively termed Septuagesima, Sexagesima and Quinquagesima. Many reasons have been assigned for these names; but to my mind the simplest and most reasonable is that of Bishop Sparrow in his "Rationale on the Common Prayer," who says: "But on my apprehension, the best is a consequentia numerandi, because the First Sunday in Lent is called Quadragesima, counting about forty days from Easter ; therefore the Sunday before that, being still farther from Easter, it is called Quinquagesima, five being the next number above four and so the Sunday before that is Sexagesima and the next Septuagesima."

These days are the first which appear in the Church Kalendar of the so-called "Movable Feasts, or Festivals" from the fact the date of each is dependent upon the date fixed for Easter.

Whatever may be the antiquity of the institution of Septuagesima and the two Sundays that follow, there apparently is no mention of them in the records of the Roman Church as to where they originated or from whence they were incorporated into the ritual of the Reformed Church — nor is there mention of them until about the close of the V. or in the early years of the VI. century. Gelasius and Gregory notice these days in their Sacramentaries and the latter assigned specific offices for each of these days ; just as the Reformers did in framing their ritual ; with a design that both the clergy and laity should prepare for Lent.

St. John of Matha, the Founder of the Order of Trinitarians, whose festival is celebrated by the Church this day, presents a very interesting story. He was born at Faucon on the borders of Provence, of a noble family, educated first at Aix in all the customary accomplishments of young noblemen of his day, such as riding, fencing, dancing, etc., as well as grammar and other things which now we would regard as but the rudiments of an education ; though then were considered all that any gentleman need to learn. But fond as John was of the sports of his companions he was both ambitious for greater knowledge and had already shown by his conduct while at Aix that love of his fellowmen that later was so marked a feature of his character. Toward the close of the XII. century

Paris became a favourite centre for religious students and while yet a young man John went there to study, passed through the various classes with great credit, graduated with the degree of Doctor of Divinity and was ordained a priest. As historical students are aware Mahometan slavery was then at its height and not a few good men gave up their time and in many cases sacrificed their lives to secure the redemption of Christian captives and to this John resolved to devote himself. With the consent of Innocent III. then in the Pontifical chair a new Order was instituted for the purpose and approved by the Pope in 1198 and took the name of the Holy Trinity, which was confirmed by a second bull in 1209. St. John was the first minister general of the Order. Their habit was a white robe with a red and blue cross on the breast. While I cannot follow the labours of these noble brethren the fact that in their first expedition to Morocco in 1201 they succeeded in rescuing 186 Christian slaves from bondage evidences their practical and earnest work. In passing let me remark that the Order of Mercy instituted by St. Peter Nolaseo in 1235, that had a similar purpose in view, was an outgrowth of the Order of the Holy Trinity. The life of St. John was given to his chosen work and has been eulogized many times for his self-sacrificing labour. He died December 21, 1213, aged sixty-one years; his festival was fixed, however, for this day. There have been many chapters of the Order instituted since, a noted one being that of the "Barefooted Trinitarians," created by "John Baptist of the Conception" in Spain in 1594.

FEBRUARY 9th.

St. Apollonia, the ancient Virgin and Martyr whom the Church remembers to-day, presents one or two features in her story quite out of the ordinary run in the lives we have been considering. Her parents had in spite of their prayers to heathen gods long been childless when three Christian Pilgrims appeared in Alexandria and preached of Jesus and his Virgin mother; and of the power of *her* intercession. The wife was led by these Pilgrims to make intercession with the Virgin and in answer to her prayers Apollonia was born. The legend continues, the child grew up under Christian teaching and "sought St. Leontine to baptise her. As he did so an Angel appeared with a garment of dazzling whiteness which was thrown over her and a voice said : This is Apollonia the servant of God ! Go now to Alexandria and announce the faith of Christ." This she did with great success.

In the last year of the reign of Philip when Apollonia had grown old and weak, riots against Christians became very prevalent and many victims fell. In their fury they seized upon the venerable saint bound her to a pillar and pulled out her teeth with pincers — Dr. Butler says they were broken out with blows upon her jaws — and because she would not pay her vows to their idols they built a huge fire threatening to burn her. She begged a moment of respite, then to show that her sacrifice was voluntary she slipped from their grasp and leaped into the burning pile, which quickly consumed her. This took place on February 9, 249, but a civil war among the pagans broke out just after and for a time put an end to the persecution of the faithful, only to be renewed under the decree of Decius in 250. The attributes of St. Apollonia are a pair of pincers or sometimes a gold tooth on a chain. She was in old days regarded as a protection against toothache and all other troubles with the teeth.

FEBRUARY 10th.

St. Scholastica whose festival is held this day, as the sister of the celebrated St. Benedict is widely respected by the Roman Church though less of her life is known than of many others who have been canonized by the church. She founded and governed a nunnery at Plombariola about five miles south of the monastery of St. Benedict. Her legend tells of the last visit St. Benedict paid to his sister that when he rose to depart she begged of him to stay a little longer and on his declining owing to other engagements she bent her head in prayer and on the instant a violent storm arose that kept him a prisoner and the evening was spent in pious discourses and on the following morning he departed. Three days later she died and St. Benedict who at the moment was alone " in silent contemplation as he raised his eyes to heaven saw the soul of his sister rising thither, in the form of a dove." From this St. Scholastica has been represented in art with a dove, either pressed to her heart or lying at her feet, while in her hand she holds a lily emblematical of her spotless purity of character.

Her death occurred in 543.

FEBRUARY 11th.

On this day the Greeks honour as a saint the Empress Theodora whom the Roman Church do not so recognise though their writers never fail to speak of her in terms of high praise as well they may. Theodora was the wife of Theophilus, Emperor of the East, who died in 842. Her influence over this brutish man was almost unbounded — strange as it sounds when we recall his life — and to her alone belongs the credit of "softening,"— though no human power could wholly control the cruel temper of this fiendish man,— and even at times protecting from harm the defenders of the Holy Images whom he so relentlessly persecuted. By the death of Theophilus, Theodora became Regent of the Empire during the minority of Michael II. who succeeded his father. And it was she who put an end to the persecutions that Leo the Isaurian had instituted 120 years before and enabled the Patriarch Methodius to restore on the first Sunday in Lent in 844, the Holy Images to the great church in Constantinople, an event which the Greeks celebrate with great pomp and ceremony calling it " The Feast of Orthodoxy." She held her sway as Regent during twelve years (842-854) and then through the machinations of her unnatural son and his infamous uncle she was banished. She spent the remainder of her life in a monastery, dying in 867.

In passing, it may not be out of place to mention this is the anniversary of the death of Caedmon about 680, the most ancient of the English poets whose name is known ; his home was near the monastery of Streaneshalch (later known as Whitby) made famous by St. Hilda and with whom the poet was a great favourite, and not infrequent guest within the monastery. This poet wrote a poem in praise of St. Hilda.

FEBRUARY 12th.

St. Benedict of Anian (as he is called, to distinguish him from others of the same name) whom the Church honours in its Kalendar to-day was the son of Aigul, Count or Governor of Languedoc, who spent his youth at the court of King Pepin (Pepin-le-Vrel) where he served as "cup-bearer," and later as an officer in the army of Charlemagne and evidently as the world terms it, was "a Favourite of Fortune," for he had both wealth family and court favour at his command. An incident, however, in an hour changed the entire course of his life. He seems to have been an amateur athlete and a proficient in manly sports and when his brother was in danger of drowning he did not hesitate to endeavour to save him, but to cut a long story short it nearly cost our saint his life before he succeeded. What it did do was to bring him to realise how valueless earthly treasures and honours are compared with a higher and nobler life. This was in 774, at which time he sought out an holy man to advise and direct him. Under his guidance he spent two years at the monastery of St. Seine five leagues from Dijon, after that becoming a hermit on the banks of the Anian where later he with some monks who had joined him in his hermitage founded a Benedictine monastery, of which he was the abbot. His first prominent public effort was at the council at Frankfurt where he combated the heresy of Felix, Bishop of Urgel, "That Christ was not the natural but only the adoptive Son of the Eternal Father." Later he wrote four treatises on this subject. But his one great aim in life was the reformation of monastic life, then at a low state, and in 817 he presided at Aix-la-Chapelle over the council that had been assembled for this purpose where the statutes he formulated were added to the rules of the great St. Benedict who founded the order. He was seventy-one years of age when he died in Inde, in 821 on February 11th. His festival is kept at Anian on this day, but elsewhere he is remembered on the 12th, the day he was laid at rest in the monastery of St. Cornelius.

FEBRUARY 13th

Is the festival of St. Gregory II., Pope. He was born at Rome to an affluent fortune, educated in the Palace of the Popes and ordained as sub-deacon by Pope Sergius I. Under Popes John VI., VII., Sisinnius and Constantine, he was Treasurer of the Church, Keeper of the library and also held many other important offices. Gregory was chosen as successor to Pope Constantine on May 19, 715. The most important events of his pontificate were his deposing of John IV. the monothelite, the false patriarch of Constantinople, the sending of missionaries into Germany and the consecration of the celebrated St. Boniface as Bishop of Mentz. Gregory held his high office nearly sixteen years dying on February 10, 731, but his festival is kept on the day he was buried in the Vatican.

This is also St. Valentine's Eve, a festival which in early days in England was celebrated by giving and receiving gifts usually anonymously presented and bearing labels such as "St. Valentine's Love" or "Good morrow, Valentine."

FEBRUARY 14th.

ST. VALENTINE'S DAY.

The endless number of times the story of St. Valentine has been told leaves little that need be said. Briefly St. Valentine was a priest of Rome who during the persecution of Christians under Claudius II., aided by St. Marius did noble work in assisting the martyrs. It was for this he was apprehended and sent to the prefect of Rome. While in the custody of one Asterius the saint performed a miracle by restoring the sight of his daughter and as a result all of the family became converts to Christianity, later proving the truth of their faith by suffering martyrdom. After a year of imprisonment Valentine was brought before the prefect, who tried in vain to induce him to renounce his faith. Whereupon he was condemned to be beaten with clubs then to be stoned and lastly to be beheaded outside the gate now called Porta del Popolo but which for a time bore the name Porta Valentini. This was about the year 270, and the greater part of his relics are preserved in the Church of St. Praxedes at Rome. His name was early enrolled among other martyrs and was retained in the Kalendar of the Reformers when the Christian church became divided.

Just why St. Valentine was chosen the patron of Love seems a little obscure. Wheatly says: "He was a man of admirable parts and so famous for his love and charity that the custom of choosing valentines upon his festival which is still practised, took rise from thence." While Dr. Butler, in his "Lives of the Saints," says: "To abolish the heathens' lewd custom of boys drawing the names of girls in honour of their goddess Februata Juno on the 14th of this month several zealous pastors substituted the names of saints on the billets that were drawn," and thus in the mutation of time the custom has grown which now takes the form of "valentines." Many learned treatises have been written on the subject but beyond the adoption of the date of St. Valentine's martyrdom the holy man had literally nothing to do with the matter of sending love messages on this day.

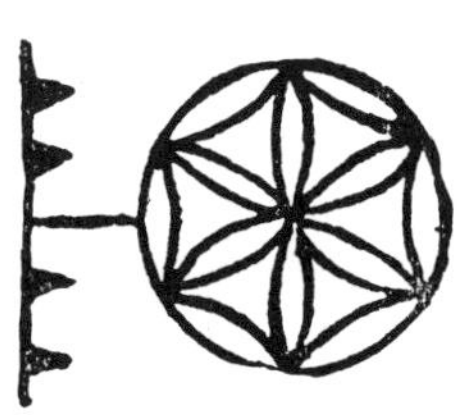

FEBRUARY 15th.

The Christian faith had been preached in Sweden by St. Auscarius as early as 830; but as was true elsewhere throughout Europe, as soon as the missionaries died, or departed, Paganism at once revived, the Christians lapsed from their faith and it became as we know was the case in England after St. Ninian died, a myth. It was so in Sweden when Olaus (Olaf Scobcong) asked of his friend Eldred, the Saxon King of England, to send some person who would revive Christianity in Sweden. Eldred selected for this purpose, Sigefride, who is mentioned as "an eminent priest of York." Yet prior to this Sigefride's name seems to be unrecorded in the ecclesiastical history in England and we find him arriving at Wexlow in Gothland on June 21st, in 950, to take up his new duties. He first we are told "set up a cross and then built a church of wood, celebrated the Divine mysteries and preached to the people." His success was very great. In a brief period the twelve leaders of the twelve tribes into which the people of South Gothland were divided became converts and it is said that the fountain where Sigefride baptised the catechumens retained for several centuries a monument bearing the names of the twelve leaders who had become Christians. Later on Sigefride widened his sphere to embrace West Gothland and finally extended it to the Midland and Northern provinces. Thus he became literally "The Apostle of Sweden," the honoured name by which he was everywhere known. He died in 1002, and his tomb at Wexlow became famous for the miracles wrought there by his relics. He was canonized by Pope Adrian IV. (who was also an Englishman), in 1158.

FEBRUARY 16th.

St. Onesimus, the disciple of St. Paul whom the Church remembers this day ranks among the earliest of those who sealed their faith with their blood. The great Apostle made him with Tychicus the bearer of his Epistle to the Colossians (Col. IV.) and ordained him Bishop of Ephesus, after Timothy. The Greeks claim he suffered martyrdom in 95, under Domitian (Consul of Rome who died in 96), while Latin Martyrology says: "Being led to Rome, a prisoner, he was stoned to death. He was first buried at Rome and later his relics were translated to Ephesus."

This is also the festival of Gregory X. who was elected to the pontificate September 1, 1271. Prior to this he had borne the name of Theobald but took the title of Gregory X. when installed as Pope. He was born at Placentia, Tuscany, and had become Archbishop of Leige. He attended the second Council of Lyons in May, 1274, when the Greek ambassadors were admitted into the unity of the Church. He was a fervent and earnest advocate of the crusades for the recovery of the Holy Land. He died at

Arezzo on January 10th, 1276. His name was inserted in Roman Martyrology by Benedict XIV. on February 16th.

FEBRUARY 17th.

St. Flavian who was a priest of distinguished merit and treasurer of the Church of Constantinople until 447, when he succeeded Proclus as archbishop is named among the saints for honour this day. At this time simony (buying and selling ecclesiastical preferment) had become a crying evil in Constantinople and Flavian had at once when he assumed the episcopate resolved to crush it, if it was in his power. For this he roused the enmity of the eunuch Chrysaphius the chamberlain of Theodosius the Younger who profited largely by the practice and when it was hinted to Flavian he should send the Emperor a present upon his promotion, he sent him — in accord with the custom of the church at that time — some "blessed bread." When the chamberlain objected and intimated that something more valuable should be forthcoming from the revenues of the church the holy bishop told him plainly they were destined for other purposes. The story is one of a long and bitter battle that culminated at the council called at Ephesus where Chrysaphius by, as we in these modern days would say, "packing the council," gained a point against Flavian and his adherents, who at once appealed to the pope-legates then present; an act that cost the bishop his life for it had so incensed certain of the chamberlain's party that at Epipus he was set upon and so beaten, kicked and bruised that in a few days he died. The general council of Chalcedon in 451 taking cognizance of the affair declared Flavian a saint and a martyr.

At Florence on this day is celebrated the festival of "The Blessed Alexius Falconeri," one of the seven who founded the Order of the Servants of the Blessed Virgin Mary, and of whom we read in Roman Martyrology: "In the one hundred and tenth year of his life being comforted by the presence of Jesus Christ and the angels, terminated his blessed career."

FEBRUARY 18th.

Aside from the fact that St. Simeon or Simon (for the names are synonymous) was a kinsman of Jesus, he was a very prominent character in the story of the Christian church after the Ascension; while there is little doubt that he was one of those who received the Holy Ghost on the day of Pentecost. When in 62 St. James, Bishop of Jerusalem, was put to death twenty-nine years after Christ's crucifixion, St. Simon was chosen bishop as his successor. In 66 the year in which SS. Peter and Paul suffered martyrdom the civil war broke out in Judea and we find the Christians seeking shelter in Pella, a small city beyond Jordan, with St. Simeon as their head and chief, as he was after they returned to Jerusalem. It was then the two first heresies entered the church known as the Nazareans and Ebonites. They recognized Christ as a great prophet but denied his divine paternity with many other added errors. While Simeon lived he was by the strength of his character and the unbounded influence he held able to hold these heretics in check, but Eusebius tells us: "He was no sooner dead than a deluge of execrable heresies broke out of hell upon the church." When we remember Simeon's great age this alone speaks in strong terms of the power he must have wielded.

During the persecutions of Vespasian and Domitian, St. Simeon escaped capture but when Trajan found him he subjected him to terrible tortures borne with such patience that even his persecutors could not restrain their admiration; in particular we have that given by Atticus. St. Simeon was 120 years old when in 107 he died, having governed the church of Jerusalem for forty-three years.

FEBRUARY 19th.

This day is the festival of St. Barbatus or Barbas, Bishop of Benevento, who was born near the close of the pontificate of Gregory the Great. He took holy orders when quite a young man and was at once assigned as curate of St. Basil's at Morcona, a town near Benevento. It was a peculiarly trying position for the people of his parish were not only noted for their irregularities but determined that no priest should dictate to or restrain them and it is not at all wonderful that young and inexperienced as he was they soon drove him from among them to return to his home in Benevento. The history of this old town is a peculiarly interesting one as Christianity had first been preached there by St. Potin who had been sent out as a missionary by St. Peter, but by 305 they like so many in the early days of Christianity after accepting the faith lapsed into idolatry and martyred St. Januarius, then bishop of the see. In 545 the Goths laid the city in ruins. When the Lombards at last obtained possession of the country in 598 they rebuilt the city and King Autharis gave it as a Duchy to Zolion, a general of the invaders with the title of Duke. These Lombards were mostly Arians but many were still idolators and even the Christians retained many idolatrous superstitions, among these a holy veneration for a golden viper, before whom they prostrated themselves. They also paid superstitious honour to a certain tree on which they hung the skin of some wild animal and worshipped it.

When these ceremonies were over there followed public games in which this skin served as a mark at which " the bowmen shot arrows, over their shoulders." Such was the class of people Barbatus found when he returned to Benevento and took up his work among them, naturally finding it no easy task. They laughed at his expostulations at their irreligious superstitions. However, he did not desist from his efforts even though they seemed to bring no results. But at last he aroused their attention when he prophesied the distress to the city which was to come from the army of Emperor Constans, who shortly after as Barbatus had foretold landed in Italy and laid siege to Benevento. Then it was they gave heed to his words and began to renounce their idolatrous practices and at length allowed Barbatus to cut down the sacred tree while they melted the golden viper into an ingot from which a chalice was made for the altar of the church. Ildebrand, Bishop of Benevento, had died during the siege and Barbatus was elected Bishop in 653. When the terrors of the siege were at their height and escape seemed to be impossible

Barbatus had once more prophesied that relief would be sent. In due time it came as foretold, and now the Bishop's influence was as great as formerly it had been of no account. Thus it was in the end the last remnant of superstition was rooted out in Benevento. In 680 he participated in the general council at Rome and the next year at the council held at Constantinople against the monothelites. But soon after his return his own summons came, for on February 29th in 682 when he was seventy years of age he died. His festival is fixed for this 19th day of the same month.

FEBRUARY 20th.

On this day is commemorated one of the most terrible scenes of which we read in the early history of the Christian church, in which St. Sadoth, Bishop of Selec, or Selucia, and Ctesiphon (then the two capital cities of Persia) took so prominent a part and in which St. Simeon, the former bishop, had, in the persecution begun in 341 by Sapor II. attained the crown of martyrdom. Hardly had Sadoth been chosen as the successor of Simeon when the edict was published which made it a capital crime with death as its penalty for any one to confess Christ. There was nothing uncertain about this edict, for all who heard it knew what their fate would be if they disobeyed and none knew this better than Sadoth himself.

Sadoth as he is named by both the Greeks and Latins, was called in the Persian, Schiadurte, which signifies "friend of the king," Schia — king, and durt — friend. He was a man of unspotted purity of character, ardent zeal and the courage of his belief. He feared naught but to sin. Yet while brave and fearless for himself he felt that for a time "prudence was the better part of valour," at least for his faithful followers, and therefore for a little he with some of his clergy lay hid from the vengeance of Sapor while still he watched over his flock. It was while in his retreat Sadoth had a vision and saw St. Simeon at the top of a ladder who called to him saying: "Mount up Sadoth; fear not! I mounted yesterday; it is your turn to-day." By this he knew he was not to escape the wrath of Sapor. And it proved so for that year Sapor came to Selucia. Sadoth with several of his priests with the monks and nuns from his church were apprehended and cast into dungeons. For five months they were thus confined but twice in this interval were they brought forth, tempted, threatened, scourged and tortured on the rack until their breaking bones could be heard to crack. On the final day chained two by two together these martyrs were led forth for execution to which they went singing psalms and canticles of joy which ceased not until the last one of this glorious company had been crowned. Sadoth, however, was separated from the noble band and sent into a neighbouring province where he was beheaded in the year 342.

FEBRUARY 21st.

The Blessed Pepin whose festival is observed this day, held the high and responsible office of "mayor of the palace," under Kings Clotaire II., Dagobert and Sigebert of France, and his story forms an interesting chapter in French history which I may only repeat in a very brief way. He was a son of Carloman one of the most powerful noblemen of Austrasia and the ancestor of Pepin (the Short) King of France in whom began the Carlovingian race.

Pepin of Landen was Lord of Brabant and his biographers say "a lover of peace, the constant defender of truth and justice, the friend to all servants of God, the terror of the wicked, the support of the weak and the father of his country." He was also governor of Austrasia, when Theodebert II. its king, was defeated by Theodoric II., king of Burgundy, in 611. When in 613 Theodoric died Clotaire II., king of Soissons, reunited Burgundy, Neustia and Austrasia he thus became sole monarch of France. It was to Pepin that King Clotaire owed the pacification of Austrasia without a bloody struggle and he was rewarded when Clotaire in 622 named Dagobert I. king of Austrasia and Neustia by making Pepin mayor of Dagobert's palace, and when by the death of his father in 628 Dagobert became king of all France save some minor provinces settled on his younger brother he continued the favours shown to Pepin, though the latter when the king lapsed as he did from the straight and narrow paths of religion and morality, did not hesitate to condemn in very plain language these shortcomings. It was a long and arduous battle between the king and his minister before Dagobert yielded. When we remember the autocratic power of kings in those days it shows what sterling character was required by Pepin to thus assail his royal master because of his wrongdoings. But Pepin was a brave man who dared to do right because it was his duty and Dagobert evidently appreciated this for he made him tutor of his son, Sigebert, who later under Pepin's careful training became one of the best of the early kings of France. Such briefly is the story of Pepin of Landen. Renowned for his probity, piety and Christian charity, he died February 21, 640. His name appears in Belgic martyrologies, though no other act of public veneration is committed than the enshrining of his relics which are still annually carried in procession at Nivelles, and his name is found in the Litany published by the authority of the Archbishop of Mechlin.

FEBRUARY 22d.

My readers will recall that on January 13th I spoke of the festival, held at Rome on that day, called "The Chair of St. Peter."

Before St. Peter went to Rome he had formed the see of Antioch. Dr. Butler places this date three years after the Ascension of our Lord.

In the early ages of the Church it was customary especially in the East but also frequently observed in the West, for every Christian to keep sacred the anniversary of their baptism when they renewed for themselves the vows others had in their infancy taken for them. In like manner priests and all ecclesiasts kept the anniversary of their consecration and thus it seemed fitting that the founding of the see of Antioch should be observed and for reasons analogous to those given for the observance at Rome of the festival of "The Chair of St. Peter," that of "St. Peter's Chair at Antioch" obtains. But this long antedated the festival at Rome. Indeed the festival of St. Peter's Chair, "Natale

Petri de Cathedra," is marked in the most ancient Kalendar extant, made in the time of Liberius about the year 354. It also occurs in the sacramentary of St. Gregory and as appears from the records of the Council of Tours, was kept in France in the VI. century; but curiously it is omitted in the ancient Kalendars of Carthage.

Therefore this day is most appropriately set aside by the Roman Church to be observed at Antioch, where the disciples were first called "Christians" for this second festival of the Chair of St. Peter.

This day is also the festival of St. Margaret of Cortona, "The Penitent." In the story of St. Margaret we have another of those romances of the saints we constantly meet in the chronicles of the early Christian church. She was a Tuscan by birth, a girl of that rich type of southern beauty we all know so well and of that hot impatient temperament from which just as they are guided in childhood are evolved noble men and women or the reverse. Unfortunately Margaret's mother died while the child was but little beyond infancy and the treatment she had from her step-mother and the unkindness of her father combined to drive her in youth to seek pleasures outside of her home. The lax morals that obtained in every city of Italy at the close of the XIII. century need no comment and it is easy to understand how a girl endowed with such rare beauty of person and vivacious spirits with a home such as Margaret had, should be led astray. For years her evil life was continued. Lovers came and went; but as the story of many an abandoned woman even in our own day proves she could and did love one man. And it was through his death that at last her salvation came. It was one of those tragedies so common in that day. A faithful dog the constant companion of his master led her to the scene where his life had been taken. On the instant her own sins, the terror of Divine justice and the treachery of the world came to her, and her first act of repentance was to seek out her father to confess to him. But her stern stepmother stood at the door and by her influence

Margaret was again driven forth into the world by her father. She wandered into a vineyard half tempted to return to her old life of sin, when the impulse to implore Divine aid came upon her, and in the solitude she knelt while still praying she seemed to hear a voice that told her what to do, and she obeyed. Rising, she went first to the parish church in Alvino. With a rope around her neck — as was then the prescribed formula — she publicly confessed her sins and then barefooted as a penitent sought out the monastery of Carlona under the Order of St. Francis and begged admission. For twenty-three years she gave herself to penance and her exemplary life and deeds of love and charity won for her at last peace and the reverence of all who knew her. She died February 22, 1297.

Dr. Butler informs us that Pope Leo X. granted an office in her honour to the city of Cartona. She was canonized by Benedict XIII. in 1728.

FEBRUARY 23d.

I can but briefly speak of a man, the Blessed Peter Damian, Cardinal, whose festival occurs this day, though from his fidelity, charity and learning he deserves a more extended notice. Born at Ravenna in 988, his childhood and youth were spent in abject poverty yet by his true force of character rising above them all, until we find him employed by four successive popes — Gregory VI., Clement II., Leo IX., and Victor II., and then by Stephen IX. in 1057 was made Cardinal Bishop of Ostia. When in 1058 Stephen IX. died, he was succeeded by Nicholas I., who recognized the rare ability of Peter Damian as his predecessors had, and used him in several delicate missions where firm purpose and rare judgment were required. Already Peter was feeling the weight of years and the arduous work he had been called upon to perform and desired to retire from his more active life but it was not until 1062 when Alexander I. filled the pontifical chair that his wishes were gratified, and in the retirement of his monastery he was allowed once more to assume the habit and duties of a simple monk and give himself to the composition of several treatises that are still held in high esteem by the ecclesiasts of the Roman Church. But even in his retirement the wise counsels and services of this highly gifted man were constantly sought. We find him sent as a legate of the pope to France in 1063 and again, in 1069, as presiding at the synod held in Frankfurt to determine upon the divorce Henry IV. of Germany desired from his wife Bertha. But in every place he proved himself something more than simply a keen, shrewd diplomat — in being an honest, upright Christian man. He died February 22, 1072, aged eighty-three years, but his festival is named for the 23d of the month the day when he was honoured as patron of the city of Faenza where he died.

FEBRUARY 24th

S. MATTHIAS.
Reredos,
Bampton Church,
Oxon.

Is sacred in all Christian churches to the memory of St. Matthias, and the Apostle St. Clement of Alexandria is the authority for saying he was the one who was chosen by lot from the seventy-two who had been assembled and from which number a successor to the traitor Judas was to be selected. There were two only who from the first seemed worthy of the great honour. One was Joseph, called Barsabas, who because of his probity and piety had been surnamed "The Just"; and the other Matthias. Tradition tells how after devout prayer for Divine guidance the "Lot" was cast and it fell upon Matthias. After the Ascension there is no perfectly authentic account of St. Matthias' life. It is only from the traditions of the Greeks as recounted in their menologies that the legend is preserved; that after preaching the faith in and about Cappadocia and later on the coast of the Caspian sea he received the crown of martyrdom in Calchis which in these menologies is called Ethiopia, where he was stoned and afterward beheaded. Another legend places his death in Judea where it is said he suffered martyrdom at the hands of the Jews, being either thrust through by a lance, or killed by an axe. In Italian art St. Matthias has as his attribute a lance, while in Germany this is an axe. But for some reason this Apostle very seldom is represented in art, and quite as rarely appears in the series showing the Apostles. For some occult reason the Clog Almanacs have assigned what may be designed to represent a leg as his attribute but no one yet has been able to understand why this was selected.

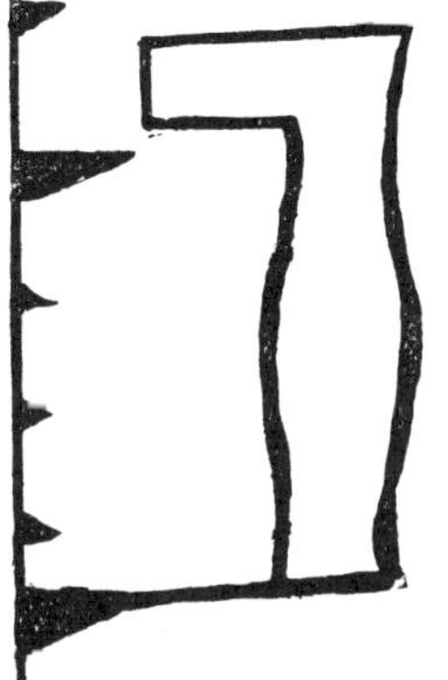

FEBRUARY 25th.

ASH-WEDNESDAY.

The first day of the season of Lent is called Ash-Wednesday and its date is dependent upon that of Easter. It is a day of strict fasting and the same is true of each of the remaining days of the week under the canons of both the Roman and Reformed Churches. The canonical colour for these days is violet.

LENT.

The word Lent is derived from the Saxon word "Lengten-tide" and from an early day applied to the customary spring fast which was kept by Christians during the forty days preceding Easter. This fast originally began on the first Sunday in Lent but since Sunday is not properly a Fast Day and by omitting Sunday there remain but thirty-six days, Pope Gregory directed that this fast should commence four days earlier, viz., on what is denominated "Ash-Wednesday."

This name arose from a notable custom intended to remind the faithful that they were all but "dust and ashes." Therefore on the first day of the penitential season the priests took ashes and after sprinkling them with Holy-water, as the worshipper came forward arrayed in sackcloth the priest took some of the ashes on his finger, made with them the sign of the cross upon the penitent's forehead, saying: "*Memento, homo, quia cinis es, et in pulverem reverteris*" (Remember, man, that you are of ashes, and unto dust will return). The ashes used were usually made from the consecrated palms which had been used on Palm Sunday of the previous year. With the Reformation in the Protestant church this custom was declared "a vain show" but the day itself was kept with great solemnity and strangely, the name "Ash-Wednesday" was retained. In the early days this first day of Lent had two names. the first "*Caput Jejunii*" (Head of the Fast), the other "*Dies Cinerum*" (Ash-Wednesday).

The Christian Lent took its rise beyond a doubt from the "Preparation for the Expiation," by the Jews, who began their solemn humiliation forty days before the Expiation. Thus the primitive Christians in the earliest days of Christianity set their great Fast at a date forty days before that of Easter, in commemoration of the miraculous abstinence of our Saviour when under temptation.

Even during the controversy about the date on which to celebrate Easter, which arose between the Eastern and Western churches, there was no dispute on this point of fasting for forty days prior to the Easter festival, the whole Church being in harmony recognising it as of Apostolic institution.

FEBRUARY 26th.

This day is held sacred to the memory of St. Alexander, Patriarch of Alexandria. It was during his episcopate that the celebrated Arius came to the front and whose heresy was to be such a sore trial to the Orthodox church. As I must often allude to this Arian heresy I will briefly speak of the man. He had been excommunicated in 300 from the Church by St. Peter, a predecessor of St. Alexander. The successor of St. Peter, St. Achillas, had been induced to restore him also making him curate of the Church of Baucales, one of the quarters of Alexandria. Dr. Butler says Arius "was well versed in profane literature, was a subtle dialectician, had an extensive show of virtue and an insinuating behaviour, but was a monster of pride, vainglory, ambition, envy and jealousy." These traits of character naturally made him peculiarly angry when Alexander was chosen as successor of St. Achillas for he knew Alexander bitterly opposed the heresy he was then publicly teaching (that Christ was not God); that he had no other soul than his created divinity. In short that he was simply a man like all other men. The heresy soon spread, drawing to the support of Arius two bishops, seven priests, twelve deacons and others. They called themselves Arians, and the Orthodox Christians Colluthians, as one Colluthus a curate of Alexandria, was the most prominent in his violent denunciations of the heresy while Alexander himself prompted by his gentle, peaceful character was inclined to be more lenient. But Colluthus was persistent and in 320 at a Council held in Alexandria Arius and his followers were excommunicated. Still this by no means ended the spread of the Arian doctrine. I may not, however, follow its history further except to speak of the celebrated Council called at Nice in June, 325, when this heresy was considered and their declaration that the Son was consubstantial to the Father embodying it in what is known as the Nicene Creed. In this Council Alexander naturally took a prominent part and was present at the magnificent entertainment given the Prelates by Constantine August 25, 325. After this Alexander returned to Alexandria but the strain upon him had been too much for on the 29th of February, 326, he died.

FEBRUARY 27th.

In the story of St. Leander, Bishop of Seville, who is this day remembered by the Church we are again confronted with the Arian heresy. I have several times stated that the Goths were all largely tainted with Arianism. The Kingdom of Seville at the time when Leander was promoted to the see was possessed by the

Visigoths or Western-Goths, while the Ostrogoths or Eastern-Goths had passed the Alps and founded their kingdom first at Languedoc in Italy. But I must not be tempted into this interesting bit of history, beyond saying that at the time of Leander's advent these Visigoths had reigned in Spain fully one hundred years and it was through Leander's efforts, the larger part of the people were reclaimed from their heresy in spite of the opposition he met with from King Leovigild then ruling.

Leander had converted Hermenegild the eldest son of Leovigild, and heir to the throne. Nothing can illustrate the fierce animosity of the Arians than the fact that a year after Hermenegild's conversion his father caused him to be put to death "because he refused to receive the communion from the hands of an Arian bishop." But later Leovigild felt such remorse for his act that he sent for Leander and committed to his care his second son, Recared, who was converted to the Catholic faith and by his aid the Visigoths were as above stated in turn converted.

It is too long a story to repeat here of the labours of this holy prelate both in Seville and in Suevi, another Spanish province. But his entire life was given up to combating the then widened heresies of the Arian clergy. One point must not be forgotten which was prominent in this good man's life, his faith in the efficacy of prayer which he constantly taught, preached and exemplified. He died on February 27, 596, and the cathedral he founded in Seville is one of the most magnificent in all Spain.

FEBRUARY 28th.

The Roman Church this day honours an unnamed and unnumbered host of men who are truly called in its martyrology "martyrs, who died in the great pestilence in Alexandria."

It is not those noble men and women who willingly gave up their lives in defence of and to testify to their faith who are alone entitled to the name of martyr, for we find them in every age, of every race and shade of religious belief. Men and women who like those commemorated to-day gave their lives for the love of their fellow men. The world's history hardly furnishes a parallel to the violent pestilence which swept over the greater portion of the Roman empire during the twelve years from 249 to 263. It is said that in one day in Rome in 262, 5,000 persons died from it. It was during this period that sedition and civil war filled the city with crime, murder and tumults, which rendered it unsafe for any one to venture upon the streets. While this state of affairs was yet at its height pestilence came upon the great city and its streets were filled with unburied dead and to the noisome exhalations from these was added the infectious vapours which rose from the Nile which came to increase the dreadful contagion, and not a house escaped furnishing its quota. It was then when the pagans, infidels and heathen fled leaving their own friends, brethren and families to perish, the Christians, who during the persecutions of Decius, Gallus and Valerian had been compelled to secure safety in hiding, came forth like angels of mercy and took up the almost superhuman task of endeavouring to bring some succour and relief to their stricken fellow citizens. Regardless of the peril their own lives were in they went from house to house, nursing the sick, comforting the dying and burying the dead. Nor did they confine their attention to those of their own faith. It was enough that one was sick to command at once such help as these heroic followers of Christ could render. "Thus," says St. Dionysius, speaking of these men, "the best of our brethren have departed this life; some of the most valuable, both of priests, deacons and laics; and it is thought that this kind of death is nothing different from martyrdom." Who can deny the saintly prelate's assertion, and if it is proper to honour the memories of other martyrs these of a surety should not be forgotten. Thus it is that to-day the Roman Church honours this nameless "noble army of martyrs."

MARCH

Sturdy March, with brows full sternly bent,
And armed strongly, rode upon a ram,
The same which over Hellespontus swam,
Yet in his hand a spade he also bent
And in a bag all sorts of weeds, y same
Which on the earth he strewed as he went,
And filled her womb with fruitful hope of nourishment.

— *Spenser*

As already said, March was for many years the first month in the calendar year and was dedicated by the Romans to Mars, called Martius, from which our name was derived. The Saxons termed it " Lenet-monat" (length-month) as referring to the lengthening of the days at this season. By some it has been claimed that the word "Lent" is derived from the Saxon name for this month.

MARCH 1st.

St. David, the patron saint of Wales, is the most prominent of those honoured by the Church this day. His name appears in the Kalendar of the Reformed church, and has been retained by the English church. He is reputed to have been the son of Xantus, a prince of Ceretica (now Cardiganshire) of the ancient regal line of Cunedda Wledig. His mythical Welsh history as told in the " Cotton MSS." makes him a lineal descendant of the Virgin Mary from whom he was of the eighteenth generation. His legends all ascribe to him the power to work miracles from the hour of his birth and some even give him the preternatural faculty while yet unborn. An angel, it is told us, attended him at all times to minister to his needs. He was early ordained into the priesthood and almost immediately thereafter retired to the Isle of Wight where for a time he led the life of an anchorite but in the meantime preparing himself for his ministry. Returning from the Isle of Wight David first built a chapel at Glastonbury but later founded many monasteries and a hermitage and chapel at Lanthony. When the Pelagian heresy sprang up a second time in Britain the bishops held a Brevi in what is now Cardiganshire, where David took a most prominent part and for this he was made Bishop of Caerleon but he soon transferred the see to Menervia (now St. David's) then a populous city where he died in 544.

An eminent English writer says of St. David: "There is no doubt of the inestimable services rendered by St. David to the British church in those early days which entitle him to a most distinguished place in its annals." He is remembered in the "Triads" with Teilo and Caturg, as one of the "three canonized saints of Britain," while Giraldus terms him "a mirror and pattern to all, instructing both by word and example; excellent in his preaching but still more so in his works." If the legends of St. David have been somewhat "extravagantly embroidered" one can hardly wonder since prior to the Reformation in the old church at Sarum in England the following collect was annually read in the service on March 1st: "Oh, God, who by thy angel didst foretell Thy blessed Confessor, St. David, thirty years before he was born, grant unto us, we beseech Thee, that celebrating his memory, we may, by his intercession, attain to joys everlasting."

St. David was canonized by Pope Calixtus II. about five hundred years after his death. Though no mention is anywhere made of St. David being at all musical his attribute on Clog sticks is always an ancient harp doubtless selected because of his name. The two given above were copied from English sticks of different dates.

MARCH 2d.

St. Ceadda, or Chad as the name is Anglicised, is honoured to-day by both the Reformed and Roman Churches. He was a brother of St. Cedd, Bishop of London, and of the two holy priests Celin and Cymbal. When St. Wilfrid went to France to be confirmed Bishop of Northumbria (or York) he remained so long that King Oswi in 666 named Chad as Bishop and he was so confirmed by Wini, Bishop of Winchester and two British prelates. But when Theodorus, Archbishop of Canterbury, came to judge the matter he decided Chad's ordination irregular and the holy man at once withdrew, later becoming the Bishop of the Mercians and fixing his see at Litchfield.

St. Chad is regarded as the missionary who introduced Christianity among the East Saxons. He was educated at the monastery of Lindesfarne or Holy Island, of which he became the bishop. When old age compelled him to retire he settled with seven or eight monks, near Litchfield, where he died in 673 from the pestilence then afflicting the land. When the old church where St. Chad was buried fell in 1788, among the few relics of old days saved was the ancient wood figure of St. Chad that is now kept in the new church at Shrewsbury.

After his canonization St. Chad became the patron saint of medicinal springs.

The emblem given above which marks St. Chad's Day upon the Danish Clogs is supposed to represent a fruitful branch.

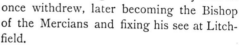

MARCH 3d

Is the festival of St. Cunegunda who was the daughter of Sigfrid, Count of Luxembourg. She was when quite young betrothed to Henry, Duke of Bavaria, whom she subsequently married. Prior to her marriage she had with the consent of Henry made a vow of virginity, which was always faithfully kept. On the death of Otho III., Emperor of Germany in 1002 Henry was chosen King of Rome and was crowned at Mentz on June 6th of that year; while Cunegunda was crowned at Paderborn on August 10, 1002 (St. Laurence Day), on which occasion she enriched the churches of the city by many lavish gifts. Henry of Bavaria was a soldier but above that — in his esteem — he was a Christian and his devotion to the Church brought on a revolt among certain powerful nobles who objected to the lavish gifts of both Henry and his Empress for religious uses. This rebellion was quickly quelled. In this love of the Church the two were most cordially united. Together they founded and endowed the cathedral and convent at Bamberg in Franconia where — I note in passing — Henry was buried in 1024.

They also founded many other religious edifices both in Germany and Italy. One was the work of Cunegunda herself that at Cafungen (now Kaffungen) which she gave to the nuns of the Order of St. Benedict. A base and wicked slander regarding Cunegunda was at one time circulated that despite her vows of virginity she had been unfaithful to her husband. Henry could not and did not for a moment believe these accusations. Yet she to vindicate her honour begged to be put to "trial by ordeal." Much as Henry objected he at last gave his consent and in public she "walked over burning ploughshares unharmed," a very common ordeal in those days. From that hour Henry's devotion and the reverence he felt for his wife, true as both had been before became unbounded. On the anniversary of the death of her husband (August 10, 1024) she, in 1025, put aside her imperial robes and had her beautiful hair, once her pride, cut off and she donned the habit and veil of the Order of St. Benedict at Kaffungen, which she had completed during the year. From that time until her death March 3, 1040, her life was devoted to her duties as a nun. She steadfastly refused every indulgence working with her hands like her fellow sisters. Her body was laid beside that of her loved husband at Bamberg. She was canonized by Pope Innocent III. in 1200.

MARCH 4th.

This day is sacred to a most interesting character, Casimir, Prince of Poland, the second son of Casimir III., king of Poland and Elizabeth of Austria, a daughter of Albert II. of Austria. Casimir's eldest brother, Uladislas, became king of Bohemia in 1471 and king of Hungary in 1490, while a younger brother, John Albert, succeeded his father as king of Poland in 1492. It was by no means want of opportunity that Casimir did not also sit upon an earthly throne. The Palatines and other nobles of Hungary were dissatisfied with Matthias Corvin, their king, and begged of the King of Poland to place his son Casimir on the throne. He was then only fifteen years of age and had almost from his infancy been religiously inclined and had no taste for the offer but would no doubt have been obliged to accept had not the differences between the king and people been adjusted by Pope Sixtus IV. who acted as mediator. Later he refused the crown of Hungary bestowed on his brother long years afterward. Instead of seeking these worldly honours, his entire life was given up to deeds of kindness and acts of love in unostentatious privacy until his name was the synonym for goodness though when he died in 1482 he was but twenty-three years of age. He died at Vilna and was there buried, but a portrait of him now hangs in the chapel of St. Germains des Prez in Paris, which, by the way, was built by John Casimir, king of Poland, the last of the family of Waza who renounced his crown and died abbot of St. Germain.

MARCH 5th.

While both profane and ecclesiastical history accords most justly to St. Patrick (of whom I shall speak on March 17th) the honour of having founded the Christian faith in Ireland, it is also true that for nearly a century before the advent of this noted saint there were Christians scattered through the island and one of these, St. Kiaran, or Kenerin (called by the Britons Piran), the Church honours on this day, and whom the Irish style "the first-born" of their saints. According to some he was a native of

Ossory, while others claim Cork as his birthplace. Usher places his birth about the year 352. His legend tells that having received some imperfect information in regard to the Christian faith he, when thirty years of age in or about 382, made a journey to Rome to assure himself of its truth. After a long sojourn "in the Holy City," where by Irish writers he is said to have been ordained as a bishop he returned to Ireland "accompanied by four holy clerks," whose names as given by these writers were "Lugacius, Columban, Lugad and Cassan." Dr. Butler, however, says: "What John of Tinmouth affirms seems far more probable, that he was one of the Twelve Apostles whom St. Patrick consecrated bishops in Ireland to aid him in planting the gospel in the island." Whichever statement is true he had evidently begun his missionary labours before the advent of the great man to whom Ireland owes her early and effectual teachings. He built himself a cell near the water at Fuaran where a town afterwards was built called Saigar, now from this saint named Sier-keran. Here he converted to the faith not only his own family but after giving to his mother "the religious veil" appointed her to a cell or monastery near his own" called by the Irish Ceall Lidain"; her name having been Liadan. In his old age he passed over into Cornwall where he led an eremitical life near to the Severn Sea not far from Padstow where he died. A tower was later built there which was called in his honour Piran's in the Sands.

This day is also the festival of St. John Joseph of the Cross, one of the later of the canonized saints of the Church, the bull for his canonization having been promulgated on Trinity Sunday, May 26, 1839. He was born in 1654 on the island of Ischia, belonging to the Kingdom of Naples and assumed the name of John Joseph of the Cross in 1671, at the time of his taking his habit. He was then but seventeen years old yet we soon see him as "Master of Novices" and by 1690 promoted to the office of "Definitor." In 1702 he rendered his Order a signal service with the Pontificate by which the Alcantarines in Italy were established in the form of a province and the arduous duties of its government forced upon our saint. Finally in 1722 the convent of St. Lucy in Naples was made over to the Alcantarines to which John Joseph retired spending the remainder of his life in good works and where he died March 5, 1734.

MARCH 6th.

To-day is the festival of St. Colette, a carpenter's daughter of Corbie in Picardy whose parents were ardent admirers of the good St. Nicholas and in his honour christened their child Colette, which is the diminutive of the saint's name. After the death of her parents she took the vows and habit of the Third Order of St. Francis called the Penitents, and three years later that of the Mitigated Clares, called Urbanists. From her earliest entrance upon her holy life her austerities were marked and severe and she early resolved to make an effort to re-establish the primitive spirit and practices of the Order. After visiting several convents she made a journey to Nice in which city Benedict XIII., then happened to be. Apparently unaided save by her own strong purpose to revive the rule and spirit of St. Francis, she received from the Pope her nomination as " Superioress in General of the whole Order of St. Clare with power to establish such regulations as she thought to be conducive to God's honour." She foretold the date of her death which occurred at Ghent on March 6, 1447. She was never canonized nor is her name mentioned in Roman Martyrology, but Clement VIII., Paul V., Gregory XIII., and Urban VIII. all approved an office in her honour by the whole Franciscan Order as the "Blessed Colette!"

MARCH 7th

Is the festival of St. Thomas of Aquino, a doctor of the Church, a man who is most highly honoured, who died March 7, 1274, at the famous Cistercian Abbey of Fossa Nuova in Terracina. The translation of his relics to France at every point presented most wonderful scenes proving the veneration in which he was held.

At Toulouse an hundred and fifty thousand people gathered to receive the sacred relics, and the procession into the city was headed by Louis, Duke of Anjou — brother of Charles V., and also by the Archbishop of the see. St. Thomas was canonized by Pope John XXII. in 1323 while Pope Pius V. in 1567, commanded his festival to be kept equal with those of the " Four Doctors of the Western Church."

This day is also the festival of St. Perpetua, a martyr at Carthage under the persecution of Emperor Severus in 303 when she, with her companions, won their crown of glory by their blood shed for the faith.

St. Perpetua is one of the saints whose names was retained by the Fathers of the Reformed church and which still has a place in the Kalendar of the Church of England.

The martyrdom of Perpetua and her companions was a peculiarly brutal affair even for those brutal times, and her fortitude during her trials was beyond praise and won for her commendation and reverence. She was thrown into the amphitheatre and tossed by a wild cow but when this had not entirely extinguished life she was put to death in the " spoliarium " (the place where the wounded were dispatched by young gladiators) by the sword. But before her death she had a wondrous vision of a ladder reaching to Heaven though each rung was beset by spikes and a dragon lying at the bottom upon whose head she was obliged to tread before mounting the first step. This vision is represented in Callot's images and has been adopted by Clog Almanacs, though in art she is usually shown with a wild cow standing before her.

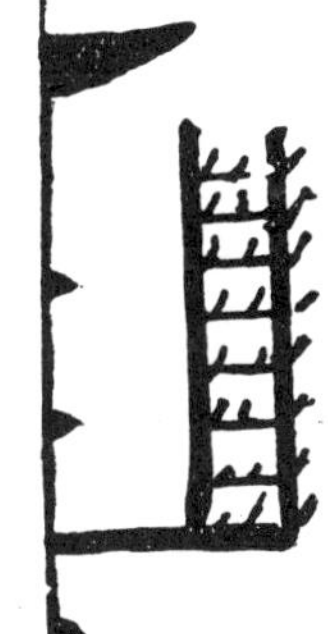

MARCH 8th.

St. John, surnamed "of God," is one of the saints honoured by the Church on this day. He was born in Portugal in 1495 of parents of the humblest class, and his early days were spent as a shepherd of the Count of Oropeusa in Castile; but in 1522 he became a soldier, serving in the wars between Spain and France, then in the Hungarian war and lastly, when Charles V. was King of Spain, against the Turks. Thus for fourteen years he lived in camps and subjected to the temptations besetting a soldier. In 1536 when his troop was disbanded he once more took up his life as a shepherd, in the service of a rich lady near Seville. Humble as his parents were they had in his youth instilled into his mind the right principles and even amid the debauchery of camp life the licentiousness of his companions had at first disgusted him; but, alas, he was only human, and like many another, by slow degrees fell but never to the depths of degradation which some of his companions did. Now in the quiet of his pastoral occupations he began to reflect upon his conduct and how he could by penance and service regain what he felt he had lost. At last he resolved to leave his present occupation and pass over into Africa there to strive to succour and comfort the captive slaves — of whom just then there were so many. At Gibraltar he met a Portuguese gentleman who was banished to Barbary and John went with him into exile serving him for two years without compensation, then returning to Granada in Spain in 1538. It was here he first heard John D'Avila, "The Apostle of Andalusia," preach and he set about the fulfilment of his purpose of striving to redeem the sins of his past life. From trading and other sources he seems to have accumulated a little money. With this in 1540 he hired and furnished a house in Granada, into which he brought such of the sick poor as he found, tending them with his own hands and providing for them as best he could. This effort came to the knowledge of the Archbishop and to curtail a long and interesting story of not only noble efforts in behalf of the sick but of reclaiming from vice many a fallen one, of surmounting endless difficulties and not a little opposition, until at last he evolved, through the aid of the Bishop of Tuy, President of the Royal Court of Judicature of Granada, the Order of Charity. John had no thought of founding a Religious Order and it was not until six years after his death it really took form and the religious vows were not introduced until 1570; but practically it had been founded and he is the recognised

"Founder." The name "John of God" was bestowed upon him by the good Bishop of Tuy.

I wish I might tell something more of his work, of how the King and princes at last came to vie with each other to aid him when he came to Valladolid, and the honours bestowed upon him. It is only one of the many stories that show how none of us are so poor or helpless that if we but will we may do good.

John of God died on his knees before the altar on March 8, 1550. He was beatified by Urban VIII. in 1630 and canonized by Alexander VIII. in 1690.

MARCH 9th

Is the festival of St. Gregory of Nyssa, Bishop and Confessor, a younger brother of St. Basil the Great and the author of many learned works still extant and which were republished in three huge folios between 1615 and 1638. As a rhetorician and orator he had few in his generation who were his equal. In youth he had been highly educated and became a married man but later resigned worldly honours and was ordained lector. In 372 he was chosen Bishop of Nyssa, a city in Cappadocia, near the Lesser Armenia. His eloquence made him a terror to the Arians, who at length prevailed on Demosthenes, the Vicar or deputy governor of the province, to banish him, but after the death of Valens in 378 the Emperor Gratian restored him to his see. Aside from his learned writings Gregory of Nyssa, as he is usually termed, was most noted for his determined opposition to the Arian heresy. He died on January 10, 400, the date on which the Greeks have always honoured him but the Latin Church has for ages kept his festival on this 9th of March.

MARCH 10th.

The Church this day holds in sacred memory the martyrdom of perhaps as remarkable a body of men as ever testified to their faith with their blood. They were Roman soldiers, brave and fearless who knowing their duty, never failed to do it for they belonged to "The Thundering Legion" so famous under Marcus Aurelius, that Twelfth Legion, the flower of the army who were in 320 quartered in Armenia with Lysias as duke or general of the army while Agricola was governor of the province. The latter, by orders of the Emperor Licinius, promulgated his command that all should sacrifice to the Roman gods. It was then these "Forty Martyrs of Sebaste," as they are called in Roman Martyrology, rose to the higher duty they owed to their faith holding it above any they were bound by, as Roman soldiers. Thus it was they appeared before Agricola telling him they were Christians and as such could not obey the order, at the same time pointing to their record as true, faithful soldiers of the empire. Agricola tried to reason with them but without avail. Then they were rent with iron hooks, scourged and cast into prison. After some days Lysias who happened to be in Cæsarea at the time returned, but no promises of wealth or aught else could make them waver. It was then Agricola conceived a horrid punishment for them. It was intensely cold and close to the town was a pond which was then frozen over and it was ordered they should be stripped naked and compelled to stand on the ice. Yet of them all only one of their number faltered, and, strangely, as he came forward to recant he fell dead. When morning broke both those who had died during the night from exposure and the living were alike cast upon a fire and burned. These are the heroes whom the Church honours this day.

MARCH 11th.

Among others that are named this day in the Roman Kalendar is St. Ængus, Abbot of the monastery of Cluain-Edneach in Ireland, and a bishop. Dr. Butler says: "It was then usual in Ireland for the abbots of the chief monasteries to be made bishops. Ængus was distinguished by the surname of Kele-De (Worshipper of God) or what came to be known as the Culdees; of whom we read so much in early Scotch history. There has been a world of historical and polemic controversy over the origin of this word Culdee. The Cele-De of Armagh Ireland) and the Colidcc of York, canons of the cathedral, seemingly were identical. In Scotland the name first took the form of Keledio, almost the same as that bestowed upon St. Ængus, who for a time lived an eremitical life, and this gives a slight reason for Burton's (the Scotch historian) opinion that the word Culdee may have come from the Celtic word Kill (a cell). But Dr. Reeves, the celebrated Celtic etymologist, glosses the word Cele-De as "Spouse of God," which apparently settles the question of name. Important, however, as the Culdees appear in the ecclesiastical history of Scotland, it would seem as though they were not under an episcopal hierarchy like the secular side of the church. That they married is patent. The gracious Duncan, who married the daughter of Malcolm II., was the son of Cronan or Crinan, Abbot of the Culdees of Dunkeld. Yet these Culdees were monks and evidently under canonical rule by the Roman Church just as our St. Ængus was whose title led me into this digression. St. Ængus is especially noted for having written several books on the Irish Saints of the church and for compiling "a longer and shorter Irish martyrology." He died at Desert Ængus, a famous Irish monastery named for him, about the year 824.

MARCH 12th

Is esteemed by the Roman Church as a festival of more than usual importance, as it is that of Gregory I., "The Great," who sat in the pontifical chair from 590 to 604.

There have been popes of every shade of human character but Gregory the Great is one distinguished by his modesty, disinterestedness and sincere religious zeal, tempered by a toleration which could only spring from pure benevolence. The son of a Roman Senator, with high mental gifts and all the accomplishments of his age, he was drawn early into prominent position but always against his will. He would fain have continued to be an obscure monk or a missionary but his qualities were such that at length even the popedom was thrust upon him (on the death of Pelagius II. in 590). On this occasion he wrote to the sister of the emperor: "Appearing to be outwardly exalted I am really fallen. My endeavours were to banish corporeal objects from my mind that I might spiritually behold heavenly joys. . . . I am come into the depths of the sea, and the tempest hath drowned me."

In exercising the functions of his high station Gregory, while he exhibited great firmness, it was always tempered by mildness and forbearance and he remembered that from his position he was "the father of the sick and needy." With him to relieve the poor was the first of Christian graces. He devoted a large proportion of his revenue and a vast amount of personal care to this object. He in a manner took the entire charge of the poor upon his own hands. He removed their necessities with so much sweetness and affability as to spare them the confession of receiving alms; the old men he out of deference, called his fathers. He often entertained several of them at his own table. He kept by him an exact catalogue of the poor called by the ancients "matriculæ" and he liberally provided for the necessities of each.

It was this Gregory of whom (before he attained his great dignity) the well-known story is told of seeing certain slaves in the market asked who they were and from what country they came; and on being told they were "Angli," he was so impressed by their beauty of person that he cried out "Verily Angeli." His one great hope and ambition from that time was to become a missionary to the heathen of Britain and he once actually started on his journey thither when on the third day he was recalled to Rome by the Apostolic Father. Missionaries, however, thanks to Gregory's influence were shortly thereafter sent to Britain.

Gregory during his pontificate was a prolific writer. Among his productions there are extant forty homilies upon the Gospels; twenty-two on Ezekiel; not to speak of others which fill four large folio volumes and are highly prized by Roman ecclesiastics. He was one of the "Four Great Doctors of the Latin Church" and next to St. Jerom the most popular, and therefore he is so often presented in art singly. In these pictures he bears the tiara of the Pope and the crosier with the double cross and the dove his *special* attribute. A legend tells that John the Deacon who was St. Gregory's secretary declared that as the saint sat writing, the Holy Spirit, in the form of a Dove, sat upon his shoulder. The legends told of St. Gregory are numerous and touching in their pathos. Especially so is the one often referred to as "The Supper of St. Gregory," which has been made the subject of several noted works of art.

Personally, St. Gregory is said to have been tall, corpulent and of a swarthy complexion with jet black hair but having a thin beard. He presented his portrait with others of the family to the monastery of St. Andrew which he founded, and which now is the Church of San Gregorio in Rome of which Mrs. Jameson wrote of that view from the "Garden of Sta Slivia" so many of us remember:

"To stand here on the summit of the flight of steps which leads to the portal, and look across to the ruined palace of the Cæsars, makes the mind giddy with the rush of thoughts. There before us, the Palatine Hill — pagan Rome in the dust; here the little cell a few feet square where slept in sackcloth the man who gave the last blow to the power of the Cæsars, and first set his foot as sovereign on the cradle and capital of their greatness."

A volume would hardly suffice to recount all that one would wish to write of this remarkable man and therefore I must let this meagre and unsatisfactory account pass as it is written.

MARCH 13th.

St. Nicephorus, Patriarch of Constantinople, is one of those whom the Latin Church honoured this day and who first came into notice after Constantine and Irene ascended the throne and gave to Christians protection from the persecution they had suffered under Constantine Copronymus. Nicephorus had early attracted the attention of the emperor and was elevated to the dignity of secretary. He distinguished himself by his zeal against the Iconoclasts and was made secretary to the second Council of Nice. In

806 he was chosen Patriarch of Constantinople and was noted for his unwearied effort to restore the old-time manners and teaching of the early Fathers, especially in regard to the reverence of images, claiming that the Iconoclasts were inconsistent when they venerated the figure of the cross and the book of the four Gospels but condemned like honour paid to the images of Christ; using the same argument which had so often been put forward, that: "For these eight hundred years, since the time of Christ, there had been pictures of Him and He had been honoured in them." In 813 Leo the Armenian, former Governor of Natolia, became emperor and being an Iconoclast encouraged his soldiers to maltreat an image of Christ on a cross on the brazen gate of the city and ordered it removed. The protests against this act and subsequent trial of St. Nicephorus by a court of Iconoclast bishops resulted in his condemnation to exile and deposition from office. He died in exile on June 2d, 828. His body was by order of Empress Theodora, brought back with great pomp and ceremony on March 13th, 846. This day was therefore selected on which to commemorate his memory.

MARCH 14th.

St. Maud or Mathildis, queen of Germany, is to-day most especially honoured in that country. In older days the names Maud, Mathildis, Matilda and Mathilda were in England and on the Continent used synonymously. The wife of Henry I. of England was styled Maud or Matilda as the writer happened to choose. In speaking of St. Henry so much of the story of the life of St. Maud has been told, how from their cradles they had been playmates and lovers, that little now need be added save a few words of eulogy of which not many women of her rank are more deserving. Her entire life outside of the beautiful domestic circle had but one great purpose in view, to visit, comfort and teach the poor, the sick and the ignorant. When at the moment of her husband's death she was at the altar in prayer for him, she saw by the eyes of those about her that he had already gone to his reward, she rose humbly bowing to the Divine will. Then in token of her resolution she cut from her garments the jewels she wore and gave them to the priest to be disposed of for the poor. From that hour her remaining life was a succession of noble deeds of charity and in the use of her wealth to build and endow churches, hospitals and monasteries. Of the latter it is told that in the one at Poldeu in the Duchy of Brunswick she maintained 3,000 monks. Indeed the charities were only limited by a lack of knowledge as to where they were most needed. She not only gave of her wealth but her personal service was at all times added to enhance the value by her example of perfect self-sacrifice.

She died March 14, 968 and her relics still rest at Quedlinbourg.

MARCH 15th.

In certain old English and German Kalendars there appears a name not to be found in either Latin or Greek Martyrology, named in the Old English Longinus and who according to mediæval legends was the centurion who under orders of Pontius Pilate pierced our Saviour's side with a spear. This strange legend also says: "This man was blind"—but fails to enlighten us how a blind man could have been a centurion, or why he was chosen for such a purpose; but adds that as the "blood and water" flowed from Christ's wounds, "some drops fell upon the eyes of this soldier and his sight was miraculously restored," and still further attributing to him the words recorded by SS. Matthew and Mark, as made by a centurion at the death of our Lord: "Truly this man was the Son of God." Then follows an account of how he, Longinus, at once affiliated with the Apostles and became "an active soldier of the faith." Soon we are told Longinus was arrested and brought before Octavius, the prefect, when he at once confessed himself a Roman soldier and a convert to Christianity. They then the legend continues discussed Paganism vs. Christianity; only resulting in Longinus being ordered into the hands of the tormentors. These torments were borne uncomplainingly until at last a curious compromise was made to which Octavius consented that Longinus might work his will upon the pagan idols and if he successfully overcame them, then the pagans should desert their gods and become Christians.

In due season Longinus "broke all their idols in pieces and trampled over them," but as the Devils were fleeing from them the old soldier stopped them and demanded of them their secret. Then they too confessed the power of God, and that they sought refuge in the idols as a place secure from having the name of Christ invoked upon them or the "sign of the Cross" made upon them. All this did not save poor Longinus from death for Octavius feared the Roman power. Yet the story tells in the end that even Octavius later became a convert. "These things," the legend closes, "were acted in the city of Cæsarea of Cappadocia on the ides of March, under Octavius the Prefect."

St. Abraham, whose festival the Church keeps this day, is another example of the fascination the life of a Hermit and Recluse had for so many in the early centuries of the Church. Abraham came from a wealthy Mesopotamian family. Of his own free will he married a woman whom he greatly admired. But the hour the wedding feast ended, he announced to his bride his resolution to lead an eremitical life and at once retired to a cell near Edessa where his friends found him after searching during seventeen days. He was not a priest but he told them he desired to spend his life in solitude and in secret adoration of God. No pleas of any kind availed and his friends were obliged to leave him in his cell where he remained for fifty years except once when the Bishop persuaded him to act as a missionary to a country town near Edessa which was given over to paganism. In this work our recluse was eminently successful but as soon as it was completed he returned to his cell. Through his friends he distributed in charity the revenues of the vast estates his parents had left him. A brother of Abraham who died shortly after the return of the recluse had left to his care his only daughter. For her Abraham built a cell near his own and placed her there teaching her his doctrines of retirement and devotion. The girl soon wearied of this life and the legend tells that under the seductions of a wily, wicked monk she fell and went to the city where she led a life of infamy, until at last to reclaim her if possible Abraham once more for awhile abandoned his cell and sought her out. With not a little difficulty he at length gained her consent to return with him where during the fifteen years of her remaining life she spent her time in penance and prayer. Abraham died five years before his niece, in or about 360. His name appears in all the early Latin, Greek and Coptic Kalendars; while that of St. Mary his niece is found only in those of the Greeks.

MARCH 16th

Is the festival of St. Julian of Cilicia. Born of a senatorian family in Anazarbus, he became a minister of the gospel, but under the persecutions of Dioclesian he, like so many thousand others, was made to suffer and prove his faith. While none escaped from the brutal torments of those edicts, Julian was called on to undergo a series of torments which it would seem only fiends could invent. He chanced to fall under the orders of a judge, who knowing his character, by a system of refined cruelty had him daily for a whole year dragged through the streets of the cities of Cilicia as a base malefactor, to be scoffed and jeered at by the populace. When threats of torture were added to this disgrace, and lavish promises were made of wealth and civic honour if he would yield and worship the idols, had all proved vain and unavailing, to quote from his legend: "The bloody executioners had torn his flesh, furrowed his sides, laid bare his bones and his bowels exposed to view, scourges, fire and the sword were used to torment him." When at last the fiends saw his life was waning and human nature could endure no more, this judge, as if to surpass all former cruelties, caused this martyr to be sewed up in a sack containing "scorpions, serpents and vipers," after which he was cast into the sea at Ægea. But the sea gave up this horrid sack and some of the faithful recovered the sacred relics, which at last were conveyed to Antioch.

MARCH 17th

Is the festival of the most noted saint of Ireland, St. Patrick. Probably no man ever lived over whom so many battles have been fought as to where his birthplace was. From a carefully translated edition of the Confessions of St. Patrick, annexed to Miss Cusack's "Life of St. Patrick," and generally accepted by ecclesiastics as authority, it seems certain that "Patricius" was born of Christian parents at Bannavem of Tabernia, a Roman provincial village in Britain. St. Patrick also proves he was of gentle birth, for in his Confessions he says his father was a "decurio," that is one of the council or magistracy of a Roman town. As near as we can learn he was born about the year 372 and until he was sixteen lived the simple life of a farmer's son. Then an event not uncommon in those days happened to him for he was captured by pirates and sold into Irish slavery where for some years he was employed as a swineherd on the Sleamish mountains in County Antrim. He once escaped but was recaptured. His second attempt was successful and he reached his native land. He had during his captivity learned the Irish language and after his escape a vision warned him to return to Ireland as a missionary but before doing so some of his biographers state he travelled into Gaul and Italy and received from Pope Celestine in 432 his Apostolic benediction. In his Confessions Patrick does not tell how or where he was consecrated as bishop but that he exercised the powers and functions of that office is clear while his authority to do so was never doubted. Yet his Confessions evidently written toward the close of his life seem to infer he had been serving as a missionary many years before he was consecrated. These Confessions Dr. Skene, the eminent Scotch historiographer, takes pains to assert are in all respects authentic and reliable but adds that at a later period "this simple narrative became incrusted with a mass of traditional, legendary and fictitious matter."

Of St. Patrick's life work in "Ierne" (Ireland), space cannot be given to speak, in detail; though we know his principal enemies were the Druid priests who then held sway. There were also magicians, the "Magi," or "Druadh" who acted as physicians and as such their influence was unbounded. From a metrical life of St. Patrick attributed to "Fiacc of Sleibhte," we learn:

> "He preached three-score years
> The Cross of Christ to the Tuatha of Feni;
> In the Tuatha of Erin there was darkness,
> The Tuatha adored the Side."

From the Book of Armagh we learn the Side, or Sidhe, were "gods of the earth, phantoms," mysterious beings who were supposed to dwell alike in heaven or on earth, in the sea, the sky, the rivers, mountains and valleys, at will. Spirits to be dreaded and conciliated, who were to be worshipped and invoked both by themselves and through the natural objects in which they dwelt. This was the secret cause of the fear that the people felt and their reverence for the sanctity of the Druid oak and stone circles we so constantly read of in early English, Scotch and Irish history. But I must not venture into this interesting story of Druidism. Still we may well believe nothing but the power of God, delegated to St. Patrick, could have overcome the dangers and difficulties these Druid priests interposed in the holy man's path. Of the endless number of miracles ascribed to St. Patrick only a volume would suffice to tell them. That of his driving the snakes out of Ireland is too patent for repetition. Another that is duly vouched for in his "Legendary Life," is not as well known when he made a fire out of ice and snowballs:

> "Saint Patrick, as in legends told,
> The morning being very cold,
> In order to assuage the weather,
> Collected bits of ice together;
> Then gently breathed upon the pyre,
> When every fragment blazed on fire."

Of the well known legend in regard to the shamrock having been used by St. Patrick to illustrate the Unity of the Trinity, there is little doubt; still less as to its fitness as an emblem but it is certainly a curious coincidence if nothing more that the trefoil in Arabic is called "shamrakh" and was held sacred in Iran as emblematical of the Persian Triads.

I may not enter on the mooted question of the date of St. Patrick's death which has been placed in two different years, 464 and 493. Mr. Skene devotes a great number of pages to show that this discrepancy comes through an error in regard to the length of his Irish captivity. Dr. Butler and most authorities place it in 464. Phillips' Biographical Dictionary revised by Weitenkamp, places it in 466.

As the birthplace of St. Patrick has been disputed so has that of his burial. But the general evidence indicates that he was buried at Downpatrick and that the remains of St. Columba and St. Bridget were laid beside him according to the old monkish Leonine distich :

> " In Burgo Duno, tumulo tumulantur in uno,
> Brigida, Patricius, atque Columba pius."

Which may be thus rendered :

> " On the hill of Down, buried in one tomb,
> Were Bridget and Patricius, with Columba the pious."

MARCH 18th.

St. Cyril, Archbishop of Jerusalem, is the most noted of the saints honoured by the Roman Church this day both for his sanctity and his wonderful writings but even more so for his gallant struggle against the heresies and schisms which had crept into the Christian Church, the chief among them being Arianism. But I must leave unsaid what is due to the learning and holy life of St. Cyril who died in 386 and is honoured by both the Greek and Latin Churches on this day.

St. Edward, King of England, who has a place both in that of the Roman Martyrology and the Church of England has his festival this day. The old story of his assassination at Corfe Castle is far too trite to repeat again in full for it has been told in every English history. The unfortunate king was by order of his mother-in-law, buried in unhallowed ground at Wareham but at once, most wonderful sights began to appear about his tomb and marvellous miracles were performed. "Then lights shone from above; there the lame walked; there the dumb resumed his faculty of speech; there every malady gave wey to health," are the words of that quaint old Saxon chronicler, William of Malmesbury. From this resting place Edward's relics were translated three years after his death, in 978, to the monastery of Shaftesbury.

MARCH 19th

Is the festival of St. Joseph, the husband of the Virgin Mary. As far back as the traditions of the Christian Church extend we find the name of Joseph honoured as a saint. The one simple fact of his having been chosen as the guardian of the Virgin and her Divine Son is alone enough to justify the esteem in which the Fathers of the Early Church held him. It was not until the bulls of Pope Gregory XV. in 1621, and Urban VIII. 1642, that this festival became obligatory. The Syrians and other Eastern churches held this festival on July 29th but the Western church observed it on this 19th day of March.

Outside of what is told in Holy Writ there is little of an authentic character known of Joseph. The legend of the Virgin and her marriage with Joseph given in the "Protevangelion" lies before me as I write, but it is too elaborate for transcribing here. When the priest Zacharius was directed "by an angel" to assemble together "all the widowers among the people" from whom was to be selected the spouse of Mary, each was commanded to bring his "rod," or staff, and Joseph came with the rest. When he appeared before the priest and presented his rod "lo! a dove issued out of it — a dove dazzling white as snow, and after settling on his (Joseph's) head, flew away to heaven."

The time of Joseph's death is a mooted point. Some, on what ground I am unable to say, put the date at the time Jesus Christ was eighteen years old. A crutched staff is the usual attribute of Joseph but I find none upon any of the Clog sticks I have seen. In art Joseph carries a wallet and a pilgrim's staff. His dress is a gray tunic and a saffron mantle.

MARCH 20th.

Few of my readers who have visited Melrose Abbey, Scotland, will have had told them the legend of "Muilros," the old Melrose and its famous Saint Cuthbert, whom the Church honours to-day. He was a Northumbrian shepherd lad born near the old monastery to whom as he watched his flock at night, "angels came and talked with him," a legend full of material for a poet's idyl though the truth is hardly less beautiful. For the shepherd lad came at last to enter the Monastery of Muilros as a novice where St. Aidan had been prior. None ever claimed for Cuthbert wondrous learning, but he had in him that which was better, "the beauty of holiness." When the time came he went forth from the old monastery as one inspired, wandering far away into mountainous regions deemed almost inaccessible and by his magnetism of voice and manner won the hearts and love of those wild, untamed people and though he became the Prior of Muilros and Bishop of Lindisfarne it is as a preacher and a missionary that his name, even now after more than twelve centuries are gone, is held in loving reverence in the "country-side" where he laboured and on the island of Farne, where he died in 687. The story of his relics is a long and most strange one until at last they were recovered from the Danes in the XI. century still as fresh and uncorrupted as at the hour of death.

By turning to September 4th of this volume the reader will find another and more extended notice of this saint.

MARCH 21st.

The Roman Church this day honours a saint who is also one whose name was retained by the Reformed church, St. Benedict or Bennett as he is at times called, Patriarch of the Western Monks, and founder of the celebrated Benedictine Order. As the father of Western monarchism and the great and durable influence he exerted both in England and upon Northern Continental Europe, it seems almost idle to try to sum up his history in the few lines I am compelled to do. He was born at Norcia in Umbria, A. D. 480. He began his studies at Rome but being disgusted with the world resolved to leave it and went into retirement in the mountains of Subiaco when he was scarcely fourteen years old. There meeting with a monk of some neighbouring community he received from him the religious habit and became remarkable for austerity and piety. It was on Mount Cassino that he founded his first monastery and bound the monks by those rules which afterward became so popular. It is related that he would often roll himself in a heap of briars as a means of self-mortification. St. Gregory tells us that the Goths set fire to his cell which burned around him without doing him the least hurt and that they then threw him into a hot oven closely stopping it up but upon coming the next day they found him safe neither his flesh being scorched nor his clothes singed.

ST. BENEDICT.

The early Anglo-Saxon monks led a very loose life, to apply no more severe term. It was St. Dunstan who restored the strict rule of St. Benedict and his Order.

MARCH 22d.

Mid-Lent Sunday or the fourth Sunday in Lent, is in England universally called

"MOTHERING SUNDAY."

This title came from one of the oldest and most rigidly observed of the earlier customs in England but long since obsolete though the name still clings to the day. On this day it was the custom for children, no matter what their age might be to pay a formal visit to their parents, but most especially the mother; at which time they carried with them a present of cakes called "Simnel Cakes," and the visit was termed: "Going A-Mothering." Upon the occasion the mother bestowed upon her child her blessing. The genial Herrick, in a canzonet addressed to Dianeme, says:

> "I'll to thee a simnel bring,
> 'Gainst thou go a-mothering;
> So that, when she blesses thee,
> Half that blessing thou'lt give me."

But the use of "Simnel Cake," was not confined to this gift brought to the mother of the family. It was almost a universal custom to make these cakes during Lent, at Easter and Christmas. They were a very rich sort of "plum-cake, with plenty of candied lemon-peel and other good things" entering into their composition. After they were made they were tied up in a cloth, boiled for several hours then brushed over with a coating of egg and sugar and baked so that when ready the outer crust was almost as hard as wood. They were sold at every "Bake-Shop." It was also an old French custom to make these cakes with a figure of Christ or the Virgin Mary.

The name Simnel is supposed to be derived from the Latin "simila," fine flour of the choicest quality.

This day is observed at Carthage in honour of St. Deogratias. In 439 Genseric, the Arian King of the Vandals, captured Carthage inflicting many cruelties upon the Christians, and banished their Bishop Quodvultdeus and a large number of others, and it was not until 454, that another orthodox prelate was allowed in Carthage. That year St. Deogratias was made Archbishop. In the meantime Genseric had plundered Rome and carried off from many places innumerable captives into Africa, where the Moors and Vandals shared them. As soon as Deogratias was installed he not only sold everything of his own but all the gold and silver vessels of the church and began the redemption of these captives. He also personally laboured in this humane service until 457, literally worn out by his arduous work, he died, on March 22d. It is for this the Church honours him to-day; though the old Carthage Kalendars name his festival for Jannary 5th.

MARCH 23d.

The Church this day remembers St. Alphonsus Turibius, a Spaniard by birth from the Kingdom of Leon. After passing through the varied gradations necessary for preparing him for the important position Turibius was named as Archbishop of Lima and sent to Peru to care for the infant Church, then struggling for existence in that far off country. His story is almost the same as that of all those early labourers in the missionary fields of both North and South America. Travelling on foot through trackless wildernesses, suffering for food, shelter and raiment, yet always without complaint or a regret for the wealth and splendour of his early life until after twenty-five years of arduous work, worn out in the service of Christ he died at Santa, a town distant an hundred and ten leagues from Lima, on March 23d, 1606, at the age of sixty-eight years. He was beatified by Innocent XI. in 1659 and canonized in 1726 by Benedict XIII., while Benedict XIV. makes especial mention of many miracles wrought through his intercession.

MARCH 24th

Commemorates the martyrdom of St. Irenæus, Bishop of Sirmium, the capital of a part of Pannonia. It is now a village twenty-two leagues from Buda in Hungary. The far reaching power of Dioclesian can hardly be better illustrated than it is by the case of Irenæus. We are apt to think of these persecutions as confined to Rome and Palestine but there was no quarter of the Roman empire that escaped. It was so with our saint, far away in a quiet hamlet teaching Christ's loved lessons and doing good to all as his hands found the opportunity. His is but a repetition of the oft told tale. A refusal to worship idols, a farce of a trial, condemnation to death. Then he was beheaded and his body thrown into the river.

MARCH 25th.

THE ANNUNCIATION.

This day is held in like reverence by the Latin, Greek and Reformed Churches everywhere, as the day when the Angel brought the happy tidings to the Blessed Virgin Mary of the Incarnation of the Son of God as told in the Gospel of St. Luke I., 28.

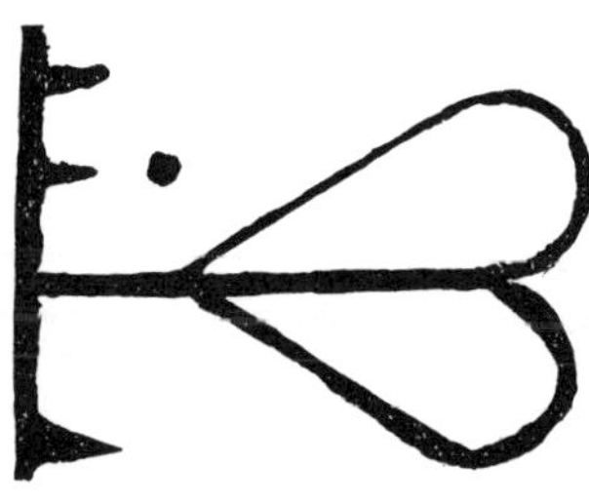

The antiquity of this festival is unquestioned for among the sermons of St. Augustine or Austin (who died August 28, 430) often called "The Greatest of the Fathers," are two upon this festival and in one of these he says: "According to ancient tradition this mystery was completed on the 25th of March." At least we know that from the V. century this has been the date upon which the solemn festival has been celebrated for Pope Gelasius I., in 492, mentions the fact. The tenth council of Toledo, in 656, calls the solemnity "The Festival of the Mother of God." Indeed at all times and in all ages the day and the festival have been devoutly reverenced by all branches of the Christian Church.

The illustration here given is the one found upon English sticks to mark the day and is not intended as the attribute of the Virgin. In representations of the Annunciation the Virgin Mary is shown kneeling or seated at a table reading. The lily (her emblem) is usually placed between her and the Angel Gabriel who holds in one hand a sceptre surmounted by a fleur-de-lis on a lily stalk; generally a scroll is proceeding from his mouth with the words "Ave Maria gratia plena" and sometimes the Holy Spirit is represented as a dove descending towards the Virgin.

In England this day is usually called "Lady Day" and in France "Notre Dame de Mars."

MARCH 26th

Is the festival of St. Ludger, Bishop of Munster, and the Apostle of Saxony. The early life of Ludger may be briefly told. Born in Friesland in 743 he was the son of a nobleman of the first rank. At his own request when young, he became the pupil of Gregory who succeeded St. Boniface in the see of Utrecht and from him he received the cleric tonsure. Readers, however, should remember that this was a common custom among students at monastic schools in those early days, and by no means meant that they were either under holy vows or in holy orders. As an ardent student and desirous of widening his education, Ludger, after leaving the school of Gregory, went to the famous school at York, England, then under that celebrated teacher, Alcuin. Here he spent four and a half years in the then customary study of ecclesiastical literature and the ancient languages. Shortly after 776 he returned to Utrecht and was ordained to the priesthood when Alberic, successor of Gregory, sent him to his native Friesland to missionate among the pagans of that country; but the ravages of the pagan Saxons at length drove him out. When however, in 787 Charlemagne overcame the Saxons, conquered Friesland and the coast of the Germanic ocean as far as Denmark, our saint saw the way open for his return to his missionary work and it was through his efforts that the Saxons in Friesland and in the province of Sudergou (now called Westphalia) were converted to the Christian faith. Thus he was able to found the celebrated monastery of Werden in La Mark, twenty-nine miles from Cologne. From this he gained the title of the "Apostle of Saxony." Ludger would gladly have rested at his monastery but in 802 Hildebald, Archbishop of Cologne, drew him from his retirement and ordained him Bishop of Mimigardeford, a city whose name was later changed to Munster. Five cantons of Friesland were also joined to his diocese. His strict rules drew down upon him the enmity of the more lax of his clergy, who brought accusations against him before the Emperor Charlemagne. But he easily proved his faithfulness to the church and his office. Ludger was favoured by a singularly clear gift of prophecy. At a time when such an event was the last thing to be dreamed of, he foretold the invasion of the Normans from Denmark and Norway and of the ravages they would make in the French empire. So, too, he foretold his own death on March 26, 809.

MARCH 27th.

In the story of the life of the Hermit St. John of Egypt whom the Church honours this day we have a picture of one of the earliest of the many holy men who adopted an eremitical life; at the same time presenting some curious features. John was born about 305, of a parentage from the lower class, and was a carpenter by trade until he was twenty-five years of age. Then impelled by a desire for a better — i. e., a holier life — he placed himself under the guidance of a venerable anchoret who, to teach him implicit obedience, imposed on him the "seemingly ridiculous task of watering a dead dry stick as if it had been a living plant." This Rufinus in his second book of the lives of the fathers, tells us John did with fidelity and unquestioning. He lived thus with his mentor for twelve years learning the lessons of humility and submission to God. After the old anchoret died John spent three or four years in neighbouring monasteries but his love for the life of a hermit had so won his heart that when he was about forty years of age he selected a rock near Lycopolis and erected for himself a cell. This he walled in save for one small window through which he received his necessary supplies. On certain days he allowed persons to converse with him provided they were men, as he never spoke to or looked on a woman; the rest of his time was spent in prayer and devotion.

Like St. Ludger he had the gift of prophecy, though he exercised it sparingly. One prophecy stands on record. Theodosius the Elder was attacked by the tyrant Maximus; emboldened by his success in 383 against Gratian, in 387 dethroning Valentinian. When Theodosius consulted John he prophesied his success, and upon this the Emperor marched into the West, crossed the Alps and took the tyrant in Aquelia, the soldiers cutting off Maximus' head. He also foretold many other events regarding the Empire all of which were fulfilled. Many miraculous powers were attributed to him such as reading the unspoken thoughts of those who came to him as was the case recorded by Dr. Butler, when, a short time prior to his death, the Bishop of Helenopolis came to him.

John of Egypt died near the close of 394. "Probably," says Dr. Butler, "on the 17th of October, on which day the Copths or Egyptian Christians keep his festival, but Roman and other Latin Martyrologies mark it on March 27th."

MARCH 28th

Is sacred in the Roman Church to St. Sixtus III., Pope, who was raised to the pontifical chair in 432 and died on this day in 440.

It is also the festival of St. Gontran, king of Orleans and a grandson of Clovis I. He was especially notable for having in those days when "might was right" governed his kingdom rather on the principles laid down in the Gospels than by the universal tyranny of his day, a man whose life and conduct kept even pace with his profession as a Christian. He was very strict in punishing offenders against the laws but to those who only offended against himself he was lenient and forgiving. During his last years he was almost a recluse amid the courtly pageant that surrounded him, spending all the time he could take from the cares of state in prayer and penance. A just and upright king living in such an age deserves mention. He died on March 28, 593 when 68 years of age after a reign extending a little over thirty-one years, and marked as one of the bright spots in early French history.

To show the bitter antagonism of the Huguenots to Romanism in the XVI. century it is recorded they dug up the relics of St. Gontran after a peaceful rest of nearly a thousand years and scattered their dust to the winds to satisfy their fury.

MARCH 29th.

PASSION SUNDAY.

This Sunday which immediately precedes Palm Sunday is the beginning of the most solemn part of the Lenten season, it being that which is devoted to the commemoration of the terrible sufferings which our Saviour was called upon to undergo before that memorable day upon Calvary; the Day of Days, never to be forgotten by Christians. It, therefore, has been most appropriately called Passion Sunday as the week is also termed Passion Week though in some of the early menologies it was identified (incorrectly) with Holy Week. Among early Christians on this day when in every orthodox church images of not only our Lord Christ were set up, but also those of the apostles and other saintly personages when these images were all invariably draped with violet — a custom still observed in the Roman Church — reference being thereby made to the words of the Gospel — for this day in the Liturgy of the Roman Church — of John VIII., 59: "Then took they up stones to cast at Him; but Jesus hid himself, and went out of the temple, going through the midst of them and so passed by." It is impossible to trace the origin of this custom though we know it is very ancient.

In connection with the celebration of Passion Sunday and Passion Week it may not be uninteresting to speak of a few of the emblems used by the early Christians to designate the Passion of Our Lord.

These are very numerous. In my own limited collection I have fully fifty combinations. As an illustration; in the celebration of the "Mass of St. Gregory" in olden days it was customary to display upon the altar of the church "The Cross, the Three Nails, the Spear, the Sponge, the Pillar and Cords, the two Scourges, the three Dice, the Thirty Pieces of Silver, the Hammer and Pincers, the Ladder, the Sword, the Lantern and the three boxes of Spice for embalming." (From "Die Attribute der Hallingen," Hanover, 1843). While the crosses used varied in form it is a fact worthy of notice that on them there was found no direct allusion to the Crucifixion or among them anything akin to what we now call

" a Crucifix." There have been many explanations of this marked omission, the most satisfactory being that the presenting of our Saviour as crucified would have given the pagans an opportunity to taunt the Christians. Whatever may have been the reason, it is authoritatively stated that prior to the VI. century no example of the crucifix had been discovered save in one single instance and that even in the VIII. century these examples are rare, but in the Middle Ages they became frequent.

The first of the emblems of Christ's Passion are the two swords, that of the Apostle and of St. Peter, in form usually as in the illustration. In many early paintings the Ear of Malchus is also shown.

These shields are copied from the " Poppyheads " in Cumnor Church, Berk's, England, XIV. century edifice, showing the

Hammer, Nails and Pincers in the first, the Five Wounds in the second, the Ladder, Spear and Reed with a Sponge in the third, and the Purse, Cock and seamless garment in the fourth.

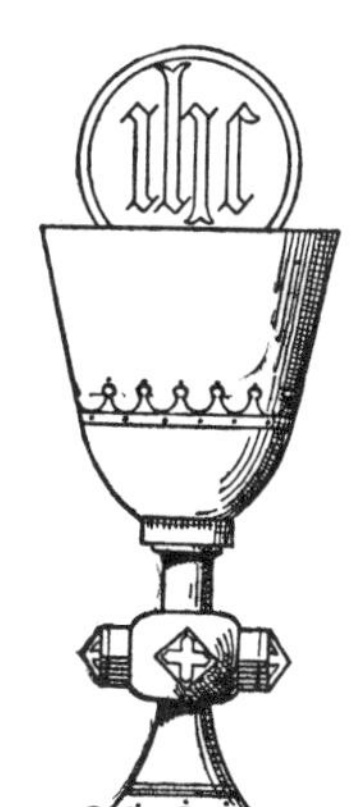

" The Agony " is usually illustrated by a chalice from which a cross is seen to rise. This cross is always the Latin Cross, the recognized " Cross of Suffering," though some artists use the cup with a contraction of the I. H. C., in place of the cross as the emblem of " The Agony."

The Betrayal of Jesus Christ is represented by eight emblems, always, however, used in combination, viz., the Sword, the Club, the Torch, the Lantern, the Ear, the Cords, the Thirty Pieces of Silver and the Head of Judas. Only five of these are usually combined or to suit artistic taste, frequently but two as in illustration, of the Head of Judas and the Thirty Pieces of Silver arranged around it.

The emblems of Our Lord's Condemnation in the Common Hall are divided into seven numbers to separately tell of His great suf-

fering. They consist of the Ewer and Basin used by Pilate, the Rope and the Pillar to which Christ was bound, the Scourge, the Scarlet or Purple Robe, the Crown of Thorns and the Reed. Separate combinations rule in the use of these as shown in the two illustrations given below which my readers can easily interpret for themselves. Yet quite often these emblems are used singly

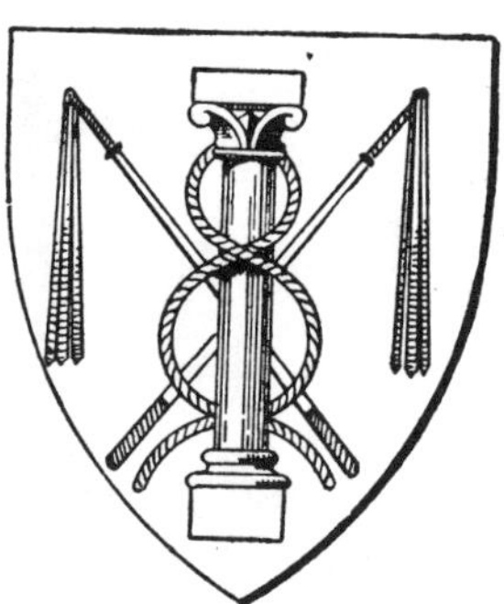

though it is seldom in art that we find the same implement represented twice in the same form, as in the case of the scourge in illustration, the two being taken from different pictures. It should also be remembered that the chances are but slender that any of these are accurate illustrations of the implements used at the time our Lord suffered but that in each case the form is doubtless the artist's own conception derived perhaps from some description he may have seen of the article.

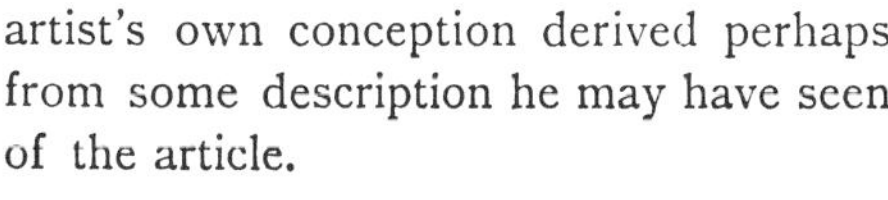

PATRON SAINTS OF COUNTRIES, CITIES, ETC.

I have several times been asked to give a list of the Patron Saints of Countries, Cities, Trades, etc. I do it now as briefly as possible and by no means complete as the list is almost endless. First, as to countries, England had St. George; Scotland, St. Andrew; Ireland, St. Patrick; Wales, St. David; France, St. Dennis and (in a less degree) St. Michael; Spain, St. James (Jago); Portugal, St. Sebastian; Italy, St. Anthony; Sardinia, St. Mary; Switzerland, St. Gall and the Virgin Mary; Germany, St. Martin, St. Boniface and St. George Cataphractus; Hungary, St. Mary of Aquisgrana and St. Lewis; Bohemia, St. Winceslaus; Austria, St. Colman and St. Leopold; Flanders, St. Peter; Holland, St. Mary; Denmark, St. Anscharius and St. Canute; Sweden, St. Anscharius, St. Eric and St. John; Norway, St. Olaus and St. Anscharius; Poland, St. Stanislaus and St. Hederiga; Prussia, St. Andrew and St. Albert; Russia, St. Nicholas, St. Mary and St. Andrew. Then as to cities, Edinburgh had St. Giles, Aberdeen St. Nicholas, and Glasgow St. Mungo; Oxford had St. Frideswide; Paris, St. Genevieve; Rome, St. Peter and St. Paul; Venice, St. Mark; Naples, St. Januarius and St. Thomas Aquinas; Lisbon, St. Vincent; Brussels, St. Mary and St. Gudula; Vienna, St. Stephen; Cologne, the three kings, with St. Ursula and the eleven thousand virgins. To give an entire list of these would include almost every town in Continental Europe.

St. Agatha presides over nurses. St. Catherine and St. Gregory are the patrons of literati and studious persons; St. Catherine also presides over the arts. St. Christopher and St. Nicholas preside over mariners. St. Cecilia is the patroness of musicians. St. Cosmas and St. Damian are the patrons of physicians and surgeons also of philosophers. St. Dismas and St. Nicholas preside over thieves; St. Eustace and St. Hubert over hunters; St. Felicitas over young children. St. Julian is the patron of pilgrims. St. Leonard and St. Barbara protect captives. St. Luke is the patron of painters. St. Martin and St. Urban preside over tipsy people, to save them from falling into the kennel. Fools have a tutelar saint in St. Mathurin, archers in St. Sebastian, divines in St. Thomas, and lovers in St. Valentine. St. Thomas à Becket presides over blind men, eunuchs and sinners. St. Winifred over virgins, and St. Yves over lawyers and civilians. St. Aethelbert and St. Aelian were invoked against thieves.

Of trades and various occupations in life, St. Joseph naturally presided over carpenters, St. Peter over fishmongers, and St. Crispin over shoemakers. St. Arnold was the patron of millers, St. Clement of tanners, St. Eloy of smiths, St. Goodman of tailors, St. Florian of mercers, St. John Port-Latin of booksellers, St. Louis of periwig-makers, St. Seveurs of fullers, St. Wilfried of bakers, St. William of hatters, and St. Windeline of shepherds. The name of St. Cloud obviously made him the patron saint of nailsmiths; St. Sebastian became that of pinmakers, from his having been stuck over with arrows; and St. Anthony necessarily was adopted by swineherds, in consequence of the legend about his pigs. It is not easy, however, to see how St. Nicholas came to be the presiding genius of parish clerks, or how the innocent and useful fraternity of potters obtained so alarming a saint as "St. Gore with a pot in his hand and the devil on his shoulder."

In the old superstitious days there was another class of saints termed medicating saints, whose power to heal disease was regarded as unquestioned, provided, always, the saint "was willing." This list is so long I can name but a few:

St. Apolin, for aching or decayed teeth; St. Otilia, for sore eyes and other ophthalmic troubles; St. Rooke, for safety from plague and infectious diseases; St. Vitus, for nervous troubles; St. Erasums heals colic and kindred trouble; St. Blase, quinsy; St. Leonard is the patron of prisoners, with power to free them; St. Perne cured quartan ague; St. Mark, from sudden and unexpected death; St. Anne, as she so wished, could give wealth to all; St. Susan protected all children from reproach and infamy; St. Romanus drove away sprites and milled devils; St. Wolfgang healed the good and kept sheep and oxen fat; St. Anthony did the same for hogs; St. Gertrude rid the house of mice and rats; St. Nicholas was the patron of sailors; St. Agatha preserved the house from fire. Nor does this list name even a tithe of this class of saints.

All saints are in a certain sense "Patron Saints," either as protectors of some particular nation, province or city, or of some avocation, trade or condition of life, or possibly of some individual selected by him for some peculiar reason. But there is a vast difference to be drawn between merely local saints and those of a nation universally accepted and revered. Again, not a few of these patron saints had neither Scriptural nor Apostolic sanction but were invested as such by a popular and universal faith which became paramount to other authority.

Many of these saints like St. George of England were patrons of both the Greeks and of chivalry from the Euphrates to the Pillars of Hercules. So, too, even the great patron saints had many minor powers tacked on to them, as for example St. Gregory was supposed to make children learn their lessons when invoked, and St. Christopher to keep servants in order. Thus the list is almost endless, and I must desist from recounting them.

The Sunday which immediately precedes Easter is

PALM SUNDAY.

The canonical colour for this day and each day during the week is violet.

This is one of the most sacred days of the entire Kalendar of the Christian Church. Nor is this feeling confined to the Roman Church, but it finds expression in the Greek and the Reformed Protestant churches of England and America, and even in modern days among many of the so-called dissenting churches of the

Protestant faith, since it commemorates that one day of brief popular enthusiasm enjoyed by our Lord, as recorded in the Gospels of Matthew (XXI.), Mark (XI.), and Luke (XIX.), but more especially in John (XII., 13) when the people "took branches of palm trees and went forth to meet Him and cried Hosanna! Blessed is the King of Israel that cometh in the name of the Lord."

HISTORICAL.

The "Procession of Palms" was customary in Jerusalem as early as 386 — when the first mention is made of it, in the life of Euthymius who died in 472 — and thence it passed to other churches of the East, soon afterward to those of the West as attested to by Isidore of Seville, who died in 636.

The custom of "Blessing of the Palms," hardly antedates the VIII. century; but its exact date is far too uncertain for me to attempt to fix it except in the above indefinite manner — the VIII. century — when it was everywhere observed.

The custom of reading one or more accounts of the Passion of our Saviour, as part of the regular service of the day, as told by the Evangelists, dates from the IV. century and beyond doubt its observance is coeval with that of the celebration of Palm Sunday, as it is first mentioned as occurring in Jerusalem. That portion referring to the capture of Jesus by the soldiers in Gethsemane was read on the night before "Good Friday." Can any one imagine a more solemn ceremony than such an one as this in the silent gloaming of the oncoming night, at the very spot where the act transpired, and told of the holy zeal of those who participated in it. Later on during the same night in the Church of the Holy Cross the story of the trial of Christ before Pilate was read; but those graphic accounts of that last wondrous scene on Calvary were reserved to be read in solemn silence on Good Friday at the morning service, while at the evening service the account of Christ's burial was given. In a sermon of St. Augustine (born 354, died 439), he says that he found it customary in Africa to read on one day in Holy Week the account of our Lord's betrayal, trial and crucifixion as given by St. Matthew and that his (St. Augustine's) ordinance to have the reading from the four Gospels occasioned considerable displeasure among the people. Since the VIII. century the Roman Church has observed the following order in regard to reading, beginning on Palm Sunday, the account as given by Matthew is read; on Tuesday, that of Mark; on Wednesday, Luke, and on Good Friday John's version of the wondrous story.

Prior to the Reformation, Palm Sunday was observed in England by the most elaborate services. The flowers and branches designed for use by the clergy were placed upon the high altar, those for the laity upon the south step of the altar. The priest arrayed in a red cope then consecrated them by a prayer that began with these words: "I conjure thee, these creatures of flowers and branches, in the name of God, the Father," etc. Later in the same prayer the blessing of God is invoked: "that the truth may sanctify these creatures of flowers, branches and slips of palms, or boughs of trees which we offer." After the flowers, etc., had been fumed with "frankincense" and sprinkled with holy water they were distributed and the procession headed by two priests bearing the crucifix marched through the streets and on their return to the church "a solemn Mass was said, communion given to the clergy, and the branches and flowers laid upon the high altar, as an offering." Of the many other customs that obtained in some places like the "Procession of the Ass," in which our Saviour's entry into Jerusalem was depicted in a realistic and reverent manner, I cannot enter into any detailed descriptions; but they are to be read in many books on "Early English Customs."

HOLY WEEK.

This ever memorable week in the Christian Church, has been the theme upon which many eminent writers, both among the "Ancient Fathers of the Church" and antiquarians of every age who have spoken of it under a variety of names such as "The Great Week," "The Week of the Holy Passion," "The Week of Forgiveness," as well as "The Holy Week." Irenæus, the Greek Bishop of Lyons, and a most celebrated writer on ecclesiastical matters, who was born in 140 and died in 202, was one of these. While Eusebius, Bishop of Cæsarea, and a celebrated historian who was born in 270 and died 338, from his writings shows he regarded the observance of this week as one that dated from Apostolic days.

In the Eastern church in primitive times each day of Holy Week was one of "strict, rigid fasting." In the "Apostolic Constitution"—a very ancient Christian work—it was prescribed that only "bread, salt, vegetables and water" should be eaten during the entire period of Holy Week. St. Epiphanius also declares that during those six days the faithful should observe the "Xerophagie" that is, to use "bread, salt and water," and these to be taken only at evening: while St. Dionysius, Archbishop of Alexandria (died November 17, 265), states that it was usual in his time to abstain wholly from food of any kind during the last two days of Holy Week, viz: Good Friday and Holy Saturday. But this strict fast was not observed as universally in the Western church.

In the Roman Church each day of this week has its especial office, as is true of the Church of England and the Protestant Episcopal Church of America.

Those of my readers who are interested in regard to these ceremonies of the Roman Church will find them fully and correctly described in "The Ceremonies of Holy Week in Rome," by Rt. Rev. Montague Baggs, published 1854.

MAUNDY THURSDAY.

In the earlier days of the Church the Thursday preceding Good Friday was always marked by especial acts of humility by Christians, in imitation of Christ's lesson, taught by the washing of the feet of His disciples on the eve of His passion. These acts of humility most naturally took the form of charity done by "one's own hand" not relegated to others :

"And here the monks their Maundies make with sundry solemn rites,
And signs of great humility, and wondrous pleasant sights ;
* * * * * * *
As he himself — a servant made, to serve us every way,
Then straight the loaves do walk, and pots in every place they skink,*
Wherewith the holy fathers, oft to pleasant damsels drink."

wrote Neogeorgus, in his "Popish Kingdom," as translated by Googe.

Again in an old history we read of Cardinal Wolsey, who at Peterborough Abbey, in 1580 : "made his Maundy, in Our Lady's chapel," etc., after which follows a description of his washing the feet of fifty-nine men and what his doles consisted of. By a natural sequence thus the word Maund and Maundy came to signify the articles given as well as the day and thus from its Maunds came to be commonly termed "Maundy Thursday." It also had in England still another title, "Shere Thursday" derived from the custom observed by the monks of shearing "their hair on this day." But throughout Catholic Europe, the day has ever been known as "Holy Thursday." Even as late as 1843 Maundy money was coined for English royalty's use on this day as shown in the accompanying illustration. But I may not take further space for an almost endless variety of customs connected with this day, both in England and upon the Continent, especially at Rome where "The Blessing of the Oils," "The Silencing of the Bells of Sistine Chapel," "The Feet Washing at

*draw.

St. Peter's," "The Pope Serving at Supper," "The Grand Penitentiary," and other solemn ceremonics are observed.

GOOD FRIDAY.

A day which beyond question has been observed by Christians of every shade of faith and doctrine since the Apostolic days; nothing need or can be said here to testify to the holy sanctity in which the day has always been held.

GOOD FRIDAY IN ROME.

At Rome the services in the churches on Good Friday are of the same solemn character as on the preceding day. At the Sistine Chapel, the yellow colour of the candles and torches, coupled with the nakedness of the Pope's throne and of the other seats, denote the desolation of the church. The cardinals do not wear their rings and their dress is of purple which is their mourning colour; in like manner nor do the bishops wear rings, and their stockings are black. The mace, as well as the soldier's arms are reversed. The Pope is habited in a red cope while he neither wears his ring nor gives his blessing. A sermon is preached by a conventual friar. Among other ceremonies the crucifix is partially unveiled and kissed by the Pope, whose shoes are taken off on approaching to do this homage. A procession takes place (across a vestibule) to the Paolina Chapel where Mass is celebrated by the Great Penitentiary. In the afternoon the last Miserere is chanted in the Sistine Chapel. After the Miserere the Pope, cardinals and other clergy, proceed through a covered passage to St. Peter's in order to venerate the relics of the True Cross, the Lance, and the Volto Santo, which are shown by the canons from the balcony above the statue of St. Veronica.

Taking up the story of the emblems of the Passion where they ended we begin with that for Good Friday the Holy Cross; or according to the period the Crucifix. Whether the T (tau) cross is used on this day, or the Latin, it is imperative that it must be either red or green.

In art like all the emblems of the Passion, artistic taste and the nature of the picture have much to do with the fact of whether some single emblem or a combination of those especially connected with the crucifixion of our Saviour are used. These combinations are varied. In the first of the illustrations given here, we have the Cross, the Spear, the Sponge — on the Reed — the Hammer, the Nails, the Pincers and the Inscription I N R I: "Jesus Nasareus Rex Judaecorum," and is more elaborate than is usually to be found. It dates from the (so-called) Renaissance of art; but I am unable to fix its exact year. Many others of a far earlier date are found; one from the catacombs near Rome of the Crown of Thorns and Three Nails; and one with the seamless garment hanging on the cross, with the Dice in the angles and in the foot of the cross. But more ancient than any of these is that of the Pelican, shedding its blood for its young.

HOLY SATURDAY.

The "Silencing of the Bells" on Holy Thursday is followed on this day by a renewal of their use.

On the reading of a particular passage in the service of the Sistine Chapel, which takes place about half-past eleven o'clock, the bells of St. Peter's are rung, the guns of St. Angelo are fired, and all the bells in the city immediately break forth as if rejoicing in their renewed liberty of ringing. This day at St. Peter's, the only ceremony that need be noticed is the blessing of the fire and the paschal candle. For this purpose, new fire (as it is called), is employed. At the beginning of Mass a light, from which the candles and the charcoal for the incense is enkindled, is struck from a flint in the sacristy, where the chief sacristan privately blesses the water, the fire, and the five grains of incense which are to be fixed in the paschal candle. Formerly, all the fires in Rome were alighted anew from this holy fire but this is now naturally impossible and is no longer even thought of. After the service the cardinal vicar proceeds to the baptistry of St. Peter's where having blessed and exorcised the water for baptism and dipped into it the paschal candle, he concludes by sprinkling some of the water on the people. Catechumens are afterwards baptised and deacons and priests are ordained and the tonsure is given.

EASTER.

The Christian Church has from its earliest days celebrated three great festivals: Christmas, Whitsuntide and this queen of festivals — Easter. In primitive times upon the morning of this joyous day when Christians met they saluted each other by exclaiming "Christ is risen!" to which the friend would reply, "Christ is risen, indeed!" Often adding "And hath appeared unto Simon." This beautiful custom was once common among all Christians but is now almost obsolete save that in the East it is still retained by members of the Greek church.

There is an opinion even now widely held by many Christians of divers creeds, that the Holy Apostles ordained the anniversaries of the Passion, Resurrection and Ascension of our Lord, and the descent of the Holy Ghost on the day of Pentecost, and therefore it may not be improbable that they also ordained the celebration of Easter. On one point all churchmen agree that the observance of the day of the "taking away of the Bridegroom" was kept from the earliest times with extraordinary humiliation and sanctity, with the strictest fasting and fervent prayer. It therefore was but natural that the fulfilment of their ardent hope, that culminated in Christ's wonderful resurrection from the dead, when hope became certainty, would be observed with reverent but joyous ceremonies. What form those glad ceremonies took on none now knows; we can only imagine them. In later times we know how elaborate they became.

With that tendency to realism which is so marked in the Miracle plays of the early drama, which illustrated scriptural legends and the suffering of the martyrs — the forerunner of the modern drama — we can easily understand why in not a few of the oldest churches in England and on the Continent they erected in the church edifice what was then called a "Holy Sepulchre," or tomb, near the altar and which at Easter-tide was the centre of attraction in the Easter ceremonies. These were of wood or stone — not a few of the later being even now preserved — supposed to represent the tomb where Joseph of Arimathea laid our Lord. Some like that at Heckington in Lincolnshire in England (still preserved) are very elaborate. This one just named has carved figures of the Roman soldiers either on guard, watching, or "the relief" sleeping around the tomb. More commonly, however, these "Easter sepulchres" were only "sepulchral recesses" in the wall by the side of the chancel near the altar; but not a few of these were real tombs. Before these tombs from Good Friday till the dawn of Easter when the choir broke forth in that glad anthem "Christ is Risen" a watch was kept and the "sepulchral or paschal light" was burned and the guard maintained with military exactitude. Prior to the Reformation this custom was invariable in all churches and even after that the custom was still kept up in not a few "Reformed" churches, but like many another old-time ceremony, it passed into desuetude even among those who had remained faithful to the elder church.

With the advent of Easter Day the church services began, varied in some respects according to locality — I refer to the Reformed church, for those of the elder church were invariable, and continued until vespers.

In the East the name first given to this festival was "the paschal feast," because it was kept at the same time as the

Pascha, or Jewish Passover. In the sixth Ancyran Canon it is called the "Great Day." Just how the festival derived its name Easter is a mooted point not likely to be settled in our day. Some suppose it was derived from the name of the Saxon goddess Eostre whose feast was celebrated in the spring about the same time when the Christian festival was observed and that while the character of the ceremonies was wholly changed, the name was retained from prudential reasons. Others believe the name was derived from the word "Oster" which means "rising." The question is one which has been so often and strenuously discussed that no possible good can come from entering upon it here.

The feast of Easter is one of those known in ecclesiastical parlance as one of the "movable feasts." While there never has been any question as to the perfect propriety of its celebration and but slight difference as to the character of its observance, as early as the II. century of the Christian era very great diversity of opinion rose as to the proper time when its celebration should take place.

In the churches of Asia Minor there were many "Judaizing Christians" who kept the paschal feast on the same day when the Jews kept their Passover, that being on the 14th of Nisan, the Jewish month corresponding with our March and April. The churches of the West knowing that the resurrection of our Lord took place on Sunday, and in order to more effectually distinguish their paschal feast from the Jewish Passover, observed it on the Sunday following the 14th of Nisan. Polycarp, the venerable Bishop of Smyrna, who had celebrated the feast with St. John on the 14th of Nisan pleaded that this proved that day to be the correct one, while Anicetus, Bishop of Rome, adduced the practice of SS. Peter and Paul of observing it on the Sunday after the 14th of Nisan. This was about A. D. 158.

The controversy was a long and heated one since neither party would grant any concessions to the other. Early in the IV. century the matter had assumed such importance that the Emperor Constantine felt it his duty to have the controversy settled so as to insure uniformity of practice in the future by both branches of the church. After a long and tedious consideration of the whole subject the great Œcumenical Council of Nice (A. D. 325) decided the question and laid down the rules to govern the fixing of Easter by directing "that the 21st day of March should be accounted the vernal equinox. That the full moon happening upon or next after the 21st of March shall be taken for the full moon of Nisan."

"That the Lord's Day next following first full moon shall be Easter Day."

"But if the full moon happens on Sunday Easter Day shall be the Sunday after."

This is the rule now observed. But it was long after the canon of the Council of Nice was decreed before it was entirely effective, for the history of the Irish Church and consequently of the Church in Scotland that as late as the VI. century they were still in opposition to the canon, a fact which proves how deep and strong the feelings of churchmen had been.

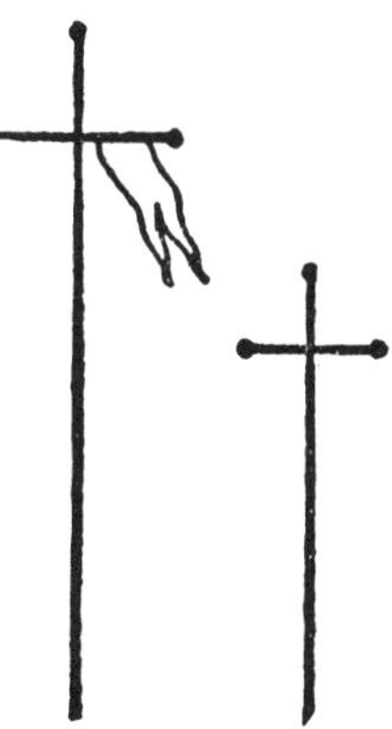

There have been a number of symbols for the resurrection of our Lord such as the Lion, Phœnix and Peacock, but the one above all others universally recognised is that which is known in Christian art and iconography as "The Resurrection Cross," a cross that differs from all others of the large number as the illustrations here show it. It is this cross that Christ holds when represented in Christian art as a symbol both when rising from the tomb and in His glorious ascension into Heaven. It is no longer the tree of suffering but it has become a staff, and those sharp pointed ends to its arms — that told of suffering — now terminate in balls, or circles like those in that form of the cross known as "The Cross Pomme." It is the form of cross almost invariably borne by the Agnus Dei, and the only one recognized in art as correct, and we find it even on the Clog Almanac as shown in the illustration herewith. It is in fact the Cross Triumphant and therefore, the proper symbol of Easter. It may be either white, silver (representing white) gold or bright yellow, since white is the emblem of purity, innocence, faith, joy, life and light. While yellow (pure) and gold signify God's goodness and also faith. A dull or dingy yellow being on the contrary symbolical of faithlessness, deceit and evil. It is for this reason Judas is almost always represented in art clad in dirty yellow.

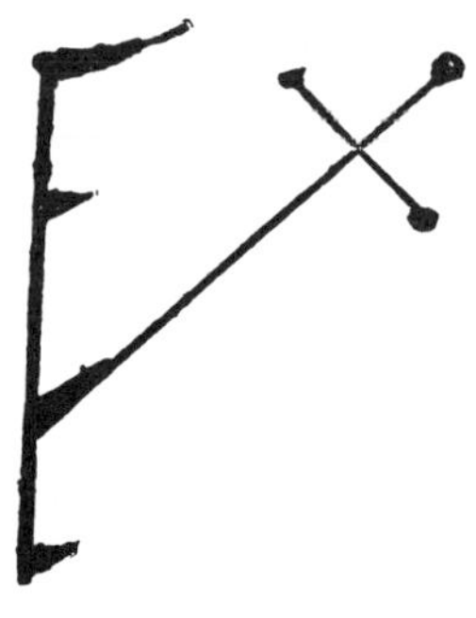

For the same reasons the canonical colours for the altar upon Easter Day are white, gold or yellow. Indeed the symbolism of colours for all holy days as recognised by the Church offers a beautiful lesson for those who can read it.

As might be naturally expected Easter Day at Rome is an event once seen will never be forgotten. It is a full half century since such was my privilege; but the magnificent solemnity of that Easter at St. Peter's lingers in my memory more vividly than any of the many, perhaps more gorgeous pageants, it has fallen to my lot to witness. Of course the magnificent old basilica was in holiday attire. The altars decked in fresh rich embroideries wonderful to behold; the lights around the tomb and figures of St. Peter after their temporary extinction were once more ablaze in full glory, and the music beyond compare — ravishing; while the Pope who had been brought in, in state, officiated at high mass at the altar; but all these externals were forgotten in the solemn grandeur of the service. Even the Pope seated in his Sedia Gestatoria, with his vestments blazing in gold and his triple crown — typical of spiritual power, temporal power and the union of the two — and the wonderful flabelli (huge fans composed of ostrich feathers, in which are set the eye-like parts of peacock feathers to signify the eyes or vigilance of the church) — all fade for the moment from sight and mind amid the sanctity of the ceremonies. We entered the sacred place amid the boom of cannons from the castle of St. Angelo to witness a pageant, but left it in reverent silence after the impressive services.

An interesting story might well be added here if space were

allowed regarding Easter customs in olden days in every country in Europe from those sweet-voiced singers which wake the traveller in the Tyrol on Easter morning to the games on some English village green. But it would fill a volume. Everywhere one feature is in evidence, the "pace," or "pascho," eggs, typical of both the mysterious birth and resurrection of our Lord. In no two countries exactly the same yet in their gorgeous colouring all are alike; a unique feature in Tyrol being the addition of original mottoes written upon the shell, each being of an individual character to fit the relations between donor and recipient. Especial dishes supposed to be peculiarly fitting for the day are also found in many countries, as in England tansy cakes, and puddings mark the Easter feast.

With Easter Monday in earlier days in England there began a variety of rather rough games in which all partook, one being what was called "lifting" of the men by the women, a compliment that was repaid by the men who on Tuesday "lifted" the women. The process being for two — men or women — to make what children call "a chair" by crossing hands, into which the victim was lifted by others and carried to the village green, when he, or she, had "to pay the carriage" as they termed it, a forfeit which those gathered there decided.

Since Easter is a movable feast and therefore no fixed date can be assigned it and the holy days that precede it, I have chosen to interpolate their stories at this point near the close of the month of March. I therefore resume the Kalendar of the Saints which the Christian Church has chosen to honour on

---

MARCH 29th.

Among the names mentioned this day is one St. Mark, a Greek whose name while it appears in all the Greek menologies, I do not find in either Roman Martyrology or in the Kalendar of the Reformed church. Yet his authenticated story reveals so truly the character of Julian (the Apostate) that I select it from others for this day.

When Constantius put to death his uncle Julius Constantius, the brother of Constantine "The Great" together with his eldest son, the two younger ones, Gallus and Julian, narrowly escaped the same fate. It was then that Mark, who had known these lads, with his instinctive dread of cruelty and bloodshed had succored and concealed them till their danger was over.

Ad interim, at the request of Constantius, and doubtless in full accord with his own feelings, Mark had razed a magnificent temple of the heathen; one held in especial reverence by the idolaters and on its site erected a Christian church.

When at length Julian became the Emperor the story needs no repetition here of how he decreed that the temples which the Christians had destroyed should be rebuilt at their expense. Thus authorised the heathen once more set out for revenge upon the Christians. How vindictive, historical readers know too well to repeat here that sad story. For the time Mark with prudence hid himself. But when he found that his brethern "in Christ" were being made to suffer for his *own* acts he promptly came to the front, throwing off all efforts to conceal his individual responsibility to shield himself thus at the cost of others.

One shudders at the torments these fiends inflicted upon him without thought or compassion and I hesitate to record even a few of these indignities. How they stripped him naked and cast him into the public jakes (cesspool), from which they drew him only to add to his torment the scourge and later, after smearing him with honey, to confine him in an open iron cage to be at the mercy of flies and wasps on a hot, midsummer day when helpless — because of his shackled hands — to defend himself in any way from these pests. The Arch-fiend could hardly have invented a greater torment. And all this that, under an edict of Julian they might exact from him something that he could not do even had he wished; to rebuild the pagan temple which under orders, he had destroyed; or that he would be bound to make his fellow Christians do so. Yet this Julian whom he had succored and saved from death, refused to interfere or in any way alleviate his suffering. Throughout it all Mark had borne himself so meekly and without even a plea for leniency that at last the brutes themselves were struck with admiration and relented even while he was still preaching to them the words of Christ. By common consent at last Mark was liberated on a pledge of a nominal payment for his act. To even this, he protested that it was "impiety;" but some of the faithful of "Arethusa" came to his rescue and the remainder of his life was spent in still teaching the religion that had enabled him to bear such trials and he died in peace in this same city about the middle of the IV. century.

Beyond doubt, the "Semi-Arian" doctrines he held had rendered him somewhat obnoxious to the Orthodox and Catholic Churchmen. But the encomiums paid to his memory by SS. Gregory Nazianzin, Theodore and Sozomen, when at the last he came into the Orthodox communion are ample evidence of the purity of purpose of this noted Greek to entitle him to a high place in the esteem of all Christians.

MARCH 30th.

St. John Climacus, whom the Church honours this day was born in Palestine about 525. He received his surname from a most remarkable book entitled "The Climax" or the "The Ladder of Perfection" which it is said is still extant but where I am unable to learn. At a very early age he was given the surname of "Scholastic" for his remarkable attainments. While he renounced the world and became a novice at the age of sixteen, his education was at a hermitage, an "afranage" to some of the many monasteries that had already been built on the summit of Mt. Sinai, under the care of an ancient anchorite named Martyrius, where he remained for nineteen years until the death of his tutor in 560. Like so many of the holy men of the early Church the attractions of an eremitical life were too great for him, and after the death of his loved mentor he built for himself a cell in the plain of Thole at the foot of Mt. Sinai and five miles from the church which had been erected by order of Emperor Justinian in honour of the Blessed Virgin. Here he spent his days in prayer and the study of the Scriptures as expounded by the Fathers, and became one of the most learned of the Doctors of the Church. Here he remained until the year 600 when he was chosen as Abbot of the Monks of Mt. Sinai. His legend tells how like a second Elias, during a period of great drouth he by earnest prayer secured for the famine stricken districts an abundant rain, and thus saved the country from certain starvation. He built a hospital for the use of pilgrims, and St. Gregory the Great, then upon the Pontifical throne aided him with gifts of money and furniture. It was here that he wrote the celebrated book above mentioned. The burden of his office at the end of four years caused him to resign his dignity and retire once more to his hermitage where he died the next year (March 30, 605) at the ripe age of four-score years.

MARCH 31st.

Isdegerdes, the son of Sapor III., put an end to the cruel persecution Sapor II. had instituted against the Christians of Persia. For twelve years the Church enjoyed immunity until in 420, a Christian bishop named Abdas with "indiscreet" zeal caused the destruction of the Pyræum (temple of fire) of the great divinity of Persia. Thus Isdegerdes' anger was roused and he threatened to destroy all the Christian churches in Persia, unless the temple were rebuilt, a thing which was not done and Isdegerdes literally carried out his threat, also putting Abdas to death. Isdegerdes died the next year but the general persecution he began against all Christians was kept up by his son Varanes and continued for forty years as the penalty of Abdas' work.

It was then that St. Benjamin, a deacon whose name appears on this day, arose in defence of his fellow Christians. It is only the old, old story, so often told of these noble champions of Christ's faith. So I need hardly repeat the cruel details. How he could have "saved himself" by renouncing his belief. But the heroic question which he put to the king, when brought before him, is one not to be forgotten: "What opinion he would have of any of his subjects who renounced his allegiance to him and joined in a war against him?"

I cannot recount the refinement of cruelty with which this martyr was treated from "reeds run under his finger-nails," and onward through tortures it seems impossible to credit — yet their record is undoubted — until a "knotty stake driven through his bowels" released the poor sufferer on March 31st, 424.

APRIL

According to the Kalendar of ancient Alban, the year consisted of ten months, and in this April was the first with thirty-six days in it. In the Kalendar of Romulus, it had but thirty and was regarded as "Venus' month" and its first day set aside as a festal day. It has, therefore, been supposed that the name was given it from "Aphrilis" which they derived from the Greek name of the goddess "Aphrodite."

APRIL 1st.

If modesty was a virtue to entitle any one to become a canonized saint then St. Hugh erst-while Bishop of Grenoble and whom the Church remembers to-day was one who should not be forgotten. He was the son of a loyal, brave soldier, born in the territory of Valence in 1053. With every advantage of family and social station to make a worldly life attractive, he, to quote from his legend, "from the cradle appeared to be a child of benediction." He went through his course of studies with a degree of applause from which he shrunk. As it was through all his life he dreaded personal notice even though he must have been aware of his remarkable attainments in many branches of learning. He had early accepted a canonry in the Cathedral of Valence in order that he might devote his life to the service of religion and his fellow men, and wholly without either the wish or hope of ecclesiastical preferment. But in the church as it is in the world at large, great merit cannot hide itself even if it tries and is also sure to be acknowleged. Thus it was when Hugh, Bishop of Die and afterward Archbishop of Lyons came to Valence he would not be content until the young man became a member of his own household.

We cannot follow in detail all the story of Hugh's life until the Synod of 1080 at Avignon when he was named Bishop of Grenoble, nor yet the state in which he found his new diocese so sunk in sin; or how church lands had been usurped by laymen, and the herculean task he was confronted with, or how bravely he performed all these duties. He prayed Innocent II. for leave to resign so arduous a task but could not obtain consent and so patiently fulfilled his duty until called to his reward April 1st, 1132. So holy had been his life that he was canonized in 1134 by Innocent II.

APRIL 2d.

In St. Francis of Paula who is commemorated this day we have an interesting example of the truth that pure goodness belongs to no rank or station in life but is largely the result of environment and often the outgrowth of early training in the home circle. Francis was born in 1416 at Paula, a small city near the Tyrrhenian sea, in Calabria midway between Naples and Reggio. His parents, poor peasants but God fearing and loving people, whose sole wish in life was to so bring up their child that he should also be like them and also have what they had not received, an education. For this last purpose, when he was thirteen years of age they placed him in the Franciscan monastery at St. Mark's, the episcopal town of their province. Two years later he returned not to his own home but to a cell built for him in the neighbourhood. Here, young as he was, he spent five years in solitary prayer and reflection; at which time he was joined by two companions. Thus was the foundation laid for the Order of the Minims which seventeen years later was to take form. Meantime they had received many accessions from devout young men and in 1454 by the consent of the Archbishop of Cosenza a church and monastery was built for these devoted self-sacrificing men and a "community" was formed, the chief tenets were "penance, charity and humility." They also observed "a perpetual Lent" and always abstained not only from all flesh food but also from all "white meats" (food made from milk such as cheese, butter, etc.) as well as from eggs, which the ancient canons of the Church forbid being used in Lent. But charity was the true motto of the Minims, and as far as possible to do this charity in secret. Personally Francis even from boyhood had sedulously sought seclusion from the world and his "humility" was his most marked characteristic for he assumed nothing for himself. The Order which he had thus founded from an insignificant following of two was first approved by the Archbishop of Cosenza in 1471. Pope Sixtus IV. confirmed it by a bull on May 23d, 1474, making Francis "Superior-General." It was at that time composed chiefly of laymen with but one priest, Balthasas de Spino afterward Confessor to Pope Innocent VIII., but in 1476 new houses for the Order began to be established which gradually increased in number until in 1480 Ferdinand, King of Naples, offended at some wholesome reprimand Francis had given him and his sons, caused his arrest "for having built monasteries without royal consent." Through the influence of a younger son of the King, Prince Frederick of Tarentum, the order for arrest was rescinded.

Francis' gift of prophecy was remarkable. In 1447-8 and 9 he foretold the taking of Constantinople by the Turks, an event that took place May 29th, 1453. He also foretold the fall of Otranto — the key of the Kingdom of Naples, — which was taken by the infidels three months later on August 31st, 1480, while he promised success to the Christians later, which was fulfilled the next year when the Turks were driven out of Italy. But I must not prolong the list of his prophecies.

On Palm Sunday 1508 he was taken ill with a fever and died April 2d, of that year, at the extreme age of *ninety-one*. He was canonized by Leo X. in 1519. In 1562, the Hugenots sacked the church of Plessis-les-Tours, where his remains had been buried, and after many indignities offered to the body burned it in a fire made from a large wooden crucifix. Not the only work of the kind which was done by the more fanatical of this noted body of men as will be recorded in these pages.

Another saint whose anniversary falls on this day was a noted Scotch Abbess, Aebba or Ebba who was the daughter of King Aedilfrid, and sister of Kings Oswald and Oserin. Her monastery was a double one, with distinct communities for men and women — as Skene in his "Celtic Scotland" describes it — and was founded by Aiden the first Columban bishop in Scotland. In passing let me say Columba was an Irish priest and at great self-sacrifice became the first Christian missionary to the Picts in Scotland and thus founded the Christian Church in the northern part of Britain.

St. Ebba's monastery Bede (the Saxon historian) located at "Urbs Coludi," the Saxon equivalent for Coldingaham now called Coldingham and was built on a rock overhanging the sea a short way south from St. Abb's Head — which, by the way, was named for St. Aebba. The monastery was destroyed by the Danes in 870, but when Edgar, the son of the Saxon Queen Margaret came to the throne in 1093, he by aid of the English refounded the monastery at Coldingham.

Aebba from all reports was a woman of great beauty and when the Danes assaulted the monastery and it was certain that they must become prisoners of the vile and lustful invaders who respected no woman the Abbess assembled the nuns in the chapter house and telling them the fate which awaited them if these brutal Danes ever secured their persons *unimpaired*, the Abbess deliberately mutilated her own face by cutting off her nose and lips. The nuns all followed her example and when at last the invaders were in possession of the monastery and after they had plundered it they sought out the nuns to gratify their baser passions but the horrible spectacle of those mutilated faces so angered and disgusted them that they penned the helpless women within their cells and set the house on fire, the nuns all being literally burned alive but saved true to their vows. It is one of those horrible pictures of early Scotch warfare like that

Mariannus describes when Thorkil Footi burned Duncans General Moddan in his "Rath."*

APRIL 3d.

St. Richard, Bishop of Chichester, England, of whom we are about to speak and whose anniversary occurs this day must not be confounded with other saints of the same name since there are no less than four whose names will appear in these Kalendars.

St. Richard died April 3d, A. D. 1253. He was born at Wich now called Droitwich near to Worcester. He was a student at Oxford and later at Paris and Bologna. After his return to England he was Chancellor of the University of Oxford and created Bishop of Chichester in 1245 though bitterly opposed by King Henry III. who was so incensed at his election that he confiscated the entire revenues of the see, leaving the bishop so utterly helpless that he was dependent even for the necessities of life upon the benevolence of others. He, however, maintained his position and went about his diocese from town to village discharging his episcopal duties with conscientious fidelity. After two years of these privations King Henry under threats of excommunication from Pope Innocent III. was compelled to restore the revenues of the see. He was not only a man of great piety and fervent zeal, but possessed a remarkable degree of executive ability by which his diocese profited largely.

His election as bishop was marked by an extraordinary event. During the celebration of the Holy Eucharist either from faintness or fatigue St. Richard fell while holding in his hand the chalice filled with consecrated wine; but miraculously the sacred

---

* Fortress

wine was preserved and not a drop spilled. For this in Christian art, St. Richard holds a chalice as his emblem but in the Clog Almanacs he has a plough-share to distinguish his day. Possibly a quaint conceit to typify his labours in the field of Christ.

APRIL 4th.

St. Ambrose, Bishop of Milan, Confessor and Doctor, died on April 4th, A. D. 397. In the entire Kalendar of the Saints of the Christan Church there are few names more deserving of especial note, than that of St. Ambrose. This extraordinary man so statesmanlike, practical and benevolent, even if somewhat despotic, was one in whose person this priestly character assumed an importance and dignity which till then had been seldom met with. He was the son of a prefect of Gaul and was born at Treves December 7th, 340. Paulinus relates that while yet in his cradle a swarm of bees settled upon his lips without injuring him — just as a similar story is told of Plato and also of Archilocus — a prophecy of his future eloquence. It is from this circumstance St. Ambrose is always represented in Christian art with a bee-hive near him.

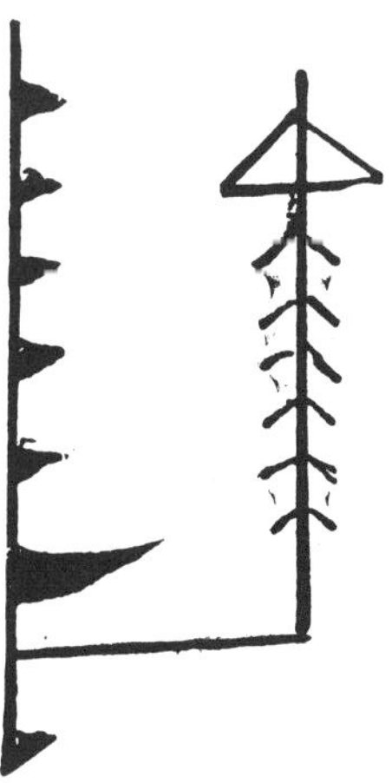

Young Ambrose was educated at Rome and at an early age was appointed prefect of Aemilea and Liguria (Piedmont and Genoa) and in this capacity had resided for five years in Milan, when in A. D. 374 Auxentius, Bishop of Milan, died. Just at this time the Church was badly disturbed by the contending factions of the Arian and Orthodox beliefs and naturally the election of a new bishop was an important event, since it meant victory to the faction that elected its bishop, A tumult, almost akin to a riot was in progress when Ambrose, as prefect appeared on the scene at the church where the people were assembled. By his persuasive eloquence the excited multitude was soon hushed into silence when he exhorted them to peace and submission to the laws. But he had hardly ceased speaking before the cry was raised: "Ambrose shall be our bishop." The cry was echoed by all in spite of his protests and attempted flight. He pleaded that although he was a professed Christian, he had never been baptized. The people would accept no excuse and eight days later, having received the rite of baptism he was duly consecrated Bishop of Milan. He at once distributed his worldly goods among the poor to render himself worthy of the new and higher dignity of his office. The grandeur and magnificence with which he invested the sacred services of the church would alone have made his name memorable. He was a great lover of music and it was he who introduced the antiphonal method of chanting the service, since called the Ambrosian chant.

His was no undecided character. What he believed he taught in the clearest and plainest words. His views upon "Celibacy" for both sexes were very strong and he advocated them in such eloquent terms that it is said that the mothers of Milan used to shut up their daughters "lest they should be seduced by the persuasive eloquence of the enthusiastic bishop, into taking on themselves vows of chastity."

Another point which in the days of Ambrose was but the assertion of the might of Christianity over heathenism and tyranny; but which has since caused infinite trouble and even bloodshed was the setting of ecclesiastical over sovereign or civil power. How he acted up to his convictions, is shown by his treatment of the Emperor Maximus and even more so in his famous conflict with the Emperor Theodosius so fully told in history that the details need not be repeated beyond calling attention to the fact that in hot-headed anger over the death of Bothius, an imperial officer in Thessalonia who had been killed in a seditious riot, Theodosius caused seven thousand men, women and children, the most of whom were wholly innocent, to be slain. For this cruel act and the staining his hands with innocent blood the bishop wrote the emperor that famous letter, which by its plain unvarnished truths fearlessly spoken — but then an unheard of act — first struck terror into the hearts of churchmen then won for Ambrose undisguised admiration. Nor did the noble bishop stop there, but he interdicted the emperor from even entering the church edifice, in fact excommunicated him. The emperor pleaded the example of David: "Then," said the bishop, "imitate him in his repentance as well as his sin." How Theodosius threatened and Ambrose stood firm, is historic and when at last Ruffinius informed him: "The emperor is coming," and the brave cleric replied: "I will not hinder him; yet if he will play the king I will offer him my throat;" is authentic as is the final denouement at once dramatic and remarkable when the powerful emperor, clad in sack-cloth bowed before the stern representative of the church saying: "I come to offer myself and submit to what you prescribe."

What a picture this! To quote Mrs. Jameson's words: "Grovelling on the earth, with dust and ashes on his head lay the master of the world before the altar of Christ because of innocent blood hastily and wrongfully shed."

The following illustration from "Callot's Images" shows St. Ambrose as he usually is represented in art with the "beehive" and the kneeling figure is Emperor Theodosius, making his submission to the bishop. A "triple scourge" in the hands of St. Ambrose is sometimes added to these pictures referring to the punishment of Theodosius.

The poetical legends and apologues related regarding St. Ambrose are almost endless, but all testify to his wonderful character and worth and not a few to his marvelous gift of prophecy.

Ambrose pleaded with the Prefect Macedonius for a condemned wretch but was refused, when he said: "Thou, even thou, shalt fly to the church for refuge and shalt not enter." This prophecy was literally fulfilled.

Again on a visit to a Tuscan nobleman Ambrose inquired as to the state of his host, who replied: "I have never known adversity, every day hath seen me increasing in fortune, honour and possessions. I have a numerous family of sons and daughters who have never caused me a pang of sorrow. * * * I have never suffered with sickness or pain," and more to the same purport.

S. AMBROSE.

"Arise!" cried Ambrose: "Fly from this roof ere it fall on us, for the Lord is not here," and the prelate hastily rising from the table fled; scarcely had he left the house and escaped in safety when an earthquake swallowed the castle and all who were within it.

It is told that Honorat, Bishop of Vercelli, attended Ambrose upon his death-bed, and having gone to sleep an angel wakened him saying: "Arise! for he departs in this hour," and Honorat had barely time to administer the sacrament when Ambrose expired.

After St. Ambrose was canonized he became the patron saint of Milan. The Basilica of Tant Ambrogio Maggiore founded by the bishops in 387 in honour of St. Ambrose is one of the oldest and most interesting churches in Christendom.

St. Ambrose was one of what are known as the "Four Latin Fathers of the Church," the others being SS. Jerom, Augustin and Gregory.

THE EASTER OCTAVE.

The first Sunday after Easter concluded the paschal feast and was long observed, with but little less ceremony than Easter itself. On this day the neophytes, or newly baptised persons laid aside their white garments and committed them to the repository of the church.

From the fact this day completed the "Octave," it received the name "Octave of Easter"; but on account of the ceremony just alluded to, it was also known as the "Sunday of Albes" (garments of white) and is mentioned by St. Augustine as such, in one of his sermons on the observance of the day.

SAINTS AND SAINT DAYS.

In an edition of Roman Martyrology the original of which was first published under Gregory XIII., the Most Reverend Archbishop of Baltimore in 1869 writes in the introduction: "If the world has its 'Legions of Honour' why should not also, the Church of the Living God?"

The question is not only pertinent but it can have only one answer. The holy men and women who in the early days of the Christian Church, whether they shed their blood as martyrs for their faith in Christ, or devoted their lives to deeds of love and charity, sacrificing those things men held most dear in life, home, friends, ambition and personal comfort for the good of their fellow men, are as truly heroes and heroines as those who have won fame and immortal names in history by valiant deeds on fields of battle, or by their sacrifice for their love of country, and it was beyond doubt this feeling which led the Fathers of the early Churches to bestow this recognition of their worth on their memories; just as we set aside a day in memory of men like Washington and Lincoln and which make us as the anniversaries of each come round, recall their virtues and the sacrifices they made and learn a personal lesson from their lives. This is the true spirit of what we term saint's days.

Only a very few of the holy men who have filled the pontificate and were later canonized have any especial symbols or emblems in most cases the usual "Triple Cross" being used. For this reason it is well to understand the significance of crosses having more than one transverse bar or arm and which are known as "Ecclesiastical crosses." The cross when worn by a prelate or it is given him as an emblem, is as an insignia of rank, (pectoral) or when carried before him (processional) as indicative of jurisdiction. The greater the number of these bars or arms, the higher the rank and wider the jurisdiction of the person to whom it is assigned. The triple cross in the illustration is that of the Pope and corresponds with the mitre. The first bar signifies *jurisdictio temporalis*; the second *jurisdictio in ecclesiam militantem*; third *jurisdictio in ecclesiam patientem*. This cross is of Greek origin and aside from this indication of rank and power has no especial significance.

The cross with two transverse bars as in the illustration, is assigned to archbishops and bishops.

APRIL 5th.

The names of two Irish saints find a place in the Kalendar for this day, SS. Tigernach and Becan. But unfortunately for our chronicles in but a limited number of cases is there much reliable information to be had regarding Irish saints, owing to the mass of mythical romance which the early Irish writers mixed with their facts. Therefore in each of the two I mention I must eliminate pages of the matter before me.

St. Tigernach was the son of Corbre, "a famous general, and his mother Dearfraych was the daughter of an Irish King named Eochod; * * * * he was baptised by Coulathe Bishop of Kildare, and St. Brigide was his God-mother. As we know the kidnapping of youths and maidens in both Britain and Ireland for the purpose of selling them into slavery was a common custom, St. Patrick being such a victim. According to his legend Tigernach thus fell into the hands of pirates and was taken to Britain where he was sold to a British King." Here follows a story too mythical to be worthy of being accepted as fact, except that the youth became such a favourite with the King that he was placed at school in the monastery of Rosnat; for in the VI. century the monastery was the only school in Britain, or, for that matter anywhere. And thus we again have presented to us the debt due to the early Christian Church in their effort to educate the peoples. The story of his manumission — if I may use the word — is also somewhat mythical for he seems to have been a somewhat "*mauvais sujet*," for we are told: "he was after his return to Ireland *compelled* to receive episcopal consecration" and later, that "he *refused* to administer the see of Clogher which had been conferred upon him" in 506. Yet he must have had "the root of this matter in him," for he soon built the Abbey of Cluanois in the County Monaghan "where he taught a great multitude to serve God in primitive purity and simplicity." In his old age he became blind, but still continued to minister to his people until his death in 550.

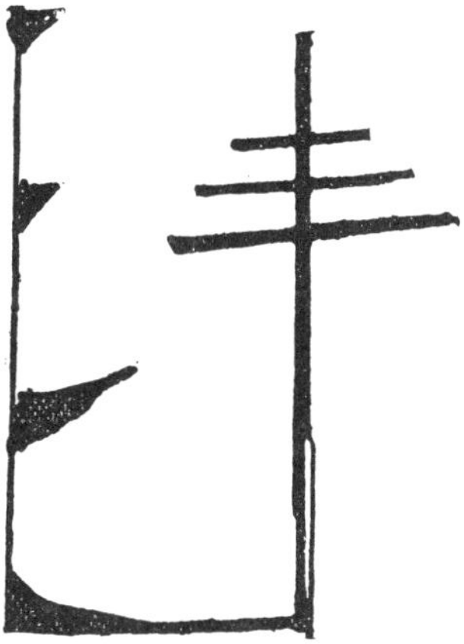

St. Becan the other saint named this day was also of royal blood being of the regal family of Munster, and his name appears as one of "The Twelve Apostles of Ireland."

APRIL 6th.

St. Sixtus (or Xistus) Pope and Martyr is remembered on April 6th. He was one of the primitive fathers of the Church chosen in 119 and dying in 128. He, like all of the Popes, has for his symbol the triple cross.

This is also the anniversary of another of the Fathers, St. Celestine I., Pope, who died in 432. A native of Rome and a man who held a high place in the esteem not alone of his fellow clergy, but of all who knew him. On the death of Pope Boniface in 422 Celestine was the unanimous choice of the people as his successor. It was this Pope who sent St. Palladius to the Scots of North Britain and St. Patrick to Ireland. He was especially active in suppressing the Pelagian heresy in Britain. He died August 1, 432, but his festival has been fixed for this day. The Clog symbol above is from the English sticks, the Danish have none for this day.

APRIL 7th

Is the saint-day of St. Albert, Recluse Bishop of Vercelli and Patriarch of Jerusalem. He was a man of deep piety but his devotions from early life were devoid of ostentation and while he attended public worship his secret and private devotions were far more frequent and it was this that led him to become a recluse in the monastery of Cropin where bread was seldom tasted, herbs being their chief diet and a fire was unknown or "any food dressed by a fire," says Butler in his "Lives of the Saints." Later he founded the "Order of Carmelites." He was murdered at Acre when on his way to Rome, and is given "the palm branch," as a symbol.

It is also the day set aside for St. Francis Xavier, Apostle of India. This noted Jesuit was born April 7th, 1506, at the base of the Pyrenees on the Spanish side and curiously, not far from which the man who was to mould his life, Ignatius Loyola, was then living. Xavier was educated at the University of Paris where he later lectured. When Loyola came first to Paris Xavier rejected his advances but when one day, exultant over a remarkably successful lecture, Loyola let drop the words: "What shall it profit a man if he gain the whole world and lose his own soul?" he was startled by the thought and he sought out the man he had repulsed. We all know the result and how from an humble quartette of earnest young men the Society of Jesuits originated in 1540 and his selection as a missionary to India and the wonderful results. Also how he then journeyed on to India intending to push on to China and how at last, by treachery he was cast on the barren island of Samian in sight of the mainland of China, and there died. The pathetic story of noble work and self-sacrifice have been too often told to need repetition. It is one continued story of heroism in the cause of Christ and an almost endless list of miracles are credited to him. He was canonized in 1662 and in 1747, by a Papal brief, was made the patron saint of East Indies His death occurred December 3d, 1553.

APRIL 8th.

Of the several names mentioned in the Roman Church Kalendar for honour this day that of the Blessed Albert, Patriarch of Jerusalem, presents an interesting story. He was an Italian by birth from the diocese of Parma and of a noble family. Highly educated he was a proficient in canon and civil laws; he received the habit of "a canon regular" in the Carmelite monastery of Mortuva; later was made Bishop of Bobio and afterward of Vercelli, over which latter see he presided for twenty years. His knowledge and integrity were recognised when he was chosen to arbitrate the differences between Clement III. and Emperor Frederick I., surnamed Barbarossa, Emperor of Germany; and when Henry VI., successor of Frederick, created him, "a Prince of the Empire." In 1204 Monochus the eleventh *Latin* Patriarch of Jerusalem died and Innocent III. selected Albert as his successor. But as Jerusalem was in the hands of the Saracens when in 1206 Albert arrived at Acon, he made this city the seat of his see.

As legislator of the Carmelites (or White Friars) he compiled the rules of the Order.

There is a curious fact connected with the Carmelite Order not generally known by the laymen of the Church, and I repeat it for *their* benefit since clerics must of course be familiar with it.

It is said that from the time of Elias the Prophet his successors had uninterruptedly as hermits occupied Mount Carmel where the Carmelites had their house. That these hermits having embraced Christianity, continued their succession to the XII. century when the Order began to extend its work into wider fields. This succession was long a contested point and neither Popes Innocent X. or XII. were willing to decide; while the latter, by a brief dated November 29th, 1698, "enjoined silence, on the subject." Yet this is the legend as it is found in ancient ecclesiastical history.

In 1214 Albert was summoned into the West by Pope Innocent III. to attend a "Council of Lateran" which was to meet in 1215. But he was assassinated on September 14th, 1214 while assisting at the "Feast of the Exaltation of the Cross." He has, however, always been honoured in Roman Martyrology on April 8th.

APRIL 9th.

St. Mary of Egypt whose festival occurs on this day, is one of the most curious in legendary history told as it doubtless was in its inception "with a purpose," its lesson has lost nothing by age.

The legend is a very old one but when vouched for by St. Jerom who, aside from his reliability as a cleric, has ever ranked as one of the most faithful chroniclers of his day — its truth is unquestioned. The story it is said even ante-dates the legend of Mary Magdalene. I must tell it, condensed and in my own words rather than in the elaborate detail in which I read it.

The story of "Mary Egyptica," appeared in written form first in the VI. century as an ancient tradition of a "female" hermit in Palestine. St. Jerom repeating it said her wickedness "exceeded that of Mary Magdalene." She was an Alexandrian noted for her beauty, for the luxury of her life, and the wiles by which she led her victims on to their destruction. "Kismet!" no doubt the Egyptians said; but as we read her legend we can clearly see the hand of Providence in the act which led to her changed mode of life.

One day in 365 she was walking by the sea when she saw a vessel laden with pilgrims about to depart for Jerusalem to attend the "Feast of the Exaltation of the Cross."

For seventeen years this woman had lived a life of shame; yet in this moment an irresistible impulse came upon her to join the pilgrims not for a holy purpose but rather for adventure. She had no money; but to quote the quaint phrase of her historian: "She sold herself to the sailors" and thus reached Jerusalem with the pilgrims. How she spent the interval before the day of the festival is not told. On that day she joined the throng around the entrance of the Basilica; yet at the moment when she was about to enter some invisible power restrained her. As often as she tried to cross the threshold an unseen hand seemed to draw her back. What it was she knew not, but suddenly, without premonition she felt the full sense of her sinful life come over her. Her utter unworthiness even to look upon that sacred emblem. She fell upon her knees there on the pavement, which was soon wet with her repentant tears and for the first time in her life she prayed. While yet praying she seemed to hear a voice that said: "If thou goest beyond Jordan to dwell there thou shalt find rest and comfort."

That night at the city gate she bought three loaves of bread and walked on until she came to the river where the church of St. John the Baptist stood. There she paid her devotions and in the morning passed over the river and for forty-seven years lived a hermit in the wilderness. As her garments worn out by age and use dropped from her, her hair became a cloak. It was thus clad that Zosimus, a holy man, at last found her. To him she confessed and from his hands received the holy sacrament; but then begged him to leave her and not return until a year had passed.

At the appointed time on Maunday Thursday Zosimus came

forth to meet her but only found her dead body; while in the sand beside her were written the words: "Oh, Father Zosimus, bury the body of the poor sinner, Mary of Egypt. Give earth to earth and dust to dust for Christ's sake."

A legend tells that as Zosimus digged the grave his strength failed him for he was an old man; but then a lion came and helped him digging with his paws.

Dr. Alban Butler in his life of St. Mary of Egypt puts the date of her conversion in 383 and her death in 421. Others place these as given above, 365 and 433.

APRIL 10th.

One of the most interesting events connected with the 10th of April is the fact that on this day in 787 King Pepin of France introduced an organ into the Church of St. Corneill at Compiegne, thus in a measure fixing the advent of this instrument into church service.

The story of St. Bademus whom the Church names this day for honour is interesting, if only for the curious means adopted to secure his "taking off" while it in no degree takes from him the claim of being a Martyr to the Faith as he is termed in Roman Martyrology.

He was a nobleman of Persia, living at Bethlapeta who out of his great estates dedicated the larger portion to found a monastery near his home, and of which he became Abbot. While Sapor the all powerful was relentless in persecuting the Christians, he hesitated before he allowed his pursuivants to apprehend Bademus and the seven of his monks. Yet hating him as he did, Sapor felt he must be prudent with the man, however merciless he was to other Christians; for Dioclesian in his persecutions of the Christians hardly equalled those of Sapor. It was for this Bademus and his monks were cast into prison rather than that more terrible penalties were inflicted. Still it was a sore puzzle to Sapor how to dispose of him.

About the same time Bademus was confined, a Christian Lord of the Persian Court was arrested, named Nersan, a Prince of Aria and imprisoned because he refused to worship the sun. He was for a time resolute but his faith at the crucial moment failed him and he promised to conform. To test him, the king through his intermediaries made proposals to Nersan who was confined in a prison that was part of the royal palace. Bademus with his chains stricken off was brought to Lapeta and introduced into the chamber where Nersan was confined with the intention that, during their interview, Nersan should slay his fellow Christian and for this purpose had been provided with a sword.

Again at the crucial moment Nersan's nerve failed him; but the Abbot had already seen through the plot and as Nersan hesitated, he said: "Unhappy Nersan, to what a pitch of impiety hath thy apostacy carried thee. With joy I run to my death; but would have wished another executioner."

Angered at the taunt implied, in a half-hearted manner Nersan strove to carry out the command of Sapor; but his strokes were so unsteady that the martyr was covered with an infinite number of wounds before the fatal blow was struck.

The monks at that time were called by Syrians and Persians "mourners" and these mourners, the legend tells us, after the body of Bademus had been "reproachfully treated by the infidels and cast out of the city" secured and buried it on April 10th in 376.

APRIL 11th

Is the anniversary of Pope Leo I. called "The Great." He was the forty-seventh in line of succession who held the sacred office. As one reads the story of his life it is easy to see how justly he was entitled to the appellation "The Great," not alone because of the manner in which he exercised his ecclesiastical powers, but in every way. The many affairs of the churches in the East during the period of his pontificate demanded in the highest degree rare executive ability and endless vigilance, but in no case was he found wanting. So too, in matters pertaining more especially to public affairs he ever stood ready not only to advise with clear, well considered judgment, but to act. The most notable event in this respect is on that memorable occasion when Attila the Hun enriched by the plunder of many nations and cities, marched against Rome just then helpless and panic stricken, and the people as with one voice called on this great man to come to their aid. How well he fulfilled the difficult and dangerous task of meeting and placating the haughty tyrant is history and cannot be repeated here; but it saved Rome in her direst hour of peril. As a scholar and a pulpit orator he was indeed "great." His sermons on the obligations of the rich not to hoard their wealth or lavish it on selfish superfluities are wonderful examples of pulpit oratory and clear logical deductions. Modern theologians often now preach on the "Love of God" as if it was some new discovery; but that was the keynote of this venerable man's teaching adding as well humility and to walk according to the spirit of Christ in charity to all.

As a pulpit orator his diction was pure and elegant, his style terse and clear, while his logic was at all times unassailable.

Another saint whose anniversary comes on this day is St. Guthlac (or Guthlake) one of the most interesting of the old Saxon anchorites and his story in his early years, was similar to that of many young men of his times; and a now nearly forgotten legend tells us that "at the time of his birth a hand of ruddy splendour was seen extending from the clouds to a cross which stood at his mother's door."

Like all youths of his day he was devoted to warlike enterprises Not what we now regard as such, but which then were not esteemed at all illegitimate. He was wild and reckless as well as fearless. Thus at the age of sixteen he became the head and commander of a body of reivers and robbers; although he seems to have been something of the "Robin Hood" order in the division of the spoils he captured and never leaving his victims utterly helpless "frequently giving back to those he had robbed one-third of the plunder he had captured." Later on he became a soldier under Ethelred, King of Mercia, with some distinction.

In his 24th year he seems to have had a change of heart, for he laid aside his warlike purposes and entered the monastery of Repanden where he studied for two years. Then he determined to lead a hermit's life selecting for his retreat Croyland Isle in the fen country. Here he built a small oratory and passed fifteen years in prayer and solitude. At this time Ethelbald, afterward King of Mercia, who was then an exile, often came to Guthlac for counsel while he was hiding in the marshes. When Ethelbald came into power he had not forgotten the saintly man in his dreary cell amid the fens; therefore after St. Guthlac died the king caused the marshes to be drained and on the site of the hermit's cell erected a monastery in his honour. This Croyland monastery must have been an immense establishment since its ruins cover twenty acres.

Croyland Isle has through drainage now wholly disappeared and rich farms now fill the place once so desolate.

APRIL 12th

Marks the anniversary of Pope Julius I. who died in 352, the most noted event of whose life was the fixing on December 25th as the correct date of the birth of our Lord. A date which until then had been celebrated by the churches at various dates. But Julius, St. Chrysostom informs us, after a strict examination of the traditions regarding the event set it on the day we now observe.

St. Zeno whose festival occurs on April 12th is styled by St. Gregory the Great, as a martyr, but by most of the chronicles of the Church is honoured only by the title of Confessor. He was by education a Latin but of the African race and made bishop in 362 during the reign of Julian "The Apostate." St. Ambrose writes of him with great admiration, especially mentioning his Easter services and the ordination of virgins "consecrated to God," who unlike the nuns "lived in their own houses."

Love-feasts at Agapis established on the festivals of martyrs and celebrated in their cemeteries were then in vogue, but had degenerated into occasions of intemperance and frivolity, if not worse. These St. Zeno severely condemned.

He is chiefly known for his boundless charity and willing poverty in his personal life as well as his sufferings and the persecution he endured for the faith.

SYMBOLS.

St. Augustine called these representations "*libri idiotarum*" (books of the simple), and beyond doubt his definition in those early days was literally correct, for outside the clergy and a few savants, none could read or write. Indeed not a few of the nobles affected to despise learning of any kind and still later relegated to their henchmen and subordinates the arduous duties and the task of acquiring a knowledge of reading, rather than devote their time to learning to do so and thereby be compelled to forego their daily pleasures. With the common people the serfs and laborers, even had they wished, teachers were lacking or refused to enlighten them. Thus these crude representations found upon Clog Almanacs came into vogue. Early in the Christian era symbols, emblems and monograms, began to be used to signify certain rites of the church and to indicate the persons of the Holy Trinity and also some of the apostles. Later many others were added as attributes for the more prominent personages of the church, and many of these may yet be seen in the catacombs about Rome and the excavations at Pompeii and elsewhere. These symbols or signs were used only for the purpose of expressing a fact or sentiment, or as an attribute of some characteristic personality, or some especial event in the life of the holy man or woman to whom they were given.

In early Christian art as seen in the catacomb frescoes they seem to aim only at a realistic representation and the crudest attempt satisfied them. With the growth of art this was all changed. The ideal gradually replacing the real, or it was idealised to a point of beauty.

APRIL 13th.

In Roman Martyrology the first name which appears on this day is Hermenegild. He was desended from a noted family, his father being Liuvigild, king of the Visigoths in Spain and professed the Arian doctrine, therefore educated his son in that faith but by his marriage with Ingondes, a daughter of Seigbert king of Austrasia in France who was a zealous Catholic, Hermenegild became convinced of the errors of Arianism and renounced its teachings. For this Liuvigild cut him off from his inheritance of the throne. But Hermenegild had inherited what his father could not deprive him of — his sturdy Goth independence — and as a sovereign prince he stood firmly for his rights. The story of the conflict between father and son is a quaint bit of history in ancient warfare. At last Hermenegild allied himself with some Roman generals who bound themselves to protect him and received his wife Ingondes and her infant son as hostages but corrupted by Liuvigild's gold they betrayed their trust. Thus it was Hermenegild was besieged in Seville where for a year he successfully resisted but then fled to Cordova with 300 faithful followers. His place of refuge was taken by Liuvigild and Hermenegild sought protection in a church where Recared his younger brother sent by King Liuvigild found him. Then by sacred promises if he would submit and ask forgiveness all would be well. Hermenegild returned and the king received him kindly, embraced him, but treacherously ordered while his promise had hardly fallen from his lips and the father's kiss was yet warm on the son's cheek, that Hermenegild should be "stripped of his royal robes; be loaded with chains and confined in a dungeon in the tower of Seville." For two years the king alternately used threats and promises to lead this faithful man to renounce the orthodox faith,

but in vain. On Easter Eve (which that year was the 13th of April) an Arian bishop came to the prisoner from the king with an offer of pardon if he would take communion from the hand of any Arian prelate. The offer was sternly refused and the bishop so reported to the king and orders were given the soldiers; who entered the prison and without further words and by a blow from an axe, ended his life. Thus while sometimes this saint has for his attribute a cross, grasped by a hand, as in the first illustration, he often has an axe as an emblem

This briefly told is the story of the heroic courage that won from St. Gregory of Tours such enthusiastic admiration of this martyr.

APRIL 14th.

On this day at Avignon there are offices celebrated in honour of their patron saint. The following from Butler's "Lives of the Saints" tells the story of St. Benezet or Little Bennet:

"He kept his mother's sheep in the country * * * when moved by charity to save the lives of many poor persons who were frequently drowned in passing the Rhone, and inspired by God he undertook to build a bridge over that rapid river at Avignon."

A gigantic enterprise for a poor boy! yet, like many another enthusiast and philanthropist he accomplished his work; beginning it in 1177 but completed after his death in 1184. "Many were the miracles which were wrought" during those years from the first laying of its foundation until its completion in 1188 four years after his death, while his tomb is appropriately placed in a little chapel built on the bridge itself

But the most remarkable part of the story that is well vouched for is that after nearly five hundred years in 1670 when repairs to the bridge made the opening of St. Benezet's tomb necessary and the body was found "without the least sign of corruption * * * and the colour of the eyes lively and sprightly though through the dampness of the situation the iron bars about the tomb were much damaged."

APRIL 15th.

Of the many saints of world-wide renown among certain classes none perhaps, is more devoutly reverenced by sailors of the Roman faith especially those of Spain, than St. Peter Gonzales whose festival day occurs on the 15th of April. Albeit he was a youth of such singular purity of character that he won the favour of his uncle the Bishop of Astorga who procured for him a canoncy; he had all the pride and haughtiness of the Spanish nobility of his day. But his pride in the very bloom of young manhood was humbled when through an accident or misstep of his prancing horse the young dean found himself wallowing in a filthy gutter. Still this mishap bore wondrous fruit, for from being proud, vain and haughty he became a model of humility and in his zeal to teach the truths of Christ he devoted himself to the peasants of Galacia and along the coast where his labours among the mariners won for him that frank generous love for which sailors the world over have ever been noted, when they encounter a brave honest self-sacrificing, unselfish man. His labours at this time and later made him the "Patron Saint of Mariners."

Many miracles have been attributed to him. While yet at court in his younger days his upright virtuous life had made him noted. It may have been in jest or banter that some of the nobles told a famous courtezan that if she ever heard Gonzales preach she would reform her life. To this she replied: "If I could but once speak to him alone he could not resist my charms, any more than some others."

To cut the story short she secured such an interview beginning by a mock confession ; but when Gonzales discovered the trend of her efforts he left her and went to an adjoining room where he wrapped himself in a cloak and cast himself on the blazing coals on the hearth calling on her to look. But the flames had refused to scorch even the hem of his cloak. Amazed, confounded and convinced, she from that hour became a penitent, converted woman.

Even more remarkable legends are told of this faithful man. An ancient galleon is the attribute usually given to St. Peter Gonzales, but none appears on any Clog stick I have ever seen.

In Roman Martyrology for April 15th we read of SS. Basilissa and Anastasia that these two "noble women were disciples of the apostles and as they persevered courageously in the confession of their faith under the Emperor Nero they had their hands and feet cut off and thus obtained the crown of martyrdom." This is undoubtedly correct ; but another authority says of St. Anastasia : "She was condemned to the flames."

In "Legendary and Sacred Art," Mrs. Jameson says :

"Notwithstanding her beautiful Greek name and her fame as one of the great saints of the Greek calendar St. Anastasia is represented as a noble Roman lady who perished during the persecution of Dioclesian. She was persecuted by her husband and family for openly professing the Christian faith, but being sustained by the eloquent exhortations of St. Chrysogonus she passed triumphantly, receiving in due time the crown of martyrdom by being condemned to the flames. Chrysogonus also was put to death by the sword and his body thrown into the sea.

"According to the best authorities, these two saints did not suffer in Rome, but in Illyria; yet in Rome we are assured that Anastasia after her martyrdom was buried by her friend Apollina in the garden of her house under the Palatine hill and close to the Circus Maximus."

The stake fagots and palm branch (as in illustration) appear on some Clogs as the attribute of this martyred woman.

APRIL 16th.

St. Druon or Drugo, whose festival the Church observes to-day has an especial place in the Kalendar as the "Patron of Shepherds." This is rather the more singular from the fact that our saint was of a noble family in Flanders. From his childhood he had evinced a desire to lead a religious life. His father died before he was born and his mother passed to the unknown "beyond" almost at the hour of his birth. Thus his youth lacked the help he needed, though in some manner replaced by the teachings and advice of the priests who directed his education. It was not, therefore, a great surprise that at the age of twenty he bestowed all his money and goods upon the poor of his neighbourhood, renounced all claim to his family estates to other heirs that he might pursue a life of poverty and penance which accorded with his views. Thus it was that clad only in poor garments worn over the "hair shirt" which he had donned, he went forth into the world. His legend does not show clearly what his purpose was so we can only follow his "trail" and each reader must judge for himself. After visiting several "Holy Shrines" he engaged in the service of a devout lady named Elizabeth de la Haire at Sebourg, two leagues from Valenciennes, as a shepherd where he spent six years. But his modesty, piety and charity had bruited his name abroad as well as drawn to him the attention of his mistress. Thus from various sources he received many presents all of which in turn went to the poor and needy; for his disguise had been penetrated and added much to the veneration in which he was held by the peasantry; who were not slow to show their feelings. It was to avoid applause like this that he at last fled once more and became a recluse in a narrow cell near the church at Sebourg; where until he was eighty-four years of age he led his saintly life, teaching and expounding the scriptures to those who came to him and in deeds of love to such as he was able to aid. Then on April 16th, 1186 he went to his reward, and his relics were laid at rest in the Church of St. Martin at Sebourg where his shrine is yet shown.

APRIL 17th

Is sacred to the memory of one of the early rulers of the Church, St. Anicetus, who succeeded St. Pius "in the latter part of the reign of Antonius Pius the Roman Emperor," as Dr. Butler tells us. Dates however conflict — as Antonius Pius died in 161 and this prelate ruled from 165 to 173. These early dates oftentimes contradict each other. But I accept without a question Dr. Butler's dates. While in Roman Martyrology Pope Pius is styled a *martyr* he did not in fact shed his blood for the faith. Dr. Butler in commentating on the life of Pius, says: "The thirty-six first bishops of Rome down to Liberius and this one excepted, all the Popes to Symmachus the fifty-second in 498, are honoured among and out of two hundred and forty-eight Popes, from St. Peter to Clement XIII., seventy-eight are named in Roman Martyrology."

Beyond the record of a faithful care of his flock the life of Pius presents few striking features beyond the trials every true Christian was compelled to undergo.

APRIL 18th.

In the story of St. Apollonius, "The Apologist" as he is surnamed, we have two somewhat curious features brought out. The first that "look for the woman" far ante-dates in fact, its use in modern literature.

Marcus Aurelius as a pagan persecuted the Christians seemingly rather as a matter of principle than from pure vindictiveness a point which strange as it sounds might I fancy be fully maintained — from his pagan teachings. But when in 180 his son Commodus succeeded him in the Empire, a new element entered for he had made Marcia — an admirer of the faith — Empress, and woman's influence stayed the tide of persecution even though the edict was in no wise changed. During this " calm " the number of the faithful was largely increased. Among these was Apollonius, a Roman senator; a man well versed in law, philosophy and the knowledge of the Holy Scriptures. It is here the second curious feature of the times and the Roman laws comes in. Ignorant of his fate; impelled by some wish for revenge against his master; a *slave* named Severus denounced Apollonius as a Christian, and he was haled before Perennis prefect of the Prætorium. By what seems a strange contradiction Marcus Aurelius had issued an edict whereby without revoking or repealing the former laws against convicted Christians the accuser should be put to death, and therefore under the terms of this law Severus was *first* condemned " to have his legs broken and then after put to death." The slave having been duly executed by the same judges who had condemned him ordered Apollonius to renounce his newly professed religion as he valued his life and fortune.

Upon the refusal of the senator to do this to secure safety, the judge no doubt gladly availed himself of the law — and sent Apollonius before the Roman Senate to plead his own case. Then it was he made his celebrated speech in the vindication of the Christian religion, which won for him the surname of " The Apologist." No record or (so far as I can learn) only an excerpt from this celebrated plea has been preserved. " St. Jerom " we are told by Dr. Butler, " who had perused it, did not know whether more to admire the eloquence or the profound learning both sacred and profane of this illustrious man."

It was ineffectual, for upon Apollonius' refusal to comply with the decree of the Senate to renounce his faith, he was condemned and beheaded in the year 186. The sixth year of the reign of Commodus.

APRIL 19th.

On this day occurs the anniversary of St. Anicetus who succeeded St. Pius I. as Pope who held the sacred office from 165 to 173 the year of his death.

ST. ELPHEGE.

The day also is set aside for St. Stephen, Abbot of Citeaux. He was an English gentleman of wealth named Stephen Harding, who became a monk and noted in the Church for his ascetic life as well as for his learning having in 1109 with some of his fellow monks of Citeaux made from Hebrew manuscripts, a "very correct copy of the Bible in Latin." In 1133 he laid down his office of abbot on account of his age. He died March 28th, 1134 but his Order, "the Benedictine," keep his festival on April 15th, while in Roman Martyrology he is honoured on the 17th day of that month the day he was supposed to have been canonized.

On this day the Church honours Leo IX. the 155th Pope. He held his high office from 1048 to 1054 the year of his death.

Again to-day comes the anniversary of another noted Englishman, St. Elphege or Alphege as it is sometimes called who has a most interesting story connecting him with the early incursions of the Danes in England and as Archbishop of Canterbury. His saint-day still holds a place in the Kalendar of the Church of England.

He was an Englishman from a noble and very wealthy famliy. Fearing the snares of riches, at an early age he renounced the world and became an enthusiastic Benedictine not in garb alone but in all that their holy vows implied. Austere and ascetic as the life of a monk of this Order was, Elphege felt it was not severe enough to satisfy his conscience therefore he denied himself in every way especially by his long and frequent fasts, until his body became so attenuated that when he held up his hand — as an old ballad says :

> "It was so wan and transparent of hue
> You might have seen the moon shine through."

In 984 St. Dunstan appointed Elphege Bishop of Westchester and he left the cloisters. For twenty-two years he governed that see until in 1006 on the death of Alfred, he was translated to Canterbury.

If my readers will turn to their English history and read of the massacre of the Danes by the Anglo-Saxons on St. Brice's day (November 13th, 1002) a massacre which only finds a parallel in the Sicilian Vespers, the atrocities of St. Bartholomew's Day, or in the barbarism of the French Revolution they will easily understand why the fierce Danes vowed revenge, though at that time they had to wait before they could accomplish their purpose it had not lessened their hatred. In 1011 the Danes came again to Canterbury; but history has not recounted their deeds of pitiless fury and Elphege's unavailing efforts to "pity the women and spare the children."

On the day before Easter in 1012 the Archbishop received notice that unless his ransom of 3,000 pieces of silver was paid within eight days, his life would be the forfeit. At last on Easter Sunday he was brought from the prison where for seven months he had suffered untold torments and stood before the commanders of the Danish ships then lying at Greenwich. It was after a banquet when these brutal men were all drunken with wine and their cry came: "Money! Money for your ransom, bishop."

With a calm voice he replied: "Silver and gold have I none; what is mine I freely offer, the knowledge of the true God."

Amid scornful laughter and angry shouts some one struck him

with the flat side of a battle-axe and knocked him down and at once the mob began to stone him. Bruised and suffering from mortal wounds yet not dead, he lay in agony when some one more merciful than his fellows raised his battle-axe and with a single blow put the holy man beyond earthly pain.

A parish church at Greenwich marks the place of his martyrdom and first burial. Ten years later when his remains were transferred to the Cathedral at Canterbury, William of Malmsbury (the historian) informs us they were found wholly incorrupt; a story an English church "year-book" incorporates in its text.

St. Elphege is usually represented in art with his chasuble full of stones and sometimes holding in his hand a battle-axe. The admirable picture I give above is from an engraving of a sculptured figure of this saint in Wells Cathedral, England.

SYMBOLS OF THE EVANGELISTS.

'Round the throne, 'midst Angels' natures
Stand four holy Living Creatures,
Whose diversity of features
  Maketh good the Seer's plan:

This an Eagle's visage knoweth,
That a Lion's image showeth;
Scripture on the rest bestoweth
  The twin forms of Ox and Man.

* * * * * *

Symbols quadriform uniting,
They of Christ are thus inditing;
Quadriform His acts, which writing
  They produce before our eyes;

Man — Whose birth man's law obeyeth;
Ox — Whom victim's passion slayeth;
Lion — Whom on death he preyeth,
  Eagle — soaring to the skies.

* * * * * *

— Translated from "Jucundare Plebs Fidelis," by Rev. J. M. Neal.

Before any especial symbol had been given to each of the Evangelists one was in use for all, a Greek cross (often of an ornamental pattern as shown in illustration) with the four gospels in the angles of it. The weird-winged symbols came much later and were beyond a doubt suggested by the four beasts named in the Apocalypse.

Another quaint symbol of this character (see illustration) is often found in the catacombs, being the Agnus Dei standing on a mount, and the four rivers of the Paradise — the Gihon, the Tigris, the Euphrates and the Pison representing the Four Evangelists and their gospels. The Gihon being St. Matthew, the Tigris St. Mark the Euphrates St. Luke and the Pison St. John.

Just when the mysterious, winged, creatures were first used is uncertain but probably in the early part of the V. century. St. Jerom (326-420) mentions them and gives at some length the reasons why each symbol was assigned the particular Evangelist. Thus St. Mark received the lion: "Because he set forth the royal dignity of Christ and His power as displayed in His Resurrection and Victory over Death." It was from St. Mark's account of the resurrection that the lion was at times used as a symbol of Christ.

The infinite variety of shapes into which these winged lions have been twisted has been limited only by the inventive genius of artists, from the early days in Greece and Rome until our own day.

After the introduction of these winged creatures as symbols of the four Evangelists they generally took the place of the books

when used to embrace all of them, and as shown in the illustration and placed in the arms of the cross instead of in the angle, but when so done a monogram of Christ or His figure was set in the center of the cross.

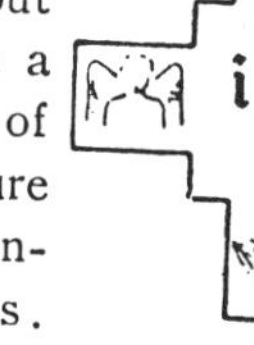

The same style of cross is also at times used as an emblem of the four great events in the life of our Lord. The following form will explain the significance in each case however used :

Symbol :	Winged Man. Winged Lion.	Winged Ox. Eagle.
Event :	Incarnation. Resurrection.	Passion. Ascension.
Evangelist :	St. Matthew. St. Mark.	St. Luke. St. John.

APRIL 20th.

St. James of Sclavonia is one of the saints which the Roman Church remembers this day. A Dalmatian by birth but as he spent the most of his life on the opposite coast of the Adriatic Sea, in Italy, his name has come down to us as "of Sclavonia." He was a lay-brother of the Observantine Franciscan Friars at Bitecto nine miles from Bari. While but an humble member of his Order his reputation and the reason for his canonization rests upon his wonderful "prophetic spirit" through the efficacy of fervent prayer, by which he made some remarkable prophecies. By nature he was extremely emotional finding vent in tears.

In his humble state he was employed like others of the Order in menial duties but often while so engaged he fell into a state of ecstacy. Once, when acting as a cook for his brethren in the midst of his duty he stood "ravished in spirit" and his tears which he could not restrain fell into the dish of beans which he happened at the moment to be preparing for the brethren. It so happened that on this day the Duke of Adria, on whose estates the monastary of Conversano stood was a guest. Unnoticed by the holy man the Duke had watched him in his moment of ecstacy — while he mechanically proceeded with his work — and had seen the tears fall into the dish he was preparing but he made no remark. When the hour for the meal came and St. James as was his place asked the honoured guest what he would eat, the Duke replied as he chose the beans: "Blessed are they whose meals are seasoned by such tears." St. James died April 27th, 1485 but his festival was fixed by Pope Benedict XIV. for the 20th of this month.

APRIL 21st.

Few English prelates have ever exercised as great an influence on the politics, literature and learning of his own age as Anselm, Archbishop of Canterbury, in whose honour services will be held on this day in the most beautiful of all England's many noble cathedrals.

Though not an Englishman by birth he became one in fact after his translation to the see of Canterbury. He was born in 1033 at Aoust in Piedmont, and from early years displayed a predeliction for study and monastic life. But his father sternly opposed this course and young Anselm secretly left home. After three years of wandering in Burgundy and France he reached Bec in Normandy and there studied under Lanfranc, later, in 1060 becoming a monk in the abbey of Bec. Six years later he was made prior of the abbey and in 1078 was advanced to the office of abbot. It was at this time he wrote many of those works which spread his fame throughout western Europe. In 1092 at the invitation of Hugh, Earl of Chester, Anselm visited England to establish monks from Bec in the new monastery the earl had lately founded.

For four years King William Rufus had kept the see of Canterbury vacant that he might enjoy its revenues. However, in 1093 William was induced to name Anselm as archbishop and he was consecrated on December 4th of that year. Within a fortnight the king and Anselm were at odds from the greed of William and the refusal of Anselm to allow the revenues of the church to be plundered. But far more important was the quarrel between the king and the prelate on the question of the temporal power of the Church. This controversy continued after Henry I. came to the throne but it is too long for record here beyond noting the prominent rôle which Anselm played throughout, until by mutual concessions the vexed question was for the time closed only, as all historical students know, later to become so important.

Anselm was a man of remarkable firmness of purpose, purity of life and of great intellectual powers. It was to him England owed the introduction of metaphysical reasoning into theology and thus a new school for the latter science.

APRIL 22d.

This day is the joint festival of two Popes of the early Roman Church although their deaths occurred an hundred and twenty years apart. The first of these was St. Soter who succeeded St. Anicetus in 173. The mention of his name brings once more prominently to mind how early "heresies" began to creep into the Christian Church. For the chief events we find regarding the Bishop — as they then were termed — was his opposition to the "heresy of Montanus." A remarkable letter addressed by this prelate to the church at Corinth drew from St. Dionysius, a letter of thanks and the words "that the letter should be read for their edification every Sunday at their assemblies to celebrate the Divine mysteries."

This bishop died in 176 — or 7 (dates conflict) — on April 22d. He is termed "a martyr" in the Roman Martyrology but like others of the earlier bishops his martyrdom was rather from the persecutions of the Church than of a death by violence.

The second of these bishops whose festival occurs this day was St. Caius, who succeeded St. Eutychian in the Apostolic see in 283. He like others of the earlier rulers of the Church did not escape from the penalties of their day but held faithful to his belief and governed the Church for over twelve years. He died April 21st, 296, but his festival is fixed by Roman Martyrology for April 22d, the day of his burial.

APRIL 23d.

This day is dedicated to one of the most noted and at the same time most mysterious saints in the entire Kalendar — St. George of Cappadocia. "He is honoured in the Catholic Church as one of the most illustrious martyrs of Christ" writes Butler in his "Lives of the Saints." Yet if we accept the account given by Gibbon (the historian), we learn that "this martial hero owes his position in the Christian Kalendar to no merit of his own." A remark which can hardly be true even though some of the legends regarding him are somewhat mythical for his fame depends on no one country. The Greek and Latin Churches alike honour him and Saxon Martyrology set aside one day as especially dedicated to him and after "the Conquest" he is thus honoured in England, while long before that Knights in France, Burgundy, Hainault, Brabant, Flanders and Germany were ever ready to "hold the lists" in honour of this saint and the Greeks entitled him "The Great Martyr." He is the tutelar saint of Genoa, and in 1222 the great national council held at Oxford during the reign of Henry III. (surnamed Winchester), ordained his feast to be kept as a holiday, and in

1344 the Order of the Knights of St. George, or "The Blue Garter" was instituted in honour of this saint.

There has long been a controversy over St. George. Calvin and the Centurcators call him an "imaginary saint," Alban Butler warning his readers not to "confound him with George, the Arian, usurper of the see of Alexandria," etc.

Indeed a cloud of mystery hangs about his whole life save on one or two points. That he was from young manhood a military man engaged in warfare with the pagans at whose hand he at last met his death, all seemingly agree. Beyond that without taking too much space to give the varied versions of the several stories as reported, I cannot here speak.

ST. GEORGE.

Endless legends are told of him, such as the apparition of St. George to Richard I. in his expedition against the Saracens and the effect of the vision on the king's army when told them; while there are few I imagine who have not heard the legend of St. George and the Dragon and have seen pictures of the gallant knight. The one given here is a rare and curious one taken from an old MS. in the Bodleian Library, England.

Even this legend is condemned as a myth, and as Butler writes like "the stories of the combat of St. George with the magician Athanasius, and other trumpery came from the mint of the Arians."

An old English ballad runs:

> "Some say there was no George,
> Some, that there no Dragon was,
> Pray God, there was at least a maid."

The scene of the legend is sometimes laid in Telene a city of Libya, and others at Berytus (Bayreuth) Syria. The inhabitants of the city were in terror owing to a terrible dragon that lived in the adjacent marshes. To prevent the monster from entering the city two children were daily chosen by lot and sent out for the dragon to feed upon. At last the lot fell on Cleodolinda the king's daughter, and whom he greatly loved. In his grief he offered anything, nay all he possessed, to save her from this horrible fate. But the people insisted and the king submitted only asking for a respite of eight days. At the end of the time decked in her royal robes the princess went out toward the place where the dragon came for his daily meal. Just then St. George on his way to join his legion, appeared. Learning the cause of her tears, the knight said to her: "Fear not, for I will deliver you." She replied: "Noble youth, tarry not lest thou perish with me but fly at once, I beseech thee."

"Think not that I will fly," said the knight. "God forbid! I will lift my hand against this loathsome thing and through the power of Jesus Christ deliver you."

Making the sign of the cross, St. George began the terrible struggle and at length pinned the dragon to the earth and bound him with the girdle of the princess and the subdued monster was led by them like a dog. As they approached the city the people were filled with terror but St. George cried: "Fear not! Only believe in the God through whose might I have conquered the adversary and be baptized, and I will destroy him before your eyes." That day twenty thousand people were baptized. After that St. George slew the dragon and cut off his head before the eyes of all the people.

After this he proceeded on his journey into Palestine, where the edict of Dioclesian against the Christians had just been posted at the temple and in the market places. Men read it with terror but St. George indignantly tore it down and trampled it under foot. He was of course arrested and taken before Dacian, the proconsul, and condemned to eight days of cruel torture. Bound to a cross, scratched by sharp iron nails, scorched and burned by torches and salt rubbed into his wounds. Then a cup of poisonous wine was given him. Making the sign of the cross and recommending himself to heaven he drank off the contents of the chalice without injury. He was bound to a wheel with sharp knives but the wheel was broken by two angels that came to his aid. He was cast into boiling oil and when they thought him subdued they brought him to the temple and bade him offer sacrifice, but he prayed to God ; and the temple and the priests were destroyed by thunder and lightning. Then Dacian in rage, ordered St. George beheaded, and the gallant Christian knight willingly bent his neck to the stroke of the executioner.

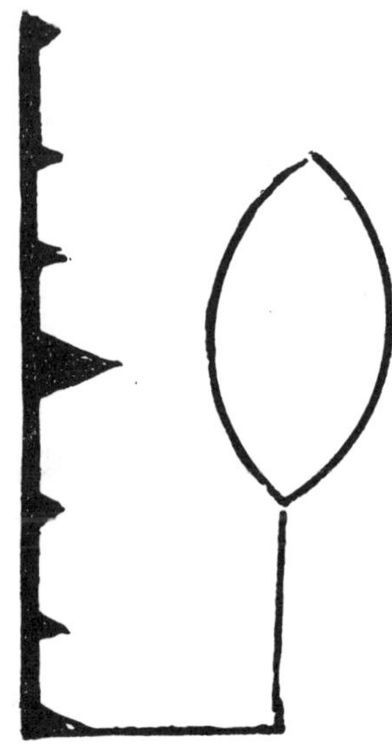

Such in brief are a few only of the many legends told of this most noted saint. In some Clog Almanacs St. George has a shield with his cross upon it; others, like our illustration, have a spearhead. In Christian art he is always represented in armour bearing a spear and shield.

APRIL 24th.

This is the festival day of St. Fidelis of Sigmarengen in Germany; one of the martyrs of the XVII. century. Thus, from an historic standpoint even to come nearer home than when we talk of those brave Fathers of the early Church. He was christened Mark in honour of the Evangelist, who is everywhere commemorated to-morrow. His name was "Mark Rey," his birth in 1577, and his education at Fribourg, Switzerland.

In 1610 after a then common custom of having acted for six years as a travelling tutor for three young men during their journeys through Europe, he resolved to become a Capuchin Friar. This Order was a reformed section (if I may use the term) of the Franciscan or Gray Friars, which was organized in 1528 by Matthew de Basei and later approved by Clement VIII., and of which in its place will be spoken of. While from youth he had been devout yet from his taking the habit of the Capuchin Friars in 1612 he became notably more humble and austere. It was at this time that he was given the religious name by which he was henceforth known of "Fidelis" or "the Faithful." Almost immediately after ordination he was sent to the convent of Weltkirchen, a district over which the Calvinists had gained almost the entire control of the people; but his earnest preaching won back from among these disciples of Calvin quite a number of converts. Even then his zeal had roused the anger of these Reformers and his life was threatened. It was at this time in 1622 "The Congregation de Propaganda" decided to send "Father Fidelis" as a missionary among the Girsons and he penetrated the territory as far as Pretigvat where he made many converts to the Orthodox faith. This added to other things, had induced the Calvinists of the province to rebel against the Emperor and to bear with them no longer. This revolt involves too many pages of history for me to enter on here, or of the demands of the Calvinists for the privilege of freely expressing their *own* religious beliefs irrespective of the rule of the Church of Rome or of the Emperor. On April 24th in 1622 Fidelis had preached at Gruch. Then he had confessed to his brethren and written several letters in which he "foretold his death." From Gruch he went to preach at Sevis where he spoke with unusual eloquence; but on his way returning to the city, a party of Calvinists met him "one of their ministers at its head," who reviled him and a musket was discharged at him as they entreated him to leave the district. His refusal drew forth a blow from "a backsword" which felled him and he lay "weltering in his blood."

He was buried the next day by the Catholics of Gruch.

He was "beatified" by Pope Benedict XIII. in 1729 and canonised by Pope Benedict XIV. in 1746.

Roman Martyrology states that the "minister" who had led this attack on Fidelis was "converted and made a public abjuration of his heresy."

APRIL 25th

Is St. Mark's day. The Evangelist was a Jew and while it is *not* mentioned in the gospels tradition points to him as having been the man bearing a pitcher of water — Mark xiv., 13-15 — and in whose room the "last supper" was prepared. His conversion apparently took place after the Ascension and when he became the companion and assistant of SS. Paul and Barnabas. He was converted by St. Peter and became his favourite disciple attending him to Aquileia and thence to Rome where tradition says he wrote his gospel. Later, during twelve years or more he preached in Egypt, Libya and Thebias. Thence he was sent to Alexandria then the second city only to Rome in all the known world. There he founded the Church of Alexandria, one of the most celebrated churches of the early Christians. But the anger of the heathen was stirred up by his miracles and teachings and they reviled him as a magician. Here it was that at Easter, when the unconverted were holding their feast in honour of their god Serapis, that he denounced their idolatry. This so incensed the Egyptians that they seized him, bound him with cords, dragged him through the highways and over stony, rocky places until he became insensible and died. A storm such as never before had been known, of hail and lightning followed and dispersed the murdering crowd.

The Christians of Alexandria reverentially gathered his remains and placed them in a sepulchre which for centuries they visited and his tomb was a shrine where the faithful worshiped. In A. D. 815 certain Venetian merchants who were then trading in Alexandria secured (not a few writers say "stole") the relics of St. Mark and conveyed them to Venice where the stately church many of my readers will remember was built over them. Since then St. Mark has been the titular saint of the city.

In Christian art the winged lion is given to St. Mark as has been stated but as St. Jerom also has a lion as an emblem, it should be remembered that this latter is in nearly every instance "unwinged," while in but exceptional cases does the lion of St. Mark appear without the wings.

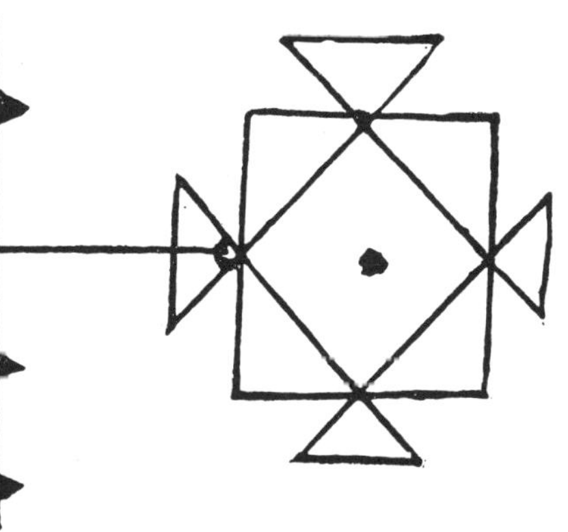

There are two Clog Almanac symbols for St. Mark, the first and more simple is given above; the other as in the illustration here. In some cases the lines intersecting the square are of irregular shape but follow the general form as above.

In portraitures St. Mark usually wears the habit of a bishop as he was the first bishop of Alexandria.

This day is observed in both the Roman and Protestant Church as a fast and the canonical colours for it are red, the colour for all "feasts of the martyrs."

The colour in general signifies divine love, power and royal dignity as well as blood, war and suffering.

In the Bodleian Library there is a rare and curious MS. "Canon Lit 99" with the annexed illustration of St. Mark, that may interest some of my artist readers and therefore is copied. It is only one among thousands extant.

APRIL 26th.

Again by the coincidence of time constantly recurring in human life; the festivals of two of the earlier bishops of the Christian Church occur.

The first is that of St. Cletus, the successor of St. Linus and the *third* bishop among those holy men of old. Beyond the fact that he governed the Church from A. D. 76 to 89, little is recorded beyond the fact of his devotion to the faith. He is like most of these early prelates designated in Martyrology as a martyr. But there is nothing to show that he really testified to his faith by his blood. To be a Christian in those days, was in fact to be a martyr.

The second of these holy men is St. Marcellinus who was chosen as the head of the Church in 296, and near the time when Dioclesian set himself up for a deity. Marcellinus governed the Church for eight years; and although he is styled a martyr in Roman Martyrology, the Liberian Calendar gives his name in the list of the early Popes, who did *not* shed his blood for the faith. He was eighty years of age when in 304 he died. But all readers will remember that this year was the one during which the brutal edicts of Dioclesian caused the death of more Christians in Jerusalem than fell within the whole length of time while they were strictly enforced. Thus his name no doubt came to be embraced in this terrible list of these faithful Christians.

APRIL 27th.

DIOCLESIAN MARTYRS.

A bit of Roman history to refresh our memory is not out of place here. After Emperor Numerian (son of Carus) was slain by conspirators in 284 Dioclesian — a native of Dalmatia and a soldier of fortune — was proclaimed emperor by the army then in Chalcedon. Dioclesian soon found himself unequal to govern the vast Roman empire therefore he selected Maximian Herculeus as his aid honouring him with the title of Augustus. This Maximian was a man of a cruel and savage temper but considered one of the best commanders of his day. There was a second and probably very potent reason for this selection in the fact that the Pretorian guard had for three hundred years indulged themselves in the playful amusement of at will murdering their emperors and as a buffer possibly Dioclesian thought Maximian Herculeus might stand between him and the guards in case the latter should again feel inclined to gratify themselves in their peculiar style of amusement. Still later these two emperors again selected two inferior emperors to aid them, naming each "a Cæsar." Dioclesian selected Maximian Galerius (a Dacian peasant by birth and a man of brutal ferocity) for the East and Herculeus chose Constantine surnamed Chlorus, for the West.

We must omit the long story of the earlier persecutions of Christians until the issuing of that famed edict which St. George is credited with having pulled down at Nicomedia where Dioclesian then had his residence and how prompted by Galerius he had despoiled the churches of the Christians, burned their Scriptures and slaughtered the people. But the insatiable brutality of Galerius demanded more victims and he so plotted that on two occasions the palace of Dioclesian was set on fire and the crime fastened upon the Christians. Then began those fearful scenes which have made this emperor's name the synomym for cruelty. Every Roman history tells the story of how Dioclesian beginning with his wife, Prisca, and his daughter Valerin, (both of whom were Christians) compelled all persons to sacrifice to idols, under the penalty of torture and death.

It began in the palace extending to the clergy, the judges, and so downward to the common people. All who refused suffering tortures till then unheard of. Altars were erected in the very courts of justice and idols placed in every market place. Therefore in Roman Martyrology the 27th of April is set aside to commemorate these martyrs of Nicomedia of whom St. Anthimus, the then faithful bishop of the city, was the first mentioned in our Kalendar as the chief martyr.

APRIL 28th.

This day is sacred to the memory of two other victims of Dioclesian, SS. Didymus and Theodora. A wonderful story if space could be given to tell it in its entirety; of the Divine aid given a maiden in her hour of trial when unsupported by friends or family, she stood alone before Eustratius Proculus the Imperial Prefect of Alexandria. Dr. Butler gives in part the details of this celebrated trial of Theodora with the questions put by the prefect and her prompt, daring answers. Charged with being a Christian she had at once acknowledged her "crime" (?) against the well-known ordinance of the emperors. Struck by her wondrous beauty of person but even more by her noble, firm reliance upon Divine power, this heartless man recognized such traits of true virtue and character that he bore with her an unusually long controversy until his patience at last wearied and possibly in the hopes of saving her from the inevitable penalty which must ensue should she persist in defying the laws, ordered: "Give her two great buffets to cure her of her folly and teach her to sacrifice." Her reply came quickly: "You are master of my body, the law has left *that* at your disposal; but my soul you cannot touch; that is in the power of God alone!" When at last neither arguments, threats of torture nor entreaties had availed, and Proculus had said he would execute the edict, adding: "*I* myself would be guilty of disobeying the emperors were I to dally any longer." Even then the prefect in his reluctancy to carry out his decision granted her a respite of three days in which to reflect and — if she would recant — "Look on these three days as already expired;" she replied: "You will find me the same then as now. * * * My only request is that in the meantime I may be secured from insults on my chastity." For she knew too well the common custom of the imperial guards.

To his credit, if hereto an act can be regarded in that light, Proculus *did* so protect her from the troop of debauchees who at such times by bribes given the soldiers were wont to gratify their vile passions.

On the fatal day an unusual event occurred when a young man, a zealous Christian named Didymus, by the liberal use of money gained access to her place of confinement. He was disguised as a soldier and after much entreaty he at last persuaded her to change their garments. Thus disguised she escaped her prison. When the guards discovered how they had been cheated of their prisoner, Didymus of course was at once haled before the prefect and in reply to the queries of why he had done this thing and where Theodora was he said: "I am a Christian and God inspired me to rescue his hand-maid" and then declared he knew nothing more of her than that: — "She is a servant of God and He has preserved her spotless. God hath done to her according to her faith in Him."

Didymus was sentenced to be beheaded and his body burned. When he heard his fate declared he cried aloud: "Blessed be God, the Father of Our Lord Jesus Christ who hath not despised my offering but hath preserved spotless His hand-maid Theodora, for God hath thus crowned me doubly."

But this was not to be. St. Ambrose in his "De Virgin" describes the wonderful and pathetic scene; how Theodora when she heard of the sentence of Didymus at once hastened to disclose herself and ran to the place of execution to die in his place, urging that she indeed owed her temporary preservation to him: "You were bail for my modesty," she cried: "*not* for my life. If my virginity yet be in danger, your bond still holds good; but if my life be required, it is a debt that *I* alone can discharge."

Again there was a halt in the tragedy while a new examination was had. But their condemnation was a foregone conclusion and although full of striking incidents I must refrain from repeating them. The two were executed on April 28th, A. D. 304.

APRIL 29th

Is the day set apart for the honour of St. Robert, Abbot of Molesme, the founder of the Order of the Cistercians. At the early age of fifteen he became a Benedictine monk. Later he connected himself with a company of monks in the desert of

Colan but they subsequently moved into the forest of Molesme where they lived in cells built from tree boughs and where St. Robert was their superior. Not to follow in detail his life we find him with other ardent, zealous followers retired to the uninhabited forests of Citeaux or Cistercium, by the side of a little river where they could live as they felt more truly in accord with the rigor of St. Bennet. They arrived there on that saint's day March 21st, 1098. From that epoch the origin of the Cistercian Order dates. They followed the strictest rules laid down by St. Bennet abstaining entirely from the use of meat at all times. The habit worn was of a tawny colour at first but under St. Alberic the successor of St. Robert, this was changed to white and the Order for the first time took the Virgin Mary as its especial protectress. It was also under St. Alberic that the Cistercian nuns were instituted. Within fifty years this Order had increased to 500 abbeys and soon after A. D. 1200 the records show they numbered about 1,800 separate houses. Under Pope Sixtus IV. in 1475 the more strict rules of abstinence from flesh were relaxed. But it *was* in 1664 under the celebrated La Trappe that the austere reformation of the Order took place. The story of this Order is an interesting one and it numbers among its devout followers many noted names not only in church history but in public life. Ancient chronicles place the date of St. Robert's birth in 1018 and his death in 1110.

APRIL 30th.

On this day the Church honours St. Catharine of Siena a woman of most remarkable strength of character as well as ardent charity and self-sacrifice. When in 1375 the people of Florence, Perugia, a great part of Tuscany and even the ecclesiastical state, entered into a league against the Holy See and were excommunicated, Catharine was selected as the mediator. Her keen wisdom and rare judgment not only brought about a reconciliation but more, since she not only saw but dared to show where some of the moving causes lay and secured their correction. Her life is full of stirring incident and without verging a hair's breadth from strict truth, it became almost a romance in some of the situations in which we find her as a nurse at the bed-side of those afflicted by the most loathsome diseases, then as the adviser of nobles and later the intermediary between thousands and the high authority of the Church. Worn out, not rusted out after an easy life, this wonderful woman died when but thirty-three years of age. She was canonized by Pope Pius II. in 1461. She died April 29th, 1380, but Urban VIII. transferred the festival to the 30th of the month.

MAY

"Then came fair May, the gayest mayd on ground,
Deckt all with dainties of her season's pryde."
— *Spenser*.

May was the second month of the old Alban Kalendar, the third in that of Romulus, and the fifth in that instituted by Numa Pompilius. The Saxons called it "Tri-Milchi" since their cows then gave milk thrice daily. At one time the name was supposed to be in honour of Maia the mother by Jupiter of the god Hermes or Mercury. But the best accepted authorities represent it as being assigned in honour of the Majores or Maiores; the Senate under the old Roman constitutions, just as "Junius" or June was a compliment to the Juniores, or minor branch of the Roman legislature. Ancient proverbs innumerable are extant about May.

The illustration here given is the one we find on Clog Sticks for the 1st of May and is supposed to represent a growing leaf or shrub.

MAY 1st.

This day holds an especial place in both the Anglican and Roman Kalendars, as the festival of SS. Philip and James Minor (or the Less), Apostles.

Of St. Philip we have little authentic imformation beyond that he was a married man and had several daughters and that he preached in Phrygia after Christ's Ascension. Nor can we be perfectly sure that he suffered as a martyr. His legend tells how when at Heiropolis in Phrygia while preaching, he saw the heathen worship a dragon or the god Mars under that form. Then the Apostle commanded the dragon in the name of the cross, which he held in his hand to disappear. When it is said it glided beneath the altar, emitting such a hideous stench, that many people died therefrom among them the King's son; but the Apostle by divine power restored him to life. Whereupon the priests of the dragon crucified him and while still bound on the cross stoned him. Thus the attribute of St. Philip is usually a T (tau) cross, the usual form used in early days. Sometimes he is given a Latin cross and more rarely a double or "Bishop's" cross. At times loaves of bread are placed in his hands in reference to St. John vi., 5-7. St. Philip's four daughters were prophetesses. See Acts XXI., 9. One of them, St. Miriamne appears in Greek calendars.

St. James Minor or the Less who is honoured to-day is also called "the Just" as well as "the Brother of the Lord." He was the first Bishop of Jerusalem. The terms Minor, or the Less may have been given him either because of his stature, or on account of his being younger then St. James the Great. Early traditions tell of his wonderful likeness to Jesus, and that this was the secret reason why Judas kissed Christ in order to point him out beyond doubt to the soldiers.

The fervour of his teaching so angered the Scribes and Pharisees especially Ananus, the high priest, that they flung the Apostle from the parapet of the Temple and then killed him with a fuller's club of a peculiar shape. He was then in his ninety-sixth year of age. In the illustration taken from the reredos of the church at Bampton, England, the two saints are shown one with fuller's club and the other with the T (tau) cross.

ST. JAMES MINOR. ST. PHILIP.

MAY 2d.

This day is the festival of St. Athanasius, Patriarch of Alexandria and a Doctor of the Church.

St. Gregory Nazianzen begins his panegyric upon this saint: "When I praise Athanasius, *Virtue* itself is my theme * * *. His life and conduct were the rule of the Bishops and his doctrine the rule of the orthodox faith." In these two brief sentences is summed up the character of this noted man though a ponderous folio now before me is filled with details that confirm the truth of the venerable prelate's assertion. But I shall hardly even sketch the outline of his life in the brief mention of some facts connected with it.

He was a native Alexandrian, born of Christian parents in 296. In youth noted alike for his virtues and "the pregnancy of his wit." While an "all round" scholar — to use a modern phrase — of rare attainments, he made especial study of the Holy Scriptures; from which he was wont to quote with such ease and aptness that his hearers almost believed he had committed the sacred book to memory. This at least is true; that he had studied it in every way from its historical point of view to those unique parables of our Saviour, which were intended each to teach its own lesson. And next to this, he had made ecclesiastical and the canon laws of the Church an especial study to which he added a rare knowledge of civil law, so unusual among clerics that Sulpicius Severus called him "a lawyer."

It was this rare combination that made Athanasius the power he was in his day in the Church and among his fellow citizens in Alexandria; feared by the pagans; while his own loveable traits, his charity and wisdom made him to be venerated and trusted and loved by his fellow Christians. Such a man was not likely to be unnoticed by the "Fathers of the Church"; especially by one like St. Alexander — then Patriarch of Alexandria, who upon his death-bed recommended Athanasius to the clergy as one worthy to succeed him. It was therefore but the natural sequence when in 326 the bishops of all Egypt assembled in council, elected him as Patriarch.

To write the story of Athanasius from this point on would be to write the history of the Church in Alexandria with all its controversies; internal and external, including the effort by Arians, to eject him from his position, frustrated by Pope Julius in 341, and at other times. It was a long and bitter struggle, therefore must be omitted since it covered a period of forty-six years, or the entire Patriarchal life of Athanasius. To quote once more from St. Gregory Nazianzen: "After innumerable conflicts and as many victories, this glorious saint having governed the Church of Alexandria for forty-six years was called to a life exempt from labour and suffering on May 2d in the year 373.

As a writer Athanasius had few in his day who were his peers for the elegance of his style and beauty of diction.

The Greeks honour St. Athanasius on this day as it is the anniversary when his relics were translated to the church of St. Sophia in Constantinople from Alexandria, and also on January 18th when they commemorate the name of St. Cyril; though Cyril died in June.

MAY 3d.

THE INVENTION OF THE CROSS

Is celebrated on the 3d of May, but the name of the festival is misleading since it was in fact the discovery or finding of the cross on which our Saviour suffered that is honoured.

The Clog Almanac symbol has the Invention of the Cross — as the ancient T (tau) cross. In an English Clog which I have seen this is shown as a Latin cross.

The history of the cross as an instrument for the punishment of criminals is one of the most curious in the whole range of archæological study. No one, not even the most erudite, pretends to know when the cross was "invented." Long before the Christian era it was in common use throughout the then known world; while legends and traditions trace the tree upon which Christ was crucified back to slips or seeds (for there are two versions of the legend) taken from the "tree of life" in the garden of Eden. All of this must be omitted here and only that part of the story told which relates to the finding of the true cross by the Empress Helena, when in A. D. 326 she made a journey to Palestine and which is strictly historical.

St. Helena, according to the best authorities, was born in England but just where is in doubt. She married Constantine Chlorus ("The Pale") and was the mother of Constantine the Great. When the latter embraced Christianity she is reported as saying: "It would have been better had he been born a Jew."

THE INVENTION OR DISCOVERY OF THE CROSS BY ST. HELENA.

Engraved from a print in a Dutch "Legendary History of the Cross," first published in 1423. Facsimile reprint 1876.

Later she too became a convert to the Christian faith. In its proper place in the Kalendar on August 18th, a more detailed account of this noted woman will be given.

As the legends regarding the cross run, after the crucifixion the cross on which Christ had hung, with the two crosses of the thieves were thrown into the town ditch, or according to some into an old vault near by and soon covered with the refuse and ruin of the city.

In her extreme old age the Empress Helena made a pilgrimage to Jerusalem to recover the cross and threatened all the Jewish inhabitants with torture and death if they did not produce the holy cross from the place where their ancestors had concealed it. At last an old Jew named Judas who had been put into prison and was nearly famished, consented to reveal the secret. He accordingly petitioned Helena. Whereupon the earth trembled and from the fissures in the ground a delicious aromatic odour issued and on the soil being removed the three crosses were discovered, and near them the superscription but it was not known to which of them it belonged. "Macarius, Bishop of Jerusalem, in company with the empress repaired to the house of a noble lady who was afflicted with an incurable disease but who was immediately restored to health by touching the true cross; while the body of a young man who was being carried to his burial was brought to life when it was laid on the holy wood." * * *

At the sight of these miracles Judas, the Jew, became a Christian and was baptised by the name of Quiricus to the great indignation of the devil for he said: "By the first Judas I gained much profit, but by this one's conversion I shall lose many souls."

This greatly abbreviated is the legend as it is told.

The temple of Venus which profaned the sacred spot where this is reputed to have occurred was destroyed by order of Empress Helena A. D. 326. Some writers on apparently strong authority say that it was beneath this temple of Venus that three crosses were found. But whichever story is true the fact is indubitable that it was through St. Helena's efforts the true cross of Christ was found. The date 326 given is by some placed in 328.

At the same time St. Helena also secured the four nails with which our Saviour had been fastened to the horrid wood. Of these four nails, two were placed in the imperial crown of Constantine, one was at a later period brought to France by Charlemagne and tradition tells of the fourth as being cast into the Adriatic to calm that stormy sea. But to attempt to follow the history of these nails as well as that of the ultimate disposition of the wood of the cross opens a too widely mooted question.

Constantine erected a basilica on the site of the temple of Venus in 335 and St. Helena herself erected in 327 the "Church of the Nativity" at Bethlehem, said to be the oldest edifice in the world.

MAY 4th.

ROGATION DAYS.

The dates of what are termed Rogation Days depend entirely upon the date of Easter and the fifth Sunday after Easter is "Rogation Sunday" so called, and the Monday, Tuesday and Wednesday following are Rogation Days. These three days immediately preceding Holy Thursday, or Ascension Day are observed in both the Roman and Protestant branches of the church as days of abstination. They originated it is said when St. Mammertus, Bishop of Vienna, about the year 452 ordained that these three days should be observed as a public fast with solemn processions and supplications to God on account of some great public or national calamity. They were continued and in time were by ecclesiastical enactment incorporated into a law of the Latin Church when it was decreed that they should be observed annually "with processions and supplications to secure God's blessing on the product of the earth and the temporal interests of men."

At the time of the Reformation the English church directed that the public processions should be discontinued, but at the same time ordained that each of these three Rogation Days should be observed as days of private fasting. The Roman Church still observes the days as of old.

At a very early day in England these Rogation Days took on also a secular type and were known as "Gange Days," from a peculiar custom of "perambulating the boundaries of each parish" during these three days before Holy Thursday. This name was given them from the Saxon word "gangen" to go. These perambulations were performed with great pomp and ceremony, the procession being composed of the priests and prelates of the church and a select number of the "substantial men of the parish" carrying with them "lights, handbells and banners," which by the law the borough was bound to furnish. During its progress the procession made frequent stops sometimes for a feast, at others to listen to an admonitory sermon from some of the church dignitaries. During the reign of Queen Elizabeth the laws regarding these perambulations were modified and it was ordered that only "the curate of the parish with certain substantial men" should make the tour of the boundaries and then "return to the church for prayers by the curate." I have before me an account of these perambulations written in 1864, in which the writer says that in his own boyhood he well remembers such a perambulation in his parish; that it was headed by the vicar and occupied "two days of merry ramble by us juveniles who followed the vicar and his substantial men." The writer then recounts a score or more of funny incidents and the tricks that were played on the processional party.

In many parts of England these Rogation Days were set aside for some special local service, as in Dorsetshire down to 1830, Rogation Monday was a special festival called the Bezant and was a sort of thanksgiving for the water supply of the town of Shaftsbury.

The canonical colour for each of the Rogation Days is violet. Its general significance is passion, suffering and sorrow; but it also signifies humility, deep love and truth, and in these it is used on the church altar on these days.

This day in May is also the festival of St. Monica, the mother of St. Augustine, and she is held in especial veneration as the patroness of the Augustine nuns. She is very often met with in

Christian art, one famous picture being in Florence. Here she wears a black robe with a coif of white. This coif is often replaced by a veil sometimes white and at others grey.

MAY 5th.

St. Hilary, Archbisop of Arles whose festival occurs on this day must not be confounded with St. Hilary (A. D. 368) who is especially honoured by the Anglican church.

Michael Ghisleri afterwards Pope Pius V., also is honoured on this day. He was from a noble Bologenese family, born January 27th, 1504 and elevated to the pontificate January 7th, 1606. He died May 1st, 1572; was "beatified" by Clement X. in 1672 and canonized by Clement XI. in 1712.

He was a man of strong marked character. He saw and knew the evils of intemperance and may be cited as one of the earliest of those who have striven to counteract these evils; as he published severe regulations regarding the "excesses in taverns" (the saloon of old Rome) and curiously, as we study his story, we see how history repeats itself; or rather that men have not changed. Yet this Holy Father did much toward checking the evil he battled against. At the same time, to further good morals, Pius V. banished from Rome or confined in safe quarters all lewd women. Indeed he was a reformer of a fearless type with but one purpose at heart, to serve his Great Master. His story would be interesting to follow but in these brief sketches I am not able to elaborate.

MAY 6th

Is the festival of St. John the Evangelist, "*ante Portam Latinam.*" This festival is named from a very early legend told by Tertullian and verified by St. Jerom and Eusebius of the persecution of St. John by order of Domitian "the last of the twelve Cæsars." A tyrant who deluged Rome in the blood of martyrs yet a creature — we cannot ennoble him by calling him a man —

of such cruel instinct that it is told of him that in his closet he amused (?) himself by catching flies and impaling them alive with needles. One so lost to all sense of morals that he hesitated not

to debauch his own niece to gratify his sexual lusts.

The legend which must be condensed into a few brief words is that when St. John was brought to Rome he was taken without the gate called "Latina " and there cast into a caldron of boiling oil. But to quote from "Butler's Lives of the Saints": "This seething oil was changed in his regard into a refreshing bath, and the saint came out more fresh and lively than when he entered the caldron."

Like all the heathen of his day Domitian believed in the art of magic and set St. John's deliverance down to that, and contented himself by banishing the Evangelist to the Isle of Patmos. On December 27th, St. John's Day, we shall further speak of him. This especial deliverance of St. John is celebrated on this day. In the Clog Almanac there are two symbols given for the day. One a bleeding heart such as is often given to martyrs. The other, referring to St. John's suffering outside the Latin gate, a caldron with the flames beneath it.

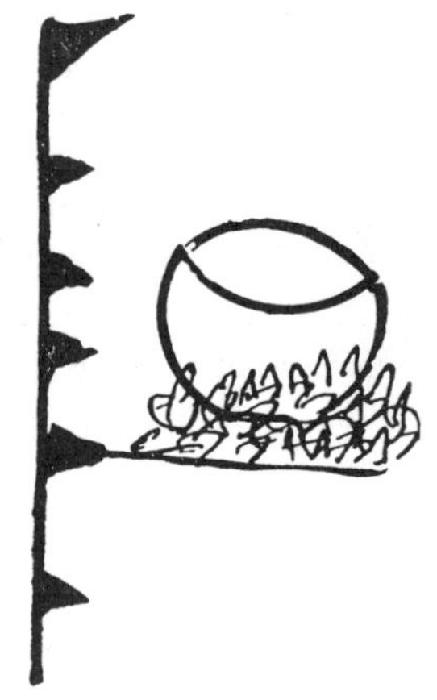

MAY 7th.

St. Benedict II., Pope and Confessor is recognised this day. His pontificate was very brief lasting less than eleven months. He died in 686.

St. John of Beverley whose festival occurs also on this day was from a noble Anglo-Saxon family and was born at Harpham, a favourite place of residence for the Northumbrian kings. The fact that he received a scriptural name instead of one of the usual Anglo-Saxon kind evidences that his family were Christians. His early education was under the Abbess Hilda of Whitby who was a great-granddaughter of King Edwin. Later he completed his studies at Canterbury. Bede (the Anglo-Saxon historian) gives a very full account of his long and peaceful life. Indeed from Bede's account his one desire was to escape notoriety and to live in seclusion, especially during the season of Lent. For this purpose he built for himself a cell in the forest of Deiri beyond the Tyne and far from the haunts of men, on a little stream where the beavers made their home and called in Anglo-Saxon Beofer — leag or the lea of beavers — which was softened in modern days into Beverley.

It was here one of the remarkable miracles credited to this saint was performed, when by his prayers he gained for a poor dumb boy whom he had taken into the forest with him, the power of speech. A monastery was built here at Beverley of which John became the abbot. Later he was translated to the archbishopric of York. He died May 7th, 721.

MAY 8th.

ASCENSION DAY.

Holy Thursday or Ascension Day is a movable feast and fixed to occur forty days after Easter Sunday. It is one of the earliest festivals known to have been kept by the Christian Church. Its first celebration was — as tradition tells us — held in the year 68.

The sacred story is too well known by all Christians to need repetition or to give any reason why the glorious ascension of our Saviour into heaven "leading captivity captive" and "opening the kingdom of heaven to all believers," should be thus held in reverence. Nor need I explain why white, the most joyous of all the canonical colours is selected as the appropriate one for use upon the altars of the church this marvelous day.

In the use of the Rosary by devout members of the Roman Church an account of which and its festival, October 1st will be duly given, this day is marked as the seventh in series of the mythical "Sorrows and Joys of the Virgin." Her legend saying that she too was present on this great day, and prayed: "My Son, remember me when Thou comest into Thy kingdom. Leave me not long after Thee, my Son."

ANCIENT ENGLISH CUSTOMS ON ASCENSION DAY.

Throughout England many quaint customs most of which have passed into desuetude marked Ascension Day. I must limit myself to brief mention of one only, which it was my privilege to witness in 1854 when I happened to be at Chatsworth that "show house" of the north of England when I heard of the festival that was to take place and drove from Matlock to Tissington, "the village of holy wells," to witness the unique ceremony of the "Well Dressing," on Holy Thursday. We entered the village about 10 o'clock in the morning but already the village had donned its gala attire and its one broad street was crowded by a motley collection of people, men, women and children and (pity them) babies in arms, who had come from miles around to take part in the "feast" as they regarded it. Booths of all kinds occupied every available space as usual at English fairs from gingerbread toys to "Brighton Tipper" ale.

Following the good advice of our landlady at Matlock we went directly to the church, but alas, too late to get inside for it was already full; thus we lost the sermon but perhaps were more than repaid by the amusing scenes outside the church until the vicar had finished and came forth to take his place at the head of the procession to the "wells."

This last word is in a way a misnomer for with but one exception they were fountains fed from the springs on the hills above the town, one only being an old-time well with its pump.

These cascades have like that of the "Hall Well" at the

Fitzherbert mansion (shown in illustration) stone arches or fronts with the fountain basin below. On this day, however, they were all hidden from view behind screens of fresh flowers fastened on wooden frames. I recall one where a text of Scripture had been traced in yellow field ranunculus on a dark background with very pretty effect. With the lavish profusion of gorgeous flowers used at each of the five wells it is difficult for my memory at this distant date to recall much beyond the general beauty of them all.

HE IS GONE TO GLORY
WHERE WE HOPE TO GO

The ceremony at each of the wells is the same. Very simple but most pleasing, while the picture made by the peasantry in their holiday attire as they stood grouped around the clergyman and the white-robed choir-boys was one not soon to be forgotten. First came an invocation for God to bless and keep pure, the waters of the well. Then the first of the three Psalms appointed for the day was read, the choir-boys chanting the responses, after that one of Bishop Heber's beautiful hymns then another Psalm, followed by the "Gloria," and the last Psalm and a prayer completed the service. From the last well the clergyman and choir-boys returned to the church.

Not so with the people for their holiday was but just then begun and from that time until the "wee sma hours" games of all kinds were kept up on the village green, with dancing round a May pole while the booths, side shows and gypsy fortune tellers did business to full houses. Full in more than one sense since the taverns and ale booths had not been forgotten.

The origin of this custom of "Well Dressing" is of very ancient date some asserting it was once a pagan festival. In its present form it seems to date from 1615. In that year a severe drought occurred throughout Derbyshire when most of the wells were dried up and the smaller streams were all dry though the wells at Tissington were never empty. The people from the countrysides for ten miles round coming there to get water to supply their cattle and stock at home. Then it was that this thanksgiving service was appointed, for Ascension Day.

THE APPARITION OF ST. MICHAEL.

The Archangel St. Michael whom the Church honours on May 8th is the acknowledged "Prince of the faithful angels." His name even in Hebrew signifies "Who is like God," has a grand sound. It was he whom God commissioned to expel from Heaven Lucifer and his associate rebellious angels when they revolted. To quote: "His office now is believed to be two-fold; that of patron saint of the church on earth, and the Lord of the souls of the dead."

The legends of St. Michael are numerous and elaborate. They begin far back in the mystic days of the Old Testament and tell of his appearance to Hagar (Genesis xxi., 17) while another describes him as the angel who forbadeAbraham to sacrifice Isaac (Genesis xxii., 11) and still another when he contested with Satan for the body of Moses (Jude 5). While in many Bible stories it is said he represented his great Master, God. These legends also tell of his announcement to the Virgin of the time when her death would occur. Of his appearance to St. Gregory both before and when the plague at Rome was stayed. These and many of the other apparitions of St. Michael are the reasons for and the title given this festival.

MAY 9th.

St. Gregory Nazianzen whose festival occurs this day holds a somewhat unique place in the Kalendar of the Saints, since not only was his father St. Gregory, Bishop of Nazianzeno ; his mother St. Nonna ; his two sisters St. Gorgonia and St. Cesarca ; but he also was honoured by the Church by canonization.

St. Gregory from his profound learning, is surnamed " The Theologian " and was one of the " Doctors of the Church." In his early years he had careful training in " grammar-learning " in the schools in Cappadocia and thereafter sent to Palestine " where the study of eloquence flourished " and subsequently studying in Alexandria and Athens. He was not baptised until he was nearly thirty years of age but from that time became an ardent earnest religious student. He was his father's coadjutor and in 362 succeeded him in his bishopric. Later in life he lived on a small estate and it was here we find him in a new rôle which gives him still another claim for being honoured. For it was here he wrote those hymns and lyrics which place his name among the very earliest of the Christian poets. These poetic effusions are like his other writings of more than usual merit and express his naturally intense imaginative nature. His death took place May 9th, but whether in 389 or 390 some doubt exists.

As a writer and chronicler he has ever been regarded as one of the most reliable of those who left on record the history of the Church during his day, as well as for the beauty of his diction.

MAY 10th.

I think I am not far astray when I say that outside of the clerics of the Roman Church certain antiquarians, archæologists and a limited class of ardent delving students only a few general readers are aware how far in advance in all educational matters many of the Irish clergy were — from the V. to the VIII. centuries — of the best educated men in or out of the church in ancient Britain ; or what grand schools of learning — for their day and generations those old Irish monastic schools were.

Indeed those of Germany, Italy and Greece were by no means so far in advance of them as we would at first suppose. One of the most noted of these educational centers was the Monastery Cluain-Aidhnech at the foot of the Bladma hills from which rise the two rivers Barrow and Nore in Queen's county. It was here St. Comgall whose festival is celebrated this day, an Ulster born man, was trained under that celebrated teacher, St. Finian, becoming by 550 one of the most accomplished men of his age there to found the great abbey of Benchor or Bangor, county Down which in its turn became another remarkable school of learning, and made St. Comgall's name famous. He later founded another monastery called Cell-Comgail now called Saynkille and attached to the archbishopic of Dublin. Comgall died May 10th, 601.

MAY 11th.

The Sunday intervening between Ascension Day and Whitsunday is termed

SUNDAY IN THE OCTAVE OF ASCENSION.

Roman Martyrology records that on this day is celebrated: "At Rome on the Salarian road the birthday of the blessed Anthimus, a priest who after having distinguished himself by his virtues and preaching, was cast into the Tiber during the persecutions of Diocletian. He was rescued by an angel and restored to his oratory;" but later was decapitated.

This day is also marked as the festival of St. Mammertus, Archbishop of Vienne, whose memory is highly venerated by the Church both for his sanctity and learning and for having instituted the three days Latines immediately before the Ascension of our Lord; and for the many miracles he performed such as the staying of the great fire by his prayers and which had baffled the efforts of men and seemed destined to destroy his city, when the archbishop took his place at the altar and ceased not his supplications until his prayers were answered. His faith in the efficacy of fasting and prayer, never for an instant failed him and this it was which led him to institute the Rogation Days. The mass and lessons appointed for these days in Gaul, are still preserved in the ancient Gallican liturgy. He was an author also of a number of noted theological works. One "On Nature and the Soul," alone would keep his memory green.

St. Francis di Girolamo who is also remembered on this day was the famous Jesuit pulpit orator of Naples; a volume would hardly suffice to record the wonderful effect of his eloquence. "His voice" says Butler "was loud and sonorous, * * * and the style of his preaching simple and impressive. * * * His descriptions forcible and graphic and his pathetic appeals were sure to draw tears while his energy astounded and terrified," yet there must have been much of the magnetism of the popular orator in his manner for whenever he spoke whether in the streets of Naples — a constant habit of his — or in the church great crowds followed him and not a few of the sudden conversions made by him of hardened sinners sound like the records of some modern "Revivalist" preachers.

He was an earnest untiring faithful worker to the very last. Born in 1642, at a very early age he became a prefect in the "College of Nobles of the Society of Jesus" and soon after his novitiate was completed took high rank in the society. It was as a preacher and evangelist that he excelled. He died May 11th, 1716. Was beatified by Pius VII. on the feast of St. Joseph in 1806, and canonized by Gregory XVI., on Trinity Sunday 1839.

MAY 12th.

On this day the "boy martyr" St. Pancras is honoured by the Church and one of the most famous churches in London was erected in his honour. Mrs. Jameson in her "Sacred and Legendary Art" sums the brief story of this youth so well that I quote it verbatim.

"In the persecution under Diocletian this young saint who was only fourteen years of age offered himself voluntarily as a martyr, defending boldly before the emperor the cause of the Christians. He was therefore beheaded by the sword and his body was honourably buried by Christian women. His church near the gate of St. Pancrazio has existed since the year 500. St. Pancras was in the middle ages regarded as the protector against false oaths and the avenger of perjury. It was believed that those who swore falsely by St. Pancras were immediately and visibly punished, hence his popularity."

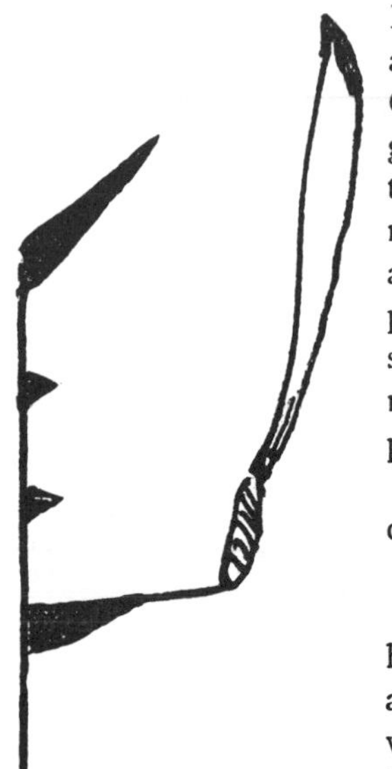

The Danish Clog Almanac marks the day as in illustration by a sword.

A somewhat peculiar trio are also honoured this day. St. Flavia Domitilla, and SS. Nereus and Achilleus (brothers) who were eunuchs or chamberlains to Flavius Clemens her uncle and herself. These latter were members of the imperial family, but because of their faith as Christians they were banished to Pontia, by Emperor Domitian. But prior to this the uncle had suffered martyrdom. The faithful eunuchs accompanied St. Flavia Domitilla in her exile. Her legend says she with Nereus and Achilleus returned to Terracina where under Trajan she was burned at the stake for refusing to sacrifice to idols. The legend of her eunuchs says they were beheaded by order of Domitian because they had persuaded Flavia not to marry Aurelian the son of the consul to whom she was betrothed because he was an idolator. Both legends may easily be true and not conflict.

Some of my readers will recall a most interesting little church, SS. Nereo and Achilleo near the baths of Caracalla. Tradition says that when St. Peter was going to execution he dropped here one of the bandages of his wounds. The watchful Christians marked the spot and an "oratory" was built which bore the name of Fasciola and later it became a small church, and in 524 the relics of the two brothers were transferred thither from Terracina by John I. and in 795 the building was restored by Leo III. and enlarged. Again in the sixteenth century Cardinal Baronius who took his title from hence, rebuilt the church as we now know it.

MAY 13th.

In A. D. 399 the Pantheon, a temple dedicated to the Roman gods was closed by order of Emperor Honorius. By permission of Emperor Phocos, Pope Boniface IV. rebuilt the Pantheon as a Christian church and in so doing preserved many of the architectural features of the old temple. Its dedication as a Christian church in 608 to the honour of the Virgin is especially observed this day in Rome. The story of the Pantheon is a very interesting one and is told in all the guide books to Rome.

MAY 14th

Is the festival of St. John "The Silent," a surname given him for his almost utter silence at all times and under every provocation to speech. Yet of him it was truthfully said, that while he was earnest and fervent in prayer, he was never slothful in business, his duties were each and all so carefully and faithfully fulfilled. One of those rare characters who have but little to say but who are always prompt to act; because they have thought rather than spoken much. When he did speak it was simply and to the point, and with a degree of wisdom that seemed inspired. Naturally a man of this character was one to be brought forward even if, as was the case with our saint, he was reluctant. Therefore in 482 when he was but twenty-eight years of age he, we may say, was driven from his retreat by the Archbishop of Sebaste to become Bishop of Coloman in Armenia. But the position was no bed of down for many reasons. The principal one being that John's brother-in-law who was then governor of Armenia, was so offensive to the Church that he was compelled to appeal to the Emperor Zeno for help. Yet for nine years he fulfilled faithfully his duties. Then he was permitted to retire to a "Laura" (an hermitage attached to or adjacent to some monastery. A sort of outlying house under the supervision of some holy man; and usually devoted to novices before their admission to the monasteries proper) — where for three years he lived in retirement. Then when promotion was again forced upon him he refused and from that time spent forty years in eremitical life save when instructing those who sought him, until he passed to the blessed company above soon after 558.

MAY 15th.

To anyone who takes an interest in hagiology there are two books to which they can turn with perfect confidence that every statement is founded on fact. One of these is the "Acta Sanctorum" and Alban Butler's "Lives of the Saints," is the other. Few laymen, I fancy, ever waded through the sixty ponderous folios of the former, but many have and will read the latter and not a few of the facts given in this series of articles are gleaned from this invaluable book; therefore it is eminently proper that his name be mentioned on this anniversary of his death, which occurred in 1773.

This ardent student devoted thirty years of his life to this work and even the cynic Gibbon is compelled to say of it: "It is a work of merit; the sense and the learning belong to the author — his prejudices are those of his profession." Yet no candid reader can fail to see how careful he has been to verify his every word.

In the Kalendar for this day are the names of SS. Peter, Andrew and their companions. Theirs is only the oft repeated story of the persecution of Christians in those early days yet in it is the material for a romance.

In the persecutions of Decius near Lampsacus, a city of Lesser Asia near the Hellespont, a young man called Peter remarkable for his beauty of person and endowments of mind was captured and by order of Optimus broken on a wheel. Thc proconsul was just setting out for Troas, a city in Phrygia when three other young men named Andrew, Paul and Nicomachus were brought before him and on confession that they also were Christians, were ordered to sacrifice to the goddess Venus. On their refusal they too were condemned to the rack. One of these, Nicomachus when put to torture recanted, and offered to sacrifice to the gods. But the legend tells us no sooner had he done so "than the Devil seized him and beat his head on the ground until he expired." Among those who witnessed this was a young virgin named Denysa who called out to Optimus: "Unfortunate wretch! Wouldst thou bring upon thyself eternal torments for the sake of a moment's ease?" Confessing that she also was a Christian the proconsul gave orders — a thing then by no means uncommon — for her punishment, in a manner that death would have been a boon instead of it for she was given to two young men to be "deprived" of her virtue. But such strength was given her that she was able to resist them until about midnight when "an angel glittering with light" appeared to rescue her and the young men overcome with fear fell before the apparition and besought mercy. The next morning the mob stirred by the priests of Diana were still calling for Andrew and Paul but when Optimus ordered them to be brought forth Denysa came with them crying: "That I may live with you eternally in heaven I will die with you now on earth." But she was taken from them and later the two martyrs Andrew and Paul were beheaded in some obscure place. The legend is silent as to the fate of the damsel Denysa.

MAY 16th.

The legend of St. John of Nepomucen or Nepomuc, canon of the Metropolitan Church and martyr, whose memory is honoured on this day is somewhat out of the customary order, since it is an evidence of the sanctity in which "the Confession" has at all times been held by the Roman Church. He was born in 1330, in

Nepomuc near Prague and educated at the University of that city which had been founded in 1356 by Charles IV., Emperor of Germany and King of Bohemia, and here St. John distinguished himself in philosophy, divinity and canon law and was also devoted to music. When he was preferred to his Canonry his attendance

in the choir did not hinder his zeal for the cause of souls. A bit of history is needed here to understand what is to follow. The Emperor Charles IV. was renowned for his wisdom and piety, neither of which his son Wenceslas inherited, instead he won for himself the infamous surname of "the Slothful" and "the Drunkard." Wenceslas had through the influence and largess of his father been in 1376 — when he was but sixteen years old — chosen by the electors as King of Rome. Later he had married the good and beautiful Princess Joan of Bavaria, daughter of Albert of Bavaria, Earl of Hainault and Holland. John of Nepomuc became her confessor. Wenceslas curious to know the secrets of his wife and utterly unmindful of the seal of confidence under which they had been confided to her confessor ordered him to disclose them. In his anger at being refused the tyrant directed he should be imprisoned in a dungeon and then tortured until he obeyed. The inhuman sufferings which John endured could not be believed if they were not proven by evidence that is beyond doubt. At last by the intercession of the Empress Joan when John was "half dead," he was released and by her majesty's own hands nursed back to life. But it was only for a time that the saint was left in peace for when Wenceslas again demanded of him to reveal the secrets of the confessional and again refused, the emperor in his anger ordered him bound and thrown into the river Muldaw from the bridge that joins the "Great and Little Prague." This occurred on the "Vigil of the Ascension" on May 16th, 1383. The legend tells of five bright stars which appeared in the sky at that moment where an instant before all had been utter darkness. In Christian art, therefore, five stars appear as the attribute of St. John of

Nepomuc; but the Clog symbol is a "pandean pipe;" doubtless referring to his love of music.

Of St. Brendan whose name appears in the Kalendar of this day the first mention we have is as a child under the tuition of St. Itha or Ita, a protégé of St. Erc. This noted woman who will be duly mentioned later is also named as the "foster-mother" of SS. Pulcherius and Cumine, seemingly was what we in later days would term the keeper of the "Dames School;" though when Brendan was committed to her care he was only a year old and remained under her care until he was five years of age. How precocious he was may be judged from the question he once asked: "What were the works in her opinion, most pleasing to God?"

"Faith out of a pure heart, sincerity of life and tender charity," was her reply.

"And what," he then asked "are most displeasing to God?"

"A spiteful tongue, a love of what smacks of evil and avarice," was her answer.

On leaving Itha Brendan for a time was under the care of Erc, Bishop of Slane, and afterward at the celebrated monastic school of Finan of Clonard while he finally founded the monastery of Clonfert.

It was natural in those early days of the Church that North Britain and the islands which lay between it and Ireland should attract missionaries to their shores. When on June 9th I speak of St. Columba I shall enter more fully on this subject in connection with the life of Columba. But among the earliest to give practical aid to such missionaries was Brendan of Clonfert.

It is at this point one of the strangest legends told of any of the canonized saints comes in since it reads like a fairy story or some of the voyages of Sinbad when St. Brendan sailed away from Ireland to find the paradise of Adam and Eve. As it fills one hundred and fifty pages I can hardly tell the story of how he and his companions after forty days and forty nights of sailing first came to the fair "Island of Sheep," where the sheep were as big as oxen and where it was never cold and the pastures ever green, how from there they went on to the "Paradise of Birds" and later to an island inhabited by devils until after seven years they found the looked for island and then they returned to Ireland. The legend is full of fabulous stories of conversation with birds, of their landing on the back of a great fish that they mistook for land and how when they built a fire on it the creature moved away and they fled to their ship in fright where St. Brendan comforted them by explaining: "That it was a great fish named Jason which laboured day and night trying to put its tail in its mouth but could not on account of its size."

The narrative of this seven-year voyage of St. Brendan and his fourteen monks who accompanied him was one of the popular "folk-lore tales" of the Middle Ages, and many editions of it are now extant. But at best it is only regarded as a romance, or a monkish dream of an imaginary voyage to some unknown regions. Still it must have had some historic foundation, of some journey of the real Brendan in his effort to extend, by missionary work the borders of the Christian Church. And further evidence of this is found in the expeditions sent out by the Spaniards to discover St. Brendan's island even as late as in 1721 the date when the last one was undertaken. Indeed there are many indications that Brendan did make some such voyage; for Fordun (the Anglo-Saxon historian) tells us that after his return from it he went to Britain to visit St. Gildas and afterward he went to the Western Isles and established monasteries "at Ailech and Heth." Of the latter Skeen says: "This land of Heth we now know to have been the Island of Tyree." Fordun also speaks of Brendan in the Island of Bute.

St. Brendan was one of St. Finan's "Twelve Apostles of Ireland."

MAY 17th.

In the reign of Valerianus who died 269 St. Restituta's name appears as one of the martyrs to the Christian faith in Africa. The fiendish ingenuity of those early Roman officials in seeking out means of torture for their victims seems beyond belief. This virtuous Christian woman, after she had endured every kind of indignity and suffering to induce her to abjure her faith under orders of Proculus was placed in a boat and bound so that she could not escape. Then the boat was filled with pitch and tow mixed and it was later taken out to sea where the pitch was set fire to and the poor woman abandoned to her fate. The skiff or boat burned to the water's edge and with the charred remains of St. Restituta, drifted to the island of Ischia, near Naples where the relics of the martyr fell into Christian hands and were reverently cared for.

Verily in those early days it required much courage to be a Christian.

MAY 18th.

As a movable feast, the date of Whitsunday is dependent upon that of Easter.

WHITSUNDAY.

THE FEAST OF PENTECOST.

Whitsunday is the third of the three greater festivals celebrated by the Christian Church and commemorates the descent of the Holy Ghost on the apostles "when they were all with one accord in one place" after the Ascension of our Lord, and when they received the gift of tongues. As this event occurred on the day of Pentecost, Whitsunday is naturally associated with the great Jewish festival held, as the name denotes fifty days after the feast of unleavened bread. A coincidence which connects the two days in our memory. The rabbinical account of this event is an ample reason for both its celebration and the importance given to it. It is a remarkable fact that in the languages peculiar to Western Europe this day seems to have had no particular name, and the English word "Whitsunday" it is said was derived from some of the characteristics of the early Roman ceremonies on the day. This fact seems more singular as Pentecost in mediaeval Western Europe was such a marked day. In the Middle Ages a great wax candle was then blessed and was supposed to be emblematic of the light of faith shown forth upon the world. Numerous ceremonies then in vogue have now passed into desuetude, especially in the English church. One of these strikes us as peculiarly unaccountable, the distribution by the church of "Whitsun ale." Yet the accounts of the church wardens of the seventeenth century show many entries where they paid for "Whitsun ale." The best explanation I have found for it is that it was a survival of the ancient Agape, or "love feast," which early Christians indulged in.

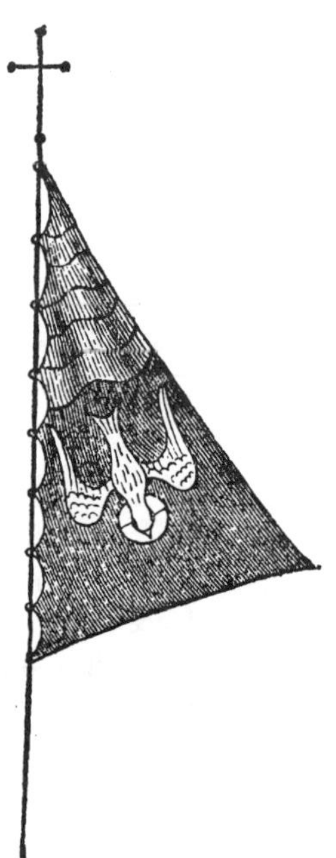

A dove descending from Heaven was the emblem of the descent of the Holy Ghost adopted by the church. The illustration is taken from a banner used at Whitsuntide in a Dorsetshire church during the seventeenth century. A dove was often suspended above an image of Christ on Whitsunday.

The canonical colour for Whitsunday is red. While this colour signifies divine love and royal dignity as well as blood, war and suffering, being thus emblematic of martyrs, it also according to Dr. Nicholas Gihr a recognised authority in such matters symbolises "that burning glowing love which is enkindled in the hearts of the faithful through the Holy Spirit, that self-sacrificing triumphant love which in martyrdom makes an offering of the greatest and dearest earthly good—even life itself. (Song of Solomon, viii. 6)." Thus on Whitsunday red symbolises the fiery tongues that came upon the apostles (Acts ii. 6), typifying that the apostles should be eloquent in words, fervent in charity. "This also," says another eminent scholar, "is the birthday of the church fructified by the blood of

Christ and the martyrs." I have been thus explicit because others like myself may have found it difficult to reconcile the canonical colour of this day with the recognised emblematical colour of suffering and martyrdom.

MAY 19th.

Of the entire list of saints whose names appear in the Kalendar of the Church, there is no one who from the different standpoints from which he has been judged, is so misunderstood as St. Dunstan. He has received such unstinted adulation that at times they bordered on the ridiculous from the ill-advised admiration of his friends; while from malevolent critics he has been pictured as not only bigoted but as utterly unscrupulous in the use of any means to gain his end that both in their extreme views are not only wrong but most unjust. That St. Dunstan was one of those remarkable men who stamp their own character on the age they live in is beyond question but that he has also like others suffered from this may be seen by any who take the trouble to study the man from an honest point of view.

ST. DUNSTAN AND THE DEVIL.

Dunstan was born in the isle of Glastonbury in 924 or 5 (dates conflict on this point) and was of noble and even royal descent. Glastonbury has always been regarded as a sacred spot. It was there King Arthur was buried and legends tell us that it was there also that Joseph of Arimathea found his final resting place on earth and that St. Patrick, the Apostle of Ireland, was buried; one of the many places assigned him as his last resting place. Here in Dunstan's youth there was a famous monastery where many Irish monks of learning resided. It was within this abbey that Kings Arthur and Edgar were buried, as well as many nobles of ancient Britain; and it is said that its last abbot was hanged, because he refused to surrender the abbey to Henry VIII. but amid the ruins the chapel of St. Joseph and the abbot's kitchen now alone can now be seen.

It was in this monastic school young Dunstan received his early education. While somewhat delicate in his bodily health he early displayed a "giant mind" far out-stripping his companions, his special studies beside Scriptural history being arithmetic, geometry, astronomy and music; but at the same time developing wonderful skill in drawing, illumination and sculpture.

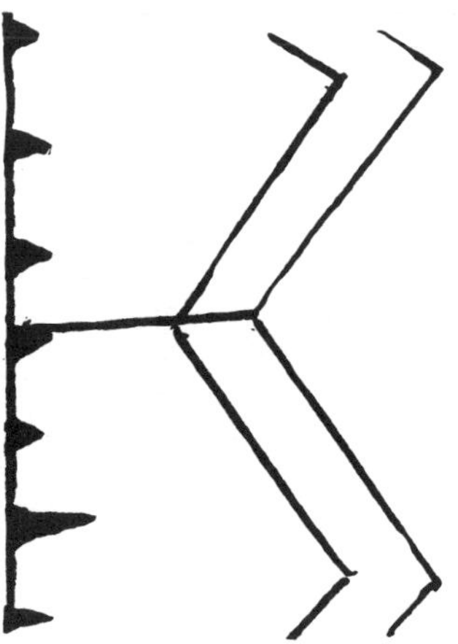

He also spent some time at the monastery of Fleury in France. As a sort of amusement he became an expert worker in metals, silver, copper, iron and brass, and in his cell at Glastonbury he set up a forge in addition to the usual appointments of a monastic cell.

He at an early age went to the Court of Athelston and later became a great friend and favourite with Kings Athelston, Edmund and Edred, as they succeeded each other, his influence over the latter being so great that Dunstan was accused by the courtiers with sorcery. One great aim Dunstan had was to establish the Benedictine rule in all English monasteries and he was therefore regarded as the father of the English Benedictines. During Edred's reign the power of Dunstan was almost supreme. With Edred's death came a change the kingdom being ruled by his profligate son, Edwy. The romantic story of Edwy and Elgiva needs no repetition here; beyond recalling that it was Dunstan's frank condemnation and remonstrance with Edwy for his shameless life that brought about the prelate's banishment from court, to Glastonbury where he erected the famous cell with its oratory, and in which occurred the temptations of the devil that gave rise to the often repeated legend. Shorn of its romantic details the legend tells us that the devil sought out St. Dunstan in his cell to lure him into sin. To effect this purpose the devil had assumed the likeness of a beautiful woman and came on St. Dunstan at a time when he was working at his forge. The saint at once detected the imposition and taking a pair of red-hot tongs from the forge seized him with them by the nose, which caused the devil to appear in his true character. The picture of this scene as shown above is from a window in the Bodleian library. With the death of Edwy his brother Edgar became king and Dunstan was restored to favour. Edgar made him successively Bishop of Worcester, London, and later Archbishop of Canterbury. Over the last he presided for twenty-seven years, and was a great promoter of ecclesiastical law and discipline as well as a patron of useful and fine arts; and his almost contemporary biographers say he was a fine musician, an architect and painter of great ability and wonderfully skilled in working metals of all kinds.

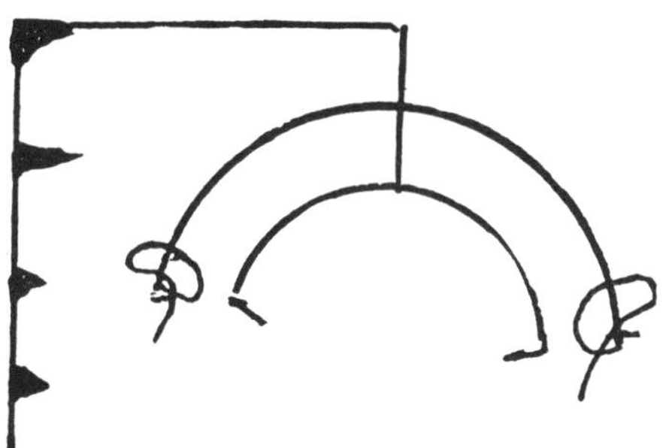

To attempt to recount the legends told of St. Dunstan one would need a small volume; while his life as told by Butler in plain, simple words leaves no doubt of his purity of life, his earnest efforts to lead all who came under his influence in the paths of peace and virtue. A truly holy and good man whose aim was ever for the good of his people and by his own life and example to teach them. In A. D. 960 he went to Rome and as Primate of the Anglo-Saxon nation received great honours. He died on May 19th, 988. The Clog Almanacs give St. Dunstan several emblems. The two given above are from English sticks and are very puzzling to know just what they intend to represent. The last is a Danish one and easily understood as the "tongs" which are regarded as St. Dunstan's proper emblems.

The origin of the Abbey of Glastonbury is lost in antiquity and I can only give the legend as it runs which is that when the Apostle Philip came to France he sent Joseph of Arimathea with eleven disciples to Britain. Arviragus, King of Britain, (said to have died in A. D. 74) was so pleased and so enchanted by the beauty of their lives and the courage which had brought them through the dangers of their journey from Palestine that he gave them the island of Avelon, as Glastonbury was then called. Here he built a church with "wattled walls" — that is by placing two rows of upright stakes, twining willow or other flexible branches between the stakes, and filling the intervening space with adobe, or earth — and they then began to live and preach as Christ had set the example. They made a few converts only at first. During the Danish invasion King Alfred found here a refuge. It was here too, so the legend runs, "the mystic thorn" first bloomed on the feast of the Nativity and that Joseph of Arimathea came to Avelon in the fifteenth year after the Assumption of the Virgin Mary. It was from this small beginning the monastery of Glastonbury at last came into existence.

This day is also the festival of SS. Prassede and Pudenziana, sisters, daughters of St. Pudens and his wife, Claudia, with whom SS. Peter and Paul lodged in Rome, and all were among the early converts. Pudens was a patrician of great wealth, with houses and public baths at the foot of the Esquiline. The first of these sisters, Prassede, died on July 21st, A. D. 146, and the last named May 19th, A. D. 148. They were not martyrs but their story is one which shows the true devotion of those early Christains. By the death of their parents and an only brother these noble women had inherited the wealth of the family. It was just then that the earliest persecutions of Christians began and the sisters resolved to devote their wealth and lives to aid the sufferers. They nursed the wounded, visited those in prison and buried the dead; aided by a holy man named Pastorus. So tender was the care they showed these martyrs that it is said they soaked up their blood on sponges and hid them in a well in their home. Pudenziana after her sister's death gave shelter in her house to a number of persecuted Christians, twenty-three of whom were discovered and martyred in her presence. She then buried their bodies in the catacombs of her grandmother, Sta. Priscilla, but collecting their blood in a sponge, placed it in a well in her own house, where she herself was afterwards buried. An oratory is said to have been erected on the site by Pius I., A. D. 160, and was certainly in existence in A. D. 499, when it is mentioned in the acts of a council. In A. D. 822 the original church was destroyed and the present church erected by Paschal I., of whose time are the low tower, the porch, the terra-cotta cornices and the mosaics. During the absence of the Popes at Avignon, St. Prassede was one of the many churches which fell almost to ruin and it has since suffered terribly from injudicious modernizations first in the fifteenth century from Rosellini, under Nicholas V., and afterwards under St. Carlo Borromeo in 1564.

This is one of the most interesting churches in Rome to-day. A mosaic in the pavement marks the grave of forty martyrs whose remains Paschal I. collected. Take down your "Walks in Rome," or any guide book of Rome, and you will be amply repaid your time in reading of its beauties, but this is not the place to repeat them.

MAY 20th.

St. Ethelbert, King of the East-Angles, is honoured in Roman Martyrology on this day as a martyr. That he was a Christian ruler we have ample evidence but his death was rather a base piece of treachery on the part of Quendreda, wife of Offa, King of the Mercias, when Ethelbert was on a visit to Offa to solicit the hand of his daughter, Alfreda, in marriage.

On this day also the Church recognises St. Bernardino of Siena, a saint celebrated alike for his devotion to the poor and afflicted and his rare learning and valuable writings upon prayer, Divine love, etc., and a " Life of Christ." It was this man who instituted the " Monte de Piete " in France, the original of the modern pawnshop. He died May 20th, 1444.

MAY 21st

Is the festival of St. Felix of Cantalicio, a native of Cittas Ducale in Umbria, a Capuchin monk, who spent his life in begging bread and wine for his fellow monks, and so successfully that never during his life was there a lack of either among his brotherhood. Many miracles were ascribed to him and he foretold the time of his own death. He was beatified by Urban VIII. in 1625, canonized by Clement XI. in 1721, though the bull of his canonization was only published by Benedict XIII. in 1724. He was the first of the Capuchins who was canonized.

The Clog symbol for this saint is a beggar's scrip, and always open.

MAY 22d.

That the two names given in the Kalendar of B.Yvo on the 21st and St. Yvo on the 22d shall not be confused, I need only call attention to the two dates; the first in 1115 and the last in 1353.

The first was connected with the monastery of the Regular Canons of St Austin's order, the last named being from Treguier in Brittany. A scholar of great parts, he was selected as official or ecclesiastical judge of Rennes. He is reputed to have protected the widows and orphans, to have defended the poor and administered justice with an impartial hand. His charities were only limited by his means. He built a hospital for the sick poor near his own house and devoted much of his time to personally caring for its inmates. The Bretons founded a collegiate church at Paris in 1348 to honour his memory.

MAY 23d.

EMBER DAYS.

The term Ember, it is said, was derived from the Saxon Embren or imb-ryne, denoting a course, or circuit, as these days occur at stated periods in the four quarters of the year. Another and fairly plausible theory is that it came from the early practice of sprinkling ashes on the head on fast days in token of humility, and from the custom on these days of eating only cakes baked upon embers and termed "ember-bread."

These ember-days or periodical fasts were, it is said, instituted by Pope Calixtus I. (219–22), to implore the blessing of God on the products of the earth. It was not until the Council of Placentia in A. D. 1095 that any uniformity in the dates for observing these fasts was determined on. Then the first Wednesday, Friday and Saturday following respectively the first Sunday in Lent, Quadragesima Sunday, Whitsunday, Holyrood day (the 14th of September) and St. Lucy's day (the 13th of December), the days observed at the present time, were chosen. The weeks when these days occur are termed "ember weeks" and in the Roman ritual the "ember days" are denominated "Jejunia quatuor temporum," or the fasts of the four seasons.

The Clog Almanac symbol is repeated in each of the four quarters. But I find none for these days upon any English Clog sticks.

This day, May 23d, is the festival of St. Julia, one of those virgin martyrs of ancient days of whom Christian women may well be proud. She was a Carthagenian who was captured when Genseric (or as some historians name him "Genzric") the Vandal King of Spain (425–455) in one of his incursions took Carthage in 439. She was sold as a slave to a pagan merchant of Syria. But being a Christian she held herself true to her faith, though faithful and obedient to her master. Her unswerving fidelity in all things and especially to her religion added to her virtues of many kinds won even from this pagan respect and trust, such as was seldom then accorded to one in her station. Therefore he treated her kindly and permitted her daily devotions. The merchant was a man engaged in commerce with many lands; and upon an occasion in about the year 445, when business took him upon a journey to Gaul, he elected that the slave Julia should be one of his suite to attend upon him and his family on the journey. The merchant was a most upright man who in addition to his tolerance of Julia's religion, had also respected her virtue and had never offered her any indignity.

On their arrival on the northern coast of Corsica, now called Capo-Corso, an idolatrous festival was in progress in which the sacrifice of a bull was one of its features. For the purpose of joining in these pagan rites the merchant and suite landed; but Julia was at her request left behind as she could not even by her unwilling presence recognise such rites. Indeed, she had openly reviled them to her fellow slaves.

Felix, the pagan Governor of Corsica, received the merchant with honour; but had noticed Julia as left behind and soon asked: "Who this woman was who thus dared to insult their gods?"

Eusebius, the merchant, told her story. Then the governor offered to buy her by giving four of his finest female slaves in exchange; but the merchant replied:—"No! all you are worth would not purchase her for I would freely lose the most valuable thing I have in the world rather than be deprived of her."

But Felix was both cunning and determined upon his purpose and resorted to the means so often used, by plying Eusebius with the wine-cup until he was drunk. Even then until he fell asleep the merchant was obdurate. Then, while he was in his stupor, Felix had Julia brought to him and strove to compel her to sacrifice, to the pagan gods. But in vain. Then he promised her liberty; but she told him she was " free " while she served Jesus Christ. In his rage the Governor ordered Julia to be hanged on a cross, and the hair torn from her head.

Thus it was the Carthagenian slave won her martyr's crown.

In 763 monks from the isle of Gorgon, now called " La Gorgona," lying between Corsica and Leghorn rescued her relics and by the order of Desiderius, King of Lombardy, they were deposited in Brescia where to-day her memory is celebrated with the utmost reverence.

MAY 24th

Is the festival of St. Vincent of Lerins; whose " *Commonitorium Adversus Hereticos* " has come down to us from A. D. 434 when it was written; and curiously some half century or so since, republished with an ENGLISH preface utilized by Dr. Alban Butler in his " Lives of the Saints," with others when he speaks of this saint.

Vincent was an officer in the Roman Army, of "Gaulish extraction," and for a long time was in active service before he began to consider seriously religious matters. When he did so he resolved to make thorough work of it. The camp, forum, or the busy city, teeming with incidents and interests of every-day life, he felt were no place for him to carry out his purpose, where ephemeral matters dominated; and no better evidence is needed to prove how sincere he was than his acts. For resigning his position as an officer he sought a place of retirement where he could work out the problem of life, selecting the smaller of the two islands which formerly bore the name of "the Lerins," to which he retired. It was here after careful study of the Holy Scriptures and with a thorough knowledge of the trend of the religious beliefs of his day that three years after the celebrated Council of Ephesus (in 431) he wrote a book in support of the decision of that Council condemning the Nestorian heresy. He entitled it "A Commonitory against Heretics"; aimed especially against Nestorians and "the Apollinarists." He disguised his identity under the name of Peregrinus; as a pilgrim or stranger who is separated from the world, his principal point being: "That all novelty in faith is a mark of heresy" when it steps aside from the traditions of the Apostles as expounded in the Holy Scriptures.

From the verdict of others his style of diction seems to have been peculiarly elegant and his logic "clear and close."

St. Vincent was never in Holy Orders though living an eremitical life and died in his retirement during the reigns of Theodosius II. "or Valentinian III." and therefore before the close of the year 456.

MAY 25th.

TRINITY SUNDAY.

The mystery of the Holy Trinity has been celebrated by the Church from very ancient days but its observance as a festival was first introduced into England by Thomas à Becket toward the close of the XII. century.

The earliest attempt at representing the Trinity by means of some symbol began in the earliest days of the Christian Church as is seen by the relics preserved from the catacombs about Rome. Here we find them the most prominent. The simple triangle; a combination of three fishes, heads and tails crossing so as to form a triangle or these circles interwoven into the semblance of a triangle. In fact, the equilateral triangle was the first accepted symbol of the Trinity. The beautiful symbol of the shamrock leaf so often used had its origin with St. Patrick, Bishop of Armagh and patron saint of Ireland who died A. D. 466. The good bishop was preaching as he often did in the open air and trying to illustrate the unity in Trinity. He read in the faces of his hearers the fact that they did not, nay could not comprehend such unity and equality. He was at a loss to know how to make it clear to these dull, simple folk. Just then he cast his eye upon the ground and saw at his feet the three-leaved shamrock. He plucked it and held it before his audience. The mystery was solved; here was the "three in one." This these simple-minded folk at once understood and from that time the shamrock became a symbol of the Holy Trinity. If, however, my reader will turn back to March 12th he will find more regarding this matter.

Drawn from a XV. Century MS.

When first the early Christians sought for some symbol for God the Almighty, they used a hand projecting from a cloud, later part of the arm and then the bust was shown. Somewhere in the V. century, the hand was displaced for a face in the cloud, but it was not until the latter part of the XI. or early in the XII. century that God was first represented in human form. Not so with Jesus Christ. Almost from the first He is represented in human form, while from the earliest days a dove had been the favourite symbol for the Holy Ghost. When at first Christian artists endeavoured to represent the Holy Trinity, God the Father and God the Son were shown as men, the Holy Ghost was shown by the symbol of the dove. But strangely for a long time, God the Father and Jesus Christ were identical in feature. Towards the end of the XIII. century the incongruity of this duality broke on the minds of the artists and from thence (as shown in the following illustration), an effort was made to show the Father as an old man and later, as is seen in the first illustration, by giving Him some outward sign of supremacy. Thus sometimes he wears the triple crown, again he bears in his hand a globe (the earth) surmounted by a cross. This history is too long to be elaborated here and I must not attempt it. Still later, artists again sought to be more explicit and evolved a symbol that embodied the thought, as shown in the Anagram copied here which also exemplifies the Athanasian creed.

The Trinity, each Person wearing the Cruciform Nimbus, 13th Century.

To be made a Pope against one's will sounds a little strange, yet such was the case with Hildebrand, afterward Gregory V. whose name is honoured on this 25th day of May. He was a man of great learning and highly esteemed by Pope Leo IX. who often consulted him. In 1073, on the death of Alexander II., Hildebrand was chosen to fill St. Peter's chair entirely against his will. "He left nothing unattempted to keep that heavy burden from his shoulders and among other expedients he wrote Henry IV., King of Germany, who was then in Bavaria, to interfere" but it was unavailing.

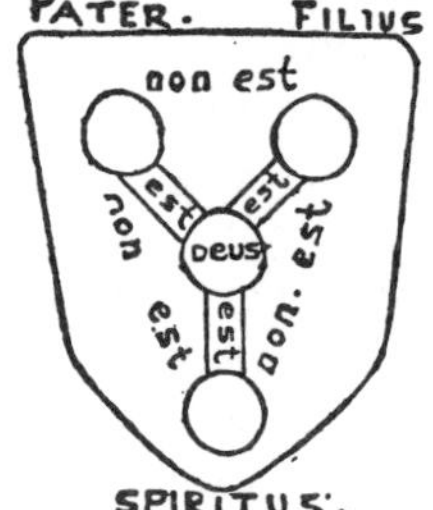

Gregory must have had a premonition of the stormy times that awaited him in his new office for he was a man of very determined character. Just then "simony," or the buying and selling of ecclesiastical preferments, was sadly common and this Gregory abhorred from his soul, and one of his first acts was to depose Godfrey, Archbishop of Milan for such a crime, and thus brought down a storm upon himself. Indeed, the whole of the twelve years he filled the pontifical chair was a continued struggle against evil and wrong in the Church even to the last, and he gladly answered the call of the Great Master when in 1085 he was called higher. His letters have been the admiration of many who have read them. "They are penned with great eloquence * * * and we boldly say no Pope since Gregory I. wrote such strong and firm letters as this Gregory did," is what Dr. Butler writes of him.

MAY 26th.

POPE GREGORY, THE GREAT.

Some thirteen hundred years ago a group of captives, women and children attracted the attention of Gregory (afterward Pope Gregory I. known as "the Great"), a monk from the monastery of St. Andrew at Rome, and he asked what nation they belonged to. The reply was "they are Angles." "And," replied the monk, "rightly so called for they have the faces of Angels, and ought to be our fellow heirs of heaven."

This no doubt lingered in the mind of Gregory and when he became Pope and saw a favourable opportunity he resolved to send missionaries to Britain. Remembering his old convent on the Cœlian Mount, and its prior, St. Augustine — whose name, both as a saint and the "Apostle of the English" is honoured this day — he selected this faithful man with a company of forty monks from the monastery and sent them forth to the pagans of Britain. Ethelbert, the Saxon King of Kent, had married Bertha, daughter of Charibut, King of Paris, a Christian. She had brought with her a French priest, Luidhard, as her chaplain, and their capital was Canterbury on the island of Thanet, for at that time an arm of the sea surrounded it. Ethelbert was still a pagan in spite of his marriage with a Christian; yet this latter fact induced Augustine to choose Thanet as the safest place for him to land.

It must have been a picturesque sight that first meeting between the Saxon king and the missionaries. "The son of the ash-tree" and his pagan warriors in one group, and the Italian prior and his fellow monks in cassock and cowl, with their white-robed choristers around them. After a long interview Ethelbert consented to the prior and his fellow monks residing for a time in Canterbury, and the strange sight was witnessed of a procession of monks headed by one carrying a silver cross on which was painted an image of our Saviour, followed by the choristers singing one of those grand Gregorian chants.

On the following Whitsunday, June 2, 597, Ethelbert was baptised; perhaps except the baptisms of Floric and Constantine, the most important baptism of a monarch that has ever taken place in its ultimate influence on the history of the Christian Church.

ST. AUGUSTINE.

In these brief sketches we cannot follow Augustine through his long and varied experiences. In 597 he was consecrated "Bishop of the English" and fixed his see at Canterbury. He died in 604, but before that had consecrated bishops to London and Rochester and laid the foundation for the Christian Church in England. Bede calls St. Augustine "the beloved of God" and Capgrave describes him as: "Tall of statue, of a dark complexion, his face beautiful, but withal majestic." He is represented usually wearing the Benedictine habit as in the illustration given above, which is copied from an Harlien Mass.

On this day also is held the festival of St. Philip Neri, the founder of the Order of Oratorians. A Florentine, born in 1515, he by his intellect, eloquence and purity of life became a leader in the religious movements of his day. He was ever employed in charity and gathered round him a company of young nobles and men of learned professions, who went about reading with and caring for the sick and needy. They were bound by no vows nor secluded from the world. They simply did what their hands found to do, in love and charity. They called themselves Oratorians, and from them sprang a similar order termed "Peres de l'Oratoire of France" and the "Oratorians of England," of whom Cardinal Newman and the poet Frederick Wilfrid Faber were zealous members.

The unostentatious self-sacrifice and earnest work of these men drew to them everywhere noble good helpers from princes and church dignitaries through all classes of community and none can read their story and not admire their work for the sick poor.

Under Gregory XIII. in 1575, the order was confirmed and afterward in 1612 reconfirmed by Paul V. Through this noble order houses of refuge and hospitals were built in many places. The story is replete with interest and instructive detail; for it tells what one godly man may do if his heart is in his work. St. Philip was canonized by Gregory XV. in 1622.

MAY 27th.

St. John, Pope and martyr, is honoured this day. He was a Tuscan by birth and in his youth among his fellow students was distinguished and regarded as an oracle. He was elected to the pontificate in 523, and in 526 died at Romania, a martyr under Theodoric.

This day is also the day when St. Bede, or Beda "the Venerable," is remembered. Of all the early Anglo-Saxon chroniclers, historians and biographers, Bede is perhaps the one above all others on whom modern writers have been obliged to rely for not only church history but for much secular matter that would have been lost save for his careful chronicles. He was born in Jarrow, Northumberland in 673. He became eminent for his learning and erudition and died dictating a translation of the Gospel of St. John. There is a legendary account of the manner in which he gained the title "venerable" that runs thus: His pupils wishing to put an inscription on his tombstone wrote:

"Hac sunt in fossa,
Bede——ossa,"

leaving the blank because they had not a fitting title to fill it. The next morning some unknown hand had inserted the word "venerable." But none can doubt he truly deserved the title. He died in 735.

Though hardly coming within the scope of these articles some may be interested to know this day also is the anniversary of the death of the noted Reformer, John Calvin in 1564.

MAY 28th.

St. Germanus, the glory of the Church of France, whose festival occurs on this day was a man of noble and marked characteristics; but by far the largest portion of his clerical life fell during troublous times in France. King Childebert, a son of Clovis, was then on the throne but until he came under the influence of Germanus had been a worldly, ambitious prince. Soon after the return of Childebert and his brother Clotaire from an expedition undertaken in 542 against Spain, Childebert was taken sick; medical aid had proved ineffectual and he sent for Bishop Germanus to come to his palace at Celles, near Melun. The good man spent the whole night with the king in prayer and in the morning laid hands on the monarch who was at once restored to health. It was not long after, however, before the king died. Clotaire succeeded his brother and was the last of the sons of the great Clovis to sit on the united throne of France. On Clotaire's death France was again divided by his sons. Paris was given to Charibert, Orleans and Burgundy to Gontran, Austrasia to Sigebert and Soissons to Chilperic. Then through their own ambitions and the intrigues of their wives trouble began.

In speaking of St. Augustine it will be remembered I mentioned Bertha, wife of the Saxon King of Kent, as the daughter of Charibert by his wife Ingoberga, but he had divorced her to marry her maid, Mariovesa. Germanus' reproof for Charibert's misconduct in this and many ways was the first of the good man's troubles which grew with the fraternal wars between the brothers. But the story is too long to tell and even our saint lived not to see the ending for he died in 576. His life had been a busy, useful one. The most noted literary work of St. Germanus is "An Exposition of the Liturgy" in which is reproduced the ancient Gallican liturgy or Mass as used in France before the Roman was introduced in the time of Charlemagne and Pope Adrian I. In this curious work St. Germanus also explains and describes the ceremonies of the liturgy and all of the vestments worn, a work which alone will keep his name alive in hagiology.

MAY 29th.

CORPUS CHRISTI DAY

Is an ancient festival in the Roman Church, but after the Reformation was discontinued by those who had separated from the "mother church," with whom it is highly honoured. It comes on the Thursday following Whitsunday and therefore is a movable feast. Its design is to honour the doctrine of transubstantiation, and was formerly observed with much pomp and show, a procession, with the pyx containing the consecrated wafer being at the head carried by the church dignitaries. In past days this procession was not confined to church and was accompanied by figures costumed to represent certain favourite saints of the Church where the festival was held. Thus St. Ursula with her many maidens, St. George leading the captive dragon, St. Christopher wading the river with the infant Saviour, St. Sebastian with his body full of arrows, St. Catharine with her wheel and others. The priests also carried in their hands pieces of sacred plate belonging to the church. The streets were decorated with wreaths and boughs and strewn with flowers. When the sacred pyx appeared every person kneeled while it passed. Later and after the procession, games and mystery plays were universal, with music and dancing. Save in certain purely Catholic countries the street processions are now seldom seen, but they are never omitted in the church.

MAY 30th.

St. Felix I., Pope and martyr, who succeeded St. Dionysius in 269 in the government of the Church is remembered this day, when after filling his high office for five years he attained the glory of martyrdom in 274.

On this day also the name of another of those royal personages whom the Church has deemed worthy of honour appears, St. Ferdinand III., King of Castile and Leon. He was the hero of many battles against the Moors and took part in that celebrated battle of Xeres, where, as the legend runs, St. Iago appeared at the head of the Spanish troops and while the Moors were slaughtered by the thousand only one Christian was slain. His daughter, Elenora, married Edward I. of England in 1253, and it was she who sucked the poison from her husband's wound for she had inherited not a little of her father's courage. It was Ferdinand who built that wondrous cathedral of Borgos which points to heaven with spires more rich and delicate than any of all the famed cathedrals of the world. He was preparing an expedition against the Moors in Africa when death called him in 1252. St. Ferdinand was canonized by Clement X. in 1671.

MAY 31st.

In the Roman Church this day is sacred to St. Petronilla, a daughter of St. Peter.

The legends of this virgin tell us that she accompanied St.

Peter to Rome. Butler says St. Peter was married before he became an Apostle and that his wife "attained to martyrdom, at which the Apostle encouraged her." The name of this virgin is Petronilla, the feminine and diminutive of Peter. She was a cripple it is said from palsy, and her legend says "that one day when the Apostle sat at meat with some of the disciples they asked why it was that while he could heal others his own child remained helpless."

St. Peter replied that it was the will of God, and therefore good that she should be thus. But that the glory of Christ should be manifested, he commanded her to rise and serve them. This she immediately did but when her service was over "she lay down as helpless as before." The legend then tells how by her own prayers she at last recovered and also that she was very beautiful, and a young Roman named Valerius Flaccus fell in love with her and wished to marry her. Feeling that she could not do this and fulfil her duties to the church, yet afraid to refuse him, she begged of him a respite of three days, when she would reply. When he came for his answer, however, he found her dead. He lamented her sorely, and with his attendants "covered her body with roses."

She was buried in a cemetery "on the way to Arden, where a church stood that anciently bore her name." Gregory III. established there a station for public prayer.

JUNE

—— After her came jolly JUNE, arrayed
All in green leaves, as he a player were;
  Yet in his time he wrought as well as played,
That by his plough-irons mote right well appear,
  Upon a crab he rode, that did him bear,
With crooked crawling steps, an uncouth pace,
  And backward rode, as bargemen wont to fare.

Spenser.

Ovid in his "*Fasti*" makes Juno claim the honour of naming this month. But standing as it does the fourth in the Roman Kalendar it was dedicated "*à Junioribus*" as May was "*à Majoribus.*" Romulus assigned to it thirty days, though in the old Alban Kalendar it had but twenty-six days. Numa robbed it of one but Julius Cæsar restored *that* and its number of days has since been unchanged.

This month since the old Roman days has been considered the most propitious for consummating marriage ties. Even down to the Middle Ages this pagan superstition was retained and if we may hazard the remark still holds good as a favourite month for "the wedding." But this passes beyond the scope of these papers; or I could fill a volume on ancient marriage customs, from the ring, to the casting of rice and old shoes for neither are of modern date.

JUNE 1st.

The first Sunday after Trinity holds an especial place in the liturgy of both the Roman and Reform Churches while its canonical colour is green symbolical of bountifulness, mirth, youth and prosperity. In its place I shall take occasion to speak of the significance of both colours and precious stones as symbols but in passing may remark that the emerald is peculiarly appropriate for this day and its significance from its glorious colour :—

"The Emerald burns, intensely bright,
With radiance of an olive light:
This is the faith that highest shines,
No deed of charity declines,
And seeks no rest and shuns no strife,
In working out a holy life."

One of the first names of noted saints which we meet in June is that of St. Pamphillus priest and martyr whose learning and erudition not only made for him a great name in those early days in which he lived but has preserved it for almost sixteen centuries. He was a native of Berytus a city famous for its schools. He came from a rich and noble family and after perfecting himself in every science taught there became a magistrate. It was not until he had passed his early manhood that he became a Christian, and then it was not upon a sudden impulse that this accomplished master of profane sciences and the renowned magistrate yielded to the convictions forced upon him by a careful study of Holy Writ. He soon moved to Cæsarea in Palestine, where he collected a vast library said to have contained 30,000 volumes. Here he also established a school of sacred literature. Dr. Butler says: "To his labour the Church was indebted for the most correct edition of the Holy Bible." In the persecutions of Galerius Maximus he was first to be tortured for his faith in Christ while later and under Governor Urbanus cast into prison, but even there he wrote several books. His imprisonment began in 307 and continued for two years, when Fermilian, the successor of Urbanus ordered him to be tortured. His flesh was torn from his bones by iron hooks; but it is said even under such torment he opened not his mouth or allowed a groan to escape him. He finished his martyrdom before a slow fire and died invoking "Jesus the Son of

God," in the year 309. Such is the brief story of this noble scholar, who gave his life in testimony of his faith in Christ.

Under this date mention must be made of St. Peter of Pisa the founder of the "Hermits of St. Jerom" who observed four seasons of Lent in each year fasting on all Mondays, Wednesdays and Fridays. He died in 1435, aged 80 years. Pius V. termed him "blessed." He was beatified by Innocent XII. in 1693.

To-day also in the Anglican Kalendar there appears the name of St. Nicomede priest and martyr in the year 90. He was a scholar of St. Peter and for conferring on his sister Felicula (a virgin martyr) a Christian burial, a thing he knew was done at the peril of his life, he was discovered to be a Christian. Whereupon Domitian ordered him to sacrifice to the Roman gods which he refused to do and was beaten to death with spiked clubs. From this came his emblem in the Clog Almanac.

JUNE 2d.

The martyrs of Lyons in the year 177 are among the most noted of the saints of the Church owing to the ferocity with which the pagans of Gaul pursued them to their death. Unfortunately the story is too long for a detailed repetition as it furnishes such an illustration of the fortitude of those heroes who took their lives in their hands and went forth to teach "Christ and Him crucified." Although they are called the "martyrs of Lyons" not a few of those who fell came from Vienne and elsewhere. After those terrible trials prior to 174 so carefully chronicled by historians of the Church God in a plain and direct answer to the prayers of Christians under Marcus Aurelius granted them for a time partial relief from their trials, but in 177 they were once more renewed by the pagans in Gaul. St. Pothinus was then Bishop of Lyons and naturally from his office was the most prominent in this tragedy though his associates Attalus, Sanctus Blandina and others were equally sufferers. Many of these were Greeks and came from Asia as a great traffic had then sprung up between Asia and Marseilles while Lyons had become a central point for the faithful missionaries of Christ. The martyrdom of these noble men is but the repetition of many similar events. Torn by wild beasts, roasted over slow fires and tortured in every conceivable way, yet always they were "faithful unto death." It is fitting then for us all to honour them on this day, named by the Church, since it is examples like theirs which show how much we of to-day owe to those early Christians.

JUNE 3d.

St. Clotildis, or Clotilda, whose name appears in the Kalendar on this day is a saint who was greatly reverenced in early days in France. Her life was a romance from her infancy. She was the daughter of Chilperic, a younger brother of Goudebald or Goudebud, fourth king of Burgundy, 491-516, a fierce brutal man who caused Chilperic, his wife and his brothers to be murdered that he might usurp the control of the entire nation. For some unknown reason Clotilda and her sister then infants were spared in this wholesale massacre. Her sister later became a nun and Clotilda though brought up in the court of Goudebald, by some providence had received a Christian education. In due time Clovis I. surnamed "the Great," the victorious king of the Franks whose reign begun in 481 when he was but fifteen years old saw and fancied Clotilda and in 493 they were married at Soissons. As the average royal marriage goes it was for those days a most happy one and the young queen set up an oratory in the palace. She evidently was a most discreet woman. She honoured her warlike husband and by slow degrees led him by her Christian meekness to respect and honour her and more to the purpose to listen to her as she discoursed on sacred subjects and discredited the idols Clovis then worshipped. She led rather than tried to drive him. At last in 496 Clovis was engaged in a battle with the Alemanni (a word intended to mean a mixed race living between the Danube and the Upper Rhine) he was near to defeat. Something inspired him to call on "Clotilda's God" for help. From that hour the tide of battle turned and Clovis won an historic victory.

The impression made upon the pagan king was so great and lasting that on his return home he was baptized. Thus stripped of verbiage we see how through the love and devotion of one faithful soul France came to have its first Christian king and to become Christianized. At the baptism of Clovis the oil used it is said, was brought to the prelate at St. Remi — where the ceremony occurred — by a dove and that an angel brought also to the king three white lilies which he in turn gave to St. Clotilda and that from this circumstance the "fleurs-de-lys," were substituted for the three crapauds (toads) which had formerly held their place in the royal arms of France. At her request Clovis built in Paris the Church of SS. Peter and Paul, but now called St. Genevieve, in this church her remains now rest. Her death occurred on June 3, 545.

JUNE 4th.

St. Quirinus who is honoured this day was one of those strong characters we are constantly meeting with among the fathers of the Church in early days. He was Bishop of Siscia a city in Pannonia upon the river Save, in what is now Hungary. Owing to his earnest fervent preaching he had fallen under the ban of Galerius Maximus as the story is related by Prudentius, and condemned to have a mill-stone tied to his neck and to be cast into the river. The legend as it is preserved states that the mill-stone instead of sinking floated and then recounts a long conversation held between the saint and Maximus who seemingly was watching and desired to save his life. But to all of the overtures the saint remained true to his great Master Christ. In this conversation Maximus said : "Now confess the power of the gods the great Roman empire adore. Obey and I will make you a priest of Jupiter." When at last Quirinus tired at the long delay while the mill-stone still floated prayed that having given testimony of his faith and trust he might be allowed to depart. Then slowly the stone began to sink and the martyr passed to his reward. This was in the year 304.

This day also marks the festival of St. Optatus, Bishop of Milevum in Numidia. A learned African educated as an idolater and who as St. Austin puts it : "Passing from the dark shades of paganism to the light of faith carried into the church the spoils of Egypt ; that is human science and eloquence." His writings yet remain as a marvelous testimony of the wisdom and learning of those early ages and the purity of purpose which actuated the Holy Fathers. St. Optatus survived the year 384 but the date of his death is not positively known.

JUNE 5th.

This day is given to one of the most noted saints in the Christian Kalendar of both the Roman and Anglican churches. St. Boniface the Apostle of the Germans. He was the son of a West Saxon chieftain born at Crediton in Devonshire about 680. He was baptised under the name of Winfrid or Winfrith as the name sometimes was then written. Showing from his infancy both remarkable powers of mind and a serious tendency he was sent when but seven years of age to the monastery at Exeter or Escancester, as it was then called to be trained by the celebrated Abbot Walphund. Later he studied at the monastery of Nutcell in Winchester and from the first was noted for his proficiency in acquiring learning. He was ordained to the priesthood in 710. From youth his great hope had been to be able to carry the gospel to the heathen of Germany and in 719 he went to Rome to secure from Gregory II. permission to become a missionary to the German infidels. This was granted, and he began his work in

Bavaria. In 723 he was elevated to the bishopric. Till then he had been known by the name of Winfrid but the pope at that time changed his name to Boniface. We cannot follow in detail the long and arduous life work among the Germans, and its wonderful success, interesting as it is, or the growing influence Boniface gained with the Church and his preferment to the archbishopric of Mentz. His entire life was one of earnest faithful devotion to the cause of Christ. His story though is that of the foundation of Christianity in Germany, of which his letters (thirty-nine in number) published in 1605 give many interesting incidents.

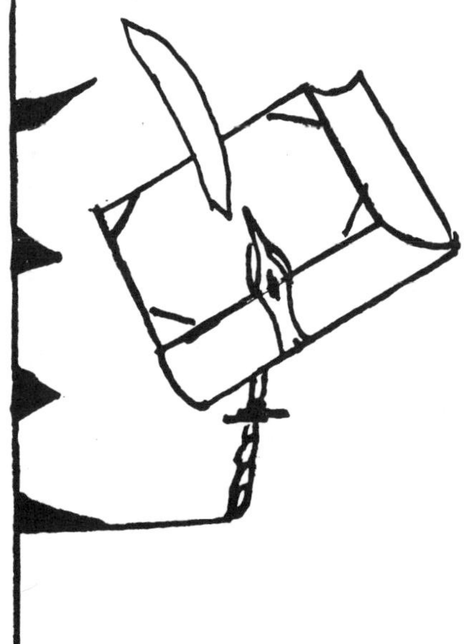

When 74 years of age he resigned his high position as primate of Germany and once more donned his Benedictine habit to resume his missionary labours only to suffer the year following with fifty-two of his companions in holy work martyrdom at the hands of the pagans of Utrecht. In Christian art St. Boniface is represented in full episcopal robes, hewing down an oak, or with an oak tree lying prostrate at his feet and an axe in his hand. In some writings he is termed "the Oak of Jupiter." His Clog symbol is a book pierced by a sword, symbolizing his learning and martyrdom.

JUNE 6th.

SACRATISSIMI CORDIS JESU.

On this day recurs a festival peculiar to the Roman Church, one that has never been recognized by the Anglican church — the Feast of the Sacred Heart.

The origin of this festival according to the traditions of the Church was that while Margaret Mary Alacoque a "religieuse" of "the Visitation of Paray-le-Monial" in France, was at her devotions Jesus appeared to her as he had often done before, and "showed her His Sacred Heart, in His open Breast, encircled with fire and flames, * * and He revealed to her that He desired to have an especial feast established in honour of His Divine Heart." In her statement written at the time in which she describes the apparition of Jesus she quotes among other words of Christ then uttered : "For this reason I ask thee that the first Friday in the Octave of Corpus Christi be set apart as a special feast consecrated to the honour of My Heart," and later He added this promise : "* * * I promise that My Heart shall be opened to shed in richest abundance the Influence of Its Divine Love."

From this the feast was in due time recognised as a sacred festival of the Church by a bull of Benedict XIV. (pope 1740-1758) and has since been observed throughout the world by the Roman Church.

The quotations given above are taken from the second of a series of six sermons on "Devotion to the Sacred Heart," by the Rev. Ewald Beirbum, D.D., an eminent German priest.

On this day also appears the name of St. Norbert the founder of a somewhat celebrated German order of the Roman Church: "Stifler der Pramonstratenser-Ordin." His father was Count Gennep and his mother a relative of Emperor Heinrich IV. being descended from the house of Lorraine. He was born at Sauten in the duchy of Cleves in 1080. His parents had early dedicated him to the service of the church but for a long time their hopes seemed doomed to be disappointed. As a young man he was dissolute and his life was given to pleasure. He was instituted to a canonry at Santen and ordained a sub-deacon, but received the ecclesiastical tonsure in an utterly worldly spirit and made no outward change in his life. At the court of his cousin the emperor he was the soul of mirth, and his wit and bon mots the life of social circles. He refused any higher orders lest they might put some restraint upon his pleasures. But the time came when this was all changed. He was riding near the village of Freten in Westphalia on a richly caparisoned horse when a sudden thunder storm burst upon him from a cloudless sky and a bolt struck directly in front of him and he was thrown from his horse and lay unconscious upon the ground for some time. Then like a second Saul, the enormity of his sins seemed to come over him as he recovered from the shock. He went no more to court but retired to his canonry at Santen leading a life of retirement and later became a missionary after having been ordained deacon and priest. This roving life of austerity and self-sacrifice he led until in 1119 by permission of Calixtus II. he founded a small monastery with a few equally devoted men in a lonesome valley called Pre-montre. After many years of faithful labour here in 1132 Norbert was elevated to the bishopric of Magdeburg and died June 6, 1134.

JUNE 7th.

St. Godeschalc who is honoured by the Church this day was one of those old time fierce warriors whose lives read like romances. In the reign of Henry the Salic whose arms with those of Knut, King of Denmark and Bernard, Duke of Saxony kept the barbarians in order about the beginning of the IV. century, one Uto a Western Vandal prince, was murdered by a Saxon chief. The son of Uto, Godeschalc had been educated at the monastic school of Lumburg under a Gothic bishop but had then apostatized from whatever of Christianity he had ever accepted. Joining two pagan princes after his father's murder he in revenge harassed without mercy the Saxons until captured by Bernard the Saxon Duke who held him prisoner for a long time. When he at last gained his liberty he found his heritage possessed by one Ratibor a powerful Slavic prince, but gathering a band of his partisans Godeschalc with them joined the Danes. Then King Knut was employed in his wars with Norway and later sent Godeschalc with his nephew Sueno, into England, where his prowess and valour won for him such favour with the Danish king that he gave him his daughter in marriage. After Knut's death Godeschalc returned from England and subdued his old enemy and the entire Slavic country. Meantime he had under the influence of a Saxon priest been converted to Christianity and reigned many years in peace surpassing all his contemporary princes in prudence, power and valour, as well as in piety and holy zeal. He built many churches and monasteries and brought over to the faith a great part of the idolaters among the nations subject to him. He extended his missions into all the dominions of Godeschalc and baptized many with his own hands, interpreting to the people in the Slavonian language the sermons and instructions of the priests.

Five years later the Vandals or Slavi who had remained idolaters, in the duchy of Mecklenburg, revolted, and began their sedition by the murder of Godeschalc, in the city of Lenzin on June 7, 1066.

CANONIZATION OF SAINTS.

The canonization of saints has only been accepted as a dogma of faith by the Roman Church since the XII. century and it was confined to those who had suffered martyrdom for their religious principles. At that time bishops were permitted to name them but the numbers increased so rapidly that it was soon necessary to limit the admission to the canon and this privilege was taken from the bishops and the pope alone was given the authority. In the same prudent spirit it was decreed that the holy man must have been dead for a hundred years before he was eligible to be canonized.

MONKS AND MONASTERIES.

From reading books like Scott's inimitable "Monastery and Abbot" and similar stories a widespread misconception has come to the general reader both as to the nature of the primitive monastic buildings but as well of the monks themselves and their usual daily occupations. This arises from no fault of the authors whose descriptions, like that of Scott speaking of Kennaquhair, are accurate as to the time of which they wrote, but far from being so in regard to earlier days. Especially is this true in reference to the primitive Irish, Scotch and English monasteries.

The description of these which follows it is proper for me to say is a sort of wholesale quotation from Skene's "Celtic Scotland"

and Burton's "History of Scotland," even where I fail to put the proper marks. A bit of literary patchwork with its pieces cut from long and elaborate description, from which I will endeavour to make a short, but I hope, clear picture.

"The primitive Celtic monastery was a very simple affair, * * * a village of rude huts," and "we must not suppose at all resembled the elaborate stone structures of the Middle Ages." In most instances the larger buildings were built with wattled walls. Thus: "A wall plate was made by upright stakes having twigs interlaced between them in the usual manner of basket making. * * * A second wall was placed within the outer one and turf or clay was filled in between these walls." The thickness varied from two to even four feet, and thus a very solid wall was constructed, the roof being of poles above which was a woven thatch of straw. Some legend, of course, lingered around each of these structures. Skene tells how Ciaran of Saighir, one of the twelve apostles of Ireland, began to build his huts and church " when he went to the wood for his material a wild boar assisted him by biting off with his sharp teeth the rods and branches he needed." Still later came the timber buildings and those constructed from hewn planks. It was not till the end of the VIII. century when the ravages of the Danes and by repeated lessons of danger from fire any attempt was made to use stone in their buildings, and then first are noticed some efforts toward the internal comforts of the monks. " The monastic system which characterised the Irish church in its second period * * * presented features peculiarly adapted to the tribal organizations and social systems of the Irish. * * * These large monasteries * * * were in reality Christian colonies into which converts after being tonsured were brought."

My readers may remember that St. Brendan was first thus cared for by St. Itha and later until he was ordained to the priesthood by Bishop Erc. It was not obligatory on these " converts " to take upon themselves at a later time holy orders. Thus when we read of 4,000 monks under the rule of Comgall, and other large numbers elsewhere we must not think of them as " monks " in the usual acceptation of the term. These were called " Muintir or familia," the elders " seniors," who gave themselves entirely to devotions and the service of the church, whose chief occupation in their cells was to transcribe the Scriptures and illuminate missals. Of one Bishop Marchata an Irish ballad says:

" Three score psalm-singing seniors,
Were his household, royal in number,
Without tillage, reaping or kiln drying,
Without work, except reading."

a somewhat strange exception. The rest of the household were divided into classes for tilling of their fields, caring for herds and such as were skilled in the use of tools in mechanical labour, and making clothing for the "family." Of this I will give other details when speaking of Iona.

These monasteries also claimed the "right of sanctuary."

JUNE 8th.

St. Maximus, the first Bishop of Aix in Provence, who is honoured in the Kalendar this day is said — but the authority for the assertion is rather vague — to have been one of Christ's personal followers and disciples. His life whether this fact be true or not is evidence of how soon the early Christians began to spread out over the world teaching the Christian faith, for his preaching the gospel in Marseilles and so establishing Christianity in Provence is fully authenticated and his successor, "St. Sedonius, the second Bishop of Arles," is said to have been the man who was born blind and healed by our Lord. St. Maximus died about the close of the I. century.

St. William, whose name also appears this day, was the son of Earl Herbert and his mother Emma was a sister of King Stephen. He received holy orders early in life and became treasurer of the metropolitan church of York. In 1144 he was elected Archbishop and consecrated in September of that year at Winchester, but through influence at Rome of his opponents, Pope Eugenius III. deprived him of his see and he lived in retirement at Winchester until in 1153 he was again elected Archbishop and went to Rome where he received the pallium from his holiness Anastasius IV., who had that year succeeded to the pontificate. His return to York was the occasion of an immense ovation. The crowd that had assembled was so great that it broke down the wooden bridge over the Ouese in York, and it was only by miraculous intervention no lives were lost and St. William has had the credit of having by his timely prayer been the means of the preservation of these people in their hour of danger. No less than thirty-six miracles are accorded to St. William. He died in 1154 and was canonized by Nicholas III. in 1280.

JUNE 9th.

This day marks the festival of the one man who above all his self-sacrificing brethren to whom Scotland owes gratitude for the first grand missionary work in behalf of the Christian religion among the northern Picts, the then dominant power in Alban. To understand clearly the grandness of St. Columba's work we must first give a very brief page from Scotch history for, singular as it sounds, the Scotch came originally from Ireland, and the word "Scotia" in the earliest recorded history, was applied only to inhabitants of Irish Dalriada. In 360, certain Scots came first to Britain, not as colonists, but as allies to the Dalriadan Picts in Alban. They soon disappeared and next are heard of in 501 when, according to Tighernac (an Irish annalist) Fergus mor mac Erc, from County Antrim in Irish Dalriada, and of the "Irish Gael," with a small colony settled in what is now "Southern Argyle" on the coast and founded the future monarchy of Scotland. I must not follow further this most interesting part of Scotch history except to add that it was among the descendants of this Fergus mor mac Erc, Columba first found friends when he came to Alban.

Now to sketch briefly this wonderful man's career as student, soldier, missionary and saint. Columba (commonly pronounced Colme) was born December 7, 521, and was descended through his father Fedhlmidh from the royal Hy Neill's, and by his mother from a long line of Irish Dalriadan kings. Innumerable prophecies attended his birth, among them one by St. Patrick who foretold his birth and :—

* * * * * * *

"That will not utter a falsehood ;
He'll be a saint and will be devout,
He'll be an Abbott, the King of royal graces,
He'll be lasting and ever good ;
The eternal kingdom be mine by his protection."

* * * * * * *

Lack of space precludes a record of his brilliant student life at Moghbile (his first school) under Gemma, a noted Bard, who inspired in him that poetic love of the beautiful of which I will later speak. His education was completed and he took holy orders at Cluin-Brad and I may say in passing became one of the historic "Twelve Apostles of Ireland."

His life soon became a busy one both in ecclesiastic and public affairs. His fervent Christian and poetic nature made him devout; yet he was a typical Irishman and allowed no one "to tread on the tail of his coat." "Athletic Christianity" was then largely in evidence, as we see by the number of "doughty men of valour" who appear in the sanguinary battles of those days. So we find Columba engaged in several pitched battles.

One feature of Columba's character from his student days was his love of rare manuscripts and it was this which under God's providence sent him forth as a missionary; for God works quite as often by human as by Divine agencies. At Moghbile, Finnian, Columba's old teacher, had a rare manuscript of the Psalter which the pupil often desired to copy — for he was a skilled penman — but was refused for Finnian was of the true "bookworm" nature which keeps secret his treasures.

About 560 Columba visited his old tutor. He had not forgotten the coveted Psalter and by some means managed surreptitiously to obtain possession of the MS. When "the theft," as Finnian termed it, was discovered and traced he demanded it should be returned, but the demand was refused and then King Diarmid took a hand in the matter uttering what became an Irish proverb: "To every cow belongs her calf."

To sum up a long story short, the Hy Neills met King Diarmid in the battle of Cuil-dreme and defeated him.

Columba's trouble was now serious; a "synod of the Saints of Ireland" was called and Columba was held responsible for the loss of life at Cuil-dreme and it was decreed "he must rescue as many souls from Paganism as lives had been lost in the battle." Thus it came that Columba went forth on that pilgrimage to the Picts which has made his name memorable. I only regret I cannot give the many interesting details which throw such clear "side-lights" on the story.

Conal, a descendant of Fergus mor mac Erc, was then king of the Dalriadan Scots who were Christians and who "by grace" the powerful pagan Picts had allowed to remain thus far unmolested in Argyle and in some of the islands along the coast; among them Mull and Hii, later corrupted into Iona.

Conal knew the tender ground he stood on with the Picts; while at heart a Christian he could not defy these fierce pagans. Indeed he stood "between the devil and the deep sea." So he gladly took a middle course and sent Columba and his associates on to Hii (or as I will from now call it Iona) to let them work out their own salvation on that utterly desolate barren strip of rocky land.

With infinite toil they built their "bothies" (huts) and began their strenuous struggle, first for the necessities of life. Even the journey from Ireland had been an arduous one in their open "cruaths," (wicker boats covered by raw skins of animals drawn over the frame and thus allowed to dry there) and in these they now carried their slender stock of provisions and other belongings to this rugged, rock bound island so often and graphically described by tourists to it.

The monastery at Iona in most respects was like those of Ireland at that time, and the household ordered on similar lines, but with some advance since Adamnan speaks of the "pincinco" or butler, and "pistor" baker, adding as a curious fact that the latter "was a Saxon." The elders and certain ones of the labourers were tonsured from ear to ear; that is, having the hair shaved from the front of the head back to a line drawn from the ear, while elsewhere it was allowed to grow. Their young men were not tonsured as in Ireland. Their dress was of but two garments, a "tunica" or white woolen undershirt and a "camilla," or sleeved woolen gown (unbleached), reaching the ankles. This had also a hood. They wore hide sandals when travelling, but in the house and field went barefooted. In such a rigourous climate such a dress we to-day would not think even safe for health. But they were hardened to this from childhood; while the Picts, save for a skin worn over the shoulders, even in winter were almost nude.

The food was of the simplest kind; bread made from crushed

barley or oatmeal, milk and fish, varied only by the addition on festivals of seal flesh, wild fowls and eggs. In honour of guests or some especial "high feast" beef would be added to the menu. I must for lack of space omit mention of their daily lives and devotions except to say that they followed in all ways the rules of the Irish monasteries. St. Columba's cell was separated from the brethren on one of those rugged "dunes" still so prominent a feature of the island. In his life he shared alike with the humblest of his brethren in everything. Gentle, kind and affectionate, yet beneath all his austerity (for he never forgot his mission) he had a deep love for the beautiful and a quaint, subtle sense of humour; as one writer puts it "with a laugh always in the tail of his eye." His teachings to the heathen were of the plainest, simplest truths utterly free from dogmas not fully set forth in the "Word of God," to use his own expression. But his real missionary work had not yet begun and it is too important to be treated within the small limit left me and therefore I must return to it later when I can also speak of St. Comgall whom I intentionally passed on May 10th, as these fellow workers can hardly be separated.

Columba was now in the flower of manhood and is described as a "type of manly beauty," endowed with a sweet, sonorous voice; a certain magnetism of manner which drew everyone toward him; yet never lacking in dignity. His fame had already spread far beyond the narrow limits of Iona among the northern Picts who from the first had been his objective point. They were a race strangely compounded. They were barbarians not savages, and possessed of wonderfully quick, clear intellects, though utterly untutored. This is shown by the manner in which they met the Romans; grasping instantly the secret of their "tactics" in war, grafting the best on their own methods and surprising their invaders by utilising them. Pagans they of course were but not unthinking. Through the Romans they had seen something of their religion and had laughed at it; refusing to be cajoled yet quick to learn the lessons the Romans had unconsciously taught them. Immured by exposure from infancy they regarded the warm, well-clad Romans as effeminate. They were a strong race wholly devoid of tenderness or sentiment, yet superstitious from their Druidic teachings; still with an inborn, high sense of honour and fidelity. Such were the people Columba had chosen to bring back from paganism. Till now his work had only been what may be termed predatory missionary labour, barely reaching the borders of the great Pictish kingdom over which Brude then reigned; a man who beyond doubt was the most powerful that had ever sat on the throne. A man of unusual penetration and perhaps the only one among his people outside of the priesthood who saw through the superstitions of the Druidical religion. How much of Brude Columba knew is uncertain; but he was well aware that between Iona and Inverness, where Brude held court, save the comparatively safe districts of Morven and Lochaber, lay the dangerous Drumalbans; beset with difficulties from unknown paths where fierce superstitious natives lurked under the guidance of the Druid and Magi priests, ready to intercept his way; yet his resolution did not fail him. Unfortunately neither Adamnan or Montelembert are able to give a clear account of this remarkable journey. We only know that Comgall of Bangor and Caimach of Achaboe were his companions. These two men were of the race of Irish Picts from whom the Dalriadan Picts had come and so to a certain extent they had kept in touch with their kinsmen in Alban.

Beyond brief mention of hunger, lack of shelter and constant opposition by the Druid and Magi priests, the chronicles are silent save for some miraculous acts of Columba by which the party were preserved until they reached the fortress of King Brude at Loch Ness and which antiquarians have positively identified with the vitrified fortress now termed "Craig-Phadrie" at Inverness, so well known to Scotch tourists.

Here again at the arrival of Columba and his companions at Inverness these chroniclers allow the miraculous to overshadow the details we desire to know. Thus we are told that the gates of the town and of the palace were closed against the strangers. But at the sign of the cross made by Comgall the town gates opened and when they had come to the doors of the royal house St. Columba advanced and, making a similar sign, these also admitted them into the presence of the king. Angered beyond measure at such intrusion, Brude raised his sword to slay them, but Caimach made the all-powerful sign of the cross over Brude's hand and it fell withered at his side, and, the chronicles continue, so remained until he (the king) believed in God. But what was spoken or how the stern Pict was brought to terms is wholly unknown. Some even declare that no such conversion took place. That at Columba's intercession, Brude's strength was at once restored, and that from then during his life he held Columba in especial reverence is historic. But Bede records that in the ninth year of Brude, or Bridius, which would be in 565 and thus correspond with Columba's dates in leaving Iona for his mission, he was baptized by Columba. The Pictish chronicles also confirm this in date and fact.

In the Irish life of St. Comgall I find an incident nowhere else mentioned, "that then Mailcu the son of the king came with his Drui (Druid priests) to contend (argue) against Columielle (Columba) through paganism; but he and his Drui with him were destroyed (overcome) by the name of God and through Columielle He was magnified."

Just here it is interesting in some measure to understand what the nature of this pagan belief was but it must be very sadly condensed. It was the same in all respects as met St. Patrick when he came to Ireland, and perhaps cannot be better summed up than by quoting from a metrical "Life of St. Patrick," by Fiacc of Sleibhte, who says:

> "He preached three-score years
> The Cross of Christ to the Tuatha of Feni.
> The Tuatha, adored the Side,
> On the Tuatha of Erin there was darkness,
> They believed not the true God-head
> Of the Trinity."

The Book of Armagh explains that the "Side, or Sidhe," were "gods of the earth, a phantom." Mysterious beings who were supposed to dwell alike in heaven, on the earth, in the sea, sky, rivers, mountains and valleys at will. Spirits to be dreaded and conciliated, to be worshipped and invoked by themselves and through the natural objects in which they were supposed to dwell.

Hence we see the sacredness of the Druidic oaks and stones. The Druid and Magi priests contended they did not worship idols, but their deities who dwelt in them; that these natural objects were not themselves powers, but that through them the Drudh could consult their deity.

The Magi added soothsaying, enchantment and divination; while as doctors they practiced on the superstitions of their patients as did the Drui. In one of these metrical accounts I find these lines:

> "The Drui of Cruithnech in friendship
> Discovered a cure for the wounded,
> New milk in which they were washed
> In powerful bathing."

And a little further on speaking of:

> "Six demon — like Druadh —
> Necromancy, idolatry and illusion,
> In a fair well-walled house.
>
> * * * * * * * *
>
> By them were taught
> The hovering of the sreod and omens,
> Choice of weather, lucky times,
> The watching of the voice of birds
> They practiced without disguise."

This word sreod Dr. Todd glosses as "sneezing." But I must not enlarge further on this strangely interesting point.

As already said we are without any details of the methods used by Columba to combat these pagan beliefs, but the conversion of their king exercised no doubt a most powerful influence in aiding Columba's efforts, and he seemed by kindness rather than by force to have first won their confidence and then by degrees to have taught the Christian faith, then following the Irish method of monastic colonies, or as they were termed, monasteries, and in many places building churches. Thus for twelve years Columba, Comgall and other faithful men worked steadily in laying the foundations of the Columbate Church as it has been called in his honour, and after these years broadening the sphere of their labours to include the Southern Picts, who under St. Ninian had been converted but who soon apostatized, all of which must be mentioned under the notice of this great teacher Ninian on September 16th.

We cannot follow through Columba's work, so full of incidents which prove his devotion; his never failing hope even under dire misfortunes and cruel wrongs, till at last he reaches his Iona family once more. Nor may I copy as I would like, the long and touching description of those last days written by his biographer, Cummene, until on the morning of June 9, 597, Columba called his faithful attendant, Diormet, to him and said: "This day is called in the sacred Scriptures a day of rest and truly to me it will be such, for it is the last of my life and I shall enter into my rest after the fatigues of my labours."

Thus peacefully passed to his reward one of God's noblest and most faithful servants, leaving behind him an imperishable memory not alone in the affection and veneration of those of his own day, but in the breasts of all true Christians who now after thirteen centuries study his character.

JUNE 10th.

Of St. Margaret, Queen of Scotland, niece of Edward the Confessor and daughter of Edmund Ironsides who is honoured by the Church this day we may read in any Scotch history.

JUNE 11th.

St. Barnabas, whose festival is celebrated this day, though not one of the twelve was through his intimate association and the prominent share he took in apostolic transactions termed by the primitive Fathers of the Church "Apostle," and St. Luke also gives him the honoured title. By birth he was a Jew of the tribe of Levi. Aside from his labours as recorded in the "Acts of the Apostles" his legend tells of his labours in Asia Minor, Greece and Italy, and in the latter was made Bishop of Milan. At last when preaching in Judea he was martyred by the Jews being stoned to death at Salamis. Tradition tells that St. Barnabas always preached from the Gospel of St. Matthew and carried with him a copy written by the Evangelist himself, and that when his remains were found this manuscript was still in his bosom. This was taken to Constantinople and a church was built "under the invocation of the saint." St. Mark and other Christians buried him there. In Christian art St. Barnabas is represented carrying the gospel in one hand and in the other a pilgrim's staff, but the Clog Almanac gives him a rake.

There is no doubt that this is from some legend or tradition as most of these emblems are, but what it is I am not able to learn.

ST. BARNABAS.

Before "the change of style" the 11th of June marked the summer solstice. Hence the old English proverb:

"Barnaby bright
The longest day and shortest night."

In "Ye olde dayes" it was customary for the priests and clerks to decorate the church with garlands of roses.

This day was appointed as a festival by St. Charles Borromeo at the sixth provincial council in 1582. The canonical colour for this day is red.

JUNE 12th

Is the festival of St. John of Sahagun; a hermit of the Order of St. Augustine.

Eremitic life had a peculiar fascination for many of the holy men of the Church; the secret of which it is hard for us with our gregarious tendencies to understand. But how strong this feeling was is seen by the number who adopted a solitary life. And it was so with St. John who early in his life as a Benedictine had preferments in the Church and noted as a pulpit orator. But he resigned each of his rich "livings" and became a hermit of St. Austin in Salamanca in 1463 and was made "Prior" of the monastery in 1471. The austerities of these monks were almost beyond belief in their devotions, prayer, penance, abstination from food and self-sacrifice in all things being their rule for daily life. When his last sickness overtook St. John he foretold his death and calmly waited it when it came June 11th, 1479. For the many miracles credited to him he was "beatified" by Pope Clement VIII. in 1601 and canonized by Pope Alexander VIII. in 1690. Pope Benedict XIII. directed an office to be inserted in the Roman Breviary fixing the date for June 12th.

JUNE 13th.

The festival of St. Anthony, or Antonio of Padua, celebrated to-day is one of the few of the mediæval saints which has been retained in the English church Kalendar as it holds its place in that of the Roman Church, and few of all the long list of the canonized saints have attained to greater celebrity. Especially is this true in Italy but most so at Padua. His legend tells us that early in his career miraculous power came to aid him. Once, it is said, that at Rimini, in order to convince a person of heretical belief St. Anthony, by calling to the fishes caused them to lift their heads from the water to testify to the truth of his assertions. But short as his life was the list of his miracles is too long a one to be re-

counted here. He was born in Lisbon in 1195. At the age of fifteen he became one of the regular Canons of St. Austin, near Lisbon. When twenty-three he became a Franciscan friar and soon after the death of St. Francis in 1226, he retired to his convent in Padua where he died in 1231, aged only thirty-six years. Yet so great was his sanctity that Pope Gregory IX., who had known him personally, canonized him in 1232. Padua claimed him as its patron saint 1307, completed a magnificent church in his honour where have been gathered a wonderful variety of sacred, saintly relics, not the least among these being a gilt urn of somewhat fantastic shape which it is said contains the magical tongue of St. Anthony, which, once in each year is, upon the day of his death, exhibited, and then solemn and magnificently imposing ceremonies are held in honour of "Il Santo," as everyone terms this eloquent silver-tongued saint.

This saint must not be confounded with another of the same title whose festival occurs on January 17th, a noted man whose memory has been recalled in its place.

JUNE 14th.

I can but briefly mention St. Basil the Great especially honoured this day in the Greek church as the founder of the Order of Basilicans. He was born in a family of great sanctity as shown by his grandmother, father, mother, two brothers and a sister, as well as himself having been honoured by canonization as saints. He was ordained priest in 362, and in 370 called to the bishopric of Cæsarea. After a life full of usefulness and good works he died on June 14, A. D. 380. His emblem is a dove, from a legend that tells that when preaching of the Holy Ghost a dove lighted on his shoulder and remained during his sermon.

JUNE 15th.

Of the several noted names the Church honours on this day none is perhaps more worthy than the Blessed Gregory Lewis Barbadigo, a Venetian of a noble family and one who for his learning alone would be remembered. But his true Christian virtues even outshone these; while his character for wise counsel is shown by his being chosen by the Republic of Venice to accompany its ambassador, Aloysius Contarini, to that famous "Congress of Ministers," when the celebrated treaty commonly called "of Westphalia" was signed by the plenipotentiaries of Germany, France and Sweden on October 24, 1648, which later was so far-reaching in its influence throughout Europe. Gregory was consecrated Bishop of Bergame in 1657; created Cardinal by Alexander VII. in 1660 and translated to the bishopric of Padua in 1664. In every state of life he was a model of zeal, watchfulness and piety. His charities were unbounded, the actual known amount being in excess of eight hundred thousand crowns; while a stately seminary and college one of the chief glories of Padua to-day was his personal gift, and those who have seen its rare library, many of its books having been selected by him or under his direction, can but wonder at the far-reaching wisdom and learning of this man, justly termed "Blessed" by the church. He was beatified by Pope Clement XIII. on February 13, 1761.

Among other bounteous gifts I must not omit mention of one, a *printing office* which was connected with the college above named.

St. Vitus, whose festival occurs this day, Roman hagiology tells us was the son of a Sicilian noble; but under the care of his Christian nurse and foster father from early infancy taught in the faith of Christ. When twelve years of age this was discovered.

The child and his foster parents were imprisoned. The legend here tells how the father watching his son through a key hole saw him surrounded by angels and the dazzling sight blinded him. By the prayers of the son his sight was restored and the prisoners were released; but later they were again subjected to persecution and fled in a boat, which the legend says: "Was steered by an angel." But they reached Italy only to meet a worse fate; for being again accused of Christianity and boldly confessing it the boy martyr was cast into a caldron of boiling oil. A chapel erected in his honour at Ulm later became famous for the miraculous cures effected upon persons (women more especially) afflicted with nervous or hysteric affection, and from this came to be known "as St. Vitus dance," when violent motion accompanied the disease. Whatever may be the truth of these miraculous cures through St. Vitus' intercession, it remains a fact attested beyond a question that this child and his nurse and foster father suffered martyrdom in evidence of their faith in Christ in 303. St. Vitus is one of the "Noth-helpers" or patron saints of Germany, as well as the patron saint of actors and dancers and also the patron saint of Saxony, Bohemia and Sicily.

I must name one other saint on this day, St. Bernard of Menthon, if for nothing more than his forty-two years of loving, faithful preaching and care for the Savoyards. Yet many will remember to have passed over the two roads, which I have, and rested in the two great hospitals he founded, the Great and Little St. Bernards. The St. Bernard dogs bred, trained and nurtured by the devoted monks of these hospices need no eulogy any more than do these faithful fathers who have so long never failed to prove their courage or their devotion to Christ and to their fellow men. Indeed, the man or woman who has passed over these roads and fails in paying due reverence to this holy, devoted man and his faithful followers is lacking in true human sympathy; for if ever a man's good works live after him, those of St. Bernard of Menthon do. St. Bernard died at Novara where his body has rested since June 15, 1008.

JUNE 16th.

The Church of Rome this day recognises one of the most distinguished members of the Society of Jesus in St. John Francis Regis. From his entry into the order he was an ardent, zealous worker in missionary fields and in his efforts to crush out Calvinism, then rapidly growing in strength. His biographers dwell especially on his labours at Vivares which for many years was the stronghold of Calvinism in France, and at Puy, hardly less noted. But to us Regis has a special interest from being one of the Jesuit Fathers who in 1634 came as missionaries to the Hurons and Iroquois tribes, even though his stay among them was brief, as his services and the wonderful eloquence of his preaching were needed in France to resist the tide of Calvinistic doctrines. In this rôle he was perhaps one of, if not the most successful workers in his order. His strenuous life wore him out quickly and he died in 1640 when but forty-three years old. St. John Francis Regis was beatified by Clement XI. in 1716 and canonized by Clement XII. in 1737.

JUNE 17th.

The Church of England honours the "Protomartyr of England," St. Alban. In Roman Martyrology the date named for this saint is the 22d of June and although the Kalendar of the English church names the 17th, the best authorities fix the date as the 22d. Alban was born in Vercelam in Hertfordshire, which then was one of the strongest and most populous cities of Britain. It is now called St. Albans and lies between the river Werlaim and the famous Roman road called "Watling street" and after the Saxon conquest fell into decay. Alban was a pagan ; a man of some renown and had travelled as far as Rome to improve himself in learning and the polite arts.

King Offa built a church for his honour in 794 and later a Benedictine monastery was established, the abbot of which had precedence over all other prelates as its tutelar saint had been England's Protomartyr. A legend tells that one of the soldiers who led St. Alban to execution was converted on the way and was executed at the same time, literally "baptized in his own blood."

ST. ALBAN.

The bloody persecutions of Dioclesian which raged with such terrible fury in most parts of the Roman empire had been held somewhat in check in both Gaul and Britain by Constantius who reigned with almost regal authority. At last these persecutions reached Britain. Alban had returned from his travels and was still a pagan when a priest of Caerleon in Monmouthshire, named Amphibalus, fleeing from persecution, sought shelter with Alban. It was granted and during the brief stay of Amphibalus Alban was converted. Dressed in Alban's garments the priest escaped but the fury of the pagans now turned on Alban and he was called on to sacrifice to their gods; but true to his new faith he refused. After the usual method Alban was first brutally tortured and then beheaded by an axe, the attribute given him in Clog Almanacs. In art he appears with sword in one hand and a cross in the other and at times with a fountain springing from beneath his feet.

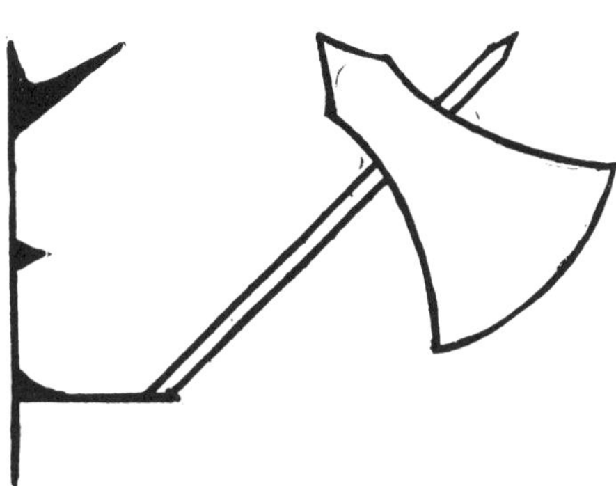

JUNE 18th.

Under the first persecution of Nero the names of twin brothers, Marcus and Marcellianus, sons of SS. Vitalis and Valeria, appear.

Arrested by Fabian, confessing that from youth they had been Christians, they were tied to posts, sharp nails driven through their feet, but still continuing their praise of Christ were at last relieved from torture by being pierced by lances.

JUNE 19th

Is the festival of St. Bruno afterward Archbishop Boniface. Descended from a noble family in Saxony, he very early displayed his inclination for a religious life and while yet a youth received the clerical tonsure. Otto III. soon made him chaplain of his person and court but the young devotee desired a more secluded life and entered the cloisters. Later the missionary spirit took hold upon him as it did on so many of the clerics of his day, and he, under the protection of St. Henry II., Emperor of Germany—having first been consecrated a bishop at which time he received the name of Boniface—he began his labours among the savage tribes of Prussia but was repulsed from among them and pushed on to the other side of Poland into Russia. From many he received rich gifts but used them all for the benefit of the poor wherever he was.

The Russians were idolators and thus had abated nothing of their ancient ferocity, and he was ordered to leave the country. But the king of a small province at last promised to listen to him "if he could see him walk through fire without it harming him." A thing which the legend tells us he accomplished, "and the king seeing the bishop thus preserved in the midst of flames, asked to be instructed in the faith, and, with many, was baptized." Thus the apostle of Russia began his work but the infidels later seized him and eighteen of his companions and beheaded them. But the seed had been sown and later bore fruit, and gave the good man his title of the apostle of Russia.

This saint is mentioned in Greek menologies on this day.

On this day also occurs the anniversary of St. Juliana Falconieri; more especially honoured at Florence where she was born in 1270, and where a little later her parents built at their own expense one of the most beautiful among the many charming churches adorning Florence to-day; the Church of the Annunciation of Our Lady. In her sixteenth year she renounced all the attractions held out before her of a life such as naturally would have come from her rank and great fortune, and consecrated her virginity to God and received the religious veil of the Mantellatae. The Mantellatae are a third order of the Servites, the religious men being the first order, and the nuns the second and third of the Servites. The Mantellatae take their name from a particular kind of short sleeves which they wear especially fitted for their peculiar duties in the service of the sick and their other charitable work for which the order was first instituted. Many devout women came to Juliana's aid, and she was obliged to accept the place of prioress of the Sisters of the Order of the Servants of the Blessed Virgin Mary; and the Sovereign Pontiff Clement XII. placed her name among the holy Virgins. Her own self-sacrifice and labour knew no rest and in her old age her early labours had so reacted upon her that she was called on to suffer great physical torment; but it was borne with that meekness that characterized her life.

JUNE 20th.

The Translation of St. Edward, king and martyr, is especially observed by the Church of England on this day. Most readers of English history will recall the tragedy at Corfe castle in 978 when the young King Edward II., surnamed "The Martyr," was by a plot of his mother-in-law, Elfrida, murdered, while he was visiting her at Corfe castle, Dorsetshire; her object being to make way for her son, Ethelred, Edward's half-brother. As the king stood drinking the usual "grace cup" from one of those huge wooden cups which required both hands to hold and so left him defenseless, he was stabbed in the back. He was privately buried at Wareham in unhallowed ground, but his legend tells of many miracles which were performed then and how; "wondrous lights shown from above; there the lame walked, there the dumb recovered speech, there every malady gave way to health."

In 980, two years after King Edward's interment at Warcham, Ælphere "ealdorman" of Mercia caused the body to be translated with great pomp and ceremony to Shaftsbury where it was reinterred. It is historic that on opening the coffin at this time, King Edward's body was found to be as fresh and untainted as when he had been so unceremoniously buried. According to the legend St. Edward appeared to Ælphere in a dream and ordered this transfer of his body to be made. In 1001 the body was once more removed, this time to Glastonbury where it has since rested. In Christian art a cup and sceptre are the usual attributes of St. Edward, while his Clog Almanac symbol is the huge wooden cup with a dagger above it.

This is also the anniversary of the birth of St. Silverius, pope and martyr, who died in 538 after but two brief years in the pontifical chair. For refusing to restore a heretical bishop deposed by his predecessor, Empress Theodora exiled him to the isle of Pontia where he passed to his reward.

JUNE 21st

Is the festival of St. Eusebius, Bishop of Samosata, capital of Comagene in Syria, now called Sempsat, and was an ancient episcopal see under the metropolitan of Heiropolis. He was elevated to his bishopric in 361 at the time when the Arian emperor, Constantius, was all powerful, and disguised under a military dress Eusebius visited his churches to continue them in the orthodox faith. Valino, however, banished him to Thrace. When under Theodosius peace was restored in the church, Eusebius was recalled from exile. But when again he was visiting his churches, an Arian woman cast down on his head a heavy tile from the roof of her house as he passed along the street, fracturing his skull and causing his death. A fact which fully illustrates the intense hatred which then existed between the Arians and Orthodox factions of the Church. His death occurred in 379 and while the Latins honour him on this 21st day of June the Greeks make his festival on the 22d.

JUNE 22d.

This day is celebrated in Roman Martyrology as the birthday in 353, at Bourdeaux, of Pontius Meropius Paulinus, a man descended from a long line of illustrious senators but who by his virtues eclipsed the honours and triumphs of his ancestors and won for him the admiration of such noted holy fathers as SS. Martin, Sulpicius Severus, Ambrose, Austin, Jerome, Gregory of Tours and many more who vie with each other in celebrating his heroism and saintly virtues. Endowed with wealth and high rank in the world, he received from nature a penetrating genius, elevated understanding, and by his carefully considered education, that needed training and culture which brought to the highest perfection his naturally rare and great gifts of mind, talents that from his infancy were cultivated by the best teachers of his day. Among these he had for his master in poesy and eloquence the famous Ansonius, the first man of his age in those sciences, and as a rhetorician renowned alike for his delicate wit and the elegant beauty of his style. Under such a teacher Paulinus even more than fulfilled the ardent hopes of his friends. "Everyone," says St. Jerom of this gifted youth, "admired the purity and eloquence of his diction, the delicacy and loftiness of his thoughts, the strength and sweetness of his style." His probity, integrity and moral worth were equally marked and everywhere recognised, as shown by the fact that in 379 he was named as consul. He married a Spanish lady of great wealth who was a sincere, faithful Christian and thus his home was equally happy and prosperous as his public life. It would seem as if both were full and that nothing was lacking for his personal happiness. Great wealth and honoured by all; yet the hollowness of earthly things already after fifteen years of success began to dawn upon him, and with his wife, still in the prime of her youth, they repaired to one of their Spanish estates where the teachings of SS. Ambrose and Martin, whom he had met at Vienne, gave him food for reflection. Encouraged by his devout wife, he sold all his and her estates and bestowed them on the poor and the church, thenceforth leaving the world behind them and going forth as poor as they had been rich. In due time Paulinus was admitted to holy orders and began his work as a teacher as well as a follower of Christ. In the pursuit of this purpose he retired to Nola in Campania, just outside of whose walls was the tomb of St. Felix with a church over it. It was here Paulinus took up his abode for the following fifteen years. In 410 the Goths in their plundering of Italy captured Nola, and in Roman Martyrology we read: "He became poor and humble for Christ, and, what is most admirable, became a slave to liberate a widow's son who had been carried into Africa by the Vandals when they devastated Campania." He died in 431.

JUNE 23d

Is the festival of St. Etheldreda, or as sometimes called "Audry." She was the daughter of Annas, or Ina, a Christian king of the East Angles and was born in Ermynge in Suffolk. She was twice married, the first time to Tonbercht, or Toubercht, prince of the southern Giroig (a tribe inhabiting what is now Rutland, Northampton, Huntingdon and part of Lincoln) who gave her as a dowry the "Isle of Ely," in the fen country. Toubercht lived but three years after his marriage. After his death Etheldreda retired to the Isle of Ely and for five years lived a saintly life in solitude. But the fame of her virtues had reached the ears of Egfrid, the powerful king of Northumberland, who sought her in marriage. Her consent to this union was "extorted" rather by force than voluntarily and for twelve years she reigned with him; being to him as Butler puts it: "As a sister, not as his wife." Then by the advice of St. Wilfrid she left her husband, took the religious veil withdrawing to the monastery of Coldingham beyond the Berwick (already mentioned), where she lived under the devout Abbess St. Ebba. Egfrid had consented to this at first, but repenting his leniency, later pursued her; but a sudden rise in the tide made the monastery inaccessible and he abandoned his quest later marrying another wife.

Freed now from Egfrid St. Etheldreda returned to her old retirement in Ely. Here in 670 she founded a double monastery for monks and nuns, becoming abbess of the latter branch. In 870 this monastery like others in England was ravaged by the Danes and pillaged. A century later King Edgar granted a charter under which the monastery was rebuilt and in 1107 Henry I. erected it into a bishopric. When Henry VIII. decreed the dissolution of the English monasteries the conventual church was converted into what has now developed into the Cathedral of Ely and which, despite its external defects from its varied styles of architecture, has but few rivals in interior beauty. Thus the festival of St. Etheldreda brings back the long and interesting story of one of England's most noted cathedrals where to-day we may see her sarcophagus, a relic of old Roman work, but which her legend assures us was "wrought by angel hands."

JUNE 24th

Is known in England as Mid-Summer Day. In the Christian Kalendar the day is held sacred as the "Nativity of St. John the Baptist." The canonical colour for the day is white.

When we remember the prominent role St. John played in both the advent and life of our Saviour it is not wonderful that this anniversary has taken such a prominent place in the festivals of the whole Christian Church. Indeed next to the Blessed Virgin, SS. Peter, Andrew and Michael, St. John the Baptist is beyond question the most popular among the saints in the Kalendar. In England alone nearly four hundred churches are dedicated to him.

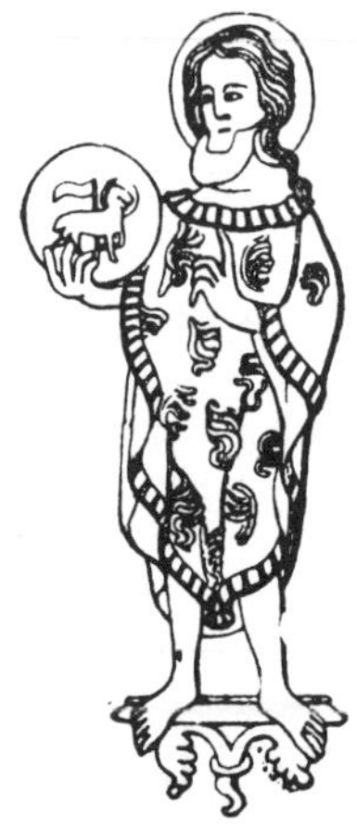

ST. JOHN.

It is the usual custom for the Church to celebrate the festival of its saints on the day of their death or to quote St. Austin "their birthday to eternal life" but St. John was sanctified even from his mother's womb (see St. Luke I. 15, 41) and the exception in his case is, therefore, most appropriate. Beyond the story of his life as told in the gospels there is comparatively little known of him. But there is no lack of evidence that many marvellous signs and wonders not only marked his birth but also preceded it. That his parents, Zachary the holy priest of the family of Abia and Elizabeth a cousin of the Blessed Virgin Mary, his mother were under especial divine protection and favour cannot for a moment be doubted. His birthplace "probably was Hebron," a sacerdotal town in the western part of the hilly country, some twenty miles from Jerusalem occupied by the tribe of Juda. And we are told that one day while Zachary was — in his turn — ministering at the golden altar in the sanctum offering incense the angel Gabriel appeared by the side of the altar and foretold the birth of this son who was to make his name sacred throughout all coming time, adding: "Thou shalt call his name John" together with other wonderful predictions all of which were literally fulfilled. We all know the remarkable story of the visit of the Holy Mother of Jesus to Elizabeth while the entire story of the life of St. John is a perpetual sermon to teach us humility, in his three prominent rôles as Prophet, Preacher and Baptist. In Christian art St. John the Baptist is usually represented wearing a long, loose mantle and carrying a tall staff or wand surmounted by a cross; accompanied by a lamb; but commonly he has a book in his hand. Frequently his mantle is formed of skins or he has "a girdle of skin about his loins," (St. Mark, I, 6) and a small pennon twined around a cross with the legend: "Ecce Agnus Dei" upon it. At times but rarely the cross is omitted. The Clog Almanac symbol is in allusion to St. John's death which his legend tells us took place two years before that of Jesus Christ at the royal fortified palace of Macheronta near the Dead Sea on the river Jordan and that he was buried at Sebaster.

MID-SUMMER DAY FESTIVALS.

From the fact that under the "old style" mid-summer occurred on the Nativity of John the Baptist there was in the early days in England a curious mixture of pagan and Christian ceremonies, since for ages the pagan's had celebrated Mid-Summer Day as a festival. Thus, in an inner court of Magdalen College Oxford, there is a stone pulpit and upon St. John's Day this pulpit was formerly transformed into a bower of green from boughs and branches out of the woods after the pagan fashion. While from the pulpit a sermon on the life of St. John the Baptist was preached. When asked why they thus followed the old Druid style the students said: "This is St. John in the Wilderness."

In many places in England down to the time of Cromwell Mid-Summer night parades were common; each man adorned with garlands of flowers, ribbons, and if possible jewels. Tradition tells of a private view Henry VIII. had of one of these processions in 1510 which so pleased him that on St. Peter's Eve (June 28th) when a similar parade used to occur, he came accompanied by Queen Catherine and a long suite of courtiers to witness it. Some very strange superstitions too, were held regarding St. John's Eve. The Irish in old days believed that on this night the soul of every person left the body and wandered on through space till it came to the spot where the soul and body would have its final earthly parting and that after thus reaching this place it returned to the mortal to whom it belonged. An English superstition was that anyone who would sit fasting all night on the church porch on St. John's Eve would see pass before him all the persons of his parish who were to die during the coming year.

JUNE 25th.

St. Prosper of Aquitain so surnamed to distinguish him from the Bishop of Orleans, is this day honoured by the Church. He apparently was a layman only but was a poet and author of great merit. Pope Leo the Great recognized this, when in 440 he called him to Rome and appointed him his secretary, while even later St. Prosper's writings against the Pelagian heresy was deemed of such value and importance that as late as 1711 a complete edition of them was republished, and a revised edition again in 1732 while in 1757 some of his writings were added to those of St. Austin, and published in Paris thus showing the value placed upon them by the Church of Rome.

The Church also on this day recognises St. Maximus Bishop of Turin, another of the lights of the V. century whose name has come down through the long centuries as one of the great and strong writers of his generation, and whose Homilies are even to-day read and regarded with veneration.

JUNE 26th.

In Roman Martyrology we read that on this day the Church honours "at Rome on Mount Cœlian the holy martyrs John and Paul who were brothers. The former was steward and the latter secretary of the Virgin Constantia, daughter of the Emperor Constantine."

I feel certain that some at least of my readers will recall this

Cœlian Hill and the view from it looking across to the ruins of the Palatine and the quaintly beautiful old Church of SS. Giovanni e Paolo, which has stood on its brow since A. D. 499 and was erected on the site of the dwelling of these two brothers, of whom Mrs. Jameson, in her "Sacred and Legendary Art," says: "They were officers in the service of Constantia, whom the old legends persist in representing as a most virtuous Christian (though I — Mrs. J. — believe she was far otherwise) * * * The site of the hill being one of the most beautiful in ancient Rome." From their rank and social position as well as from their offices these brothers naturally carried great influence and trust. When Julian the Apostate came to the throne he attempted to persuade them to sacrifice to Roman idols but they refused, saying: "Our lives are at the disposal of the emperor but our souls and our faith belong to our God." Then Julian, fearing to bring them to public martyrdom lest their popularity should cause a rebellion and the example of fortitude be an encouragement to others, sent off soldiers to behead them privately in their own house. Hence the inscription on the spot "Locus Martyrii SS. Joannis et Paoli in ædibus proprus." This church was built by Pammachus the friend of St. Jerom on the site of the house of the saints.

In this church lies the body of "St. Paul of the Cross," who died in 1776, and who was the founder of the Order of Passionists of whom I shall speak later.

In devotional art SS. John and Paul are always represented in the ancient Roman military custom with sword and palm. In the Clog Almanacs they also bear the sword and palm crossed as in the illustration.

There is also a famous church in Venice erected to these martyrs by the Dominicians who emigrated from the convent in Rome which stands near the church on Cœlian Hill.

JUNE 27th

Is the festival of St. Crescius who was a disciple of the Apostle St. Paul. He was born in Galatia and became a missionary in Gaul where he was most successful in converting many to the Christian faith. When the strength and vigour of his manhood began to fail him and he was unable longer to endure the hardships of his missionary work in Gaul he once more returned to Galatia, where he became Bishop and laboured faithfully to the end of his life confirming his people in the faith until Trajan condemned him to suffer martyrdom. Only one more of that devoted band of early Christians whose name is hardly known in these later days but it is to just this class of noble martyrs that the Christian Church owes its preservation nay even existence to-day.

Another royal personage St. Ladislas I. King of Hungary, is also honoured this day, though we can give him but a brief mention. He was a younger son of Bela I. who died in 1063 and, much against his wishes after his elder brother's death, Ladislas was compelled in 1077 to assume the sovereignty of his country. While of a quiet retiring nature, when once he had put his hand to the plough he looked not backward but devoted himself to his country and yet more to his Divine Master. To his prowess in war, his wisdom in diplomacy and his watchfulness at all times, Hungary under his rule was freed from the Huns whom he drove out of his domains as well as from the Poles, Russians and Tartars, whom he vanquished. In 1095 Ladislas was about starting at the head of his army on an expedition to the Holy Land against the Saracens, when death suddenly came to him on July 30th. Roman Martyrology, however, has changed the date of his festival to June 27th. His life was full of good deeds and endless number of miracles were placed to his credit, both before and after his death. He was canonized by Celestine III. in 1198.

JUNE 28th.

St. Irenæus the noted man whose name is honoured this day by the Church, was by his own statement born "near the times of Domitian," or about the beginning of the reign of Adrian A. D. 120, still his fame seems to rest largely upon his power as a writer against the heresies that even at that early day had begun to creep into the church. Of these writings St. Gregory of Tours and St. Jerom speak in most enthusiastic terms: for his zeal and earnest work in the vineyard of the Lord was very great and we find him in 177 selected as the second bishop of Lyons at a time when as already alluded to the Christians at Lyons were being sorely tormented and persecuted. It is thus we find St. Irenæus named as one among the "martyrs of Lyons."

Dates disagree somewhat as to the exact year when he testified to his faith by yielding his life but most writers make the date in 202, but some fixing it in 208.

THE REASON THE POPE CHANGES HIS NAME.

A pertinent and proper inquiry as to why the popes change their names when elevated to the pontificate is often asked. Prior to 884 this was not done, but in that year Peter di Porea was elected pope and took the name of Tergius II. from a feeling of humility: since he did not deem himself worthy to bear the title of Peter II. and from the same sentiment no pope who has ever yet occupied the pontifical chair has ever assumed the name of Peter. Just why each successor of Peter di Porea has followed the example which he set is not very clear, yet the fact remains that each of the holy fathers upon assuming their high office have adopted a name by which they chose to be known.

SYMBOLS OF THE APOSTLES.

From the earliest period to which archæologists have been able to trace Christian art the "Four Holy Evangelists" who recorded the words and acts of our Lord have naturally taken precedence of others. Next to them came those Apostles whom Christ chose to preach His gospel "through all nations." The first representation of those twelve apostles like those given the evangelists were purely emblematical. They were figured as twelve sheep, with Christ as the Good Shepherd standing in their midst bearing a lamb in his arms. Soon we find Christ represented as Himself the "Lamb of God," standing on a slight eminence, crowned with a cruciform nimbus, with the apostles as sheep standing on either side of Him. In some of the oldest of the Roman churches this form is in a degree varied and Christ is seen as "the Lamb" standing on a hill from which the four rivers of Paradise are flowing (see illustration in article of April 19th), with six sheep coming out from Jerusalem on the one side, and six more sheep issuing from the city of Bethlehem, on the other side of the hill. The next step shows the twelve apostles as men, each however, accompanied by a sheep; and still later the apostles stand with scrolls in their hands, and the sheep left out from the picture. The several especial emblems by which we in these later days have come to recognize each apostle were assigned them at a far later period, not a few having been given long after their death. Of these, I will speak as I record the life of each one and therefore omit them here; except for convenience of the reader I will make a list of them:

THE CRUCIFORM NIMBUS.

St. Peter — Keys, or a fish; St. Paul — One, or at times, two swords; St. Andrew — A transverse cross; St. James (Major) — A pilgrim's staff; St. John — A chalice with a serpent; when an eagle is given it is in his character of an evangelist; St. Thomas — A builder's rule or square; but sometimes a spear; St. James (Minor) — A club; St. Philip — A staff or crosier surmounted by a cross; or a small cross in his hand; St. Bartholomew — A large knife; St. Matthew — A purse; St. Simon — A saw; St. Thaddius, or Jude — A halberd or lance; St. Matthias — A lance.

S PETRUS

JUNE 29th

Is the day which has been fixed upon by the Church as the "birthday" of "The Prince of the Apostles," as St. Peter is sometimes termed.

In both Biblical and profane history the names of SS. Peter and Paul are naturally, constantly and intimately connected. The early Christian Church was at all times considered under its two great divisions; that of the converted Jews, and that of the converted Gentiles, the former represented by St. Peter and the latter by St. Paul, and this combined for the universal Church of Christ, not as Apostles only, but also as founders of the church. For this reason, in correct Christian art we find them constantly seen together; or where our Lord is introduced into the picture, they are standing on either side of Him. The same is true where the Blessed Virgin appears or where they are at the altar, one being seen at each end of it.

ST. PETER.

In the Greek types the portrait of "the Pilot of the Galilean lake" is taken from the description (so often quoted) given by Nicephorus. He is: "A robust old man with a broad forehead and rather coarse features, with an open, undaunted countenance, short gray hair and a short thick beard, silvery white and curled." But, strangely, according to this description Nicephorus adds an unexpected feature that "he had red, weak eyes," a peculiarity which has not been preserved in his portraits. Mrs. Jameson says: "In some of the early pictures he is bald on the top of his head and the hair grows thick around in a circle, somewhat like a priestly tonsure, and in some examples this tonsure has the form of a triple row of curls, close to the head, like a tiara." The same authority says that in Anglo-Saxon art: "St. Peter is always beardless and wears the tonsure."

One of the legends of St. Peter says the Gentiles shaved his head to make him an object of derision, and that from this the tonsure originated. In Greek art St. Peter's dress is a blue tunic with white drapery thrown over it, but blue and green are now regarded by the best artistic authorities for the saint's robes.

Of the two keys now universally recognized as St. Peter's peculiar attribute there seems to be no mention until after the beginning of the VIII. century. In all the ancient mosaics and upon the early catacomb sarcophagi St. Peter (as in the illustration) bears in his hand a scroll or book, and later examples show him still with the gospel in one hand and the cross in the other.

The keys seem to have been given St. Peter only after the commencement of the VIII. century. While in rare cases he bears a single key, in general he has two, one of gold and one of iron, opening the gates of Heaven and Hell. Or these keys are of gold and silver, which is interpreted to signify his power "to absolve or to bind." A mosaic on the tomb of Otho II. (Lateran Mus.) shows St. Peter with a third key, expressing dominion over Heaven, Earth and Hell. But such examples are very rare.

At times St. Peter wears a papal tiara and carries his key, as Milton drew him:

> "Last came and last did go
> The pilot of the Galilean lake;
> Two massy keyes he bore of metal twain,
> (The golden opes, the iron shuts amain)
> He shook his mitred locks, and stern
> bespake."

It would be a work of supererogation, (if not conceited on my part), after the many and graphic sketches of this wonderful man's life and character which have been written by theologians of every possible shade of Christian faith, for me to re-tell his remarkable story, while a volume would be needed to recount the many legends of his varied career.

Of his death we are all familiar with the story of how Nero after the burning of Rome accused the Christians of the crime, and how St. Peter, under the counsel of friends started to flee from the city but was met by a vision of our Saviour who warned him to return, as he did only to be seized by Nero's soldiers and, with his fellow apostle, St. Paul cast into the Mamertine prison from which he emerged only to meet his death. The records of this event vary somewhat. According to one St. Peter suffered martyrdom in the Circus of Caligula at the foot of the Vatican and was crucified between two metae (i. e., the goals or terminal) in the circus, round which the chariots turned in the races. Another tradition says he was put to death in the courtyard of a barrack or military station, on the summit of Mons Janicula where the Church of San Pietro in Montoreo now stands on an eminence above the site of the Circus of Caligula. Of this event Dr. Butler writes: "St. Peter, when he was come to the place of execution, requested of the officers that he might be crucified with his head downwards, alleging that he was not worthy to suffer in the same manner his Divine Master had died before him. * * * Accordingly the executioners easily granted the apostle his extraordinary request. St. Chrysostom, St. Austin and St. Austerius say that he was nailed to the cross; Tertullian mentions that he was tied with cords. He was probably both nailed and bound with ropes."

JUNE 30th

Is the festival of St. Paul the apostle and martyr, the fellow prisoner of St. Peter as he had been his companion and fellow worker in earlier days.

There must have been as striking a contrast between St. Paul and St. Peter in person as there evidently was in character. That images, or what we to-day would call "statuettes" of noted persons even those of Christ, were common with the Romans is seen by St. Augustine's allusions to the "Lalarium of Marcellina," when he names among her household effects images of "Homer, Pythagoras, Jesus Christ and Paul the Apostle," from which pictures later were made. Lucian refers to St. Paul as "the bald-headed Galilean with a hook nose." According to several ancient traditions St. Paul was a man of "small and meagre stature," with an aquiline nose, a high forehead and unusually bright, sparkling eyes. In the early Greek pictures of him his face is long and oval, the nose aquiline, the forehead high and quite bald. His beard is always long, flowing and pointed and of a dark brown colour, Mrs. Jameson saying: "I recollect no instance of St. Paul with a gray beard." In dress the pictures of St. Paul give him the same blue tunic and white mantle accorded to St. Peter. As attributes, St. Paul in all the earliest pictures bears a scroll or book, or twelve rolls intended to designate his epistles. Later on he was awarded the sword, as in illustration, as a double attribute, first to evidence the manner of his death, and next as emblematical of the faithful battle fought with "the sword of the Spirit which is the word of God," (Ephesians vi., 17) for, as we all know, his life from the time of his conversion was one long spiritual struggle. The position of the sword in every case is the point to be noticed. If, as shown in illustration, the saint leans or rests upon it, it is his attribute as a martyr. If held aloft or brandished it is then his attribute as the apostle of Christ. Sometimes two swords are given St. Paul to indicate the dual attributes, but this is not frequent. The traditions regarding the martyrdom of SS. Peter and Paul, (although in Roman Martyrology the death of St. Peter is marked on the 29th and that of St. Paul on the 30th of June) as generally accepted is that the two apostles attained their glorious immortality on the same day, but in different places. As a Roman citizen, St. Paul escaped the ignominy attached to public execution in the circus, as well as the prolonged torture of death upon the cross. That he was beheaded at a point two miles from Rome beyond the Ostian way known as "Tre Fontane," is generally accepted, his legend running that as his head fell beneath the sword it struck the earth three times before resting and at each of these spots a fountain sprang forth that continues flowing even now. Legends of St. Paul are far less numerous than those of St. Peter, one, the last, being that a Christian Roman matron named Plautilla stationed herself on the Ostian way to look upon him for the last time and ask his blessing. As the apostle turned from her he begged that she would loan him her veil to bind his eyes at the fatal moment, promising to restore it after his death. It was given him amid the mocking jests of the laughing soldiers. But, the legend continues, after St. Paul's death, true to his promise, he did appear to Plautilla and returned her the blood-stained veil.

ST. PAUL.

A great monastery was later erected on this dirk and marshy spot where a church "St. Paolo alle Tre Fontane," was built in 1590 for Cardinal Aldobrandini, which contains, it is said, the marble pillar St. Paul was bound to when beheaded.

The following description of this historic martyr is from Conybeare and Housons' long and graphic account of the event: "Through the dust and tumult of that busy throng, the small troop of soldiers threaded their way silently under the bright sky of an Italian midsummer. They were marching, though they knew it not, in a procession more really triumphal than any they had ever followed in the train of general or emperor along the Sacred Way. Their prisoner, now at last and forever delivered from captivity, rejoiced to follow his Lord 'without the gate.' The place of execution was not far distant, and there the sword of the headsman ended his long course of sufferings and released that heroic soul from that feeble body. Weeping friends took up his corpse, and carried it for burial to those subterranean labyrinths where, through many ages of oppression, the persecuted church found refuge for the living and sepulchres for the dead."

For the same reasons I failed to comment on the life of St. Peter, I must omit any remarks on that of St. Paul; but no Bible reader need search long for such details.

JULY

This month was originally the fifth month in the Roman year and hence denominated Quintilis. In ancient Alban Kalendars it had thirty-six days. Romulus gave it thirty-one and Numa reduced it to thirty; but Julius Cæsar restored the lost day and it has so remained. After Cæsar's death, Mark Anthony changed the name to July in honour of the great Julius. Among the Romans the influence of the "Dog-Star" was believed to be all powerful. Our illustration is from an antique Roman gem and pictures "The Dog-Star" as the Romans were used to call it.

The Saxons termed July the: "Hey Monath" and also the "Maed Monath," this being the time of their hay-harvest and when the maed was in bloom.

JULY 1st

Is the Octave of St. John the Baptist, and has a typical office in the liturgy of certain churches of the Roman faith.

Among a long list of saints the Roman Church honours this day is St. Theobald, or Thibault, as he is sometimes designated. His legend is only another which illustrates the peculiar fascination that seemed to hang round devoutly inclined men and women down to the Middle Ages, and was confined to no rank or station in life.

Theobald belonged to a family of the "Counts Palatins" of Champagne; born at Provins in Brie in 1017, and was a nephew of "Theobald Archbishop of Vienne" for whom he was named. In his youth the lives of St. John the Baptist, St. Paul, the Hermit St. Antony and St. Arsenius in their retreats in the wilderness were always his favourite books over which he spent days and nights "in ecstasies of delight" and they so charmed him that "he sighed for the like sweet retirement." Frequent converse with a hermit named Burchard who had a cell on a small island in the Seine, only added to his fervent desire to become also a hermit. The many days he spent with this holy man confirmed him in his desires and strengthened his resolve to follow a life of solitude in prayer and holy study. No attraction of Court life nor the brilliant marriage his family had arranged for him could wean him from his set purpose. In 1034 Rodolph (the last King of Burgundy), an uncle of Theobald died, and a cousin Eudo claimed the crown and the sovereignty over Provence, Savoy, Viennois and Burgundy, (though the Duke by a sort of vasselage yet held Burgundy) but the Emperor Conrad "the Salic" seized upon it by virtue of the will and testament of the late King and a war ensued in which Theobald's father wished him to take the head of an army he had raised to aid his cousin Eudo. Then it was Theobald informed his father of his intended eremitical life and declined in any way to take part in the struggle. Theobald then was barely eighteen years old; but with a young nobleman named Walter the two, having given their courtly garments in exchange for the robes of beggar pilgrims set out for their quest of a hermitage. It all reads like one of those old tales; how they wandered barefooted through Germany and on to Rome and at last found a spot named Salanigo near to Vincenza, Italy where they built their cells and "Walter" died. For years Theobald then led his lonely life known far and wide as "the Hermit of Salanigo" whose sanctity had attracted the notice of the

Bishop of Vincenza through whom at last the parents learned for the first time of the whereabouts of their son.

The dénouement is somewhat dramatic when the father and mother found their son in rags, and came away with the enthusiasm of his pleadings, the mother resolved to become a hermit and the son built for her a cell near his own. Theobald died in 1066 and was canonized by Clement III.

JULY 2d.

On this day is commemorated in both the Roman and Protestant churches the "Visitation of the Virgin Mary," to her cousin Elizabeth as recorded in St. Luke's (I., 39, 40) gospel, when the Virgin went into the mountains of Judea to see the mother of St. John the Baptist. This festival had been observed for some time by the devout members of the church, but with no degree of regularity, when in 1383 Urban VI. instituted it as a prescribed festival. The council of Basle in 1441 enjoined it to be observed in all the churches and fixed the date. It is also called "The Salutation of Elizabeth." This scene has so often been reproduced by artists, that few tourists will not recall some one of the many pictures in the galleries of Europe.

JULY 3d

Is the festival of an humble but devoted servant of our Lord, St. Phocas of Sinope, only a gardener, whose field served to furnish food for his Christian brethren, and his cottage a shelter from the storm. Yet this was enough to bring upon him the wrath of those persecutors who in those fateful years of 303 and 4 pursued every Christian with relentless hate. His legend tells of his unremitted charities and self-sacrifice, until one stormy night when two strangers sought shelter and received it. They told him they were in search of one Phocas ; to slay him for his faith.

From his humble stores he fed them and later, with his blessings, sent them to rest. Then he went to his garden and beneath his vines dug his own grave. In the morning, when questioned, he led his guests to the open grave and told them who he was. The strangers, loth as they were to slay so saintly a man, dared not to disobey the orders they had received and therefore beheaded him by the grave he had prepared in which he was buried. He is only to be found represented in Byzantian art; where he is shown in his gardener's dress holding his spade which in Clog Almanacs is given him as an attribute.

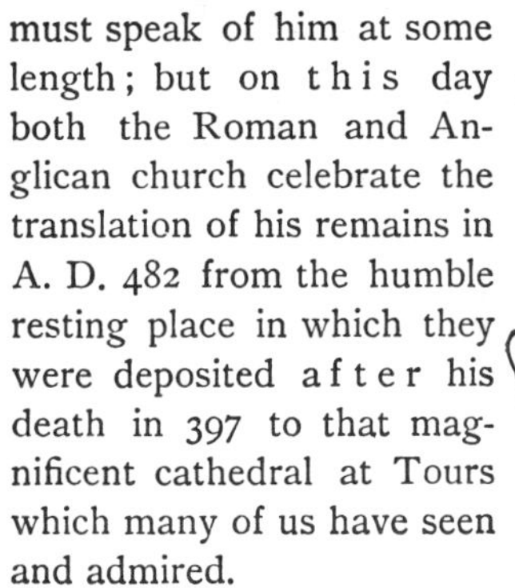

JULY 4th.

On November 11th the festival of the Great St. Martin of Tours occurs at which time we must speak of him at some length; but on this day both the Roman and Anglican church celebrate the translation of his remains in A. D. 482 from the humble resting place in which they were deposited after his death in 397 to that magnificent cathedral at Tours which many of us have seen and admired.

ST. MARTIN OF TOURS.

JULY 5th.

I will mention to-day only St. Peter of Luxemburg though he is one who well deserves more extended notice. One "whose miracles" Dr. Butler says, "would fill volumes;" one of which made him the patron saint of Avignon.

The same is true of St. Modwina, a noble Irish virgin who migrated to Scotland and there founded two monasteries, one at Sterling and the other at Edinburgh. Later she came to England and about A. D. 840 founded a monastery in the forest of Arden where she secured and educated the daughter of the pious King Ethelwolf, which bore her name, "St. Editha" and who became its second abbess.

THE CHRISTIAN RELIGION IN BRITAIN.

While I in no way pretend to trace the story of the church, it naturally is interwoven with our subject matter, and before speaking of St. Palladius, whose name is a prominent one in the Kalendar of both the Roman and Reformed churches it is necessary to speak of the progress Christianity had made in Britain before the advent of this holy man. During the occupation of the island by the Romans the Christian religion had unquestionably made some progress in such provinces as were under the domination of Roman arms; but beyond or outside of this influence the natives were pagans. When Severus, the Roman general, made his advance northward and came among the southern Picts there are found some slight traces of Christianity having been taught the conquered tribes. But it was nearly two centuries later that any material progress seems to show itself in this direction; or to be more exact, a few years only before the Romans in 410 finally evacuated Britain. Ptolemy places a tribe of the Novantæ of the Southern Picts along the north shore of Solway Frith at a point he terms, "Leukopibia," on the west side of Wigton Bay. Before that time a Christian missionary named Ninian had appeared among them and built a church. Several important facts are connected with this church. First, Ninian tells us he sent to Martin,

Bishop of Tours, for workmen to build his church "after the Roman manner." That is, of stone and cement. Thus this is the first stone structure we have any authentic record of built north of the Solway Frith. Next from the fact that Ninian heard of Martin's death while he was building his church we get an almost exact date, not usual in those days; for we know Martin died in 397. On September 16th, on St. Ninian's festival, I shall have more to say of this church and man.

Whatever advance may have been made after Ninian's death the Novantæ and any other of the Picts who had listened to Ninian quickly apostatized and lapsed into paganism, for we hear no more of Christianity till we come to the record of Palladius.

JULY 6th.

There is a long, dark interval of more than a century between the death of Ninian and the advent of Columba (lately mentioned) among the Southern Picts. In the meantime the only break referring to Christianity is the advent of St. Palladius, who we are told was sent by Pope Celestine in 430 as a missionary "to the Scots." Now unfortunately as history shows, there were "no Scots in Scotland," as both Burton and Skene tell us so conclusively; perplexing as the assertion sounds, for the land now called Scotland was then called either Alban or Pictavia according to the writer who was speaking of it, and the only Scots then known were the Dalriadan Scots of the north of Ireland who later colonized Argyle under Fergus mor mac Erc. Indeed the story of Palladius taken from either ecclesiastical or profane history is at best a very tangled skein which I cannot undertake to straighten out in these pages.

After careful study of a translation of a portion of the "Book of Armagh" (compiled in or about 801), which contains the oldest authentic life of St. Patrick, one cannot fail to be struck by the fact that there is here no mention of St. Palladius. Again reading the fictitious account of Fordun in which the Scots colonized Scotland several centuries before Christ and had been converted to Christianity by Pope Victor I. in the year 203, we wonder what sort of a church they had until in 430 Palladius became their first bishop. After thus sifting the various phases of the story of Palladius it seems the most natural to accept the one that he first had gone to Ireland; that while there, according to Fiech of Sleibath, he founded three churches. "Nevertheless, (says Skene) he was not well received by the people, but was compelled to go round the coast to the north," and thus on his homeward way to Rome came into Pictavia, where at a place called Forddun in the plain of Girgin he died. Whether a martyr or not seems quite too uncertain to be asserted. This place, Forddun, is beyond doubt in Mearnes, and it seems a natural sequence that, driven northward from Ireland through the Pentland Frith along the east coast, Palladius reached Kincardineshire, to die at Forddun, fifteen miles from Aberdeen.

Of the character of this saint who is termed in Roman Martyrology "the apostle of the Scots," it is hard to pass judgment upon it with the scant material available; but none can deny that only heroes in those early days gave themselves to a missionary life such as his was. In some of the old Scotch and English Kalendars the festival of St. Palladius is named for December 15th, but later English and Roman Kalendars agree upon July 6th as the proper date.

JULY 7th

Marks the anniversary of St. Pantænus one of the noted "Fathers of the Church" in its early struggles. He was by birth a Sicilian and by profession a Stoic philosopher, so remarkable for his eloquence that he gained the name of the "Sicilian Bee." Attracted by the virtuous lives and the character of their conversation, he entered the celebrated school which the disciples of St. Mark had established at Alexandria in Egypt in order to study the Holy Scriptures. Once convinced of their truth he delved still deeper in the study of sacred learning. His natural ability and habits as a critical student early won for him the rank and reputation he deserved. By choice he would have remained in obscurity devoting himself entirely to his sacred studies; but the need of such men as he was urgent, and before A. D. 179 he was called to the head of one of the schools where his rare ability as a teacher and his depth of learning quickly raised the reputation of his seminary to the first place among "the schools of the philosophers." His reputation had long before extended beyond the confines of Alexandria and Christian envoys from India begged him to visit the East to confute the subtle arguments of the Brachmans (Brahmins), and Demetrius, who had been made Bishop of Alexandria in 189 appointed him "preacher to the Eastern nations," and he spent several years in preaching and teaching in India. Then he returned to Alexandria where the remainder of his arduous life was passed as a leader and teacher in those famous schools, ending his noble career, still "in the harness," about 216, leaving a well earned reputation for his erudition and faithful labours in the cause of Christ.

To-day is also sacred to the memory of St. Willibald, a son of St. Richard one of those early Christian kings of West Saxony. Willibald as early as 721 with one of his brothers made a pilgrimage to the Holy Land and later becoming a missionary to Aichstadt in Franconia, where he was ordained as Bishop and for nearly forty-five years served his Great Master. He died the 7th of June 790, but his festival has been held on July 7th. He was canonized in 938 by Pope Leo VII.

This day also is the festival of St. Benedict XI. Pope and Confessor. He was born in 1240 and when fourteen years of age took on the habit of St. Dominick. In 1298 he became a cardinal and on the death of Boniface VIII. on October 11, 1303, was chosen to fill the pontifical throne but he only occupied it for eight months and seventeen days dying July 7, 1304.

JULY 8th

Is set apart by the Roman Church as the festival of Queen Elizabeth of Portugal. She was the daughter of the King of Arragon and wife of the profligate King Dionysius of Portugal to whom she was married when but twelve years of age thus for forty years compelled to do penance for the misdeed of those who had thus condemned her to this life of suffering. Yet through it all, bearing her trials with such saintly submission as to win for her the love and reverence of all who knew her. Indeed she won for herself by her patience the title of "Sant Isabel de Pez." It may interest some of my readers to know that she was the original of Schiller's "Fridolin," a German, though the scene is laid in Germany and the name given her: "Die Grafin von Savern." Her story is one long sad romance. She died July 4, 1336. For her virtues and charities she was canonized by Urban VIII. in 1625 who at that time appointed this day as sacred to her memory.

To-day also is remembered for St. Grimald of St. Omer who has the especial honour of being the first professor of divinity ever appointed to the University of Oxford. On the death of Eldred, Archbishop of Canterbury, King Alfred strove to secure Grimald's consent to accept the archbishopric, but he refused it. He died in holy sanctity on July 8, 903, at the ripe old age of eighty-three.

One other name, that of St. Procopius, appears in the Kalendar of this day and must not be passed if for no other reason than that he was the proto-martyr at Bethsan under that fatal decree of Dioclesian which reached Palestine in 303. He was an interpreter of the Greek into the Syro-Chaldeac tongue; but a devout Christian and being brought before Paulinus prefect of the province was, as usual, ordered to sacrifice to the heathen gods or the four great emperors, Diodesius, Herculius, Galerius and Constantius but true to his faith refused and won the crown of martyrdom.

By a coincidence the festival of St. Procopius King of Bohemia who relinquished his crown to become a hermit also falls on the same day with that of his namesake, St. Procopius of Bethsan. I find for King Procopius a Clog Almanac symbol, given here which is almost identical with that of St. Giles and was given for a similar reason, his kindness to the wild animals around his hermitage.

JULY 9th.

According to the Martyrology of the Venerable Bede this day is the festival of St. Ephrem of Edessa of whom Dr. Butler in his "Lives of the Saints" says: "This humble deacon was the most illustrious of all the doctors who by their doctrines and writings have adorned the Syriac church." He was a hermit in Syria; but his wonderful writings even now after over fifteen centuries are yet read; while as late as 1743 they were esteemed worthy of being republished in six folio volumes at Rome, a fact which fully justifies Butler's assertion.

This day is also recognized as the festival of St. Veronica Guiliani, virgin, who must not be confounded with the St. Veronica whose festival occurs on Shrove Tuesday; since St. Veronica Guiliani was born in 1660. She was christened Ursula and from her infancy was noted for her devout character. At the age of eighteen she became a novitiate of the Capuchine nuns of Citta del Castillo when she took the name of Veronica. She successively filled every office in the community until when thirty-four years of age she was appointed "Mistress of the Novices" becoming in 1716 Abbess.

Without relating the legend in its entirety, mention should be made of St. Veronica's remarkable vision and the terrible suffering she endured but it would be impossible to explain how after *that* she bore upon her brow marks that were the counterpart of those left by "the Crown of Thorns" which our Saviour bore after His Crucifixion; and to which those who were duly to examine her "testified under oath" she bore these marks until her death, as evidence of her "espousal" of Christ; Butler, explaining this word "espousal" as denoting: "A more intimate union formed between God and the soul, by the most perfect love."

The legend is one of the most remarkable ones found in the Lives of the Saints; and yet is verified by authorities that it seems impossible to question. Her death came from consumption.

Veronica was beatified by Pius VII., and canonized by Gregory XVI. on Trinity Sunday, May 20, 1830.

JULY 10th

Is somewhat remarkable as the festival of seven brothers the sons of a noble and wealthy Roman widow who all fell victims to the persecutions of Christians in the reign of Marcus Aurelius Antoninus. One by one these noble young men were brought before Publius the prefect first tempted then threatened and tortured, but without avail for their mother St. Felicitas stood by and exhorted them to remain faithful to Christ. One brother was scourged to death with whips whose lashes were loaded with lead; two were beaten to death with clubs and one cast over a precipice while three were beheaded. These are commemorated this day; but the noble matron, their mother, is remembered on November 23d.

JULY 11th.

Pius I. Pope and martyr is this day honoured by the Roman Church. He was elevated to the Papacy in 142. From the records of Tillemont we see he had served with the clergy at Rome a number of years and succeeded St. Hyginus in the government of the Church. The records of his life are meager some contending against his title as a martyr. As there are eminent writers on both sides I prefer not to judge. All that seems certain regarding this early Pope is that he was born in Aquileia and died in 157; being buried at the foot of Vatican Hill.

This day is also devoted to the honour of St. James, Bishop of Nisibis. He was one of those early saints to whom according to his legend had been given the gift of prophecy and who is credited with many remarkable miracles. The most wonderful of the latter being when he saved the city at the time it was besieged by the Persian Sapor; and utterly helpless. Then in answer to the prayers of the Bishop as in the days of the Egyptians under Moses clouds of gnats and flies came. They entered the ears and nostrils of the elephants and horses stinging them to madness and putting the army into utter confusion and disorder. After this followed pestilence and a famine which in time caused the barbarian Persian to withdraw his hosts and the city was relieved.

Much confusion covers the date of the death of St. James ranging from 301 to 350 the date accepted by Dr. Butler. Thus the festival of the saint is recognized by the Latins on the 11th of July by the Eastern and on the 15th of July by the Western Churches, by the Greeks on the 13th of January and 31st of October; by Syrians on the 18th of January and by Assyrians on a Saturday in December. Certainly a variety of days to choose from.

The writings and learning of St. James have given him a rank among the doctors of the Syriac Church, next to that of St. Ephrem, while the Armenians honour him as one of the principal doctors of their national church.

JULY 12th.

St. John Gualbert came of a rich and noble family in Florence. He was given in his youth to all the usual follies of wealthy men until in an hour he was suddenly taken from his worldly life. A brother had been murdered. Impelled by a spirit of revenge he sought for the assassin to mete out to him the vengeance which then honour seemed to require. At last the two met but to his surprise the assassin fell on his knees and craved mercy in the name of Jesus Christ. The plea seemed to touch an unusual chord in John Gualbert's heart. He could not resist it. His feeling of revenge was gone. Not only did he grant forgiveness but promised future friendship. From this interview he hastened to the monastery of St. Minias of the Order of St. Bennet and applied for admission to the order. Despite his father's protest and pleading he was at last admitted but in humility he never would take even "Minor Orders," though he might have been abbot of the monastery at a later time.

Sometime after this with a single companion he sought out solitude where they could in privacy indulge in such austere devotions as met their wishes happily finding two devout hermits in a valley called Vallis Umbrosa a half day's journey from Florence in Tuscany when the four established their new order which in 1070 Alexander II. approved and from which the Order Vallis Umbrosa grew. The order received lay brothers as well as monks "who were exempt from certain penances and silence and were employed in external offices." This, Dr. Butler says: "Is said to be the first example of such distinction; but it was soon imitated by other orders." The holy man died at Passigrano at the age of seventy-four in 1073. Pope Celestine III. canonized him in the year 1193.

JULY 13th.

When the 13th day of July falls on Sunday (or upon the Sunday immediately following the 13th) there is celebrated at Brussels in Belgium, a local feast called

THE FESTIVAL OF THE MIRACLES.

The legend very much abridged runs as follows:

In 1369 a Jew named Jonathan lived in Enghien in Hainault who was very rich. For the purpose of profanation he desired to secure some of the consecrated wafers used in the Holy Sacrament of the Eucharist. To accomplish this he hired a poor Jew named Jean de Louvain who after a time on an October night, managed to steal from the altar of St. Catherine's Church in Brussels the pix which contained the sacred wafers. In somewhat graphic words the legend tells of Jean's adventure. He must have been a very stolid dolt or a most brave man to have carried out his purpose as he did amid the strange demonstrations that accompanied the theft. But he did so and duly delivered to Jonathan his spoils receiving the reward the rich man had promised. Jonathan did not live to carry out his sacrilegious purpose for very shortly thereafter while walking in his garden he was murdered by unknown hands. His widow seems to have known his wishes and soon after his death delivered to a coterie of Jews the pix with its sacred contents. Upon a day, evidently selected with the utmost malice for it was Good Friday in the year 1370 these Jews assembled and taking from the pix the sixteen wafers it contained spread them out on the table around which they stood. At a signal they began to stab the wafers with their poinards. It was then the Miracle occurred, for from each wafer there flowed a stream of blood as the poinard was withdrawn. Affrighted and amazed the sight struck them dumb as they stood unable to move. At last they fled in terror; but like all cowards they began to take counsel with each other how to conceal their vile work. A woman was found who was engaged to carry the defiled wafers to Cologne. Just what was to be done with them there by some strange inconsistency the legend does not tell nor yet where they were left when the woman returned to Brussels. It was her own conscience began to reproach her and she confessed to the clergy of St. Guduli her share in the sacrilege and how the sacred emblems could be recovered.

Later this was done and the sacred wafers confided to the care of St. Guduli church where they yet may be seen bearing the blood stains and marks of the Jewish poinards. Later the miscreants were captured, tried and condemned for their sacrilege and on May 22, 1370 were burned at the stake for their crime.

On several occasions thereafter these holy wafers proved their miraculous powers in staying epidemics. One most notable instance being in 1529 when they caused a grievous epidemic which then raged in Brussels to cease. From that time a festival in their honour was ordained and duly observed; until during the political struggles of half a century later in the Netherlands, from 1579 to 1585, they were omitted. Again during the Revolution of 1789 to 92, they were neglected, but in 1804 with due solemnity, they were renewed and have since been observed.

This day is set aside in especial memory of St. Eugenius and his fellow martyrs who won their crowns of glory in 505. The Roman provinces in Africa were for years the richest and most favoured of the entire Roman empire. Cartagenian barbarism had given place to the lights of science and the true religion of Christ had dispelled heathenism. African princes vied with their kings in their efforts towards a higher and better life when the Romans, to preserve Italy, abandoned many of their outside provinces to preserve its great center from the onslaughts of the Goths and Vandals. Already they had as our historical readers know though they had abandoned Britain thus felt no fear for Africa though Geneseric, King of the Vandals and Alaus had gained a foothold in Spain. Strange as it sounds these Vandals were mostly Christians but of the Arian types of faith. When in 454 Geneseric late returned from plundering Rome he allowed them to choose St. Deogratius for their bishop after he had razed the public buildings of Carthage, while still persecuting those of the Orthodox faith. After a reign of thirty-seven years this tyrant was succeeded by his son Huneric if possible a more barbarous persecutor of Orthodox Christians than his father. But in 481 Huneric so far relented that he allowed the long vacant bishopric to be filled. The universal choice fell upon Eugenius. From thence on life was indeed a burden to the good bishop though he came safely through the first stormy conflicts with the Arians. It was Dr. Butler says, during this quarrel that the Orthodox church took the name of "Catholic" they have since retained. We cannot follow Eugenius in his arduous life; while constantly opposed by Thrasimund the African king then reigning, until with St.

Vindemial, Bishop of Cuspa in Africa, he was condemned to die unless he would accept the Arian heresy. Both he and Vindemial refused and the latter was beheaded; but for some reason the king chose to send Eugenius into banishment in the Languedoc under the King of the Visigoths where he died in 505.

JULY 14th.

St. Bonaventure who is honoured by the Church this day was one of the "bright lights" of the order of St. Francis who for his attainments in sacred learning was given the title of "Seraphic Doctor." He advanced rapidly in the church and in 1256, was made "Doctor of the Church" by Pope Alexander IV. King Louis IX., (St. Louis) held Bonaventure in very high esteem; frequently sending for him to consult upon intricate points and always having a place for him at his table.

The writings of Bonaventure hold a high place in the literature of the Roman Church. Especially is this true of his homiletic writings, though not a few of his controversial efforts show deep learning and a great command of language.

The last public function where St. Bonaventure appeared was the Council at Lyons to which he had accompanied Pope Gregory X., which he addressed on May 7th. Later his fatal illness came, and he died when fifty-three years of age on this day in 1274, leaving a memory for his learning, humility and loving charity such as is not often accorded even to canonized saints.

JULY 15th

Is the festival of St. Swithin (as the Saxons called him) or Swithun, Bishop and patron of Winchester, a city which even in the early days of the Romans in Britain had attained some note, and is mentioned by Ptolemy under the name of Venta. Later it was the chief seat of the kings of West Saxony, one of whom in 625 built a church here. When, under Egbert, King of

Wessex, in 828, Britain came under one rule Winchester was the capital of the kingdom, and it was here that King John in 1214 to save his crown, under orders from Pope Innocent III. did homage to the Papacy.

This is an historic spot where Kenewalch, son of Kinegils, in 643 completed the church his father began and founded the monastery where St. Swithin received both his education and took upon himself monastic orders;

being ordained by Helinstan, Bishop of Winchester, and made provost or dean of the "Old Monastery." Such was Swithin's reputation thus early in his career that King Egbert committed to his care the education of his son Ethelwold, and also often consulted him in affairs of his kingdom. After Egbert's death (837–8) Ethelwold (who had been ordained a sub-deacon) by a dispensation from Pope Leo returned to secular life and succeeded his father as king, and in 852 procured for his old teacher, Swithin, the Bishopric of Winchester, and also made him Chancellor. Swithin accompanied Alfred the Great (the youngest son of Ethelwold) when he went to Rome to be confirmed. Through the influence of Bishop Swithin King Ethelwold bestowed a tithe or tenth part of all his lands in the kingdom on the Church.

After presiding over the see of Winchester for nearly eleven years the good man departed this life on July 2, 862, and through humility requested his body should be buried outside of the Cathedral, "Where the feet of passersby might tread and the rain of heaven fall on his tomb." This request was complied with and his tomb was on the north side of the church, where it received the droppings from the eaves, and there it rested until on July 15, in 971 his relics were with great pomp and ceremony translated to the tomb within the church, and again in 1094 to the (then) new Cathedral where they now remain. It is said the old-time quartrain:

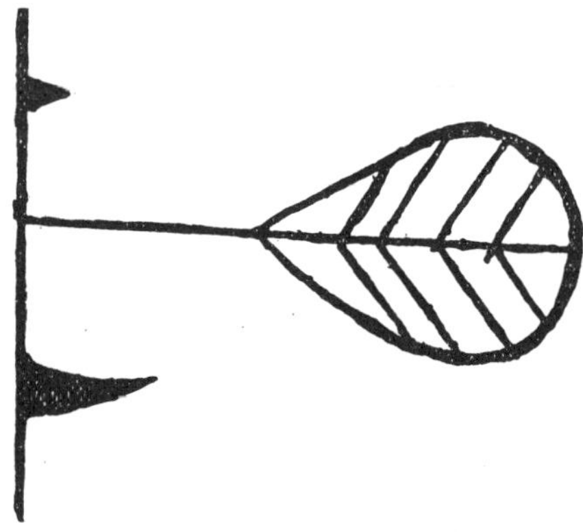

"St. Swithin's day, if thou dost rain,
For forty days it will remain;
St. Swithin's day, if thou be fair
For forty days 'twill rain nae mair."

originated from the eaves dripping on the saint's tomb and has been repeated in a score of different ways. We find it in Poor Robin's Almanac of 1697 in a poem of twenty lines. The poet Gay also in his "Trivia" recounts the story, but cautions in finishing:

"Let not such vulgar tastes debase the mind;
Nor Paul, Swithin, rules the clouds and wind."

The Clog Almanac symbols given to St. Swithin are three in number. The first is supposed to be his attribute as a bishop. But it is beyond my power to guess even what it or either of the other two are intended to signify. They no doubt had some runic signification to the possessors of these Clog sticks, and no doubt it was cases like this which gave these sticks the name of "runic."

JULY 16th

Is the festival of St. Eustathius, a native of Sida in Pamphylia, who from being Bishop of the insignificant Beraea in Syria while under the rule of the Arian emperor Constantius, by his learning, sanctity and zeal for the orthodox faith became famous and in 324 he was made Patriarch of Antioch. Here as elsewhere the ardent efforts of Eustathius against heresy made him many enemies among the Arian bishops who laid a plot to secure his removal from Antioch. In 331 these plotters assembled at Jerusalem, and in a synod there convened tried and condemned Eustathius of an heinous sin upon the testimony of a debauched woman, suborned for the purpose. They also accused him of "Sabellianism." Whereupon Eustathius was first sent to Constantinople whence he was banished to Trajanopolis in Thrasia (Thrace), where he died in exile. Before his death the base woman confessed her crime.

In a foot note Dr. Butler refers to the opinion St. Jerom held of St. Eustathius and quotes from Sozomen to show the wonderful eloquence of this saint and the inestimable value of his elegant writings, though most of them have been lost.

JULY 17th

Commemorates St. Alexius, the son of Euphemian, a rich Roman senator, whose story reads like a romance. From youth he had been devoutly inclined and his life was patterned after the highest types of virtue and true nobility. At the urgent solicitation of his parents Alexius was induced to marry a young, beautiful and rich maiden; one whom he respected and it is said — but herein is the strange inconsistency — loved. But even while consenting his mind was ill at ease, for he felt that the fascinations of such temporal happiness and honour as then awaited him would draw him aside from the higher purposes of his life. By what course of reasoning he at last was led to act as he did is unknown. But while he consented to follow out his parents' wishes even to the point of permitting the ceremony of a marriage to be performed, he on his wedding night, quietly slipped out of his house and was seen no more. Disguised as a pilgrim he wandered into a distant land, "living in poverty and sanctity." At last he returned to Rome not as the Prodigal Son, for he did not disclose himself, but as a beggar sought refuge in his father's house. He was received as a mendicant by his father who never suspected his identity. In those days it was no uncommon event for rich men to support several mendicants in their great houses, and so for seventeen years Alexius lived under his father's roof bearing meekly the contempts of the pampered servants. Only after his death was the truth made known by a letter his son left.

This day is also the festival of Leo IV., who was elected to the pontificate in 847. To him the Roman Church owes the restoration of St. Peter's after it had been plundered by the Saracens, and also for his fortifying the city against future disasters from similar causes. Among many miracles attributed to Leo was the extinguishment of the great fire in 853 which threatened the destruction of the Church of St. Peter. He died July 17, 855.

JULY 18th

Is sacred to St. Bruno, Bishop of Segni, and noted as the founder of the famous Order of Carthusians and the first Abbot of that Order.

He was from the illustrious family of the Lords of Asti in Piedmont. Studying first at the monastery of St. Perpetuus in Asti, later he was taught theology at Paris under "Raymond," and then later himself taught as a theologian at Rheims, where Urban II. was his pupil. When Urban became Pope he sent for Bruno and bestowed many honours on him. Already, in 1081, Gregory VII. had made him Bishop of Segni and Urban wished to make him Archbishop of Reggio, but the honour was declined. With six companions in 1101 Bruno established the first Carthusian monastery at Chartreux. Its rules are among the most severe of all the many monastic orders, almost perpetual silence being imposed as the monks may talk with each other but one day in each week. They never eat meat and take but one meal daily, and this is eaten alone. The robes and hoods of the order are white, and the entire head of each monk is closely shaven.

One curious fact is worthy of note, that in spite of their asceticism they are great lovers and patrons of art. Indeed no other monastic order in early days did as much for pure art as the Carthusians.

St. Bruno died on August 31, 1125; was canonized by Lucius III. in 1183, but his festival is kept on July 18th.

JULY 19th

Marks the saint's day of St. Vincent de Paul, one of the most romantic as it is one of the most beautiful stories of a pure, spotless, Christian life, and a true philanthropist. Happily his story has been often and well told so my brief mention is all that is needed.

St. Vincent was born in Gascony near the Pyrenaen mountains on a small farm. His father seeing in the lad such evidences of talent placed him in the Franciscan monastery school at Acqs. At the age of twenty he went to the University of Toulouse where he spent seven years, and his course of study was marked by many exhibitions of his great talent. In 1605 a legacy of 500 crowns was left him and he went to Marseilles to receive it. On his homeward journey the fellucca in which he and his companions were was captured by African brigands and Vincent was sold as a slave to a fisherman, but later was bought by an alchemist and physician who died within a year, and finally was sold to a "renegado" Christian from Nice, whom in time he brought back from his apostacy and the two crossed the Mediterranean sea in a small open boat. Vincent reached Rome in June, 1607, and entered the Convent of Fate — Ben-Fratelli. In 1609 he came to Paris. The story of his founding of the "Lazarites," or "Fathers of the Mission," and later "The Congregation of the Sisters of Charity," and the wonderful work done by these good people and his own self-sacrifices, have been so often and fully told, as well as the story of his work for "The Magdalenes of Paris" and the "Hospital La Magdalen" and the first of the "Foundling Hospitals" for which Paris is noted it needs not be repeated. As a friend of Cardinal Richelieu and of Louis XIII., he became a most influential man. I will therefore add no more, only to record his death at St. Lazare, September 27, 1660, at the great age of four score and five years; and was buried in the Church of St. Lazarus in Paris, leaving a memory sacred to every true Christian of whatever faith. He was canonized by Clement XII., in 1737.

JULY 20th.

St. Margaret, virgin and martyr, in whose honour both the Anglican and the Roman branches of the church hold this day sacred has for ages been regarded as the special type of maiden innocence and humility. The name signifies a pearl. Her legend is one of the oldest among the many of the saints of the early days; and even from the Middle Ages was one of the most popular. She was the daughter of a pagan priest named Theodosius of Antioch; but being a delicate child she was sent into the country and placed in the care of a nurse who proved to be a Christian and who educated her young charge in that faith, a fact that was unknown to her family. As she developed into maidenhood she

displayed such wonderful beauty both of feature and person, that when by chance Olybrius, the Roman governor of the province saw her, he was captivated and wished to marry her; but the young girl rejected his offers and to free herself from his attention declared herself to be a Christian. The anger of her relatives knew no bounds and when Olybrius in order to overcome her opposition cast her into prison, they did not interfere. As she remained obdurate, the governor next tried torture and imprisonment in a dungeon, but still she was inflexible. While thus confined, the legend tells us the devil in the form of a dragon appeared to her to frighten her from her faith, but when she presented the cross before the fiend he fled. Another form of this legend says, the dragon swallowed her bodily; but immediately thereafter she burst from him unhurt. Next, the devil appeared to her as a man; but she overthrew him and with her foot on his head compelled him to confess his base purposes. The fame of her wonderful power was spreading and under its influence many were being converted. Once more she was tortured but with no result except to confirm her more surely in the faith, and to prevent further trouble she was condemned and beheaded. From her miraculous delivery from the dragon St. Margaret became the patron of women, who call on her in time of childbirth. Her attributes are usually the palm and a dragon. She is often shown in art standing on the dragon and piercing him with a tall cross with a sharpened foot. Occasionally she is seen burst from the body of the dragon. The Clog Almanac symbol is as shown above, two white crosses on a black background. St. Margaret's popularity in England is best shown from the fact that her festival-service is one of the very few found in the "MSS. of Hours" and that 238 churches are named in her sole honour. Only as interesting by comparison I add St. Nicholas has 380, St. Laurence 250, St. George 170, and St. Martin 165.

ST. MARGARET.

St. Joseph Barsabas, whose festival is also held this day, was one of the disciples of our Lord who competed to be the successor of the traitor Judas.

JULY 21st

Is the festival of St. Praxedis, a sister of St. Prudentia of whom I spoke May 21st. It was at the house of Pudens, the father of these noted sisters, that St. Peter dwelt when he came to Rome. After the death of their father these noble women devoted their great wealth to the succour of suffering Christians in Rome, adding thereto their time and personal services in nursing those of the faith who were sick or wounded by the persecuting Romans.

To-day also is the festival of a noted soldier, Victor of Marseilles. When the Emperor Maximian arrived in Marseilles with the blood of the Thebæan legions and other martyrs in Gaul yet fresh upon his garments, he found there the most flourishing and in numbers the most numerous church of the provinces. One of the officers of the German army then stationed at Marseilles was named Victor, who was a Christian and who in spite of his position as an army officer dared to proclaim the fact, thus proving his courage for it required brave men to profess Christianity in those days. The emperor heard of Victor and directed him to be brought before him, later ordering him to be tortured on the rack. Faithful even in prison, Victor by words and example converted two of his guards. When Maximian heard this he was more incensed than ever and once more ordered Victor into his presence, having previously had a statue of Jupiter placed in the presence chamber and an altar by its side. Here Victor was commanded to worship, but instead the brave soldier kicked over the altar and statue. For this act his foot was first chopped off and later his body placed under a millstone and he was crushed to death by its revolution. Even this did not abate the fury of the vindictive emperor for he caused the lifeless body to be beheaded. In art Victor is represented as a Roman soldier with his foot on a millstone.

JULY 22d

Is the day set apart both in the Roman and English Church Kalendars for the festival of St. Mary Magdalene. Of all the persons who figure in sacred history and in Christian art, Mary Magdalene is one of the most difficult to treat of. So unreal, if we attempt to fix her identity; so real as the accepted and recognized impersonation of the penitent sinner absolved through faith and love. Whether Mary Magdalene, "out of whom Christ cast seven devils," Mary of Bethany, and "the woman who was a sinner" be, as some assert, three separate persons or, as others affirm, one and the same individual, under different designations is one of those mooted points that it is not likely will ever be settled, and since the doctors of the church like St. Chrysostom hold one view and SS. Clement and Gregory another, it is hardly fitting for a layman to presume to decide. An eminent English writer says in speaking of the matter "that since St. Gregory wrote a general opinion prevails that if not all three, two at least, 'the woman who was a sinner and Mary Magdalene,' are identical."

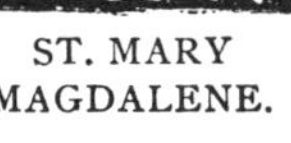

ST. MARY MAGDALENE.

This day in memory of Mary Magdalene was retained in the first Book of Common Prayer of Edward VI. and the Collect, Epistle and Gospel — this last from St. Luke vii., 36, to end of the chapter — most appropriate; but the identity of the person being questioned the service was omitted in the second of Edward's prayer books. Nothing of any moment in the history of Mary Magdalene which is perfectly authentic is known beyond what is told in Holy Writ; but it is believed that after our Lord's Ascension she dwelt in Ephesus with the Blessed Virgin and St John. There is a widely credited legend and not wholly unsupported by evidence that Mary Magdalene, the Blessed Virgin, Martha and Mary of Salome, finding themselves much persecuted by the Jews of Ephesus, set sail to cross the Mediterranean; that their boat was a poor and leaky craft, and that it was only by a miraculous intervention the party was saved and landed on the south coast of Gaul; where they separated and Mary Magdalene went to Marseilles and finally returned to St. Baume where she spent the remainder of her days, and that it was in this retreat she closed her earthly pilgrimage. The finding of her relics at a place now called St. Maximin's, and those of St. Martha at Zarascon on the Rhone as related by Dr. Butler, seems to bear out the truth of the legend as above told. Another legend, possibly a part of the first one for these tales often become sadly mixed by their being frequently orally repeated, tells of St. Mary Magdalene living for thirty years in a cave near Marseilles weeping for her past sins, while angels daily ministered to her wants.

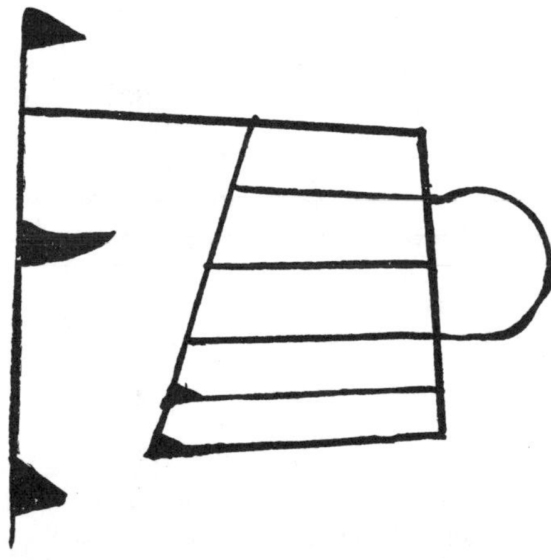

In art Mary Magdalene is always represented carrying a vase, or a box of a peculiar form supposed to contain the "precious ointment." At times this box lies at her feet and in some rare cases an angel is bringing it to her. Her hair is always golden in colour and very abundant, falling down and covering her shoulders. Again, she is represented as kneeling before a "death's head" and clasping the foot of a cross, but the "alabaster box" and her long, beautiful hair are never forgotten. From her being the first witness of the Resurrection she is especially reverenced by the Greek Church while both the Greek and Latin Churches honour her on the same day.

The Clog Almanac symbol given is supposed to represent the "alabaster box," yet like many of these it requires a great stretch of imagination to see it.

JULY 23d

Is the festival of St. Apollinaris, who, according to Bede, "was crowned with martyrdom" during the reign of Vespasius — Roman Emperor from 9 to 79 — "after having sat as Bishop for twenty years." The saint had gone with the Apostle Peter to Rome from Antioch. While at Rome St. Peter, "after having laid hands upon him, sent him into east Italy to preach. Here, later, he became the First Bishop of Ravenna. While Dr. Butler styles Apollinaris "Martyr," he does not agree with Bede for he thinks the "martyrdom," of the faithful bishop consisted in the usual suffering and privations every true Christian must pass through.

This day also is the festival of a very remarkable woman, St. Bridget of Sweden, widow of Ulpho, Prince of Nevicia, who died July 23, 1372. She seems to have been peculiarly favoured in that she received a far higher degree of education than most women of her times and is termed a "scholar," while her voluminous writings on religious subjects are yet quoted and regarded with esteem. She founded the Order of Brigantines, a peculiar one from the fact that it associated under the same roof nuns and monks. The regular establishment of a "House of Brigantines" numbered sixty nuns and thirteen monks, four deacons, and eight lay-brothers, all under the control and government of a "Lady Abbess." Henry V. at about 1420 founded the "Brigantine House of Sion," on the bank of the Thames (now the palatial residence of the Duke of Northumberland) as a memorial of the battle of Agincourt, the nuns being almost entirely ladies of rank. It flourished until about 1589 then seems to have gone into decadence, and the nuns there remaining went to sister orders on the continent. St Bridget of Sweden was canonized by Pope Boniface IX.

JULY 24th.

SS. Romanus and David, Patrons of Muscovy, are this day honoured by the Church. They were brothers and sons of Uladimir, Muscovite Prince and a Christian, and were named Boris and Hliba, or Cliba; but in Latin were called Romanus and David. Uladimir had in 908 founded a great monastery near Klow, where these two for their faith were basely murdered in 1010 by their brother, Suatopelch, who had usurped his father's throne. If for no other reason these two are worthy of mention, in that they alone are honoured by the Catholic Russians of Lithuania and Poland who keep this, and no other saints-day festival except of these brothers, the Patrons of Muscovy.

JULY 25th

Is the anniversary of St. James (Major), the Apostle and brother of the Evangelist St. John. Beyond what is told of him in the gospels very little is known save that by order of Herod Agrippa, sometimes called Herod the Great, he was beheaded about fourteen years after the crucifixion of Jesus Christ, and that he was the first of the Apostles who suffered martyrdom. But in Spanish legends as the patron saint of Spain they enter into other details of his life that a volume would hardly suffice to repeat. They say that Santiago (James) was not a poor fisherman, but a nobleman's son who for pleasure accompanied his father and brother attended by servants in their boat, but attracted by the miracles of Christ he followed Him. That at thirty-eight different times St. James after his death appeared at the head of the Spanish army. That after Christ's death for a time he preached in Judea, then came to Spain as a missionary. I may repeat here the Spanish legend of his victory over Hermogenus, a noted sorcerer, and how he converted him, and that they were beheaded at the same time.

According to these Spanish legends St. James after preaching the gospel in Spain returned to Palestine and was the first Bishop of Jerusalem, and that it was while preaching there he was seized and thrown from the battlements of the temple and killed by the Jews. The recovery of his body was more miraculous than any event in his life as was the voyage of the ship from Joppa, through the Pillars of Hercules and its final arrival at Iria Flavia, or as sometimes called, Padron. Here the body was laid upon a stone which became like wax, and the body sank into it until at last it enveloped it and it became St. James' sarcophagus. This stone was, the legend continues, revealed by a vision to a priest in 800 and the sacred remains moved to Comportella where a church was built, and many wonderful miracles wrought for pilgrims. Of these it is said often an hundred thousand persons visited the shrine in a single year. Dr. Butler says: "It was the accuser of St. James who, repenting, was beheaded with the Apostle," and the same authority gives the place of the burial of St. James at: "Iria Flavia" on the border of Galicia, and that the relics were translated to Comportella to which place Pope Leo III. transferred the see of Iria Flavia. The military Order of St. James, surnamed the Noble, was instituted by Ferdinand II., in 1175.

ST. JAMES MAJOR.

JULY 26th

Is sacred to the memory of St. Anne, the Mother of the Blessed Virgin. This name Anne, in Hebrew signifies "gracious."

Among the Hebrews for a woman to be barren was looked upon as the greatest possible affliction, and according to the legends of St. Anne, this was her case, and it was only in answer to her prayers that "the curse" was removed. No doubt, therefore, that the earliest representations we find in Christian art of St. Anne in the attitude of prayer with her arms extended, refer to this. From the very earliest records of the Church St. Anne and her husband St. Joachim have been honoured, and their names appear in both the Roman and English Church Kalendars; though both history and Holy Writ are silent as to their lives and acts. As early as 550 a magnificent church was erected in Constantinople in her honour and in 710 her relics were translated from Palestine and placed there. Even in the Catacombs about Rome St. Anne's figure appears as above mentioned in the attitude of prayer, often accompanied by a dove. In later times (as in illustration) she holds a book and is teaching the Blessed Virgin to read. Occasionally St. Joachim stands by St. Anne's side. The Clog symbol here given some may be able to decipher; I am obliged to confess I cannot. There is yet another of these Clog symbols quite as mysterious as the one given and I copy it though I cannot explain it. There must be as I have said before, some "runic" significance to some of these symbols lost to us of modern days.

ST. ANNE.

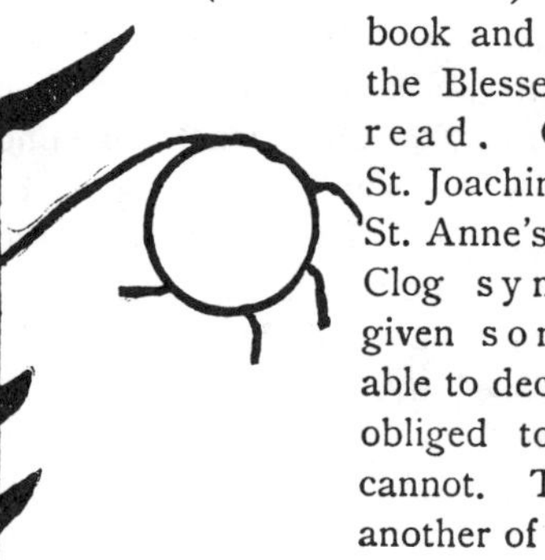

JULY 27th.

THE LEGEND OF THE SEVEN SLEEPERS

Whose festival the Roman Church celebrates this day, is a curious story, as the legend runs, transmitted orally as all those old Folk Tales were. The Emperor Decius set up a statue in the city of Ephesus (191-251) commanding every one to worship it. Seven young men who were Christians disobeyed the mandate, but unambitious to become martyrs they fled to Mount Cœlius and concealed themselves in a cavern. Decius, unable to locate them, caused all of the caves on the mountain to be sealed up. From that time nothing was heard of them until in the year 479, when persons digging for the foundation of a stable they intended to build disturbed the stones with which the cavern had been sealed and the young men were awakened by the noise. Feeling hungry they with due precaution sent one of their number into the city to buy food. The strange dress and the antiquity of the coin the young man offered for the food he had bought aroused the curiosity of the merchant, and he was tracked to the cave where all were found well and alive after a miraculous sleep of two hundred and twenty-nine years.

Like others of these legends there is in it a soupçon of truth. The young men were walled in and it was the discovery of their relics in 479 that gave rise to the fable. A similar one may be read in the Koran, only in the Mohammedan legend a dog named Kratius accompanied the sleepers who were all animals, and he, with eight other animals, yet sit in the Mussulman paradise. These are the ass of Balaam, the ant of Solomon, the whale of Jonah, the ram of Isaac, the calf of Abraham, the camel of Falch, the cuckoo of Belkia, the ox of Moses and the mare of Mohammed.

These Seven Sleepers are highly honoured by the Greek and Oriental nations and in early martyrology have a prominent place and are commemorated on this day.

JULY 28th.

Among those early fathers of the Church to whom we all owe a great debt is St. Victor, who is this day remembered. He was a native of Africa and succeeded St. Eleuthenus in the pontificate in the year 192 and the XIX. of Commodus. Already heresys and schisms had begun to enter the church one of which, "that Jesus Christ was but a man," was then being taught, and which Victor by his earnest efforts checked, even if he could not overcome. A watchful, faithful servant whose strenuous life had but one purpose in view. It was during Victor's pontificate too, that the first questions about the time for celebrating Easter began and councils were held in Rome, Gaul, Palestine, at Corinth and elsewhere. The edicts of Severus for Victor's persecution were issued in 202 but the good man had already gone to his reward in 201. Some place this date in 197 and others in 202. The date given is from Dr. Butler's "Lives of the Saints."

Another Pope, Innocent I., is also honoured this day. He ascended the pontifical throne as successor of Anastatius in 402 when Alaric the Goth threatened to overrun Italy, and Innocent personally strove to effect a reconciliation but in vain. The overthrow of Alaric in 403 for a time gave Rome rest and after the last struggle of the Goth in 410 the good Pope devoted himself to his pontifical duties and to combating the Pelagian errors, which brought forth those letters which have so long kept him in memory. He died in 417.

JULY 29th.

St. Martha, the sister of Mary and Lazarus, is the saint whom the Church honours this day. Beyond the story told of her in the Gospels there is little known of her. After the Ascension of our Lord her legend tells us that she accompanied Mary Magdalene to Provence and, according to all the Provençal legends Martha was the first person who founded a convent for holy women. This it is said was at Aix. One of the legends told of Martha at this time is that a fearful dragon called Tarasque ravaged the country lying concealed during the day in the river Rhone. Martha watched for him, and meeting him, overcame him by sprinkling holy water over the beast. Then she bound him with her girdle (some say with her garter), and when thus he was helpless she slew him. A magnificent church was built in the city of Tarasçon, the alleged scene of Martha's conflict with the dragon, which was richly endowed by King Louis XI., who also gave the church a gold bust of St. Martha and which is reputed to contain her head. The usual attribute of St. Martha is some implement for cooking. Sometimes she is shown holding the asperge and the dragon lying bound at her feet. St. Martha is the recognized patroness of housewives and cooks.

JULY 30th

Is the festival day of St. Julitta, one of the many martyrs who proved their faith in that fatal year 303. When Dioclesian issued his first edict against Christians in the year 303 he disbarred them from all protection by the laws and to be without any of the privileges of citizens, thus by one unjust act opening the door for fraud of many kinds, as was the case with Julitta. She was rich, had estates about Cæsarea in Cappadocia with flocks and herds, coveted by a wicked man who, when all other means had failed him to obtain possession of her property haled her into court where he accused her of being a Christian. The judge ordered fire and incense brought into court and demanded the woman to sacrifice to the Roman gods. Exasperated by her refusal the usurper was awarded her estates. Because she bore her poverty with such meekness exhorting her Christian brethren to hold firm to the faith, she was condemned to be burned in the vault where they confined her. Strangely though while stifled to death by the dense smoke her body was untouched by the flames and her friends buried her remains entire.

JULY 31st

Is the anniversary of St. Ignatius Loyola, a man whose influence has been more far-reaching in its results than many who have filled the papal throne. The story of his life has been told many times and from many points of view, from those who almost idolize his memory to those who treated him with vindictive bigotry. He has been pictured as an angel of light and as the incarnation of evil. Space permits only a brief outline in which many of the most dramatic scenes must be omitted.

He was born in 1491 of an ancient and noble family. Bred at the court of Ferdinand V. as a page, but emulous of his brothers he became a soldier and hidalgo, his veins full of hot Biscayan blood when in 1521 in the defense of Pampeluna against the French he was wounded. From boyhood he had high, noble ideas free from avarice. He hated gaming but was addicted to gallantry (as that word then implied) and full of the maxims of worldly honour and a genius for poetry. His confinement during convalescence was long and painful. We cannot undertake to follow the train of his thoughts which upon his recovery led him to seek the ancient monastery of Mount Serrat, where he hung up his arms and on the morning of the Annunciation of the

Blessed Virgin in 1522 took on himself the holy vows which ordered his future life and started on a pilgrimage as a beggar to Jerusalem, reaching there September 4th, 1523. On his return to Spain he completed his university course and in 1528 went to Paris. But let no reader think that either his pilgrimage or the years since have been devoid of incident. Indeed they are full of remarkable happenings though I cannot recall them here. At Paris Ignatius completed his study of Latin and his course in philosophy. It was here he met and became intimate with the five young men — Francis Xavier, Peter Faber, (a Savoyard), James Laynez, Alphonso Bodadilla (a Spaniard), and Simon Rodriguez (a Portuguese)—who with Loyola were to found his famous Society of Jesus. By degrees Loyola inspired these young men with his ardent spirit of devotion. It is a long and interesting story which at last culminated in an underground chapel of the Church of Montmartre where they took solemn vows of celibacy, poverty, and the devotion of their lives to the care of Christians and the conversion of infidels. Such on the night of August 15th in 1534 was the beginning of the most world renowned order but it was only completed at the time fixed for the closing of their studies, the Feast of the Assumption of Our Lady, January 25, 1537.

The plan of the new order was laid before Pope Paul III. who after some objections finally approved it and a bull granting them a constitution was issued September 27, 1540.

To write the story of Ignatius Loyola's life from this point would be to write almost in its entirety the early history of the Jesuits, as he was elected the first president and established at Rome as the director of all the movements of the society. Even the most casual reader must be aware of the vast and varied manifestations of this famous society, but few can imagine the wonderful executive ability required in its inception. The planning of the thousand and one details for the success which, to quote from an ultra-Calvinistic writer, they secured "as sharpshooters and skirmishers, that made them the most dangerous antagonists of Protestantism." The rules which Ignatius ordained show his far-reaching foresight as well as the purity of his intentions, whatever the world may think or in later days may have been the aim of the order, and no true Christian can read the "Spiritual Exercises" Loyola wrote and not be sure the author was inspired by only true and holy motives, for it is the man we are considering and not the order he instituted. One of his best and most truthful biographers gives us in a single sentence the true inwardness of this man's character when he says: "This interior strength he chiefly maintained by an eminent spirit of prayer and the constant and closest union of his soul with God."

Worn out by his labours Loyola died July 31, 1556, aged sixty-five years. He was beatified by Paul V. in 1609 and canonized by Gregory XV. in 1622, though the bull was not published until the following year by Urban VIII.

AUGUST

The eighth was August, being rich arrayed
In garment all of gold, down to the ground:
Yet rode he not, but led a lovely maid
Forth by the lily hand, the which was crowned
With ears of corn, and full her hand was found.
— *Spenser.*

In the old Roman Kalendars August bore the name of Sextilis as the sixth month and it contained but twenty-nine days. Julius Cæsar in reforming the Kalendar, added a day to it; but when Augustine conferred upon it his own name he took a day from February and added it thus making the thirty-one days now accorded it.

AUGUST 1st.

LAMMAS.

This was one of the four great pagan festivals of Britain, the others being on 1st November, 1st February and 1st May. The festival of the Gule of August as it was called most probably celebrated the realization of the first-fruits of the earth and more particularly that of the grain-harvest. When Christianity was introduced the day continued to be observed as a festival for the same reason, a loaf being the usual offering at the church service, and consequently the day came to be called Hlaf-mass, subsequently corrupted into Lammas, just as hlaf-dig (bread-dispenser) was applicable to the mistress of a house and came to be softened into the familiar and extensively used term lady. This we would call the rational definition of the word Lammas. There is another, but of a somewhat uncertain derivation pointing to the custom of bringing a lamb on this day as an offering to the cathedral church of York. Without doubt this custom which was purely local had its rise from the term Lammas, after the true original signification of that word had been forgotten.

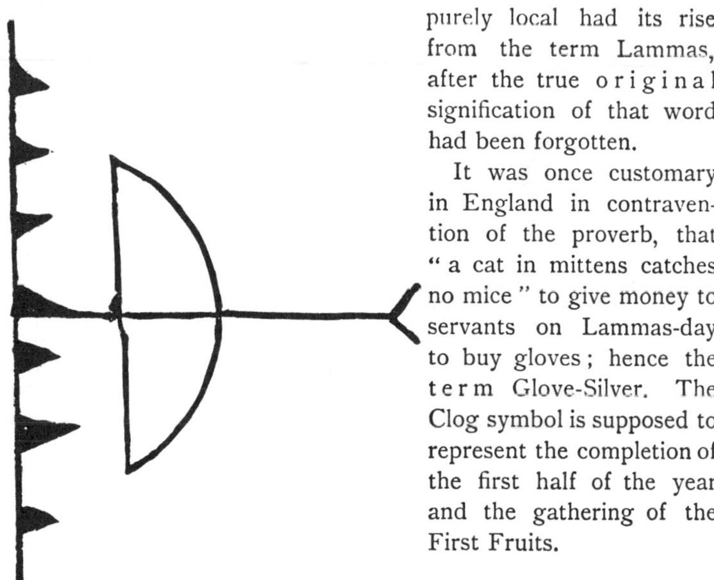

It was once customary in England in contravention of the proverb, that "a cat in mittens catches no mice" to give money to servants on Lammas-day to buy gloves; hence the term Glove-Silver. The Clog symbol is supposed to represent the completion of the first half of the year and the gathering of the First Fruits.

The Roman Church to-day celebrates the feast of

THE SEVEN MACHABEES.

This word is sometimes written Maccabees. These were seven brothers but their mother must not be confounded, as is often the case with St. Felicitas and her seven sons mentioned on July 10th.

These seven brothers were holy Jewish martyrs who suffered death in the persecution of Antiochus Epiphanes the impious king of Syria 164 B. C. Why they have a place in the Roman Church Martyrology is a most natural question. In the Catholic Dictionary of Addis and Arnold many Old Testament saints are mentioned and attention is called to the fact that "Abel and Abraham are invoked by name in the Liturgy for the dying prescribed by the Roman ritual." The same authority says: "The list of feasts given by Manuel Comnenus mentions one feast of an Old Testament saint Elias, though the Church of Jerusalem had many such feasts and at Constantinople churches were dedicated to Elias, Isias, Job, Samuel, Moses, Zacharias and Abraham. But the Machabees are the only Old Testament saints to whom the Latin church assigned a feast to be kept by the whole church; though the Carmelites keep the feast of St. Elias and at Venice there are churches dedicated to Job, Moses, etc."

In a personal letter from an eminent professor at St. Bernard's Seminary to whom I wrote for reference, and to whom I am indebted for the above quotation as well as for an endless number of kindly acts in citing to me historical authorities; he replies to my query why these Jewish martyrs who fell victims for the faith of their Church, as truly as ever a Christian fell for his faith—were thus included in the Roman Church list of martyrs, he says: "The reason, as Thomassen thinks for the exception in the case of the Machabees is that the mode of their martyrdom so closely resembled that suffered by Christian martyrs and that the date of their suffering was so near to the Christian era," later adding: "I suppose that as the Old Covenant or Dispensation was but a preparation for the new the church authorities did not consider it inconsistent to select certain personages of the Old Testament as models of virtue even for Christians."

To-day at Rome, there is an especial office in honour of

ST. PETER AD VINCULA.

The chains and prisons of the saints have ever been their greatest joy. All Bible readers are familiar with the story of St. Peter when after Herod Agrippa had slain St. James the Great he cast the Prince of the Apostles into prison and loaded him with chains and how he was delivered the night before the day when Herod had expected to win for himself great applause by permitting the Holy Apostle to be put to death. Thus this is naturally a great festival and kept by the Church in memory of that miraculous event. The celebrated church Roman tourists are familiar with

St. Pietro in Vincoli is said to have been originally founded in A. D. 109 by Theodora a sister of Hermes Prefect of Rome. A bolder legend attributes the foundation to St. Peter himself who is believed to have dedicated this church to his Divine Master. But history can assign no earlier foundation for this church than that in 442 by the Empress Eudoxia wife of Valentinian III., from whom the church takes its name of the Eudoxian Basilica and who placed there one of the famous chains which now form its great attraction to Roman Catholic pilgrims.

Hemans gives also the following legend:

"The chains left in the Mamertine prisons after St. Peter's confinement there are said to have been found by the martyr, St. Balbina, in 126, and by her given to Theodora, another sainted martyr, sister to Hermes, Prefect of Rome, from whom they passed into the hands of St. Alexander, the first Pope of that name, and were finally deposited by him in the church erected by Theodora, where they have since remained."

AUGUST 2d

Is sacred to the memory of St. Stephen "Pope and Martyr." When St. Lucius was going to martyrdom he urged upon the brethren to choose Stephen as his successor. Accordingly in May 253 this was done; though Stephen filled the high office only a little over four years. But they seem to have been four busy anxious years. Between the internal disturbances in the Church and persecution from without the holy Father had little rest. It is a weary story of those early heresies which had entered the Church and which Stephen was called on to combat, and my readers would find scant satisfaction in them unless I told the story in detail so that the merits of the controversy could be understood; a thing I cannot do.

But the fact remains that through all these troublous times Stephen was ever true and loyal to the Catholic — Orthodox — Church. In passing let me say, that in its proper place in the course of these articles, I shall give readers the story of the origin of this word Catholic, and the significance attached to it by the Church, as a distinguishing title.

St. Stephen died August 2, 257 and was buried in the cemetery of Calixtus, Rome. He is styled martyr in the Sacramentary of St. Gregory the Great, and in many ancient Martyrologies, though nothing of a definite character is given. We know the persecution of Valerian began in 257 and it is but natural to suppose Stephen would be among the first to be sought out as a victim.

St. Stephen's relics were translated to Pisar, in 1682, and Dr. Butler says: "His head is kept with great respect at Cologne."

AUGUST 3d.

This day is sacred to the memory of the discovery of the relics of St. Stephen the proto-martyr; or as it is termed in Roman Martyrology, "The Invention of St. Stephen." The same puzzling term that is used about the finding of the Cross of our Lord.

Through some fatality, neglect or whatever it was, the place of burial of the First Martyr of the Church had been forgotten and neglected though it was found to be but twenty miles from Jerusalem at a spot called Capahargmala (the borough of Gamaliel) and while the story of St. Stephen had so often been related the place where his mortal remains rested had seemingly been blotted from the memory of those who told of his glorious martyrdom.

The legend is an interesting one. At Caphargamala in 415 there stood an old basilica in the charge of a venerable priest named Lucian who slept in the baptistry. On the night of December third in 415 the old man lay half-waking, meditating upon some sacred theme when he saw by his couch a tall comely old man, of venerable aspect. He wore a long white beard and was clothed in a garment of white bordered with plates of gold whereon were crosses and in his hand he held a golden wand.

"Who" asked Lucian, "art thou?"

"I" was the reply "am Gamaliel who instructed Paul the Apostle in the law. But go thou to Jerusalem and tell the Bishop John to come here and open the tombs in which on the east side lieth Stephen who was stoned by the Jews without the north gate. His body lay unguarded for a day and a night but was untouched by birds or beasts. Then I caused his relics to be secretly carried to my house in the country, by the faithful and for forty days funeral rites were celebrated when I had him laid here in my own tomb. Nicodemus who came to Jesus by night did I also bring into my house and he lies honourably buried in my tomb where I likewise buried my son Abibas. His body is in the third sarcophagi on higher ground next to that of my own. My wife and my eldest son, Semelias lie in another spot called 'Capharsemalia.' Go therefore and tell this to the bishop."

Lucian fearful lest he might be regarded as an impostor hesitated. But Gamaliel appeared to him again this time with two baskets one of gold filled with red and white roses and one of silver full of saffron of delicious smell. Asking what they meant he was told: "The red roses represent St. Stephen and the white Nicodemus who was without stain."

But Lucian still hesitated, until, on the same day he was upbraided by Gamaliel for his neglect. To cut short the voluminous details of the legend Lucian at last did repair to Jerusalem and told of his visions. Thus it was that the relics of St. Stephen were recovered.

The relics of St. Stephen were first translated to the Church of Sion and later by the younger Theodosius to Constantinople and, lastly, by Pope Pelagius conveyed to Rome and when lowered into the tomb where St. Laurence lay the legend continues: "St. Laurence moved aside to give the place of honour on his right hand." This was the origin of the Spanish title conferred upon St. Laurence (of whom I will speak August 10th) the title "Il cortose Spagnuolo" the courteous Spaniard. In art St. Stephen is represented as young with a mild and beautiful aspect always habited in the rich dress of a deacon, the Dalmatica being of a crimson colour covered with delicate embroidery. The sleeves are loose and flowing, while heavy gold tassels hang from his shoulders, both over his breast and at the back. But the attribute that is everywhere recognized as the one most fitting for the glorious protomartyr is the simple palm branch of victory. On December 26th St. Stephen's Day I spoke at length of this holy man.

Naturally the festival day selected for St. Gamaliel and St. Nicodemus was that of the discovery of the relics of St. Stephen. Outside of what we read in Holy Writ regarding these two men with what is told in the legend there is no record, beyond the fact that Nicodemus when turned out of the synagogue and deserted — possibly persecuted — by his former companions, sought out Gamaliel and was by him given a home and Christian burial.

AUGUST 4th.

In the long list of the canonized saints of the Roman Church it would be a difficult task to select the favourite one. But I run no risk when I name St. Dominic as one of the foremost in the affections of the laity of the Roman Church and of not a few of the English church as well. Imprimis he was born a Spanish gentleman, and I think that we of to-day, hardly realize the true significance attached to those words in the XII., century; for they implied then the best type of a true noble-man. Not a hidalgo or bravado to whom might made right.. A class of men to whom Spaniards now look back upon with justifiable pride. He was born in Old Castile at Calaruega in the diocese of Osma; of the famous family of Guzman of whom the ex-Empress Eugenia is a descendant. Had Dominic de Guzman so chosen there were few honours at the Spanish court he could not have with a fair degree of security looked forward to; but he preferred to resign worldly honours for the service of his Great Master. I have before me as I write a sketch of the life of St. Dominic written by a clergyman of the Church of England forty years ago in which he says: "Protestants hardly do justice to such men. Think of their objects as we will we must own that in confining themselves to a diet of pulse and a bed of boards, in giving away everything they had to the poor, in depriving themselves out of every earthly indulgence and giving nearly their whole time to religious exercises they established such a claim to popular admiration, that the influence they acquired was not to be wondered at." And I am fain to believe with him as I read the life of this man.

He was fourteen years of age when he entered the public schools of Palentia from which he went to the University of Salamanca. Even then we know the associations a young man met at those universities were not such as to lead them in the paths of holiness. Yet one incident in Dominic's life at the university when he was but twenty-one years of age which is no legend or fable shows the earnest heartfelt longing he had, to sacrifice himself when in his walks one day he met a poor woman who begged alms to help secure for her brother the ransom needed to save him from becoming a slave to the Moors. Dominic had not money to secure this yet at once offered himself as a substitute to take the place of the captive. Happily this end was gained without such a sacrifice but it proved the metal the man was made of. Let my readers turn to the Gospel of St. John and read xv: v. 13.

Alphonsus IX. King of Castile, chose the Bishop of Osma as Ambassador to arrange the marriage of Prince Ferdinand with the daughter of the Earl of La Marche — some claim this was a province of North Germany and others of Sweden, while still other historians make it France — and the Bishop took Dominic with him. As they passed through Languedoc then the center of the Albigneses heresy Dominic's heart took fire. It was this Waldensian "heresy" that first put him into great activity. His success in restoring many of the Vaudois to the Church seems to have suggested to him that he, and others associated with him, might greatly advance the interests of religion by a practice of going about preaching and praying continually, while at the same time abstaining in their own persons from every sort of indulgence. In the course of a few years he had thus established a new order of religious called the Black or Preaching Friars, or later after his own name the Dominicans (the term black referring to the hue of the cloak and hood which they wore). This order was sanctioned by Pope Innocent III. in 1215 and very soon it had its establishments in most European countries. There were in England at the Reformation forty-three monasteries of the Blackfriars, and in Scotland fifteen. Dominic was unremitting in his exertions to extend, sustain and animate his institution. He performed many journeys always on foot. He braved every sort of danger. He never showed the slightest symptom of pride in his success for all with him was for the glory of God and the saving of men. The contemporary memoirs which describe his life are full of miracles attributed to him. He had on several occasions restored to life persons believed to be dead. Often in holy raptures at the altar he appeared to the bystanders elevated into the air. It was his ardent desire to shed his blood for the cause he had espoused, but in this he was not gratified. The founder of the Dominicans calmly died of a fever at Bologna, at the age of 51. He was canonized by Gregory IX. in 1224. St. Dominic has several attributes. A dog is often given him as a symbol of fidelity. He is also represented in the full canonical robes of a Bishop and holding a lily in one hand and a book in the other while in Danish Clogs he has a star as in illustration.

AUGUST 5th.

There are three patriarchal churches in Rome in which the Pope officiates upon different festivals and in one of which he resides when in the city. These are the Basilica of St. John

Lateran, St. Peter's on the Vatican Hill and Sta. Maria Maggiore, the last named because of its antiquity and was the first church erected in Rome to the honour of God, that was dedicated to the Virgin Mary. It is sometimes called Liberian Basilica, as it was founded by Pope Liberius and John a rich Roman patrician to commemorate a miraculous event which has sometimes given it the name of Sta. Maria Ad Nives. The legend was that on the 5th day of August there was a fall of snow that covered the plot where the Basilica now stands and that the Holy Virgin appeared there in a vision and that the snow covered no other ground than that she had selected for the site of a new temple.

It is in commemoration of this event that on Mount Esquilin in each year the "Festa La Madonna della Nive" is celebrated at Sta. Maria Maggiore when, during a solemn high Mass in the Borghese chapel, showers of white rose-leaves are thrown down constantly through two holes in the ceiling "like a leafy mist between the priests and worshippers."

This church, in spite of many alterations, is in some respects internally the most beautiful and harmonious building in Rome, and retains much of the character which it received when rebuilt between 432 and 440 by Sixtus III., who dedicated it to Sta. Mater Dei, and established it as one of the four patriarchal basilicas, whence it is provided with the "porta santa," only opened by the Pope with great solemnity four times in a century.

It is in this basilica that the manger from Bethlehem, in which our Saviour lay, has been preserved and upon Christmas day it is taken from its silver case and shown.

AUGUST 6th.

The Transfiguration of our Lord on Mount Tabor in the presence of St. Peter and the two sons of Zebedee, SS. James and John, who were later to be also witnesses of his bloody agony in the garden, is one that marks a Holy Mystery as told in Mat. xviii., Mark ix., and Luke ix. And thus the day has been selected by all branches of the Christian Church as a sacred festival.

Just when the festival was first observed is not quite certain. The Greeks as their records show made it a holy day in the VI. century and according to Dr. Butler: "The ninety-fourth sermon of St. Leo which is on this mystery shows this festival to have been observed at Rome in the middle of the V. century." Pope Calixtus III. made it more universal by a bull dated in 1457. The only Clog symbol I find for this day is an English one, a simple Latin cross.

This day also commemorates St. Xystus, or Sixtus II. the 25th successor of St. Peter. He only filled the high office for a single year and fell a martyr under the persecution of Valerian in 258.

AUGUST 7th.

The early Christians made constant use of a variety of monograms of the name of Christ in endless varieties. These monograms were of Greek origin and the Latins long used the Greek letters only modifying them to conform to the Roman letters at a very late period and as in Clog symbol given, thus combining both the Greek and Roman letters. A monogram of Christ was written at Chartres in Latin in the XIII. century; but the first two letters are Greek, the third and fourth might be either Greek or Latin, and the last two are exclusively Latin XPITVS.

"The first sigma is omitted. Here (referring to the illustration) the monogram of Christ is Greek, while the adjective noster is Latin." It will also be observed that the Greek letter chi takes on the form of the Latin Cross, whereas in the usual monogram of the letter X (chi) P (rho) the Greek Cross is used in some of the raised familiar forms like these, or by contracting the names of our Lord by using the first and last letters I C which stood for Jesus. The I (Iota) and C (ancient sigma) of IHCOYC are Christ, the X (chi) from XPICTOC and these combined read Christ. In the West, however, they altered the original Greek letters into those used in their country and time, and by using the first two and the last letter of the name of Jesus in Greek and the clever device of making the sign of contraction intersect the h (Eta), added the significant Cross.

In another common form the same result is arrived at by crossing the Iota and using the later form of the Greek letter Sigma (S).

Referring to the very commonly used monogram given here I wish to quote from the calendar of the Book of Common Prayer, edited by the Rev. W. D. Macray of Oxford, England: "It is a mistake to suppose that these initials were originated to convey the meaning of 'Jesus Hominum Salvator' (Jesus Saviour of Men), for they were not, being of Greek and not Latin origin." A verd simple form known as the Vesica Picis (in illustration) is also often used as an emblem of the name of Jesus.

The dedication of the 7th of August to the name of our Blessed Lord was introduced into the English church calendar at the time of the Reformation from the Office Books of the Sarum Use. In the Roman Church this feast, of the name of Jesus is fixed for the second Tuesday after Epiphany.

AUGUST 8th.

Under that fatal edict of Dioclesian in 303 the number of victims who suffered seems to be endless. Again to-day the Church honours SS. Cyriacus, Largus and Sinaragdus, who with twenty companions had been executed on the 16th of March and hurriedly buried by friends on the Salarian way; but on this day brought to the sacristy of Sta. Maria in Via Lata and placed at rest. This is therefore a day of abstination.

AUGUST 9th

Is observed in the Roman Church as the "Vigil of St. Laurence Martyr."

To-day the Church remembers St. Romanus, a Roman soldier who was so convinced of the truth of Christianity as taught by St. Laurence, while this holy man was in prison, that he begged of him to be baptised then and there knowing as he did that the act meant nothing less than death, that by making even the request he was signing his own death warrant. If we needed evidence of the potent power of St. Laurence as a preacher and earnest worker in his master's vineyard, St. Romanus gives the proof for the soldier was instantly arrested, tried, condemned, and on the day before his worthy preceptor he won his crown of glory.

AUGUST 10th.

Of St. Laurence, the principal saint whom the Church honours this day, Mrs. Jameson truthfully says: "It is singular that of this young and renowned martyr honoured at Rome next to SS. Peter and Paul, so little should be known and it is no less singular that there has been no attempt to fill up the lack of material by invention." Even Dr. Butler who terms him "the glorious St. Laurence," confesses that "the ancient fathers made no mention of his birth and education," while at the same time he also says that with St. Maximus "the whole church joins in a body to honour." Nor is this honour confined to the Roman Church, for again to quote from an eminent writer of the English church: "This saint has ever been famous throughout all Christendom. His heroic firmness and constancy under intense suffering having caused him to be most highly honoured since mediæval days."

ST. LAURENCE.
From painted glass
Nettlestead Church
Kent.

The claim of the Spaniards that St. Laurence was of Spanish birth is generally conceded, but beyond this Laurence appears as a deacon at Rome under Bishop Xystus (Sixtus II.) while his legend much condensed from the "Flos Sanctorum," is as follows though my version is not verbatim.

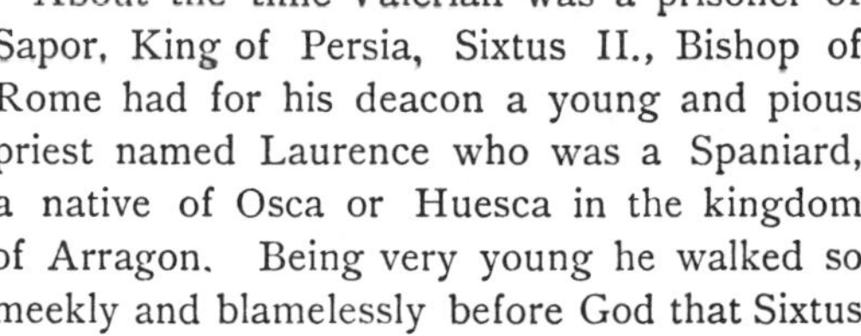

About the time Valerian was a prisoner of Sapor, King of Persia, Sixtus II., Bishop of Rome had for his deacon a young and pious priest named Laurence who was a Spaniard, a native of Osca or Huesca in the kingdom of Arragon. Being very young he walked so meekly and blamelessly before God that Sixtus chose him for his archdeacon and gave into his care the treasures of the church as they were then styled, consisting of a little money, some vessels of silver and gold and copes of rich embroidery for the service of the altar which had been presented to the church by certain great and devout persons.

Sixtus, on being denounced to the prefect at Rome, was imprisoned and soon after condemned to death. When Laurence saw this he was in great affliction and clung to his friend and pastor, saying: 'Whither goest thou, O my father, without thy son and servant? Am I found unworthy to accompany thee to death, and to pour out my blood with thine in testimony to the truth of Christ? St. Peter suffered his deacon, Stephen, to die before him. Wilt thou not suffer me to prepare thy way?' All this he said and much more, when the holy man replied: 'I do not leave thee, my son. In three days thou shalt follow after me and thy battle shall be *harder* than mine for I am old and weak and my course shall be soon finished; but thou who art young and strong and brave, thy torments will be longer and more severe and thy triumph the greater, therefore grieve not. Laurence the Levite shall follow Sixtus the priest.' Then he commanded Laurence to take all the possessions of the church and distribute them among the poor. Then Sixtus was put to death and Laurence walked through the city seeking out the poor, the sick, the naked and hungry fulfilling Sixtus' command, arriving at night at a house on Cœlian Hill where dwelt a Christian woman named Cyriaca, who sheltered many fugitives and ministered to their wants. When Laurence reached there he found her sick, but healed her by laying his hands upon her. The legend follows Laurence for several days in his good work before the satellites heard that the possessions of the church had been confided to him and searched him out (these details I omit) and arrested him, confining him in a dungeon under a man named Hippolytus whose whole family had been converted.

When brought before the prefect and the question put where he had hid the treasures of the church, Laurence said that in three days he would show them. To quote from this point as I have not done before: "The third day being come, St. Laurence gathered together the sick and poor to whom he had dispensed alms and placing them before the prefect he said: 'Behold the treasures of Christ's church.' Upon this the prefect, thinking he was mocked, fell into a great rage and ordered that St. Laurence should be tortured till he made known where the treasures were concealed, but no suffering could subdue the patience and constancy of the holy martyr. Then the prefect commanded he should be carried by night to the baths of Olimpias, near the villa of Sallust the historian, and that a new kind of torture should be prepared for him more strange and cruel than had ever before been used or had entered the heart of a tyrant to conceive, for he ordered him to be stretched on a sort of bed formed of iron in the manner of a gridiron and a fire to be

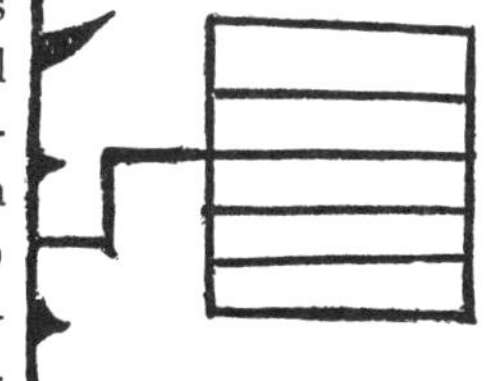

lighted beneath which should gradually consume his body to ashes," an order that was carried out literally, and is told in all its horrid details and then continues thus :

" In the midst of his tortures Laurence, to further triumph over the cruelty of the tyrant said : ' Seest thou not, oh foolish man, that I am already roasted on one side and that, if thou wouldst have me well cooked, it is time to turn me on the other."

The well-known attribute of St. Laurence is the gridiron (lagraticola), to which the palm branch is often added. Sometimes the gridiron is omitted and St. Laurence bears a dish with gold and silver coins in it.

AUGUST 11th.

As we turn the pages of history the terrible persecutions of Dioclesian seem to meet us everywhere. In Roman Martyrology we read to-day : " At Rome between the two laurels is celebrated the birthday of St. Tiburtius the martyr, who under the judge Fabian in the persecution of Dioclesian, after he had walked barefooted on burning coals still confessed Christ with great constancy, and was led three miles from the city and there struck with the sword." Dr. Butler locates the scene of the martyrdom on the Lavican road. With Tiburtius' name is coupled that of Chromatius and the somewhat curious cause for the conversion of this man, erstwhile " vicar to the prefect of Rome," as told in Butler's " Lives of the Saints " is that " in the first year of Dioclesian, St. Tranquillinus being brought before him," Agustins Chromatius, vicar to the prefect, " assured him that having been afflicted with the gout he had recovered a perfect state of health by being baptized. Chromatius was troubled with the same disease and being convinced by this of the truth of the gospel sent for Polycarp, the priest who had baptized Tranquillinus, and receiving the sacrament was freed from that corporal infirmity, * * * and resigned his dignity and was succeeded by Fabian," only to become himself a martyr. This Tiburtius above mentioned was a son of Chromatius and while all details are lacking, it is easy to see how as in other Roman families the truth of Christ had been discussed between father and son, and whatever first led up to their convictions they were among those true heroes who gave up their earthly lives rather than to recant and lose their life eternal.

AUGUST 12th

Is especially recognized as the festival of St. Clare virgin and abbess named in Roman Martyrology to be honoured on this day. "At Assisi in Umbria St. Clare Virgin who was the first of the poor women of the Order of Minorites and being celebrated for the holiness of her life was numbered among the holy virgins by Alexander IV." But the story of St. Clare or Clara cannot end with such brief mention. It has been told for ages as a folk-tale repeated in grave severe form by the fathers of the church in the middle ages and half-satirically told by an English clergyman of late days. Each in their way do this noble woman injustice. Let us strive to sift the true story, of a maiden born of a rich and noble family in Assisium, in Italy whose father Phavirino Sciffo had proved his prowess as a knight on more than one stricken field. The period when St. Francis, (Francisco d'Assisi founder of the Order of Franciscans, 1182-1226) appeared was one of great darkness in the history of the Roman Church though the enthusiastic faith of some barbarian kings and nobles, "bred of the self-devotion and earnestness of the missionaries had led to their endowing the church largely so that bishoprics begat wealth and men of noble birth sued for them to the power which accompanied these places." The Church as we know from Dean Milman and others, was not then prosperous. But the story of St. Francis must not be intruded upon here beyond the point of the influence the Saint had over St. Clare.

The first great gathering of the order St. Francis had founded was in 1212 on Palm Sunday and that day Francis spoke from the pulpit.

Among those who heard him were Phavirino Sciffo, his wife Hortulana (sometimes written Ortulania) and their daughters

Clare, Agnes and Beatrix. As Francis expounded his "golden thought" of the duty of each to cast aside the world, wealth, luxury and personal aggrandizement and accept even poverty for the love of Christ, none listened with more rapt attention than Clare Sciffo. The desire to serve her master had penetrated her soul. She had all that wealth beauty and worldly station could give; but what were these compared to that "priceless treasure." From that hour her mind was fixed and she would give her whole life to the service of Christ.

ST. CLARE.

That night she went to the Chapel of the Portiuncula where Francis was installed, and implored to be received and given work to do no matter what, at the same time taking off her jewels and rich garments. Francis was as unable as he was unwilling to refuse the maiden, and casting over her a coarse habit, she was enrolled among the Champions of Poverty. As Francis had no other female adherent, he took Clare to the Benedictine convent of St. Paolo for the time being and in spite of the protestations of her parents, when Francis had completed a dwelling for her and others who also had joined her, established the Order of Franciscan nuns, as they were later called, the "Poor Clares," and she became the "Madre Serafica" in October of the year 1212. As the rules of Francis enjoined strict poverty, the only support of the nuns at St. Damian as the little nunnery was called, was brought them by the monks. Gregory IX. objected to such free intercourse as thus obtained, but Clare was firm, telling him "that if the holy brothers may not minister to us the Bread of Life, they shall not provide us with the bread that perisheth." Gregory, who could defy an emperor as he did Frederick at Barbarossa met his match in this determined young woman and finally had to yield to her. But I may not elaborate the long and interesting story of St. Clare and the wonderful results attained by the Franciscan nuns. She died in 1253 at the age of sixty. She was canonized by Alexander IV., in 1255.

AUGUST 13th.

It is but the natural sequence that the bold Roman soldier Hippolytus converted by St. Laurence while awaiting his own crown of glory, did not escape the fury of Decius, and it is equally fitting that the Church honours him as it does this day.

The respite given Hippolytus was brief, between the horrible death inflicted on his instructor and the time he and his family, even to his aged nurse Concordia, stood before the implacable tyrant — not judge — it could have been hardly less than torture for the noble soldier to see the nurse he had loved from infancy actually scourged to death because she would not yield her faith, and then one by one to see nineteen of his own family beheaded before him for the same cause, while he, not knowing yet his own doom, was obliged to witness the horrid sight. We may well reverence Roman courage with an example like this set before us, when this hero, despising clemency if he would apostatize preferred to be, as he was, "tied to the tails of wild horses and thus perish by a cruel and terrible martyrdom."

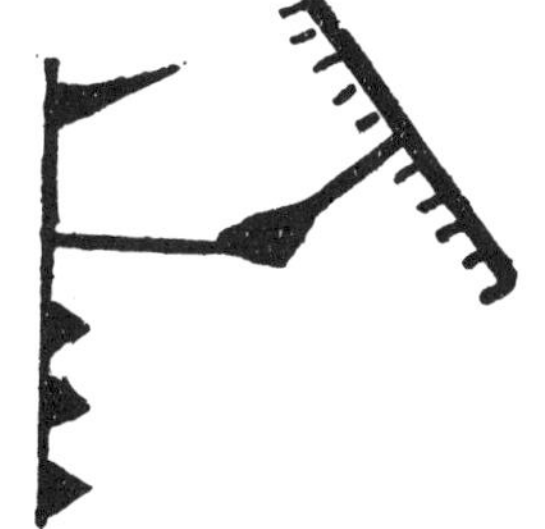

By a curious mingling of pagan mythology and Christian traditions this Christian Hippolytus has received the attributes of his pagan namesake, the son of Theseus, and is the patron saint of horses. The name in Greek signifies "one who is destroyed by horses." In art Hippolytus is usually represented as a Roman soldier with a bunch of keys at his belt. On the Clog sticks he has as an attribute the same as is seen in St. Hippolytus' hand in a picture in the Academy of Florence and is said to be an ancient curry comb. There are several noted paintings of the martyrdom of

St. Hippolytus showing him fastened to the wild horses' tails, who are rearing before starting on their mad race.

AUGUST 14th.

By a curious coincidence two saints bearing the same name are honoured this day. One, St. Eusebius, who for his defense of the Catholic faith was confined by the Arian emperor Constantine for seven months and died from the effects of it. The other St. Eusebius was a martyr of a time antedating the decrees of Dioclesian so often mentioned, and still his martyrdom in all its essential features is like those of other days a few years later, his offense being a refusal to sacrifice to the Roman gods. The exact date of his death is not known, but was not far from 295.

AUGUST 15th.

On this festival the Church commemorates the translation of the Mother of our Lord into His kingdom. There is literally nothing known regarding the life of the Blessed Virgin after the Ascension of our Lord. An endless number of legends exist and not a few with more than a soupçon of truth in them. I wish I might quote some of them, but I cannot. Still I can refer my readers to Mrs. Jameson's invaluable and reliable "Legends of the Madonna" that will more than repay the time required for their perusal.

There seems little doubt that St. John the Evangelist fulfilled the sacred trust committed to him. We find ample evidence that St. John in his old age retired to Ephesus, but whether the Holy Virgin went there with him is too "vexed" a question to enter upon; or whether, as many believe, she died at Ephesus or Jerusalem and was laid in "her sepulchre cut in the rock at Gethsemane." All authorities agree that she lived to an advanced old age before she paid the debt of nature. The festival of her Assumption is one of the oldest recognized in the Roman Church as well as that of the Greeks, mention being made of it in pontifical records of the early part of the VI. century. The Assumption of the Virgin had even before this been recognized, as mention is made of a sermon by St. Proclus in 428 "on the day of her festival."

This festival is by far the most sacred of the many paid by the Roman Church to the Blessed Virgin.

AUGUST 16th.

The saint which the Church honours this day, and whom ecclesiastical historians call "the apostle of the North and the Thaumaturgus of his age," is St. Hyacinth. He was descended from an ancient house of the Oldrovans, one of the most illustrious of all Silesia, then a part of Poland. He was born in 1185 in Breslau, educated at the celebrated universities of Cracow, Prague and Bologna, taking his degree as doctor of laws and divinity from the last named university. Then he became prebend of the Cathedral of Cracow. After that in 1218, accompanying his uncle Yvo of Konski, chancellor of Poland, to Rome, Hyacinth there met St. Dominic and took upon himself the habit and vows of the Dominican Order and became a missionary on the banks of the Baltic, and founded churches in Prussia, Pomerania and adjacent countries, including the Isle of Rugen and the peninsula of Geden. Later he pushed on to Denmark, Sweden, Norway and Gothia, and yet later to Little, or Red Russia and penetrated the Tartar country.

A typical man among that great army of those early missionaries that we of to-day do such scant justice to, who not only "took his life in his hand," but forgetting self in the service of his great Master, stands forth justly glorified among saintly heroes of those bygone ages, to whom the Christian Church owes a debt I am fain to believe few recognise. After travels which covered over 4,000 leagues, he at last reached Cracow in 1257 when seventy-two years of age and upon the feast of the Assumption of the

Blessed Virgin passed to his reward. He was canonized by Clement VIII. in 1594.

AUGUST 17th.

In Roman Martyrology this day is named as

THE OCTAVE OF ST. LAURENCE.

Perhaps no one story can better illustrate the bitter vindictiveness of the so-called Arian Christians toward their Orthodox brethren than that of St. Liberatus and his six Brothers of the Church who occupied a small monastery near Capsa in the province of Ryzacecena, whom the Church honours this day. In 483 under Huneric, the Arian Vandal King in Africa, because they would not abjure the orthodox faith of one baptism, they were dragged from their quiet monastery and subjected to unheard of torments. Lastly, when they refused to acknowledge any change, they were bound to the wood by which they were to be burned. Again and yet again did these vandals strive to light this wood, but in vain; the wood would not take fire. Then in his anger Huneric commanded that they should be beaten to death by iron bars, an order faithfully carried out. The event is worth remembering to emphasize the bitterness of these Arians toward their fellow Christians.

AUGUST 18th

Is the festival day of St. Helena, wife of Constantine Chloris (the Pale) and mother of Constantine the Great. But perhaps the one act of her varied life which has and ever will make her name memorable was that, when over four score years of age, through her agency the true cross upon which our Lord Christ had suffered was discovered after nearly three centuries, during which time its hiding place had been kept a profound secret.

Naturally the life of this woman has been often told, but it can never fail to be of interest to every true Christian.

French historians have vainly tried to prove that at the time she married Constantine Chloris she was "an inn-holder" (Stabularia) in Bithynia, but the most reliable traditions show her to have been a Briton by birth and probably a native of Colchester, though some eminent English historians name York as her birthplace. To understand clearly the story the reader should turn to his Roman history and read up the events which led the two Roman emperors, Dioclesian and Maximian, in 293 to choose two other "inferior emperors" to aid them in the government of the vast empire. Dioclesian chose one Galerius and Maximian took Constantine Chloris for assistants. Prior to this Constantine had married Helena the Briton. Then read on through those long pages of events which rendered it necessary from a diplomatic standpoint, for Chloris to divorce Helena in order to marry Theodora, the daughter of Maximian, and thus follow the wonderful story by which Constantine the Great, the son of Chloris and Helena, rose to power. All history of a most interesting nature and which carefully read would add greatly to the clear understanding, not only of St. Helena's story, but of scores of the saints referred to.

The Empress Helena and her son were not separated by the divorce and he always honoured her, as shown by calling her "Augusta," or empress of his armies. But Helena was not converted at the time her son was; indeed it was only after his miraculous victory that she renounced paganism. I will not give details of her interesting life down to 325-6, when Constantine became master of the East and concurred in the assembling of the Council of Nice and resolved to build a magnificent church on Mount Calvary. It was then that St. Helena took charge of the enterprise and, although over eighty years of age, went to Jerusalem, to discover if possible where the true cross was then hidden. As the legend is told under date of May 3d when speaking of the "Invention of the Cross" it need not be repeated here.

The temple of Venus which profaned the sacred spot where this is reputed to have occurred was destroyed by order of Empress Helena A. D. 326.

On her return to Rome after this wonderful discovery, the noted empress passed quietly away in the year 328, on August 18th. The "Church of the Nativity" at Bethlehem was built by St. Helena in 327, and is the oldest church in the world.

AUGUST 19th.

While Dioclesian yet reigned and during the second year of the great persecution of the Christians, Urban, then president of Palestine, became especially vindictive against the faithful, visiting condign punishment upon them for the most trivial offense against Roman law, or in not a few cases on suspicion only that any one was a Christian. This was so with the several saints whose names are to be honoured by the Church grouped together this day. In regard to St. Timothy no pretext seems to have been offered for the cruel treatment he received except that he openly avowed his faith, and for that was stretched upon the rack and his flesh torn with iron combs to make him recant; upon his refusal, he was burned to death before "a slow fire," at Gaza, on May 1, 304, while SS. Agapius and Thecla, upon similar grounds were sent to Cæsarea under guards, where after being tortured, they were condemned to be torn to pieces by wild beasts in the amphitheater. Thecla was the first to fall a victim to this barbarous punishment; then with a refinement of cruelty, Agapius was remanded to his prison and only after two years of constant torment did he gain his martyr's crown in the same manner. By common consent both the Latin and Greek churches have united the festivals of these three saints and named the 19th day of August for its celebration.

AUGUST 20th.

In every age and class of society there are men who seem to be born leaders, men whom their associates recognize at once and willingly follow. It has been thus in the Church as well as in the world at large, as is seen in so many cases; but never perhaps, more strikingly illustrated than in the case of St. Bernard of Clairvaux, whose festival occurs this day, and who is often styled "the last of the Fathers," while he was beyond question one of the greatest men of the Middle Ages.

He was the son of a knight of a ancient and noble family, and was born at Fontaines near Dijon in Burgundy, in 1091. His mother Aliz was a devoutly pious woman and encouraged her son in his religious tendencies which he began to show at a very early age, and when he was still but a lad he declared his intention of leading a monastic life. His mother died in 1110 when Bernard was but nineteen years of age, and he soon thereafter entered the Cistercian monastery of Citeaux, though his brothers and friends plead against such a course. Instead — and this early incident shows that gift of leadership above spoken of — in the end he persuaded thirty of his companions including his brothers to join him in his monastic life. The discipline of the Cistercians is very rigourous but did not reach the standard Bernard set for himself, and he imposed many restrictions on his life which the order would permit but did not command, while in every way he was rising in the estimation of his superiors.

A capable man like Bernard was not to be lost in privacy. As Citeaux became crowded with devotees, the Abbot, a shrewd judge of character, selected Bernard and sent him into the wilderness at the head of twelve companions to found a new settlement. After wandering northwards for ninety miles they fixed their abode in a woody valley called Wormwood in Champagne, and erected a log hut that, under Bernard's genius, grew into the renowned Abbey of Clairvaux, of which he became abbot when he was but twenty-four years of age.

I may not follow the interesting details of this great man's life. An incident or two must suffice.

The saintly rigour of his life, his eloquence as a preacher, and his courage in attacking civil and ecclesiastical wrong-doers gradually raised Bernard into European fame, and letters and visitors from far and near drifted to Clairvaux. The force of his influence became especially manifest in 1130 when on the death of Pope Honorius II. two popes — Innocent II. and Anacletus II.

—each claimed to be the true and only vicar of Christ. The rulers of Europe were at a loss to decide between the rivals. Louis VI. of France convened a council to consider the question to which Bernard was invited. The assembly waited with awe for his opinion, believing that the Holy Spirit would speak through his mouth. He declared for Innocent, and the council at once broke up perfectly satisfied.

When Wordsworth wrote he no doubt imagined he had originated a thought, but St. Bernard anticipated him by centuries when he wrote one of his pupils: "Trust to one who has had experience. You will find something far greater in the woods than you will find in books. Stones and trees will teach you that which you will never learn from masters. Think you, you can suck honey from the rock, and oil from the flinty rocks? Do not the mountains drop sweetness, the hills run with milk and honey, and the valleys stand thick with corn?" One of his most notable controversies was with Abelard, the Rationalist of the XII. century, who was accused of unsound doctrine and dangerous speculation on the mystery of the Trinity. Abelard challenged Bernard to a public logical disputation. At first Bernard hesitated and refused. "When all fly before his face," said Bernard, "he selects me, the least, for single combat. I refuse, because I am but a child, and he a man of war from his youth." These fears were overcome by his friends and a council was called at Sens to which the king of France and a crowd of nobles and ecclesiastics repaired. Abelard came with a troop of disciples; Bernard with two or three monks, as it behoved a Cistercian abbot to travel. Abelard seems to have discovered that he had made a mistake. He was used to address the reason of scholars, and the gathering at Sens was made up of men on whose minds his logic would have slight effect whilst his adversary's impassioned oratory would be irresistible. Bernard had scarcely opened his discourse when, to the speechless astonishment of all, Abelard rose up, said he refused to hear more or answer any questions. He appealed to Rome and at once left the assembly. The council, nevertheless, proceeded to condemn Abelard, and the pope affirmed the decree. Two years afterwards, in 1142, Abelard died.

Perhaps the crowning glory of St. Bernard's life was his efforts for the second crusade when our saint was fifty-five years of age.

The writings of St. Bernard fill many volumes and are highly prized. His first published book "On the Twelve Degrees of Humility" even now widely read, was followed in 1120 by his "Homilies on the Gospels." But I cannot enumerate. Perhaps his masterpieces are "The Cross of Abelard" and his "Five Books of Consideration." All of his writings are characterized by their vigour, terseness and a high degree of literary ability, even when judged by our modern standards.

St. Bernard died at Clairvaux, August 20th, in the sixty-third year of his age, and was buried before Our Lady's high altar in the monastic church.

He was in every way a truly great man whether we view him from an ecclesiastical or moral standpoint; one of those rare men whose virtues and accomplishments cannot be justly summed up in a brief sketch like the present.

AUGUST 21st

Is the festival of St. Jane Frances De Chantal, the grandmother of the celebrated Mme. de Sevigné. The father of St. Jane was a man of some note being one of the presidents of the Parliament of Burgundy, but more particularly for his loyalty to Henry IV. in his struggle with the league. While Jane Freniot was still an infant she lost her mother by death, but her father by his prudent, pious care, as far as possible supplied the mother's place. When Jane was twenty years of age, in obedience to her father she was married to the Baron de Chantal, an officer of distinction in the French army and a favourite with King Henry IV. While thus complying with her father's wishes the union was one that she would have avoided not from any just reason so far as the baron went, for he was in all ways a thoroughly acceptable man and proved a kind husband, but that the maid had earnestly desired to lead a religious life. In those days a father's command on such a subject was recognized as supreme. She therefore yielded, but in so doing made a mental vow that if in God's providence she became a widow, from that hour she would devote her life to the service of God and the poor.

A happy, contented life followed for eight years during which four children were born. Then on a day when the baron and a friend were hunting deer in his forest at Bourbilly (the name of his estate), this friend in the dim light mistook the dull, dun color of the baron's hunting coat for a deer moving behind a clump of bushes and shot him. The baron lived nine days only and then the baroness found herself at twenty-eight years of age, the widow she had pictured herself; but hampered by her duty to four young children, a duty she did not either shirk or deny, and though her inclinations for a religious life were unchanged she recognized where her paramount duty lay. After her year of mourning was over she began her consultations with her old friend, St. Francis de Sales, who after months of careful consideration at last broached to her his project for the establishment of "a Congregation of the Visitation of the Virgin Mary." In the formation of this order the baroness lent him her aid and contributed largely from her wealth. But her children were neither neglected nor forgotten, and before she left the world to assume the direction of the new order as "La Mere Chantal" she saw her eldest daughter happily married to the young Baron de Thouns, a nephew of St. Francis; a second daughter also married to the Count de Touloujon, a nobleman of great virtue, prudence and honour; while God, in his wisdom, had taken to himself the third daughter. Her son the young Baron de Chantal, then fifteen years old, she committed to the care of her father, President Freniot. Thus when her children no longer needed her care, she took upon herself the arduous duties she had determined upon. The vicissitudes of her life from this point would fill a volume and be the entire early history of the Order of the Visitation, as it was known. How faithfully she fulfilled those duties is well known in the Roman Church. She died December 13, 1641; was beatified by Benedict XIV. in 1751, and canonized by Clement XIV. on September 2, 1769, who then fixed the day of her feast for the 21st of August.

AUGUST 22d.

Of St. Hippolytus, the primitive prelate and illustrious doctor, who flourished in the beginning of the III. century, and whom the Church honours this day, outside of his writings very little is known. Even St. Jerom was obliged to say that he was unable to learn of what city he was bishop, yet such was the force of his wonderfully gifted pen that not a few of its products live even now after seventeen centuries have come and gone, and we are apt to wonder if the writings of any of the prelates of the twentieth century will be found so wise and valuable that men will read them in the thirty-seventh century, as a half score of this man's writings are read to-day. Even in his own day or very near it, his fame must have been beyond that of most of his contemporaries for there stands now in the Vatican library a statue of St. Hippolytus which was dug up in 1551, and which bears evidence of its having been erected far back in the dusty days of the past, in his honour. "The Greeks and Ethiopians," Dr. Butler says, "honoured St. Hippolytus on our 29th of January; the Latins on the 22d or 23d of August."

AUGUST 23d.

Of the several saints named in the Kalendar of this day I will take space to mention but one, St. Philip Beniti, or Benize as he is sometimes called, the principal ornament and propagator of the religious "Order of Servites" in Italy.

As a young man St. Philip had studied medicine in Paris and later took his degree of doctor from the University of Padua, whence he returned to Florence.

The Order of Servites or the servants of God had been founded some fifteen years before his return. Some very rich merchants of Florence by mutual agreement, had retired from the world to Monte Senario, six miles from the city; where in little cells they lived, having all things in common. To St. Philip their lives seemed to be peculiarly attractive as meeting his own ideal of self-sacrifice for others. Attending service one evening at their chapel the Epistle was from Acts viii., 29, and in it the words occur "Draw near and join thyself to the chariot," which were addressed to his namesake, Philip; and which he felt were addressed to him in person. A vision which came to him that night confirmed him in this, and with no little dread he applied, and in due time was "admitted to the habit of the order by Father Bonfilio," the superior of the community. This was in September, 1233. From thence his life was devoted to charity and the propagation of his order, passing through every grade from that of servitor to that of definitor and at last in 1267 he became the fifth General of the Order.

After the death of Clement IV. he was sought for by many as a successor to the pontifical throne; but when he heard of this he fled to the mountains and lay concealed until after the election of Gregory X., and thenceforward gave his life to the service of his order. He died in 1285 and for his sanctity was canonized in 1726 by Benedict XIII.

THE NOBLE ARMY OF MARTYRS PRAISE THEE.

In opening the chapter on early martyrs Mrs. Jameson says: "When in the daily service of the church we repeat these words of the sublime hymn I wonder sometimes whether it be with a full appreciation of their meaning. Whether we do really reflect on all that this noble army of martyrs hath conquered for us?" As I record in the Kalendar the names of these "noble" martyrs this question constantly recurs to me, and how utterly, except for the Roman Church we in this utilitarian age should forget them and let the memory of their sacrifices sink into oblivion. From our comfortable, well upholstered pew, with a due and reverent mien we echo back the glorious words as they fall on our ears; yet how many of us in the privacy of our own homes ever give this "noble army of martyrs" a second thought, much less to stop and compute the debt every Christian no matter what his creed may be, owes them, or reflect on the true heroism they displayed.

Their names even are but empty sounds while their noble deeds are quite forgotten though done in imitation of their Divine Master and to prove their faith in His promises.

AUGUST 24th.

This is St. Bartholomew's Day. As this apostle is not mentioned in any of the canonical books except when enumerating the names of the twelve, legend has filled the gap with the usual result, and we find ourselves much at a loss in regard to his true history. One of these legends makes him the son of an husbandman, while another makes him the son of Prince Ptolomeus, supposed to be the Tholomew or Tolmai family mentioned by Josephus, while Jensenius and other learned writers take the apostle to have been the same person with Nathaniel, a native of Cana in Galilee, a doctor of Jewish law. All legends agree that after the Ascension of Christ he travelled into many distant lands preaching the gospel; some saying he even reached India in his journeyings. It was at Hierapolis in Phrygia he met St. Philip. It is said that in all of his travels he carried with him a copy of the Gospel of St. Matthew from which he constantly quoted. Returning from his travels he preached in Armenia and Cilicia and while in the city of Albanopolis he was seized and condemned to a most cruel death; for he was first flayed alive and later crucified. The proper attribute of St. Bartholomew is a knife of very peculiar form. If we could get an exact copy of an ancient Jewish "flesher's knife"

ST. BARTHOLOMEW.
Winchester Glass.

we should have it in its proper shape. The illustration copies the knife in an old Florentine picture of St. Bartholomew and I give it as found, not assuming to vouch for its correct form. The other illustration is from an English Clog-stick, for I find none of this saint on the Danish sticks.

The martyrs of Utica who had suffered under the decree of Valerian in 258, are this day honoured by the Roman Church, in Carthage. St. Austin places their number at one hundred and fifty-three persons, and this holocaust is universally spoken of as the "White Mass" and the question is often asked why. The following, taken verbatim from the American edition of Roman Martyrology, not only answers the query but shows the propriety of the appellation: "Among other torments inflicted on them, a limekiln was set on fire by order of the governor and live coals with incense being brought to him he said to the confessors: 'Choose one of these two things, to offer incense to Jupiter on these coals or to cast yourselves into the kiln.' Armed with the faith and confessing Christ to be the son of God, they each with a rapid step precipitated themselves into the kiln and amidst the vapours of the lime were reduced to dust." It is difficult to conceive of a higher degree of moral courage and heroism than this "Noble Army of Martyrs" displayed on that memorable 24th day of August in 258. Even those gallant three hundred Spartan heroes at Thermopylae,

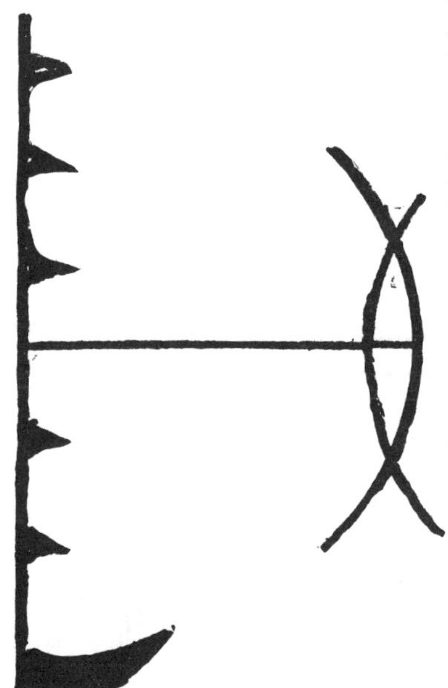

who for ages have been held up as models of courage were not superior to these humble Christians.

AUGUST 25th

Is the feast of St. Louis, King of France, a saint who in France has had few that have been held in greater esteem. He was born in Poissey, in 1215, and therefore often signed himself "Louis of Poissey." By the death of his grandfather, Philip II. in 1223 his father, Louis VIII., became king, but only for three brief years as he died November 7th, 1226, and our saint when only in his twelfth year of age became nominally King of France.

His mother Blanche, a daughter of Alphonsus IX., (sometimes called VIII.) King of Castile, was proclaimed regent during his minority, and happily for the young monarch she proved herself a woman of more than ordinary worth and ability. She was not only a devout church-woman, but a most devoted mother from the hour of the birth of the heir to the French throne. From infancy Louis was a docile, loving child, and from the earliest dawn of his intellect Queen Blanche directed and personally supervised his education. Even the burden of care which the regency placed upon her was not allowed to interfere with this — as she felt it — her paramount duty. She must have been a woman of— for that period — unusual education, and to her care, and in part we are told, by her personal teaching, young Louis became a perfect master of the Latin language, as well as to speak with a grace, ease and dignity in public. But over all the teachings of the Church at all times dominated; while the tender, mutual love between the mother and her son is one of the pleasantest pictures of the life of St. Louis. In a like manner Louis was most fortunate in the wife that was selected for him, Margaret of Provence, whom he married May 27, 1234. But I must not enlarge on biographical matters. In Dr. Butler's notice of St. Louis I read the following: "Baldwin II., the Latin emperor of Constantinople in 1239, made St. Louis (in gratitude for his great largesses to the Christians in Palestine and other parts of the East) a present of the Holy Crown of Thorns which was formerly kept in the imperial palace but was then in the hand of the Venetians, as a pledge for a considerable loan of money borrowed of them and which St. Louis discharged," and following this the author tells of the disposition of this holy relic.

The story of the Crusades of King Louis to the Holy Land are too trite to repeat here save to mention the date, when after having gone to the Abbey of St. Denis "to take the Oriflame" (the ancient standard borne by the kings of France in war and so called from its being of a red or flame colour) he set sail from Aiguesmortis on August 27, 1248, for Palestine and not to return until after over six years of this terrible war, to Vincennes on September 5, 1254.

The second crusade was undertaken March 25, 1267, but King Louis only finally sailed with his army from Aiguesmortis July 1, 1270, with his sons Philip, John (Count of Nevers) and Peter (Count of Alençon) and a numerous retinue among whom was Theobald, King of Navarre, a son-in-law of St. Louis.

It was to be the last of the great king's efforts, for he died from "distemper" on August 25th in 1270 and his relics were brought to Paris and deposited in the Church of St. Denis. He was canonized by Benedict VIII. in 1297.

AUGUST 26th.

The Church to-day remembers St. Zephrinus, one of those early fathers who filled the pontifical chair in 202 when Severus raised the fifth of those bloody persecutions which mark the entire history of the Christian Church from the day when our Lord suffered upon Calvary. Like so many of those devoted men, little is known of him beyond the fact of his having suffered for the cause of Christ and that during the sixteen years he was looked up to as the Head of the Church, he comforted the suffering, giving strength to the wavering and at the last won his own immortal crown of glory in 218.

Another saint who is also this day honoured is St. Gelasinus; who is one of whom we wish we knew more. At best his story is a mythical "Folk-Tale," told from the chronicles of Alexandria. The man was an actor and for a jest in a warm bath, in a scene in a play given on an Alexandrian stage, he had been in mock solemnity baptized. From that moment a strange solemn feeling had seized upon him. The thing which had begun as a jest had materialized into a solemn reality, and as he came forth from his bath he proclaimed himself a Christian in truth. The story of his arrest, trial and condemnation is without any marked features from others of its kind and the chronicle of his execution briefly states "he was stoned to death."

AUGUST 27th.

In Roman Martyrology for this day we read of the death of St. Joseph Calasanctus, Confessor: "Illustrious by the innocence of his life, who to instruct youths in piety and letters founded the Order of the Poor Regular Clerks of the pious schools of the Mother of God." His life had been one continued self-sacrifice for the sick and destitute; for whom he gave up the wealth and social station of the noble family in Arragon from which he came. He was, in short, a man with an ideal priesthood in his mind which he sought by both precept and example to establish. He had laboured for this twenty years when in 1617 Paul V. allowed him and his companions to form themselves into a congregation under simple vows, which in 1621 Gregory XV. changed to religious vows and gave them the name they bear. The Order passed through many vicissitudes. Alexander VII. in 1656 brought them back to the simple vows of 1617. Clement IX., again in 1669 raised them to a religious order which Innocent XI. confirmed in 1689. They teach philosophy, divinity, mathematics, the learned languages and all the classics as well as the elementary branches. They have houses in most cities of Italy, Austria-Hungary, Poland and Spain. St. Joseph Calasanctus died at the wonderful old age of ninety two in 1640. An office in the Roman Breviary was established for him in 1769.

AUGUST 28th.

St. Augustine, to whom this day is dedicated is often called "The Greatest of the Fathers" and is one of those saints who are held in equal reverence by both the Roman and Protestant Churches. He was one of the "Four Latin Fathers" who as logicians and advocates wrote and suffered for the church militant in its early and fierce struggle, and who fixed the articles of faith which thereafter were received for their guidance. Of these "Latin Fathers" St. Augustine appears as the third in usual order, SS. Simon and Ambrose occupying the first and second places and St. Gregory the fourth.

ST. AUGUSTINE
of Hippo.

Augustine was an African being born at Tagaste, a city of Numidia, in 354. His father was a pagan and his mother, Monica, a Christian of earnest piety who longed with exceeding desire for her son's conversion. In his boyhood falling seriously ill, he desired to submit to the rite of baptism, but the danger being averted, the rite was deferred. As he grew up, his morals became corrupted and he lapsed into profligate habits. In his nineteenth year the perusal of Cicero's Hortensius (a work now lost) made a deep impression on his mind, and stirred within him aspirations after a nobler life. At this juncture he became a convert of the Manichaens and for nine years an able advocate of their opinions. The Manichaens were a set founded by one Manes, about 261. He confounded the teaching of Christ with that of Zoroaster and held that the government of the universe was shared by two powers, one good and the other bad; the first, which he called Light, did nothing but good; the second, which he called Darkness, did nothing but evil. Meanwhile, Augustine taught grammar at Tagaste and then rhetoric at Carthage, but growing disgusted with the vicious character of his pupils he determined to go to Rome, much against the will of his mother. In Rome he attracted many scholars, but finding them no better than on the other side of the Mediterranean, he removed to Milan where he was elected professor of rhetoric. The intrepid Ambrose ruled at that time as Archbishop in Milan and by his ministry Augustine was delivered from the Manichaen heresy. The vacation of 386 he spent at the country seat of his friend Verecundus, in the diligent study of the Scriptures; and in the Easter of the following year he and his son, Adeodatus, a youth of singular genius, were baptized by Ambrose.

It was on this occasion it is said, that the "Te Deum" was composed and chanted by Ambrose and Augustine alternately as they advanced to the altar At the request of his mother, St. Augustine accompanied her (who had been in Milan to witness his baptism) to Aplina, but she died on the way and he retired to a villa near Hippo where after three years spent in monastic seclusion in 391 he took on himself holy orders, and in 396, was made Bishop of Hippo, where he presided nearly thirty-five years until in 430 when the town was besieged by the Vandals. It was during this siege that he died in the month of March. When the city some months after his death was captured and burned, his library was fortunately saved, which contained his voluminous writings — two hundred and thirty-two separate books or treatises on theological subjects, besides a complete exposition of the psalter and the gospels, and a copious magazine of epistles and homilies. The best account of Augustine is found in his Confessions, in which with unflinching and sorrowful courage he records the excesses of his youth, and the progress of his life in Christ.

It is these writings which have made St. Augustine the patron saint of theologians and scholars. The representations of St. Augustine in Christian art make too long a list for me to venture upon them, beyond mentioning that such great names as Reubens and Vandyke head the list of artists, while Albert Dürer was proud to be the engraver of Vandyke's picture.

AUGUST 29th.

This day in the Roman Church is held an office in memory of the beheading of John the Baptist. The story as told by SS. Matthew and Mark are like household words. We all have heard it from our childhood. Pointing as this event does, to both a great moral and an historic event of no ordinary character, it is eminently fitting it should be remembered with suitable offices by the Church.

Well authenticated traditions tell us that after the decollation of John the Baptist his disciples secured his body and that they entombed it at Sebasti, or Samaria, but that during those troublous days when Julian the Apostate reigned, the tomb was devastated and rifled by the pagans who then burnt a part of the sacred bones, but that faithful Christians secured the rest and sent them to Alexandria whence in later days they were distributed to many places. Theodosius in 386 had built a church in honour of St. John the Baptist on the site of the ancient temple of Serapis, which had been destroyed. It was here the remainder of the relics were preserved. But the head of John had never been found, until it was discovered in Emesa in Syria.

According to a tradition for which I am indebted to my kind friend at St. Bernard's Seminary, Herod in grief over his act had the head of St. John the Baptist concealed and buried in his palace to spare it from further indignities on the part of his courtiers. There it remained until after the discovery of the holy cross by St. Helena which, as history tells us, brought many pilgrims to Jerusalem, and the head was found by two pilgrims to whom St. John had appeared in a vision, and it was brought to Cilicia under Emperor Valeses and later to Constantinople under Emperor Theodosius. From Constantinople it was stolen by a Greek and brought to Emesa in Syria, and its location was unknown until the year 453 when it was again brought to light by the Archimandite Marcellus.

Emesa was captured by the Moslems in 635 and the head of the Baptist was saved from their hands by being taken to Cappadocia or Armenia, and kept until in the year 850 it was again brought back to Constantinople. Here it was at first kept in the imperial palace but was afterwards confided to a monastery (Kloster Studuim) where it still was in 1025. The front part of the head was taken to Amiens, France, in the time of the Holy Roman Empire, where it is still kept in great veneration. Dr. Butler says: "Part of the head is said to be kept in St. Sylvester's Church in Campo Marzo, Rome, though Sirmond thinks this to be the head of St. John the Martyr of Rome."

The celebration of the feast of "the Decollation of St. John the Baptist," according to the "Kirchenlexikon" seems to have originated from a particular festival that has been observed in Sebasti, Palestine, since the IV. century on the 29th of August, though the event itself may have taken place earlier in the year; "possibly in February." It has according to ancient Sacramentaries been observed in Italy since the V. century. In some churches it was celebrated within the octave of the "Festurn Nativitatis of St. Joannes." But it was introduced into the Roman Missal from the Sacramentaries of Pope Gelasius, and Gregory extended it to all churches of the West, fixing the date (IV. Kal. Sept.) on August 29th. The Greek Church in addition to this festival celebrates the Synalis St. Joannes (Synalis "getting together") as a triple festival. The first, "the Inventio Caput Joannes" on February 29th, another on the 3d, or 6th of May. The Clog symbol for this festival is an axe

of an ancient form, doubtless the invention of the Clog-stick maker.

AUGUST 30th

Is the festival of the only canonical saint yet chosen from the western shores of the Atlantic, St. Rose, or "Santa Rosa di Lima." She was christened Isabel, but from the wondrous colour of her complexion as she lay in her cradle, which resembled the delicate tints of a rose, her mother called her: "My Rose," a name which clung to her through life and by which she was canonized. From infancy her life was one beautiful story of love and patience. At a very early age she took the habit and vows of the third Order of St. Dominic, and her legend tells that to keep constantly her mind intent upon her Saviour she wore a thin circlet of silver on her head within which were sharp points or nails to remind her continually by their tiny prickings of the crown of thorns. She died when but thirty-one years of age at Lima, Peru, on August 24, 1617.

The Peruvian legend regarding her says that when Clement X. was asked to canonize her he refused, exclaiming: "India y Santa! asi como blueven rosas." (India and saint! as likely as that it should rain roses). The words had hardly left Clement's lips before a literal shower of roses began to fall in the Vatican and "continued until the Pope acknowledged his incredulity." This was in 1671 when, after the examination of one hundred and eighty witnesses, Clement X. canonized St. Rose and named August 30th as her festal day.

AUGUST 31st.

This day is the festival of St. Raymund Nonnatus. The surname appended from the peculiar circumstances attending his birth. His legend unfortunately is devoid of many details we would like to know. He was a Spaniard born at Portel, in Catalonia, in 1204.

As Raymund passed from youth to young manhood, with his ability and agreeable manners he might, if he would have done so, by pushing his fortune at the court of Arragon, backed by the influence of his friends and his family who all urged him to such a course, have easily attained to almost any reasonable ambition, either for wealth, rank, or official position he desired; but he would not consent. Almost from his cradle, certainly from the time when he could reason with himself, he had a higher aim than worldly power. It was only after strenuous opposition, and through the mediation of his relative, the Count of Cordova, that his father at last consented and young Raymund took the vows and habit of the then newly organized "Order of Our Lady of Mercy for the Redemption of Captives," an order which came from the necessities of the time when so many Christians were suffering captivity under the Moors. One of those organizations which offered neither personal glory nor honour, whose members were prompted and stimulated to action by pure love of their fellowmen. Their convent was at Barcelona and Raymund early took rank among his associates, so that hardly had three years elapsed after his entry there before he was named by his superiors to the office of "Ransomer," a position which demanded a high degree not only of executive ability but a clear, cool head and great judgment.

His first assignment to active service sent him into Barbary with a considerable amount of money to negotiate for the release of Christian slaves. This accomplished, he still found so many captives remaining that his heart was wrung with pity, and to secure their release he himself became a hostage that they might go free while he remained until their ransom was paid. From our standpoint Raymund's conduct during this interval may not have been wise; for urged by the love of Christ he preached to the Mohammedans the doctrines of the Christian religion only to be punished by chains, torture and imprisonment, and he would have been put to death but for fear that by such an act the ransom he was an hostage for would be lost. At last this was paid and Raymund returned to Barcelona but his sufferings had brought upon him disease and when barely thirty-seven years of age he died. He was made a Cardinal but he never took upon himself either the dress or the usual equipage of his high office. "Pope Alexander II. inserted his name in the Martyrology in 1657."

SEPTEMBER

Next him September marched eke on foot,
Yet was he hoary, laden with the spoil
Of harvest riches, which he made his boot,
And him enriched with bounty of the soil.

—*Spenser.*

When the year began in March as the seventh month, September was properly named, but when the Kalendar was changed by placing two months before March, the name, like those of the three following months, October, November and December, all seem inappropriate, but through all the mutations their names have not been changed as others have, though Julius Cæsar added a day to the month which Augustus again took away, and it has since remained so. In old English days this month was called Gerst monat or barley month, because of the barley harvest.

SEPTEMBER 1st.

To the denizens of London there is no name in the entire list of saints mentioned in the Kalendar more familiar than that of St. Giles who is this day honoured by all branches of the Christian Church, especially in France, Germany, England and Poland, as well as in Greece and Rome, for he was by birth an Athenian of noble extraction who in Latin is called Aequidius.

From a desire to secure perfect isolation from the world St. Giles migrated into France and set up a hermitage in a forest near the mouth of the Rhone in what is now the diocese of Nismes, devoting himself wholly to his prayers and holy reflections. His legend tells us of a hind who came daily to his cell and thus furnished the hermit with milk. One day the King of France while hunting happened to stalk this hind and chased it until it found refuge in the cave of St. Giles and it was thus the secret of his retirement was discovered; but nothing could induce him to leave his loved solitude. He did, however, consent to allow a few disciples to join him, and a monastery, which at its inception was like the early Irish monasteries, was begun and St. Giles became its abbot. From this later grew an abbey of the Benedictine order bearing his name and the town of St. Giles which was famous in the wars of the Albigenses. The church, it is said, still remains and is a remarkable example of the architecture of the VIII. century, being "covered with bas-reliefs on the outside and has a remarkable staircase in the interior." St. Giles is the patron of cripples from his refusal to be cured of an accidental lameness, in order that by his deformity he might be able the more thoroughly and completely to mortify his pride. St. Giles' Cripplegate is one of the many churches that have been dedicated to this saint. This church antedates the Conquest. Where the Church of "St. Giles-in-the-Fields" now stands Queen Matilda, wife of Henry I., erected a hospital for lepers. While in Scotland to this day on one side of the coat-armorial of the city of Edinburgh you may see figuring as a supporter the hind which ancient legend represents as nurturing the holy anchorite in the forests of Languedoc twelve hundred years ago.

ST. GILES.

In art St. Giles is usually represented in full canonical dress with a crosier and hind as in our illustration. In some cases the hind has an arrow in its neck, but the usual Clog symbol is a mysterious emblem given above, the form often being varied into the shape shown here and supposed to be some old Athenian symbol or hieroglyphic. St. Giles died at his abbey some time between the years 720 and 725. The exact date is unknown but for centuries the feast day of September 1st has been observed both by the English church and in Roman Martyrology in honour of this saint.

SEPTEMBER 2d

Is sacred in the Roman Church as the festival of St. Stephen, the first Christian king of Hungary. His father, Geysa, was the fourth duke of the Hungarians, and with his wife, Sarloth, under the teaching of Adalbert, a Northumbrian missionary and who afterward became Bishop of Prague, were baptised. The legend of St. Stephen tells that Sarloth, his mother, was warned in a dream to give her son the name of the great proto-martyr and when in 977 he was born he was at once thus christened, and from his infancy educated in the tenets of the church. In 997 his father, Geysa, died and the young duke set about the task of Christianizing his province, he himself often acting as a missionary. As his strength grew he added by conquest much territory, and at last asked Pope Sylvester II. to confirm him as king of Hungary. Not only was this done, but the pope sent him a present of a cross which was to be carried before him, and the legate of the Vatican, Astric, placed the crown on Stephen's head. This was in the year 1000. I am reminded in passing of an interesting historical fact connected with this crown, which was preserved at Presburg, that it was used to crown Maria Theresa as empress. But I must not try to follow the intricate story of this first Christian king of the Hungarians beyond referring to his remarkable "code of laws" in fifty-five chapters, which even to-day are noted for their justice, wisdom and moderation, and which are the foundation of Hungarian law. Of Stephen's fidelity to the church and of his own personal purity of life, one can hardly speak too highly. For three long years he suffered from painful maladies borne with the true Christian patience, yet never failing to watch his kingly duties. At the last on August 15, 1038, he passed to rest after forty-one years of rule and when over three-score years of age. He was canonized by Pope Benedict IX., but Pope Innocent XI., in 1686 fixed his festival for the 2d of September with an office for the whole church, that being the day Emperor Leopold recovered Buda out of the hands of the Turks. But in Hungary the festival is kept on August 20th, the day on which his relics were translated to the great Church of Our Lady at Buda erected in St. Stephen's honour by the holy King Ladislas.

SFPTEMBER 3d

Is devoted to St. Simeon Stylites the Younger, of whom I may make but brief mention. He was one of those famous "Pillar Saints" of whom I already have made mention. His legend reads: "For three-score and eight years he lived successively on two pillars within the inclosure of the monastery in the exercise of assiduous contemplation." He died in 592.

SEPTEMBER 4th.

St. Cuthbert, who died March 20th in 687 or 8, and was Abbot of "Old Melrose," is again especially honoured on this day, the anniversary of the translation of his relics in the year 995.

Readers must not confound "Old Melrose" with the well-known ruins of Melrose Abbey. Back in the VII. century in a rude woody country occupied by a few half-savage tribes of southern Picts and Angles, on a high promontory around two sides of which flows the Tweed, stood the monastery of Mailros, a small connection of "wattled huts" such as before described. This was "Old Melrose" as it is termed, in order to distinguish it from its successor whose beautiful ruins many of my readers have seen. It was of this monastery of Mailros that Cuthbert, who had entered it as a shepherd-boy, at last came to be its Abbot. The incursions of the Danes had come before the death of St. Cuthbert often disturbing the monks of Mailros, and the Abbot had commanded if after his death the monks should be driven out by these Danes, they should take his remains with them wherever they went. The holy man was much honoured during his life, but when eleven years after his death, in order to give his remains a more prominent place, his tomb was opened, they found his body untouched by decay; the monks became convinced that he was indeed a saint, and not a few miracles are recorded as having been performed at his new shrine where his body remained until 875 when the monks, driven out by the Danes, took St. Cuthbert's relics to find rest at Chester-le-Street.

But even this resting place was in a certain sense temporary, for in 995, a new incursion of the Danes sent them off once more upon their travels. They were kept some time at Rippon in Yorkshire, and when the danger was past the monks set out on their return to Chester-le-Street, bearing the relics with them. They were miraculously arrested, at a spot called Duirholm (the deer's meadow), on the River Wear, and there they finally settled with the precious corpse of their holy patron, giving rise to what has since been one of the grandest religious establishments of the British empire, the cathedral of Durham. This is the event which was for some ages celebrated as the Translation of St. Cuthbert.

For upwards of an hundred years the tomb of St. Cuthbert with his uncorrupted body continued to be visited by devout pilgrims, and in 1104 on the erection of the present cathedral of Durham it was determined to remove his remains to a shrine within the new structure. Some doubts had been expressed as to the permanence of his incorruptibility, and to silence all such misgivings the clergy of the church, having met in conclave beside the saint's coffin the night before its intended removal, resolved to satisfy themselves by an actual inspection. After preparing themselves for the task by prayer, they removed, with trembling hands, the external fastenings and opened the first coffin within which a second was found, covered with rough hides and enclosing a third coffin enveloped in several folds of linen. On removing the lid of this last receptacle a second lid appeared, which on being raised with much fear and agitation, the swathed body of the saint lay before them "in a perfect state."

For the greater part of three centuries more the body of St. Cuthbert lay here undisturbed. He was not forgotten during this time but a legend prevailed that the site of his tomb was known only to the Catholic clergy, three of whom, it was alleged, and no more were intrusted with the secret at a time, one being admitted to a knowledge of it as another died — all this being in the hope of a time arriving when his shrine might be re-erected, and the incorrupt body presented once more to the veneration of the people.

In 1827 St. Cuthbert's tomb was opened once more and lying on the breast of the swathings, was found the gold cross St. Cuthbert is reported to have worn, and it is shown in the illustration copied from an illustrated description of Durham Cathedral. But as on March 20th I spoke of this saint I will not enlarge further upon his story here except to mention the legend of "St. Cuthbert's Beads," as told in "Marmion":

On a rock, by Lindisfarne,
Saint Cuthbert sits, and toils to frame
The sea-born beads that bear his name;
Such tales had Whitby's fishers told,
And said they might his shape behold,
    And hear his anvil sound;
A deadened clang — a huge dim form,
Seen but, and heard, when gathering storm
    And night were closing round.

It was an ancient Northumbrian legend a thousand years old when Scott wrote, and while modern science shows these beads with which the shore is strewn after every storm to be the fossilized remains of animals called crinoids which once inhabited the deep in myriads, now seldom found complete, yet if the reader examines these illustrations, selected from thousands no two alike he will not wonder back in the old days when superstition reigned, men could believe the legend that St. Cuthbert forged these beads in his cave under the sea for the faithful to use on their rosaries.

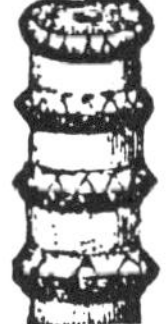

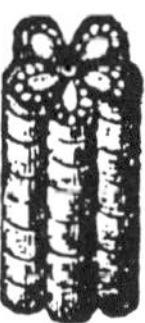

ST. CUTHBERT'S BEADS.

SEPTEMBER 5th.

St. Laurence Justinian who is honoured by the Church this day was a native of Venice, born in 1380 of an illustrious family, even amid the host of Venetian nobles of that period ; but from his earliest childhood he constantly desired to lead a religious life. His mother, a devout woman, had been left a widow and therefore hoped to see the family honour perpetuated in her son, and thus an honourable alliance had been arranged for Laurence when he was nineteen years of age. But this was never completed as the young man then secretly fled to the monastery of St. George in Alga and was admitted to the religious habit. From that time on his life was that of the usual novice save that it was marked by an unusual degree of humility, a trait which he never overcame even when his profound wisdom and learning had placed him among the leaders of the church.

Talents such as Laurence Justinian displayed never are long without recognition, and his reputation spread far beyond the walls of his monastery. Pope Eugenius IV. in 1433, much against the wish of Laurence, not only nominated him to the episcopacy of Venice but insisted upon his accepting the high office which he so worthily filled until 1451, when Dominic Michelli, the Patriarch of Grado, died, and Nicholas VI. transferred the patriarchal dignity to the see of Venice, and invested Laurence with it; thus conferring on him the high honour of being the first Patriarch of Venice, an honour which he held until January 8, 1455, when he passed peacefully to rest. The ceremony of beatification was performed by Clement VII. in 1524, and that of his canonization by Alexander VIII. in 1690, when September 5th, the anniversary of his consecration as bishop was fixed upon for his festival.

SEPTEMBER 6th.

The especial name honoured at Rome in Martyrology on this day is St. Eleutherius, a man noted for his beautiful simplicity of character and noble virtues which won for him the friendship of St. Gregory the Great, nay more, his love and reverence, and we read in Roman Martyrology of "this servant of God who, according to the testimony of Pope St. Gregory, raised a dead man to life by his prayers and tears." St. Eleutherius died at the Monastery of St. Andrew's in Rome about 585, and his remains were translated later to Spoleto.

SEPTEMBER 7th

Is the saint-day or festival of St. Evurtius, or Evurchus who holds a place in the Anglican Kalendar, as well as in that of the Roman Church; yet singularly almost nothing is known of him. His brief legend tells that during the reign of Constantine (the Great) he was sent to secure the release of some captives; but fails to tell by whom held, and that he arrived at Orleans just when the faithful happened to be electing a bishop; that as he waited and watched the ceremony, a dove twice came and lighted upon his shoulder and the last time remained there.

The incident so impressed the congregation as to his sanctity that they elected him —*nem. con.*— Bishop of Orleans. This election was duly confirmed and he assumed his office. Still later, the legend tells when he was about to erect his Cathedral Church of the Holy Cross he directed the men where to dig for its foundation, and that as the workmen dug they came upon a spot containing gold amply sufficient to meet the expense of the edifice. Dr. Butler says: "His name is famous in the ancient Martyrologies; but his history has no authenticity, as Stilting complains," and adds, "his relics had three translations," but beyond this furnishes us with no details. He is supposed to have died in 340.

St. Cloud is another saint also honoured this day, a prince of the royal family of the first race in France, a son of Chlodomir, King of Orleans and a grandson of St. Clotilda, of whom and of whose machinations to secure the control of the entire country I spoke lately. In 524 Chlodomir was killed in Burgundy when St. Cloud was hardly three years old. His grandmother at that time came to Paris bringing with her his two older brothers, Theobald and Gunthaire.

Childebert, King of Paris, and Clotaire, King of Soissons, the brothers of Chlodomir, at once conspired to kill their children and thus to secure Burgundy to be divided between them. They succeeded in murdering Cloud's two brothers, Childebert killing one by his own hand and Clotaire in turn the other; but by a mysterious Providence, Cloud escaped and was hidden in a monastery until all danger was over. It is a long and interesting bit of French history how Cloud might have gained the kingdom of Burgundy until in 551, of his own wish he was ordained to the priesthood by Eusebius, Bishop of Paris, and later built a monastery at Nogent (now St. Cloud) and collected pious men to join him in his efforts for the good of mankind, and his holy life, and his death in 560, when his inheritance was by his directions divided among the poor of Nogent and the churches of the see of Paris. It is a true and beautiful story of one who might have been a king, but preferred to serve his Great Master, and while I would gladly tell it cannot do so here. The monastery built by St. Cloud is now changed into a Collegiate Church of canons.

SEPTEMBER 8th.

THE NATIVITY OF THE BLESSED VIRGIN

Is a sacred festival which is observed alike in the Greek, the Roman and the English branches of the Christian Church.

In the birth of the Holy Virgin we come one step nearer to the accomplishment of those prophecies which abound in the Old Testament and to appreciate duly the wonderful importance of this event "we must," as Dr. Butler says, "consider her transcendant dignity and the singular privileges by which she was distinguished above all other pure creatures." Her dignity is expressed by the Evangelist when he says; "Of whom was born Jesus, who is called Christ." (Matthew i., 16). Again the venerated St. Bernard says: "Choose which you will most admire, the most beneficent condescension of the Son or the sublime dignity of the Mother, etc."

The legends of the Nativity of the Virgin are almost endless in number, a favourite one describing the Concert of Angels who hovered over the mother and child. In Le Clerc's Almanac this concert is presented and the Angels at the same time are seen strewing flowers over them.

Most of the traditions regarding Joachim and Anne tell us that they were "exceedingly rich," and thus in many of the early works of art that present "La Nascita della B. Vergine" the room is full of gorgeous furniture and magnificent decorations of the ancient Hebrew type, and the child Mary as she rests on her mother's breast is surrounded by "a Glory" and never without "a Nimbus." The Clog symbol is a simple heart without any adornments.

The Nativity of the Blessed Virgin has been kept by the Church with great solemnity from very early days. The "Roman Ordo" mentions homilies and litanies appointed by Pope Sergius (687-701) in 688 and a procession to be made on this day from St. Adrian's Church to the Liberian basilica (Sta. Maria Maggiore, lately mentioned) and a prescribed office for the ceremony, not to speak of them in detail, many especial prayers and collects, at close intervals from the feast as mentioned by St. Idlefonsus in the VII. century down through intervening ages. The Greeks, the Copts in Egypt and all Christian Churches in the East kept this feast with the utmost solemnity and when after the Reformation the ceremonials of the dissenting church were revived, this feast was retained.

On this day also the festival of St. Adrian is observed. He was a Roman officer and the church above mentioned was erected in his honour. He suffered martyrdom under Maximian Galerius in the year 306.

Under this date Dr. Butler speaks of "The Festival of the Holy Name of the Virgin Mary" to be observed "on the Sunday within the Octave of her Nativity." This festival was appointed by Pope Innocent IX. and the occasion was a solemn thanksgiving for the relief of Vienna when it was besieged in 1063.

SEPTEMBER 9th.

Again this day the cruelties of Dioclesian are brought before us by the names of SS. Dorotheus, Gorgonius and their companions, who as martyrs for the faith of Christ suffered under those terrible edicts of this brutal Roman emperor. Dorotheus was the first chamberlain of the Emperor Dioclesian while Gorgonius and Peter were under chamberlains. These three were the principal eunuchs of the palace and had sometimes borne the weight of the most difficult affairs of State and been the support of the emperor and his court. When the palace of Nicomedia was set on fire, an event already mentioned, which readers will remember was charged to the Christians by Galerius, the joint emperor with Dioclesian, Dorotheus and a number of his companions who knew how unjust and untrue the assertion was had the manhood to deny boldly the falsehood. The anger and suspicions of the emperor were aroused and he accused his eunuchs of being Christians. This was not true in fact yet once these three men had been nearly converted to the faith. They were thoughtful men not time servers and were considering in their own minds the weighty question of the salvation of their souls. By a mere word, an assertion and a vain act they could then have saved their earthly lives but with solemn deliberation they saw the truth and their noble Roman blood knew no deceit. They had decided for themselves and the inexorable Dioclesian sacrificed these men, true to him in all matters of state, but who refused to sacrifice to Roman gods they knew were but myths. The cruelties they were subjected to seem beyond the humanity of man to inflict on a fellow man. The fiendish cruelties of the wildest savages are gentle when compared with those these sturdy brave men were called on to endure as the price they paid for holding fast to the faith of Christ. The details of these horrors are told in the narrative of their persecution and death that lies before me as I write, but they are too brutal to transcribe. Yet I cannot help asking myself whether I would have endured them as these "saints" did.

SEPTEMBER 10th.

St. Pulcehria, the Virgin Empress of the East whom the Roman Church has chosen for honour on this day is one of those remarkable and exceptional characters that from time to time come to light as we turn the pages of ancient history. She was born in 399, the granddaughter of Theodosius the Great. Her father, Arcadius, was a weak man governed by his wife, Eudoxia, and his eunuchs; but his daughter, Pulcehria, had evidently inherited from her grandfather the noble traits which marked her character.

She was hardly fifteen years of age when in 414, she with her brother Augustus — two years her junior — were jointly invested with imperial power; while the care and education of her brother devolved upon Pulcehria at an age when we to-day would regard her as hardly more than a child herself. We must not forget the fact — too patent for debate — that the women of the East mature both mentally and physically at a much earlier age than with us of the West. Yet there was a certain precocity of wisdom and a provision of her future which induced Pulcehria to make a public vow of chastity, and thus warn off possible suitors for her hand. In like manner she induced her sisters to take similar vows and thus save the empire from being embroiled by some marriage that would be disastrous to the State. Her influence over her brother was unbounded and whatever else may have been the outcome of her teaching she at least held him true to the faith of his grandfather, Theodosius, at a time when many heresies were creeping into the Church. A writer very near to this period says: "The imperial palace under her discretion was as regular as a monastery," while another of later date says: "Far from making religion subservient to policy, all her views and projects were regulated by that virtue, and by this the happiness of her government was complete." She was skilled in both the Greek and Latin tongues, proficient in history and other branches of science and literature, and a generous patron of art, but above all, a just and generous ruler who by her wisdom had kept her people at peace and in prosperity and won their love.

When her brother was about twenty years of age, an Athenian

lady appeared at Court seeking aid to secure justice in her father's will by which she was disinherited. The young man was captivated by her beauty and he married her.

At first there was no change in any way so far as Pulcehria was concerned. But soon the story, as old as the institution of kingly powers, was again reenacted. The Queen Eudosia, jealous of the influence Pulcehria exercised, plotted for her downfall. She had neither grounds nor reason for so doing since the devoted sister already weary of power was only too happy for an excuse to be relieved and quickly sought retirement.

Eudosia had been brought up and educated by her father, an Athenian philosopher, as an idolator; but before her marriage had been baptized, and as soon as Pulcchria was removed from her path began those historic presecutions of 447 and 449. This providentially was of but short duration, for the emperor died in July of 450 and Pulcehria again resumed her control over the Empire of the East and brought peace to the Christians. It was then the Empress felt the need of help in her duties and was married but with the agreement that she yet should be permitted to keep her early vow. The man thus chosen was worthy of the confidence reposed in him and to their joint efforts the Church owed much of the peace it enjoyed in the East during this reign, while Dr. Butler says of her: "Historians assure us that volumes would be required to sum up all the churches, monasteries and especially the hospitals which St. Pulcehria founded and richly endowed."

She died upon September 10th in 453, and for centuries both the Greek and Latin Churches have celebrated hers as the feast of a holy virgin.

SEPTEMBER 14th.

The history of the "Invention of the Cross" has been told already (see May 3d) and how from this discovery by St. Helena, Constantine the Great was led to build a magnificent church on Mount Calvary for its preservation. But before this came the wonderful "Labarum." This story as briefly told is that when Constantine (who was not then converted) was about to meet the Emperor Maxentius, he put up a prayer "to the One True God," for help and in response to this prayer there appeared in mid-day the monogram of Christ known as the Labarum (see first illustration) and caused a banner to be made, that bore upon it the monogram of Christ and beneath it the portraits of himself and his two sons. This was the banner carried in the decisive battle when Maxentius was defeated and after which as history tells us, he drowned himself in the Tiber. Still another form is given which is said to have born upon it the inscription (as in illustration) in Greek the words: By this Conquer.

Here foloweth the Exaltacion of the holy Crosse

The first form, however, is beyond doubt the one placed upon the banner.

Naturally the discovery of the true Cross, made Christians of Jerusalem and the hosts of pilgrims who flocked to the city anxious to see the sacred piece of wood. Therefore in 338 it was determined that the Holy Rood, (cross) should be "raised" or "exalted" in full view of the people.

Our illustration given is taken from a reprint in 1876 of a Dutch Legendary History of the Cross originally published in 1423.

This custom of the Exaltation of the Cross on this day was continued annually through several centuries.

In 603 Phocas, the cruel and covetous Emperor of the East, was reigning, when Chosroes II., King of Persia, broke peace with him upon a specious pretense and meeting no serious opposition plundered Mesopotamia and part of Syria. Heraclius, then Prefect of Africa (afterward Emperor of the East) was begged by the people to assume the purple and rid them of the tyrant Phocas. This he did — though I may not tell the story here — and sought for peace with Chosroes. But the barbarian refused all overtures and pushed forward until in 613 he captured Damascus, and in 614 Jerusalem, and in so doing secured the sacred relic of the Cross. It was then that as history tells us Chosroes defiled the sacred relic and carried it, among his plundered treasures from Jerusalem. Then, by his wonderful victory over Chosroes, Heraclius once more secured the Holy Cross and brought it to Jerusalem. The next illustration taken from the same Dutch book already spoken of is in two parts, the left showing an angel closing the gates of the city, on account of the pomp and show of Heraclius, and the right where the veil hides the Cross as it is being taken into the Basilica. This last event occurred in 629 when the ceremony of Elevation of the Cross was for a time resumed but with the late prostitution of the holy relic it ceased at Jerusalem until revived by decrees of the Church.

THE LABARUM.

THE LABARUM BANNER OF CONSTANTINE.

Many churches in Britain were dedicated to the Holy Rood or Cross. One at Edinburgh became the nucleus of the palace of the Scottish kings. Thus Holyrood Day was one of much sacred observance all through the middle ages. The same feeling led to a custom of framing, between the nave and choir of churches what was called a rood-screen or rood-loft, presenting centrally a large crucifix with images of the Holy Virgin and St. John on each side. A winding stair led up to it and the epistle and gospel were often read from it. Some of these screens still remain, models of architectural beauty but numbers were destroyed with reckless fanaticism at the Reformation, when the people did not distinguish between the objects which had caused what they deemed idolatry and the beautifully carved work which was free from such a charge.

THE CONSTANTINE BOOM.

SEPTEMBER 15th

Is the Octave of the Nativity of the Blessed Virgin and is observed in the Roman Church by an especial office.

In the "Ordo" for this day, I note an office for St. Nicomedes, a holy priest, who during the persecution of Domitian, was beaten to death with clubs, because of his aid and comfort to other martyrs and his refusal to sacrifice to idols, saying: "I do not sacrifice except to the Omnipotent God, who reigns in Heaven."

Saints Sabas and Nicetas are the two most famous saints among the Goths. The first of these — Sabas — is honoured on April 12th and the last on this day; especially by the Greeks, who name him as one of the "great martyrs." When Valens became Emperor of the East in 364 the nation of the Goths was divided into two kingdoms. Athanaric, King of the Eastern Goths, whose territory bordered on the Roman empire toward Thrace, in 370, raised a furious persecution against the Christians. By his orders an idol was placed in a chariot and carried through the towns and villages and any Christian who refused to adore it was

put to death; their usual custom being to burn them and their children in their houses. Thus Nicetas, a noble Goth, who had accepted the Christian faith and proved his constancy within the holocaust of his own dwelling.

SEPTEMBER 16th.

This day the Roman Church honours another of those noble men of whom she has so many to be proud of, St. Ninian, the Apostle to the Southern Picts, and to whom I already have alluded. Of his early life, as is the case with many of those old-time worthies, little seems to be known beyond the fact that he was the son of a Cumbrian Briton prince in or about Galloway; in the borderland between what is now England and Scotland, but then was in North Umbria and a part of Bernecia. The same section I have spoken of as that occupied in the II. century by a tribe which Ptolemy termed the "Novantæ" and who came to be known as "the Picts of Galloway," and still later as the *locus habitat* of the "Wild Scots of Galloway." How Ninian's house had come to know anything of Christianity is untold and we can only infer that it had come about through intercourse with his Irish neighbours. Thus in a vague, uncertain way we are told how Ninian had quitted "court and its attractions" and made a journey to Rome where he spent many years. The next we hear of him is toward the close of the Roman occupation of Britain, as a missionary located on the north shore of Solway Frith and on the west side of Wigtown Bay, at a town which Ptolemy calls "Leukopibia," now called Whithorn. St. Ninian's story here first connects him with St. Martin of Tours for whom we know through many incidents in his later life he had a great veneration and love. It also first mentions the foundation of the "*Magnum Monasterium*" founded by Ninian at Whithorn, and variously called "The House of Martin" and "Candida Casa," the latter probably from the white stone of which the church edifice was constructed. The legend tells us that Ninian sent to St. Martin of Tours for workmen to build this church "after the Roman manner," and it is the first stone structure of which we have any authentic account north of the Solway Frith. While no date is given in regard to this we know St. Martin died in 397, and therefore this could not have been at a later date. This monastery became known as a great seminary for secular and religious learning. It was here that St. Finian, or Finbarr, was educated and later established the great school at Magh-Bile, or Mogbile in county Down, Ireland, of which I spoke on June 9th, when describing the life of St. Columba.

From this great monastic school both Ninian and his pupils went forth as missionaries among the Southern Picts and pagan Britons from Mount Grampus — as it was then called — through Cumbria and Northumbria; and from this gained the title of the "Apostle to the Southern Picts."

In early days the residence of the Picts alternated between the Northern and the Southern Picts and also the capitol of the nation changing with each alternate dynasty, an interesting subject I can not enter on here. Ethnologically these Picts were one race and descended from the same cruithnigh; but while united in general purpose they were dual in certain essential points. In Ninian's time the king was a Southern Pict, Tudivald by name; as fierce an idolater as Columba encountered in Brude at Inverness. Yet Ninian seems to have overcome him as it was by his aid the wonderful church which Ninian built was completed. It is singular though, that there is no account of the conversion of King Tudivald to be found either in Bede's or Siacginui's Chronicles, or in any of the Folk-tales of the time as was the case when the doors and gates fell before SS. Columba and Conegal at Inverness.

Whatever of Ninian's teachings resulted in had passed by St. Columba's time and the tribes again lapsed with Ninian's departure into a state of semi-paganism.

Again there comes an aggravating hiatus in the life of Ninian; yet in an old "Irish Life of St. Ninian" it is recorded that he left Whithorn and went to Ireland where he founded a church in Leinster called Cluain Couairc, and in "Bollaudus Acta Sancta" it is recorded he is commemorated on September 16th under the name of Morenn. "Mointnd Tomain hi tuaiscert h Fallan" glossed — Monenni of Cluain Toman in the north of Hy-Fallan in Leinster. The Martyrology of Talsnacht says "Monenni" is merely Nenn, or Ninian, "i. e., Ninianus Episcopus Candida Casa." Bede, the Saxon historian, is the authority — now universally accepted — for the date of St. Ninian's death in 432; but no details of any kind exist, as to when, where or how he died except that Montelambert's, "Monks of the West" says Ninian died at Whithorn 432.

Another honoured name this day is St. Cyprian, one of the most famous of the Latin Fathers and second only in eloquence to Lactantius. He was a native of Carthage and became a convert to Christianity at an advanced period of life having been led to renounce paganism through conversation with an aged presbyter called Cecilius, whose name he adopted as an addition to his own. The enthusiasm which he displayed on behalf of his new faith caused him soon to be admitted as a priest, and within less than a year afterwards to be raised to the dignity of Bishop of Carthage as successor to Donatus. In the exercise of his office he manifested such zeal that the pagans, in derision styled him Coprianus, in allusion to a Greek term for filth; and on the commencement of the Christian persecution under the Emperor Decius the heathen populace rushed into the market-place shouting: "Cyprian to the lions! Cyprian to the wild-beasts!" The danger that threatened him seemed so imminent that he deemed it expedient for a time to retire from Carthage though in doing so he exposed himself to some severe animadversions from his brother-clergy of Rome for thus shrinking from the storm and suffering his flock to perish. From his place of retreat, however, which seems to have been carefully concealed, he despatched numerous letters to guide and animate his people under their trials. At last on an abatement of the persecution taking place, Cyprian returned to Carthage and continued his episcopal ministrations with great zeal and success till a fresh season of tribulation commenced for the church under the Emperor Valerian, in A. D. 257. On this occasion the Bishop of Carthage showed no disposition to cower before the blast but bravely remained at his post to encourage and strengthen his hearers. In the autumn of the last-mentioned year he was himself apprehended and brought before the African proconsul, who ordered him into banishment to the city of Curubis, about fifty miles from Carthage. After remaining there for about a twelve month the expectation of still bloodier edicts arriving from Rome caused him to be brought back to Carthage and lodged for a time under surveillance in his own country-house near the city. On the reception of the fatal orders, the Proconsul Galerius Maximus caused Cyprian to be brought before him at his country-seat of Sextus, six miles from Carthage. The tide of popular opinion had now turned entirely in favour of the bishop ; who had while a pestilence was raging in the city, exerted himself with the most heroic ardour both personally and by calling forth the co-operation of others in relieving the sufferings and ministering to the necessities of the sick. A noble large-heartedness had also been shown by him in proclaiming to his people the duty of assisting all sufferers in this terrible visitation without regard to the circumstance of their being Christian or pagan. An immense and sympathizing crowd accompanied him on the road to the proconsul's house. The proceedings before that functionary appear to have been of a very summary description as Cyprian on having replied to a few interrogations and steadily refusing to conform to the pagan ceremonies, was forthwith ordered to be beheaded. This was in the year 238.

SEPTEMBER 17th.

In Roman Martyrology mention is made and in the Ordo for this day there is in the Roman Church an especial office directed in commemoration of the "Impression of the sacred wounds which St. Francis, founder of the Order of Minorites, received through a wonderful favour of God, in his hands, feet and sides on Mount Alvernia." St. Francis' festival occurs on October 4th, but this day is a special occasion to mark this event which won for him the title of "the Seraphic." The legend is a very long one and must be condensed into a few words devoid of the incidents which make it a graphic picture. After a fast of fifty days in his cell on Mount Alvernia he had a vision of a seraph with six wings descending from Heaven and standing beside him. When the angel left he found indelibly impressed on his hands, feet and side imprints of the wounds our Saviour Lord had received on the Cross of Calvary, imprints he carried with him until his death. It is this event that the Roman Church celebrates to-day in especial honour of St. Francis, though his festival occurs later in the year when I shall have much to say of this notable man.

SEPTEMBER 18th.

The Roman Emperor Domitianus can hardly be counted a saint but since the name of this heartless monster is closely connected with the death of so many of the "noble Army of the Martyrs" it seems proper to mention this as the anniversary of his death. He was foully though no doubt deserving of his fate — assassinated in the year 96 as Roman history tells us, but I must forego giving the details.

This day is the festival of St. Thomas of Villanova, or Villanueva, surnamed "The Almoner;" the glory of the Church of Spain in these later days. He was born at Fuelana in Castile in 1488. When fifteen years of age he was sent to the University of Alcala which was founded by Cardinal Ximenes, Prime Minister under both Ferdinand and Charles X. Later on, after graduation he taught moral philosophy at Alcala and at the celebrated University of Salamanca. In 1518 he took the habit and vows of the Hermits of St. Austin at the house of that institute at Salamanca. His legend tells us the singular coincidence that "he pronounced his vows on the very day and in the same hour," when Luther publicly renounced his connection with the Roman Church. The title Almoner was bestowed upon him because of his generosity to the poor. It is told of him that from a child his one aim in life seemed his desire to help others. That as a lad he would disrobe himself in the street even, in order to clothe some poor child he met in rags and that throughout his life he was ever ready to forego any comfort, deny himself every luxury and endure privation, even to the extent of personal physical suffering, if thereby he was able to alleviate the necessities of others. As a pulpit orator he was wonderfully eloquent and Charles V. held him in such veneration that in 1544 he named him Archbishop of Valencia. Thomas reluctantly accepted the exalted position but secretly resolved to use the wealth the office would inevitably bring to him for the good of his fellow men. He arrived at Valencia so poorly clad and provided for that his canons sent him a purse of four thousand crowns with which to equip himself for his new state. He thanked the donors and then sent the money to a hospital for the sick and appeared wearing the same hat he had worn for twenty-six years. He classified as philanthropists to-day might well do; the poor, dividing them into six classes to be treated accordingly. First the bashful poor who once had been independent and were now ashamed to beg. Second, poor girls whose poverty enforced them to temptation, sin and shame. Third, poor debtors. Fourth, orphans and foundlings. Fifth, the lame, sick and infirm. And lastly strangers who found themselves without the means to secure for themselves food and lodging.

While he gave all his income save barely enough to maintain his simple establishment, barren of every luxury or anything ostentatious, his charities were not indiscriminately bestowed. A professional beggar (tramp or hobo we term them) found no mercy at his hand; but the deserving never left him empty handed. Had I the space to tell the story, some of his methods would give points to our generous but unsystematic philanthropists.

But the choicest gift this holy man bestowed was given all unconsciously to himself by his personal visits to the poor, sick and suffering, where his presence seemed to bring comfort and peace at all times. I regret thus to briefly memorize a life so full of love and charity. He died in 1555 and was beatified by Paul V. in 1618, who then directed St. Thomas' attribute should be "An Open Purse." He was canonized by Alexander VII. in 1658.

SEPTEMBER 19th.

This day is the festival of St. Theodore, the first Archbishop of Canterbury after St. Austin, who had been consecrated by Pope Vitilian in 668.

The Roman Church holds this day in honour of SS. Januarius, Bishop of Beuenvento ; Sosius, Deacon of Miseno ; Provennilus, Deacon of Puzzuoli and two eminent laymen named Eutychius and Acutius of Puzzuoli, all victims of the cruel persecution of Dioclesian. This is but the repetition of the oft-told story of chains, imprisonment, exposure to wild beasts in the ampitheater, and they were at last beheaded in 305 because they had visited and comforted Christian prisoners, and that they themselves held firmly to the faith of Christ. The body of St. Januarius was brought to Naples and with it a bottle which contained some of his blood, and his legend says that even to-day after these centuries of time have elapsed when this bottle is placed by the head of its martyr the congealed blood at once liquifies. Pope Pius II. mentions this as a fact in 1450.

SEPTEMBER 20th

Is sacred to the honour of St. Agapetus, Pope and Confessor. In 535 when Pope John II. died, Agapetus was only an Archdeacon of the Church of SS. John and Paul of Rome, but his learning and sanctity were widely known and he was elected successor to the Holy See and ordained on May 4, 535, ten days after the death of John II. His influence was at once felt for by his interposition the unhappy schism of Diosconis against Boniface II. in 529 was quickly healed. Justinian not only recognized him but sent to him an especial profession of faith which Agapetus received as orthodox and the two became warm, loyal friends. In February, 536, Agapetus went to Constantinople to interview the emperor, where he died on April 17th of the same year after a brief but eventful period of only eleven months and a few days as a dominant power of the Church. His festival has been fixed for this day.

THE SIBYLS.

The author has been asked several times in regard to the Sibyls and their connection with the Church. While it cannot be said the Church recognised these mythical personages it seems clear it used them as a quasi-argument in the early and middle ages as shown by this verse, from a hymn said to have been written by Pope Innocent III., (172d Pope, 1198-1216) and translated in the English version of the Missal as follows:

> "The dreadful day, the day of ire
> Shall kindle the avenging fire
> Around the expiring world;
> And earth, as Sibyl said of old,
> And as the prophet king foretold,
> Shall be in ruin hurled."

Both the origin and number of the Sibyls is obscure and uncertain. Varro one hundred years B. C. gave their number as ten and their names came from their habitation: Sibylla Persica, from Persia, Libyca (Libyea), Delphica (Delphi), Eryhaea (Erthyrae), Cumana (Cumae), Samia (Samos), Sinomeria (Black Sea), Tiburtina (Tivoli), Hellespontina (Hellespont), and Phrygia (Phrygia). There were others afterward named like the Agrippa, the Hebriaca and the Europas; while the Queen of Sheba is also termed one of these wonderful creatures. They were prophetesses and foretold the coming of Christ to the Gentiles as the Prophets of old did to the Jews. Much disagreement existed among the Early Fathers as to the value of their prophesies. Some even regarded them as emissaries of the devil. Traditions and legends innumerable are told of these Sibyls; but I can make room for none, and only mention the especial office of a few.

The Sibylla Persica was supposed to be a daughter-in-law of Moses. She predicted the coming of the Messiah. She is represented as holding down a serpent beneath her feet and with a lantern in her hand.

The Sibylla Libyea prophesied the manifestation of Christ to the Gentiles. Her legend says she was twenty-four years old at that time. Her attribute is a lighted torch.

The Sibylla Eryhaea seemed to have a varied mission. She appears as the prophetess of divine vengeance and of the Trojan war, and as such bears a naked sword as her attribute. But she is said to have also foretold the Annunciation, and in this character has for her attribute a white rose.

The Sibylla Cimmeria when eighteen years old prophesied the crucifixion of Christ, and for this bears as an attribute a cross or crucifix.

The Sibylla Cumana foresaw and foretold the Nativity and that it should take place in a stable, and thus her attribute is an ancient stone manger.

The Sibylla Delphica for her prophecy of the mock regal adornment of Christ, has for her attribute a crown of thorns.

The Sibylla Cania was of the time of Isaiah, and has as attribute a reed and a cradle. Just why is not apparent in her legend.

The Sibylla Phrygia prophesied the Resurrection of Christ, and therefore bears the Resurrection Cross with its banner.

The Sibylla Tibertina is represented as dressed in skins of animals. Her attribute, a bundle of rods, seemingly symbolizes Christ's flagellations, and in like manner the Sibylla Agrippa has a scourge in her hand.

The Sibylla Hellespontina prophesied the incarnation and also the crucifixion of Christ, and thus has the double attributes of a crucifix and a budding rod.

Finally the Sibylla Europa is represented as but fifteen years old. It was she who prophesied the massacre of the Innocents and thus has a sword for her attribute.

From this brief mention of the Sibyls we can easily understand the quasi-recognition given them by the Church, mythical though they were.

SEPTEMBER 21st.

This is the festival of St. Matthew, the Apostle and Evangelist. Among the Apostles St. Matthew ranks as the seventh or eighth, but as an Evangelist is placed first, since theologians in general concede it was the first of the Gospels written. Others place it as

ΚΑ ΠΙ ΤΩΝ ΠΑΡΑΒΟΛΩΝ:

Ο ΑΓΙΟΣ

ΜΑΤΘΑΙΟΣ

ἰδοὺ ὅσα ἡμῖν θεὸς ἐξέβαλε· καὶ τὸν ἐχθρὸν κα
τηφρονήσει· Ὀνομία ὁ θεὸς θεὸς δοῦ
λενειν καὶ μαμμωνᾷ

the third and its date is fixed by these in A. D. 66. There is very little positive knowledge about St. Matthew's personality. He alludes to himself but once in his own Gospel, while in the Gospels of the other Evangelists he is named but twice and then only incidentally. He was a Hebrew, the son of Alphaeus of the tribe of Issachar; by profession "a publican" or tax-gatherer under the Romans, an office which while very lucrative to him was peculiarly odious and offensive in the eyes of his fellow Jews. His original name, Levi, in Hebrew signifies "Adhesian," (See Genesis xxix., 34) while the name Matthew in the same language means "Gift of Jehovah." To the point where Christ bids Matthew follow him, the sacred records as well as traditional and legendary history are equally scant. Beyond this we have almost wholly to depend on tradition for everything we find regarding St. Matthew. From the "Perfecto Legendario" and other traditions that confirm it, we learn that St. Matthew wrote his Gospel to satisfy the wishes of the converts in Palestine and that after the Ascension when the Apostles were dispersed, he went into Egypt and Ethiopia to preach; that while at the capital of Ethiopia he lodged at the house of the eunuch who had been baptised by Philip. At that time there were two terrible magicians who by their spells and enchantments held the Ethiopians in terror and subjection. St. Matthew quickly overcame these magicians, and having baptized the people they were free from the diseases which the incantations of these sorcerers had inflicted on them. St. Matthew

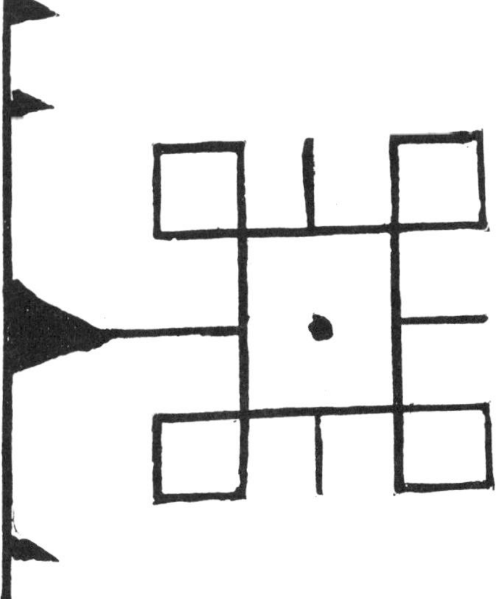

spent twenty-three years in Egypt and Ethiopia, and during that time is reported to have performed many miracles.

Both Eusebius and St. Epiphanius in their chronicles claim that St. Matthew spent several years preaching in Judea before he went to the East and was richly rewarded by the number of converts he made and that his Gospel was written before he departed on his long mission.

That St. Matthew reached a very old age and died in the ninetieth year of the Christian Era seems to be generally believed; but the manner of his death is uncertain. The Greek legends tell of him dying in peace in Parthia, but Venantius Fortunatus relates that he suffered martyrdom at Nadabar. According to Dorotheus he was honourably interred at Hierapolis in Parthia. His relics, were long since brought to the West, Pope Gregory VII, in 1080, saying they were kept in a church bearing his name at Salerno.

In art St. Matthew as an Evangelist, holds in his hand a book, (see illustration) or a pen while an angel — his proper attribute — stands by pointing toward heaven. As an Apostle he usually holds a purse or money-bag as significant of his former vocation. The grotesque winged-man, his frequent symbol, I have before spoken of, while the Clog Almanac symbol is purely "Runic."

SEPTEMBER 22d.

The story of St. Maurice and his noble companions of the Thebean legion of which Maurice was the commandant may be somewhat trite to readers of ancient history, but it is peculiarly fitting to be told now as it marks the inception of what have come to be known as the Dioclesian persecutions.

Among the troops which accompanied Maximian into Gaul was the Thebean legion raised in Thebais, Upper Egypt, a country then full of zealous Christians. Maximian's expedition was wonderfully successful and when the army had crossed the Alps and reached Octodurum on the Rhone (now Martini in the Valais), Maximian issued an order that the whole army join in sacrificing to the gods for their success.

It was then the Thebean legion rose in their might, inspired by the heroic Christian Maurice, and withdrew from the main army to Agaunum (a village now called Maurice in honour of this brave man) and to a man openly but firmly refused obedience to the

order to sacrifice to the Roman gods. They were loyal, as soldiers; would fight the battles of the Empire "a la mort," but they would worship only the one God, whom Christ represented. The anger of the emperor knew no bounds. He ordered the legion decimated, one in every ten as the lot fell to be put to death, and that the rest return to camp and obey his order. Encouraged by their officers not one man faltered in his given purpose even after that first decimation. Again the emperor threatened them with death to every man of them if they refused to sacrifice to the gods. Their reply was as before, adding: "We have arms in our hands, but we shall not resist because we would rather die than live by any sin."

This Thebean legion was six thousand strong, the finest soldiers of the Roman Army when by Maximian's order they were surrounded. Although well armed and while their officers were skilled men of war and brave; yet when the final order came they silently submitted without one blow in self defense but allowed themselves from their commanders Maurice, Exuperius and Candidus, down, to be slaughtered. Save to encourage each other to stand firm in the faith and submit to their martyrdom they opened not their lips. The camp was literally filled with their dead bodies lying in pools of bood.

Maximian, to encourage his army to this brutal massacre, had given them permission to loot the Thebean camp and each to retain such spoils as he could secure. While thus engaged a veteran Roman soldier who had held aloof from the bloody work, came among them. This soldier, Victor by name, they invited to join the revels as they feasted on the viands they had secured, but he refused. They taunted him and cried: "Art thou then, too, a Christian?" to which both he and a companion named Ursus replied: "We are, and glory in our profession." Whereupon they, like their Thebean friends, were cut down.

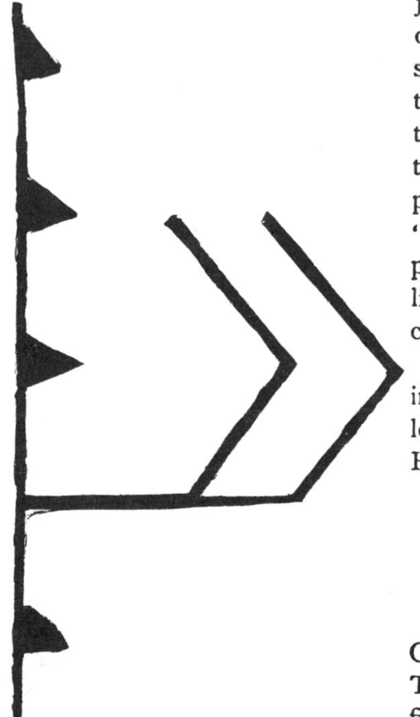

SYMBOL OF THE HAPPY LEGION.

This was on September 22d in 286 and their festival was long known as that of "the Happy Legion."

SEPTEMBER 23d.

On this day the Greek Church especially honours St. Thecla, a virgin martyr of the first century. The Latin Church as well reverences her with but little less veneration. She was a native of Isauria, and St. Methodius in his "Banquet of Virgins" tells us she was "well versed in profound philosophy and the various branches of polite literature." Her legend is that she was betrothed to a youth named Thanryris; but on hearing St. Paul preach she resolved upon leading a religious life and to do so refused to marry the young man. At last tired of entreating Thecla, Thanryris applied to the governor, and this caused Paul to be imprisoned. Bribing the jailor with her earrings and a silver mirror, she gained access to Paul and sitting at his feet listened to his words and became all the more convinced in her resolves. In the end Paul was scourged and driven from the city, but St. Thecla was condemned to be burned. She was brought naked to the stake and though a huge fire was built round her, it burned itself out leaving the virgin unhurt. After this her legend tells, but does not say how she escaped and went with Paul to Antioch where she was again arrested and condemned by the governor to be torn to pieces in the amphitheatre by wild beasts. The day came and she was again stripped of her clothing and led by a chain fastened to a girdle around her waist. But as the flames had refused to burn her, so now the wild beasts came and lay quietly at her feet as if they slept. The governor marvelled as well he might, and cried out: "Who art thou, woman, that no beast will harm thee?" "I," she replied. "am a servant of the living God and His Son, Jesus Christ." The governor ordered her clothing brought and said: "Put on thy garments and get thee hence."

Then Tinsinia, a widow, took Thecla to her house where she entertained her giving her "much money" to aid Paul in his work, and with a store of clothing for the poor, she sent her again to Paul.

At last Thecla retired to a mountain cave to dwell as a recluse but the sick sought her out and she healed them by her prayers. The physicians of Silicia said she was a priestess of Diana and healed others by reason of her perfect chastity of thought and deed. So they sent evil men to do her violence but as she ran within her cave for safety a great rock rolled itself before its mouth and shut the wicked men out from harrassing her. Her long legend adds that thus, partly in journeying and partly in the monastic seclusion of her cave, she spent seventy-two years of her life having been eighteen when she left Iconium and ninety "when God translated her." Thecla was the first female honoured by the Greek Church. Her attributes are a palm branch in her hand and wild beasts of every kind lying quietly at her feet.

SEPTEMBER 24th

This day is marked in the Roman mass as the Feast of Our Lady of Mercy.

In the English church the day is recognised as

THE FEAST OF INGATHERING.

Wherever throughout the earth there is such a thing as a formal harvest, there also appears an inclination to mark it with a festive celebration. The wonder and gratitude felt towards the great Author of Nature when it is brought before us that, once more, as it has ever been, the ripening of a few varieties of grass has furnished food for earth's teeming millions, make it natural that there should everywhere be some sort of feast of ingathering. In England this festival passes under the endeared name of Harvest Home. In Scotland where that term is unknown the festival is hailed under the name of the Kirn. In the north of England its ordinary designation is the Mell Supper. And there are perhaps other local names.

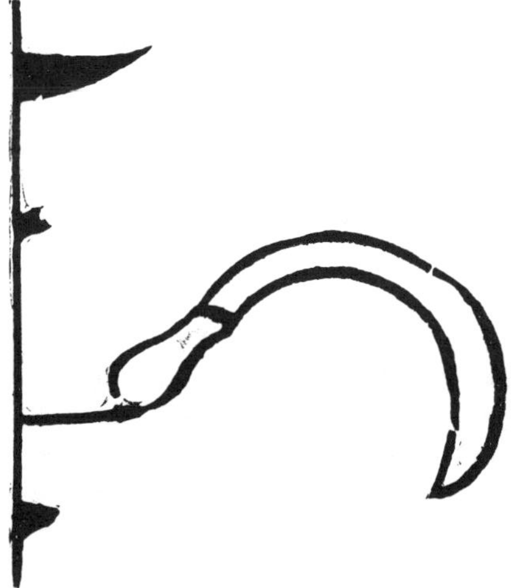

While this day is marked in the ritual of the Church it is not like our Thanksgiving a national feast, but rather it may be called a movable feast which every farmer regulates to suit his own Harvest Home, that few of the great estates or larger farmers even now fail to observe.

But if you would read of the old-time Harvest Home take down your volume of Herrick, that quaint, genial, lovable English poet of the old days, and read his lines beginning

"Come, sons of summer, by whose toile,
We are the Lords of wine and oile;
By whose tough labours, and rough hands,
We rip up first, then reap our lands."

* * * * * *

The only Clog Almanac symbol I find for this day is an English one, which represents a sickle, the reaper's implement from the earliest days.

SEPTEMBER 25th.

To St. Barr or Finbarr, as he is at times called (or yet again Barrus, or Barrocus; for in those old days seemingly, no two persons spelled the same name in the same manner), every Irishman, born in Cork, pays reverence on March 17th and December 1st, for it was to this saintly man, who established a monastery at Lough Eric, that the city of Cork owes its inception. The church has named this 25th of September his festival day. The name by which he was baptized was Lochan; that of Fin-bar, or Bar the White was given him afterward. He served as Bishop at Cork seventeen years and died at Cloygen, fifteen miles from there, but his relics rest in a silver shrine in his cathedral at Cork. The old monastery is called Gill Abbey, or Gill Acda o Mugin after the famous Bishop of Cork in 1170, who had so increased its importance that it bore his name as if he had founded it.

SEPTEMBER 26th

Is dedicated to SS. Cyprian and Justina who were brought together under somewhat peculiar circumstances. St. Cyprian has as a surname the title "the Magician," for the reason that prior to his conversion he was a soothsayer and practiced the arts of magic. It was in this capacity that a young pagan nobleman came to consult him and employed him to use his art of divination to enable the young man to overcome the objections of a beautiful young Syrian lady named Justina with whom he was in love. Her father was a "Priest of the Idols" in Antioch. But she had been converted to Christianity and through her influence both her parents had become Christians, and she naturally was very averse to granting the wish of the young pagan. Cyprian was not loth to make the trial and put forth every artifice he knew to accomplish his purpose; but soon found himself smitten with the charms of the young lady as well as surprised at his want of success. Justina was well aware of what Cyprian's purpose was, and in his "Confessions" the Magician says: "She armed herself with the sign of the Cross and overcame the invocations of the demons," and wondering what the secret power could be began in earnest to search for the truth. He consulted a priest named Eusebius who encouraged him in the work of conversion which he ultimately consummated by burning all his magical books, giving his substance to the poor, and enrolling himself among the Christian catechumens. On the breaking out of the persecution under Dioclesian, Cyprian was apprehended and carried before the Roman governor at Tyre. Justina, who had been the original mover in his change of life, was at the same time brought before this judge and cruelly scourged, whilst Cyprian was torn with iron hooks. After this the two martyrs were sent to Nicomedia to the Emperor Dioclesian who forthwith commanded their heads to be struck off. The history of St. Cyprian and St. Justina was recorded in a Greek poem by the Empress Eudocia, wife of Theodosius the Younger, a work which is now lost.

SEPTEMBER 27th.

This day is the festival of another somewhat remarkable couple. Saints Elzear, Count of Arian, and his wife, Delphina. Both were from rich and noble families in the kingdom of Naples.

When Elzear was but ten years old, Charles II., King of Sicily and Count of Provence, caused him to be betrothed to Delphina of Glandeves, the daughter of the Lord of Pui-Michel, a girl of twelve years of age. In 1308, three years later, the marriage was celebrated with great pomp. But as it happened, Delphina as well as her husband was a devotee to religious life; for the two had been brought together solely for the aggrandizement of their respective families and for state purposes. By a mutual agreement, the newly wedded couple resolved to live together in perfect chastity and sanctity as brother and sister, a compact which was never broken. When Elzear was twenty-three years old, by the death of his father, he inherited his rank, titles and great wealth. But these the noble couple looked upon only as "talents" entrusted to them for the benefit of the poor, sick and needy. Delphina had also inherited the great estates of Glandeves. From that hour their lives were unostentatiously given to the work of their Master; as in the meantime they both had been enrolled in the "Third Order of St. Francis," of whom and his Orders of Franciscans I shall speak on October 1st.

I must omit all further details of his advancement at Court though still living for the great purpose he set before him, until we find Elzear, attended by the flower of the nobility of Naples, as the ambassador of King Robert, at Paris, to demand of Charles IV. the hand of Mary, the daughter of the Count of Valois in marriage for the Duke of Calabria. It was in Paris he sickened and died on September 27th, 1323, when in his twenty-eighth year of age, leaving a memory for his brief life redolent for its true beauty and sanctity.

After Elzear's death, Delphina spent some time at the court of Naples as the friend and companion of Queen Saucia, wife of King Robert. But on the king's death in 1343, Delphina was retired to the nunnery of St. Clare, where she died, in the seventy-sixth year of her age, on September 26th, 1369, but her festival has most appropriately been kept on the same day with her sainted husband.

SEPTEMBER 28th.

St. Lioba, who is this day honoured by the Roman Church, was held up by them, both in England and Germany, at the close of the X. century, as a model of Christian perfection which was to be followed. She was of an illustrious Anglo-Saxon family and born in West Saxony. At an early age she was placed in the monastic school of the great double monastery of Winburn in Dorsetshire where she was under the care of the Abbess Zetta. For her day she was an unusually learned woman. St. Boniface was fully aware of both her learning and her virtues, therefore was anxious to secure her services for his infant church in Germany; a wish which Lioba shared most heartily, and which at length was gratified and St. Boniface quickly placed her at the head of a small monastery, called Bischafsheim, or the Bishop's House. Her teachings and precepts soon made the little nunnery famous and many nuns were sent from it to other parts of Germany to be taught by her; while kings and princes recognized her worth and virtue. Especially among these was Pepin, the King of the Franks, and later his son, Charles, or Charlemagne, when he came into power, often sent for her to come to Aix-la-Chapelle for consultation, and his wife, Hildegardis, would have kept her perpetually by her if she could have done so. The departure of St. Boniface to Friesland and his martyrdom was a crushing blow from which Lioba never fully recovered, and in her old age she resigned her cares and retired to a little nunnery at Scornscheim near Mentz, dying there in 779.

S. MICHAEL.

SEPTEMBER 29th

Is the feast of St. Michael and all the Angels, or as it is popularly called, Michaelmas Day.

Michael is regarded in the Christian world as the chief of angels, or an archangel. His history is obscure. In Scripture he is mentioned five times and always in a warlike character ; namely, thrice by Daniel as fighting for the Jewish church against Persia ; once by St. Jude as fighting with the devil about the body of Moses ; and once by St. John as fighting at the head of his angelic troops against the dragon and his host.

The festival is one which is strictly observed by both branches of the Christian Church : the Anglican and Roman.

On the Clog Almanac St. Michael has for his attribute a pair of scales of the earliest type.

According to St. Dionysius (called the Areopagite) and other theologians there are three classes of angels, each division consisting of three orders, or choirs, thus making nine orders ; viz. :

1st THE COUNCILLORS OF THE MOST HIGH.

And of these First, SERAPHIMS. Usually represented as covered with eyes. Second CHERUBIMS, each having six wings. Third THRONES.

IId GOVERNOR.

Of these First, DOMINATIONS, who bear a sword, triple crown and sceptre. Second VIRTUES, in complete armor. Third POWERS, chaining devils.

IIId MESSENGERS.

Of these First, PRINCEDOMS. These hold a city, or are in complete armor and bear a pennon. Second ARCHANGELS.

St. Michael and St. Raphael, bearing a pilgrim's staff. St. Gabriel, Angel of the Annunciation, and St. Uriel. All these wear complete armor and sometimes carry trumpets. Third ANGELS. These generally carry a wand.

CAEDMON MS.
X. CENTURY.

WINDOW IN ANTE-CHAPEL, MERTON COLLEGE, OXFORD.

Of the endless variety of conception by artists as to the forms of the Angels and Archangels I cannot here speak, though it is a most interesting subject. The two illustrations given are from the painted glass windows in the Chapel of New College, Oxford, while the two others, a Cherubim and Seraph, are from sources as shown in the subscription of each. The canonical colour for this Feast of St. Michael and All Angels is white.

I cannot take space to speak of why : —

> " September, when by custom (right divine)
> Geese are ordained to bleed at Michael's shrine "—

save to call attention to the custom.

SEPTEMBER 30th.

The day is especially sacred to St. Jerom in all Christian churches ; not alone because he stands as the first, of the " Four Latin Doctors of the Church," but because of his importance and dignity as founder of Manachism in the West ; and also as the author of the universally received translation of the Old and New Testaments called " The Vulgate."

Jerom — as his name is spelled in the earlier writings of the Fathers — was born at Striddonium (now Idripui) on the confines of Pannonia, Dalmatra and Italy in 342. His father, Eusebius, was rich and as young Jerom displayed especial aptitude for study he was sent to Rome for his later education, where he had for his tutors the famous pagan grammarian Donatus and the celebrated Victorinus, the rhetorician, who by a decree of the Senate was honoured with a statue in Trajan's square — later perfecting himself in logic by studying the works of Aristotle and Porphry. Jerom tells us, that while thus engaged: "I was wont to visit the tombs of the Apostles and Martyrs," and of the deep impression they made upon his mind, In spite of it all, he like other students even in modern days, fell into temptation and for a time abandoned himself to the pleasures of gay Roman life. But his inborn love of virtue and learning at last triumphed over this youthful lapse from "the straight and narrow way." His perfect knowledge of the Greek and Latin languages and his naturally critical mind led him to study for the bar, and he early became eminent for his eloquence as a pleader before tribunals and his accurate knowledge of law. When past thirty he began his travels in Gaul, visiting the various schools of learning of Marseilles, Toulouse, Bordeaux, Autun, Lyons and the then imperial city of Triers. It was at this latter place he became converted and was baptised, a most interesting story, as read in the "Chronicle and Letters of St. Jerom;" though too long for repetition here; but culminating in his vowing perpetual celibacy on his return to Rome, where for a time he was secretary to Pope Memasus.

In 373 he traveled in the East later studying divinity with Gregory, Nazianzen, Epiphanius and Didymus, and the Hebrew with a learned Jew named Barraban, but spending most of his time at the monastery in Bethlehem in deep study; later retiring into the deserts of Egypt and Syria among Amhorites to gain instruction and edification from their conversation.

But we cannot follow the details of his studious life though from the day of his consecration in Holy Orders in 377, there is no period that is not replete with interest. Twice before he began the work that has made his name immortal, he had corrected from the ancient Italic, books of the Old Testament and Psalter, once at Rome in 382 and next in 389 while yet in Palestine.

The new and correct translation of St. Jerom's Vulgate was published only when Dom Martiany (1647-1717) the French Benedictine and Commentator brought it before the world under the title of "The Sacred Library" though the council of Trent had in 1546 declared it to be the authentic version of the Bible. But the history of this would of itself fill a volume to cover it in detail, and cannot be crowded into a few lines, such as are at my disposal.

After three years of residence in Rome, Jerom once more returned to the monastery he had founded in Bethlehem, where he died in peaceful old age in 420.

(From an ancient Venetian edition of his writings and life.)

The legends and traditions of St. Jerom are replete with interest, but like the brief story of his life which I have so unsatisfactorily to myself told must be curtailed.

Sitting at the gateway of his monastery in Bethlehem, St. Jerom saw a huge lion come limping toward him holding one front paw in the air. The holy man did not move until the lion crouched at his feet and held his paw before him. On examining, St. Jerom found the paw had been penetrated by a sharp thorn which he carefully removed and then applied some healing ointment, bound up the wounded foot and assigned to the lion to lie down within his own cell where he attended him until the paw was healed. From that time the lion became the saint's constant companion, following him like a dog everywhere. Later an ass that used to bring fire-wood for the monks, was confided to the care of the lion while he grazed in a neighbouring meadow, but while the lion slept the ass strayed away. The lion searched in vain and returned to the monastery shame-faced and with a drooping head. Jerom, thinking the lion had devoured the ass, ordered that the daily burden of fire-wood should be packed on the lion's back, to which the beast humbly submitted and performed the duties of the ass. One day the lion having performed his duties, set out again to search for the ass. A caravan was just then passing and the lion saw it was led by an ass in whom he recognised his erstwhile charge, and the ass also remembered the lion. At once the lion drove the camels, merchants and attendants into the gates of the monastery, where the merchants at last confessed to having stolen the ass. St. Jerom pardoned them and set them free. From a score of such legends the lion early became the attribute of St. Jerom and appears in all pictures of the saint. Another reason being that the proud, fiery nature of the lion was peculiarly characteristic of St. Jerom.

OCTOBER

Then came October, full of merry glee;
For yet his noule was totty of the must,
Which he was treading in the wine-fat's see,
And of the joyous oyle, whose gentle gust
Made him so frolic and so full of lust:
Upon a dreadful Scorpion he did ride,
The same which by Dianae's doom unjust
Slew great Orion, and eeke by his side
He had his ploughing-share and coulter ready tyde.

—*Spenser.*

October received its name from bcing the eight month in the old Alban or Latin Kalendars when there were but ten months in the year. The ancient Saxons styled this month the "Wyn-monath," or "wine-month," yet there was no wine made at that time in old Saxony. The early Germans termed it "Winter-fyllith," as being the precursor of winter.

OCTOBER 1st.

St. Remigius, who is this day honoured by the Roman Church, was the great Apostle of the French, and one of the brightest lights of the Gaulish Church; alike illustrious for his learning, eloquence, sanctity and miracles. His name still has a place also in the Calendar of the English church. Youthful precocity did not, as it does sometimes, belie the future in Remigius; for at the age of only twenty-two years we find him (reluctantly on his part) made Bishop of Rheims. The result proved that the pontificate, in insisting upon his accepting the perferment, made no mistake. Clovis was at this time king, and though yet a pagan, held Remigius in high esteem and listened to him as he did to his wife Clotildis, who was a Christian. It was not until after the battle of Talbiac in 496 that Clovis was converted as the result of securing Divine interposition, the legend running that: "When Clovis was starting to meet the Sueve and Alemani, Clotildis had said: 'In the hour of your need, if you cry to our God He will help you.' The battle was going against Clovis; his troops had already begun to retreat before the enemy, when Clovis in desperation cried: 'Oh Christ! whom Clotildis invokes as Son of the living God, I have called on my gods, but they have no power; I implore Thy succor. Deliver me from my enemies and I will be baptized in Thy name.' From then the legend said, the tide of battle changed, and Clovis won his great victory and soon after fulfilled his vow." Many bishops came to Rheims for the remarkable ceremony, Remigius performing the solemn rite. After his baptism Clovis bestowed many lands and much wealth on Remigius who distributed them among the churches. King Clovis died in 511 but Remigius survived him many years, dying in 533 when ninety-four years of age and after he had served as bishop and archbishop of Rheims over seventy years.

S. REMIGIUS.

OCTOBER 2d.

In the Ordo of the Roman Church to-day is an office for "SS. Angelonim Custodium," or "The Feast of the Holy Angel-Guancaus."

This day is also the festival of a somewhat noted Englishman whose name is alike honoured in the one English church and in Roman Martyrology, St. Thomas Cantelupe, some time High chancellor of England and Bishop of Hereford. His father was the celebrated William Lord Cantelupe, one of those generals who succeeded in the overthrow of the Barons and the French, thereby fixing the crown on the head of Henry III. The family was descended from one of the Norman Knights who made up the train of William the Conqueror, and had by many felicitous marriages by the XIII. century become one of the most powerful families in England allied to the earls of Pembroke, the Fitz-Walters, earls of Hereford, the Brenses, earls of Abergavany and others. Thomas was first placed under the care of Walter Cantelupe, Bishop of Hereford, later under that remarkable man Robert Kilwasby, the learned Dominican who was successively Archbishop of Canterbury, Cardinal, Bishop of Porto, and the Founder of the Black Friars of London.

When Thomas resolved to consecrate his life to the church after his studies in England, he perfected himself at Orleans in the study of civil law as a preliminary to a better knowledge of canon law. Pope Innocent IV. recognising his ability nominated him as his chaplain but he within a few months resigned his office and returned to England to complete his course of canon law at Oxford and later was chosen chancellor of that famous university; an office he held when King Henry III. created him lord high chancellor of the kingdom. At his own request Thomas was granted leave by Edward I. to resign again and retire to Oxford where his time was given to study and devotion. In 1275, he was canonically chosen Bishop of Hereford, an office he filled until his death in 1282. The sanctity of the man and the reverence in which he was held is testified by the fact that in 1287 Edward III. personally attended the translation of his relics to the marble tomb where he now rests. He was canonized by John XXII. in 1310, when his festival was fixed for October 2d.

OCTOBER 3d

Is sacred to St. Dionysius, the Areopagite.

Among the judges of that most venerable and illustrious senate of the Areopagites who listened to St. Paul on that memorable day described in Acts xvii. about the year 51, was a noted scholar, named Dionysius, an Athenian philosopher. The convincing logic of Paul added to his own knowledge of the facts in regard to the life and death of Jesus Christ left the philosopher no alternative and he frankly and publicly acknowledged the same, receiving from the Apostle the rite of baptism, and from his great learning at once became an active and most valued assistant and later was appointed by St. Paul as bishop of Athens.

Of the death of this holy man not a little uncertainty exists. The Greeks in their menologies say he was burned at the stake in Athens for his faith.

A long list of works written by St. Dionysius the Areopagite is to be found in Butler's "Lives of the Saints."

OCTOBER 4th

Is the anniversary of one of the most interesting characters in the entire list of the canonized saints of the Roman Church. St. Francis of Assisi, "The Seraphic" as he was termed for his fervid eloquence and his devout love and service of his Divine Master. Yet with it all such a miracle of personal humility. A large volume that lies before me finds scant room to record the events of his noble life of self-sacrifice; therefore this brief mention can be but a testimony of his worth. The son of a merchant of Assisi near Florence, he was baptized Giovanni (John) but gained his name of Francis (the Frenchman) from his being taught French as a preparation for the business he had been intended for by his father; but Providence changed this. In one of those local provincial quarrels Francisco was taken a prisoner, and for a year, held a captive in the fortress of Perugia. Sickness followed upon his release, and as he lay upon his sick bed he resolved to devote his life to God. From thenceforth his whole life was one of poverty, for his father had cast him off; yet he in the midst of his own poverty still went bravely on in his life's work until he succeeded in founding the Order of Friar Minors, or better known as Franciscans, one of the three Mendicant Orders of Friars, that later was supplemented by the Order of "Poor Clare's" described in the account already given of St. Clare of Assisi, the "Grey Sister." The fundamental character of each being either personal poverty; relying wholly upon the charity of others not alone for their own meagre wants, but as well for the means whereby to carry on their own great work for the benefit of the sick, the suffering and the poor whom they fed. It is a wonderful story which I regret not to repeat; but it would involve the entire early history of this noted order of Franciscans.

OCTOBER 5th.

THE FESTIVAL OF THE ROSARY.

The first Sunday in October is fixed by the Ordo of the Roman Church as the Festival of the Rosary. By means of its beads and their arrangement the rosary is used by members of this church to assist their memory in the repetition and counting of the prayers said in accordance with its ritual. These consist of fifteen Pater Nosters and a hundred and fifty Ave Marias which, for the convenience of worshippers, are counted on a string of beads. Each rosary or string of beads consists of fifteen decades, each of these decades contains one Pater Noster marked by a large bead, and ten Ave Marias, marked by ten smaller beads. The festival of the rosary was instituted to implore Divine mercy in favour of the church and all the faithful and to return thanks for the benefits conferred on them, more especially for the victory of Lepanto in 1571 over the Turks.

Pope Pius V. ordained the festival for all the churches under the title of Sta. Mary de Victoria, but Gregory XIII. changed the title to that now used.

The rosary itself in its present form is said to have been invented by St. Dominic; though it had its first origin in the East and had long been used by hermits, anchorets and the Benedictine monks before its introduction into the use of the church as a body.

The Roman Church pays honour this day to St. Placidus, the Abbott of Messina in Sicily and his companion martyrs. Placidus was the son of Tertullus, a Roman senator, and like so many sons of noble Roman families was at the age of seven committed to the care of St. Benedict at his monastery at Sublaco. It was here, legend tells us, St. Benedict performed a wonderful miracle. The lad Placidus in some way had fallen into the water of the lake and when St. Benedict was told of it he called a monk, named Maurus and blessing him sent him to the rescue. The child, "was floating a bow-shot from the shore when Maurus, walking on the water, seized the lad and drew him ashore, his (Maurus) melote (a sheep-skin the monks wore on their shoulders) not even having been wetted." This power having been given Maurus through the blessing of St. Benedict.

How much influence this rescue had on young Placidus in determining his future is not told in direct words; but it could not have failed under all the circumstances and his surroundings to have impressed him deeply; for he took upon himself the monastic vows at an early age. In or about 541 he went to Sicily where he founded a monastery at Messina; he then being twenty-six years of age. In this act he was nobly aided by his father Tertullus. Here, too, he was joined by his two brothers Eutychius and Victorinus, with his sister, Floria, devoting their lives to devotion and to works of charity. A few short years only were granted them when a party of Arian Goths headed by a pirate named Manrechas landed on the island and some thirty or more monks with Placidus, his virgin sister and his brothers were brutally murdered and their monastery plundered and destroyed on October 5, 546.

OCTOBER 6th

The memory of St. Faith to whom a crypt in the cathedral of St. Paul in London is dedicated, is one of the saints which both the Anglican and Roman Churches select for honour on this day. Among those Christians whose invincible constancy triumphed over the malice of Dacian under Dioclesian and Maximian, none better deserves notice than the — almost — child whose parents had named at her baptism " Faith." A girl endowed with such exquisite, wondrous personal beauty of both face and form, that even passing strangers stopped and watched her with longing, lingering eyes that they might fix in their memories her pure, saintly face. No woman, however young, is insensible of her own charms, nor was Faith so. She knew also what such beauty as hers could win for her in the outer world; but hers was a higher, purer and nobler ambition for she had been taught only the simple faith of Christ crucified, risen and all powerful to save. Thus when apprehended and brought before Dacian she needed none to instruct her how to answer him. Her legend purports to give these verbatim as she stood sturdy and steadfast to her name and all it represented.

ST. FAITH.

Nor could all the wiles, threats or promises of Dacian avail against her strong purpose. Even the on-lookers were struck with pity and horror as they exclaimed: " How can this tyrant torment this innocent young virgin!" For which many were then and there arrested and suffered death as the penalty of their sympathy. Of course St. Faith's fate was sealed from the moment when she refused to sacrifice to Diana and she was beheaded on October 6, 290.

To-day is also the festival of the celebrated St. Bruno, Founder of the Carthusian Monks.

The story of how St. Bruno with his companions first conceived the project of the order at Rheims and at a later date retired to the wilderness of Chartreaux and founded a church and small monastery from whence the order was finally evolved is a long and interesting one. The event is said to have occurred in 1085 or 86, authorities differ, Dr. Butler naming June, 1084.

The rules of the Carthusians are the most severe of any of the monastic orders. Almost perpetual silence is maintained among the brothers, for they never speak if a sign can serve the purpose except on one day in each week when for a time they may converse together. They never taste meat and a single meal of "pulse, bread and water," is allowed daily. This too is eaten separately. Their dress is white.

St. Bruno might have had preferment in the Church but he declined all to carry out his cherished ideal community. He died in 1101. Pope Leo X. instituted an office for St. Bruno in 1514 for the church of St. Stephen; but in 1623 when he was canonized by Gregory XV. the office was extended to the whole Church.

This St. Bruno must not be confounded with St. Bruno, Bishop of Segni, mentioned July 18th, as he sometimes is, even by writers, for I have a volume before me, purporting to be "Stories of the Saints," in which the lives of the two saints are sadly jumbled.

OCTOBER 7th

Commemorates St. Mark, Pope and Confessor, who held the high and holy office but for eight months from January 18th, 336, when he was placed in the Apostolic chair, until his death on October 7th of the same year.

The day is also sacred to St. Justina, the patroness of both Padua and Venice who like the gentle St. Faith was yet another victim of the terrible persecutions of those twin monsters Dioclesian and Maximian; who recognized neither youth, beauty nor virtue as an excuse for the heinous crime of being a Christian. This beautiful virgin was the daughter of King Vatalicino of

Padua, a Christian who educated her in his faith. On his death Maximian accused the princess of holding the faith of her father. Far from denying it, she boldly affirmed her belief in Christ. As usual, no mercy was given and she was condemned to death and her legend tells how when the executioner appeared, "she opened wide her arms and received without flinching the fatal sword thrust in her bosom."

OCTOBER 8th

The Church honours St. Bridget of Sweden, the Founder of the Order of Brigitines, or Brigitta. She was the wife of Ulpho, Prince of Nericia, who died in 1344. After her husband's death and when she had distributed his estate among her children she instituted the Order bearing her name, whose object was, in addition to charity and other good works, to observe particular devotions for the Passion of Our Lord and in honour of His Holy Mother. She built the great monastery of Wastein in which were housed sixty nuns, and in a separate building friars numbering thirteen priests, four deacons, four doctors of the Church and eight lay brothers of the Order. The Order itself apparently was not confirmed until after her death when it was approved by Martin V. (Pope 1417-1431), while she died in 1373.

The Order of the Brigitines appeared as the Third of the Order of St. Augustine. One monastery only of this Order ever was founded in England, that of Sion-house built in 1413, by Henry V. and of which I have already given an account in a previous article.

St. Bridget was canonized in 1391 by Boniface IX., and her canonization confirmed by Martin V. in 1419.

This day is also the festival of St. Pelagia, the penitent comedian, who is such a prominent character in Charles Kingsley's remarkable novel, "Hypatia."

OCTOBER 9th.

This day is sacred to St. Denis, Denys, or Dionysius, who must not be confounded, as is often the case, with St. Dionysius the Areopagite spoken of on October 3d.

St. Denis was of all the Roman missionaries in Gaul the individual who, in preaching the doctrines of the Cross, penetrated furthest into the country, and fixed his seat at Paris of which he became the first bishop. He is said to have been put to death during the persecution of Valerian, and a well-known legend is related regarding him, that after suffering decapitation, he miraculously took up his head, carried it in his hands for the space of two miles and then lay down and expired.

ST. DENIS.

The bodies of St. Denis and his companions are recorded to have been interred by a Christian lady named Catalla not far from the place where they had been beheaded. A chapel was thereafter erected over their tomb and in the fifth century a church which was greatly resorted to by pilgrims. St. Denis is the patron of France.

To-day is also kept the festival of St. Lewis Bertrand. He was one of a noble band for whom too high praise cannot be spoken, who in those early days dared the dangers of crossing the broad Atlantic to carry the gospel to the Indians of the New World.

He was a Spaniard by birth, born in Valencia, where as a youth he became a novice in a Dominican monastery, passing through the various degrees in the order with credit both to himself and his teachers. For years his one ambition had been to become a missionary to the savages of America. He was not ignorant of the discomforts and dangers which attended such a life or the probability of its costing him his own life. It was not until 1352 when he was thirty-six years of age, that he received permission to undertake such a mission, and South America was selected for his field of work when accompanied by one of his fellow friars he started, and after a long and tedious voyage landed at Golden Castile. The scene of his labours for the next three years lay in the Isle of Tobago, the province of Carthagena, and upon the Isthmus of Panama. Even at that early day the Dominicans had established themselves in South America but the territory St. Lewis Bertrand penetrated was new ground and the hardships he and his companion endured from hunger and exposure were beyond description. A stone for a pillow, Mother Earth for a bed, and wild fruits for their food. It would seem as if the "gift of tongues" had been bestowed on this man, so quickly did he acquire the varied dialects of these untutored savages; but it was this above other things which won for him their confidence. The next objective point of our missionary was the Caribbees, where in the mountains of St. Martha he baptized over 15,000 persons. Again in the country of Mopaia and on the Isle of St. Thomas he gained many converts to Christ, protected always by unseen hands from dangers only later discovered. In 1569 to protect these savages from ruthless plunder and persecutions of lawless Spanish adventurers who infested these new countries, St. Lewis Bertrand resolved to sail for Spain and seek from the Spanish throne the needed relief in which he was partially successful; but his superiors thought they had other and more needed work for him in Spain, and he could not therefore return to his missionary work, much as he desired to; but devoted himself to preparing others for the Master's vineyard by his holy life, example and teachings, until in 1580 when one day preaching in the cathedral at Valencia, he was taken ill and carried from the pulpit to what proved to be his death bed. He was beatified by Paul V., in 1608, and canonized by Clement X. in 1671.

OCTOBER 10th.

This day is kept sacred to the memory of another of the noted men of the Jesuits, St. Francis Borgia, the Fourth Duke of

Gandia and the Third General of the Jesuit Order, and named by his mother out of love and devotion to St. Francis of Assisi. He was a precocious child. At the age of seven he read fluently his native Spanish language and as he advanced in years no pains or expense were spared to furnish him with the best and most learned tutors and masters in each branch of learning. He early disclosed a desire for a strict religious life; but his father opposed it (his mother had died in 1520) and in 1528 when he was eighteen, in order to turn his thoughts into other channels he was removed from Saragossa and placed at the court of Charles V., then one of the gayest courts in Europe. Here he gained the esteem of the Empress, who planned to marry him to Eleanor de Castro, a Portuguese lady of the first rank, with great wealth and very accomplished as well as possessed of rare beauty, while added to these she was a woman of fervent piety, and Francis' father gave him no opportunity to decline so advantageous an offer.

In 1539 the pious Empress died and shortly thereafter the Marquis was made Viceroy of Catalonia, and created knight of the order of St. James or the "Red Cross," the most honourable order of Spain. Barcelona was the seat of the government and it was here that Francis first became acquainted with the tenets of the Jesuit order and began to study their objects. Encouraged as he had always been by his wife, Francis' life had at all times been a devout and religious one; but now he began to strive for something beyond the life he was then living. In the meantime Francis' father had died, and he now was Duke of Gandia, and in 1543 he returned to his native town where he soon founded a college for the Society of Jesus. In 1546 his devoted wife died and about that time Peter Le Fever, one of St. Ignatius Loyola's associates in founding the order, came to Gandia and laid the first stone for the new college. It was then the Duke resolved on the most momentous act of his life and applied for admission to the Society of Jesus, laying aside wealth, honours, and rank to be a servant and to renew his studies in order to become a doctor of theology.

In 1549 St. Francis visited Rome and with the money he had brought from Spain built a church for the "Professed House" and laid the foundation (though he declined the honour and title of Founder) of the great Jesuit institution called the Roman College completed by Pope Gregory XIII., then resigned his Duchy to his eldest son and in January, 1551, took his final vows as a member of the Society of Jesus.

The zeal with which Francis carried out his vows during the succeeding years justly entitles him to the title given him by Dr. Butler as "the second founder" of the Order, for while his gifts in money had been lavish, his wisdom and prudence had done even more for the Order.

On July 2, 1565, on the death of St. Laynez, the second General of the Society, Francis Borgia was elected the third General in succession, an office he filled until his death in 1572.

ST. ETHELBURGE.

St. Francis Borgia was beatified by Pope Urban VIII. in 1624, canonized by Clement IX. in 1671 and his festival fixed for October 10th by Innocent XI. in 1683.

OCTOBER 11th.

This is the festival of St. Ethelburge or Edeliburge, the virgin Abbess of the first Benedictine nunnery founded in England by St. Erconwald, Bishop of London. Ethelburge was an Anglo-Saxon princess, and a sister of Erconwald. Although there were then no English houses to which she could repair to carry out her vows of religious life, she secluded herself from the world, even in her father's "Rath" in the privacy of her own apartments. When, however, her brother, Erconwald, then Bishop of London, founded a Benedictine nunnery at Barking in Essex, she consented to become its head and was its first Abbess. Her life was one of those quiet, unostentatious ones we sometimes see devoted to silent and secret good works; her greater and more sterling qualities only once being called out when in 663 the plague appeared within the walls of the Barking nunnery. Then her true heroism displayed itself in a most marked manner by her attention and devotion to her sick and dying sisters. Giving herself no rest, performing even the most menial duties without complaint and giving succor and support to all until the last victim had been claimed by the dread disease no earthly power could resist.

When at last the survivors were safely removed from danger and her hour of rest seemed near, she herself fell a victim to her devotion to others and went to her reward, on this 11th of October in 664.

OCTOBER 12th.

Both the Anglican and Roman Churches commemorate on this day the memory of St. Wilfrid or as the Anglo-Saxons wrote it Willferder, Bishop of York, who was born in the ancient kingdom of Northumberland in 634 and educated at the monastery of Lindisfarne, then one of the noted monastic schools. Indeed these monastic schools were, down to the tenth century, the only ones in Britain where any high degree of education was to be obtained. At the age of nineteen in 653 ambitious still to attain a degree of knowledge beyond that of Lindisfarne Wilfrid started for France and Italy and in passing through Kent met the noted Bennet Biscop the founder of the celebrated monasteries of Wearmouth and Jarrow into whose churches this advanced thinker and theologian introduced the first paintings ever placed in a church in Britain. In company with this learned man young Wilfrid traveled to Rome, where by good fortune he met St. Boniface then an archdeacon and through him was introduced to the pope. From Rome he proceeded to Lyons where after three years of study he received the ecclesiastical tonsure and was ordained returning to Britain in 658 when the great controversy over

Easter was at its height and in which he had a part. From thence on his was a busy missionary life, not only in Northumberland but in Bernecia and the North which if I might tell it in detail would show how constant and earnest were those faithful men who laid the foundation for Christianity in Britain. The contest over his bishopric was long and tedious and would interest none save ecclesiastics therefore I omit it. Yet even during all this persecution Wilfrid was never idle in his Master's work literally "dying in the harness" in 709.

OCTOBER 13th.

TRANSLATION OF THE RELICS OF EDWARD THE CONFESSOR.

ST. EDWARD THE CONFESSOR.

Towards the close of 1065 this pious monarch completed the rebuilding of the Abbey at Westminster and at Christmas "he caused the newly-built church to be hallowed in the presence of the nobles assembled during that solemn festival."

The king's health continued to decline till on the 5th of January he felt that the hand of death was upon him.

Every reader of history knows how the Confessor's last hours were embittered by the bickerings of his court as to who should succeed him until worn out he at last told Harold and the rest to settle the matter any way they could, then turned on his bed commending his soul to God thus dying on January 5, 1066.

The Confessor's first burial place was in front of the high altar in the church dedicated to St. Peter (now called Westminster Abbey) begun by Ethelbert and completed by his son Edward surnamed "The Confessor." This tomb was then a very simple affair and the early Chronicles tell us that William the Conqueror presented a pall to cover it: "Very richly was it worked in fine gold and silver, which King William had made to the honour and fame of St. Edward."

When Westminster Abbey was rebuilt by Henry III. the coffin of the Confessor was for a time placed in the palace of Westminster from whence it was brought to the gorgeous new shrine the monarch had prepared for it, in the new Abbey, on October 13, 1269. The coffin on this occasion was carried by King Henry, his brother Richard, Earl of Cornwall (King of the Romans), his two sons, Edward (afterwards Edward I.) and Edmund, Earl of Lancaster; the Earl of Warren; Lord Basset and as many other nobles "as could come near to touch it." And we are told, "this was the first time that Divine Service was celebrated in this Church after the King rebuilt it."

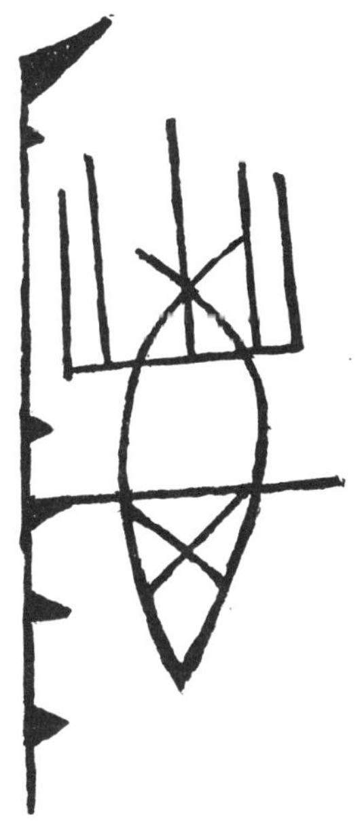

The present tomb that some of us have seen is but the mutilated remains of the magnificent structure erected by Henry III. for only the basement of that XIII. century work is now standing. It was Italian design erected in Purbeck marble then profusely adorned with glass mosaic. The material and workmen were brought from Italy by Abbot Ware and an inscription may yet be seen that tells us "Peter the Roman citizen finished the work in 1269." On either side of the shrine north and south are the niches wherein in old days they laid sick persons in hope of a miraculous cure from St. Edward whose body *now* actually lies above those niches.

To quote from Mr. Troutbeck's valuable monograph: "The body formerly lay in a golden shrine above the marble and mosaic base and this shrine was adorned by many splendid jeweled images. There were among others an image of St. Edmund King and Martyr, his crown set with two large sapphires a ruby and other precious stones, a figure of the Virgin and Child set with rubies emeralds and garnets, a figure of St. Peter holding in one hand a Church in the other the keys; upon his breast there appeared a large sapphire, meanwhile the saint was trampling on the heart of Nero." This will give my readers a faint idea of the splendors of this now vanished shrine.

Henry VIII. in 1536 despoiled the shrine of its treasures, while all that he left of any value the "Reformers" of Cromwell carried away. Lest these vandals should even desecrate the tomb itself the Monks for a time, secreted the Confessor's body; but in time of Queen Mary it was restored to its proper place. This Queen presented many jewels and images for St. Edward's shrine but its pristine beauty had forever departed.

OCTOBER 14th

Is the festival of St. Callistus, or Calixtus as that name is sometimes written. He was elected to the pontificate August 2, 218, and held the high position for five years and two months; but the uncertainty of these early dates lead others to limit this time to four years and a few months.

OCTOBER 15th

Is held sacred in memory of St. Teresa, or Theresa, Virgin Foundress of "The Barefooted Carmelites." Her story, if I could tell it in extenso is one of the many real romances that are to be found among the devotees of the Roman Church. I take space for but an epitome of it.

She was Spanish, born at Avila in Castile in 1515. Her parents were of gentle blood but not wealthy yet not in that most unhappy of all lots in life, in any age or country, "genteel poverty." In one of the fortress-houses of Avilon says Miss G. C. Graham in her life of Santa Teresa: "Where on the shield over the gateway the bucklers of the Davilas were quartered with the rampant lion of the Cepedas she was born and passed her childhood."

For a time after her mother's death Teresa was in the Convent of Encarnacion not as a novice but pupil. It is right here a pretty love story comes in had I place for it. For in spite of the dearth of eligible suitors for many maidens owing to the hegira of the more enterprising young Spaniards to the Eldorado of the New World Teresa had no lack of them. Then, too, she had fallen into the habit of reading those old-time thrilling anecdotes of Knight-errantry then so much the vogue in Spain. But the romances and fiction each were ended by a sudden and for a time dangerous illness. During her convalescence at the manor-house of her Uncle Pedro de Cepeda, a grave formal man who read religious books only; she was called upon to read to him. The courteous respect of the young for their elders, left her no alternative while she concealed her dislike to such books as best she could. At last the epistles of St. Jerom were given her to read and it was from the reading of these that her resolution came to take upon herself the vows of a Carmelite nun. It was not the inspiration of a moment but after a long struggle which fills many pages in her own writings in describing; for unlike many who

ST. TERESA.

in those days entered religious retreats she was sincere and earnest. The nunnery of Encarnacion it may be said in passing was then far from being what many think of such retreats.

Under her newly inspired devoutness this far from met Teresa's ideas though perforce she for a long time endured it. In fact, twenty years lapsed, full of many interesting experiences, failures and falterings before the hoped for time came.

Even the story of the Reformation of the Carmelite Nuns must be abridged. The discipline of the Encarnacion was lax, lacking in almost every way the essential features of a religious house during the twenty years St. Teresa waited before her opportunity came and then, it was accomplished only through difficulties she might well have shrank from. Briefly told it came about thus: An elderly nun of the Carmelite Order had observed St. Teresa often talking with her regarding the restoration of the primitive rules that once governed houses like the Encarnacion. It was not without hesitation that the Superior and the Provincial were induced to give their consent that Teresa and thirteen nuns should start a convent to be governed by the old-time strict rules. Indeed the Provincial very quickly changed his mind and forbade the new enterprise to be entered upon. But Teresa had forestalled this. A house had been secured and through friends both a Papal brief and the consent of the Bishop had been obtained and on St. Bartholomew's Day in 1562 the little band of enthusiastic ascetics set up their altar in their new home. What followed seems to us to-day a sort of comedy. The Prioress had taken alarm, the Town-Council and Chapter of the Cathedral joined in the fray when St. Teresa was ordered by them to return to the Encarnacion and close the new house. But she held the Papal brief and the authority of the Bishop, which she flourished in the face of the Provincial and to quote from a descriptive verse before me of this affair: "The city magnates in high dudgeon appealed to the sovereign Philip II." In the end but not until after a year Teresa came off victor.

This then was the origin of the Reformation of Barefooted Carmelites. But her eager active mind now that she had her discalceated nuns, resolved to enlarge her field and secure an order of friars as well which through a General of the Society of Jesus at Medina she later succeeded in founding in 1568. A story quite as curious in all its details as had been the founding of her discalceated nuns. But I will not enlarge beyond saying that through the aid of an excellent priest Antonio de Heredia and St. John of the Cross the foundation for the Order of the Barefooted Friars began in Medina and the Order soon began to spread under St. Teresa's earnest work. For she was practical as well as enthusiastic and from the hour she started out from the Encarnacion convent for her new purpose her life was one of incessant toil until in October 1582 worn out with her labours for the Carmelites Brothers and Sisters of the Strict Observance she went to her reward. She was canonized by Gregory XV. in 1621.

OCTOBER 16th

Is devoted to the memory of St. Gall, one of those learned Irishmen who went forth from those remarkable monastic schools of Ireland as missionary to the pagans of the continent in the year 585; first preaching in Austrasia and Burgundy finally settling with a few devoted brethren on the banks of Lake Constance in the Switzerland of to-day: where they dwelt in their little cells. The legend tells us " by the casting out of a devil, from the beautiful daughter" of Gunzo, the Duke or Governor of the surrounding country, St. Gall had won them great favour so that the Duke as well as the Bishops, would have placed him in the Episcopal see of Constance; but he preferred his mission work and cell by Lake Constance from which he only emerged to preach among the pagans many of whom he brought to the knowledge of Christ. He went out to be a missionary and as such he faithfully remained, in spite of hardships and all tempting offers of ease until his death October 18, 646.

His festival has been fixed for the 16th of this month.

OCTOBER 17th.

The Angelican Church honour in their Kalendar on this day St. Etheldreda, Abbess of Ely for whom the Roman Church holds a festival June 23d, on which day I told her history.

On this day the name of St. Hedwiges, Duchess of Poland, appears in Roman Martyrology. A remarkable woman who despite her almost royal birth saw nothing in the pomps and vanities of Court life worthy to compare with the love of Christ in the soul. Her father Bertold III. of Andectia, Marquis of Meran, Count of Tivol and Prince of Carinthea had bestowed her in marriage on Henry, Duke of Silesia when she was but twelve years old. Henry was also descended from a great and noble family and himself a man of note. Not to dwell on the early years of her married life in which she faithfully fulfilled her marital duties we hasten on for those stirring times in Poland. Henry of Silesia proved himself no pawn on the board while the great game was being played. In 1235 as all readers of Polish history know, the crisis came started in 1233 when the nobles of Greater Poland expelled Ladislas Ortonis who had made Henry their Duke. His wife urged him not to accept the flattering offer for she foresaw what only too surely came as it did in most of the governing houses of that period when her own sons would be quarreling for supreme authority in the State.

S. HEDWIGES.

This conflict came even sooner than Hedwiges had anticipated for Duke Henry having marched against Cracow and some other provinces of Poland had easily overcome them. Out of love for his second son Conrad the Duke wished to place him in control. To this Hedwiges demurred regarding the rights of the elder brother Henry as paramount. To make our story brief the armies of the two brothers met in deadly conflict and despite the support Conrad received from his father Henry was victorious and Conrad died soon afterward in retirement. But I must not follow Polish history any further.

For years before Duke Henry died it had been the wish of the Duchess to found a great monastery for Cistercian nuns at Trebuitz, three miles from Breslau the capital of Silesia. To this the Duke although at first opposed at last consented, but to secure her end Hedwiges sacrificed her entire dower while her husband aided by settling upon the new monastery as an endowment the town of Trebuitz, and other estates thus providing for the maintenance of *one thousand* persons. It was hither she retired after her (amicable) separation from Duke Henry took place that she might more earnestly fulfil her charitable and religious ambitions. From this time her life was devoted solely to penance and good works too numerous for detail here. Her death took place on October 15th, 1243. In 1266 Pope Clement IV. canonized her, but it was Pope Innocent IX. who fixed the date for her festival.

OCTOBER 18th.

St. Luke, the third in rank among the Holy Evangelists is this day remembered and honoured by Christians throughout the world. He was not one of the Apostles having been converted after Christ's ascension. But he was the companion and beloved friend of Paul and after his death Luke preached the gospel in Greece and Egypt. He was a proficient in the science of physics and also an artist of no mean talent, as the pictures he drew of both our Saviour and the Virgin Mary prove. One of these pictures of the Blessed Virgin ascribed to the pencil of St. Luke, Pope Paul V. had placed in the Borghesion chapel of Sta. Maria Via Lata in Rome, where it is still shown. While Mrs. Jameson (see her Sacred and Legendary Art) does not credit St. Luke as having been an artist she concedes that he is the recognized Patron of Painters.

His gospel was — it is generally believed — written much later than either St. Matthew or St. Mark. His symbol is the "Winged Ox." Callot's images represent him as painting the Virgin and Child. His death occurred on or about A. D. 63. The illustration above is the Clog Almanac symbol of St. Luke and purely Runic.

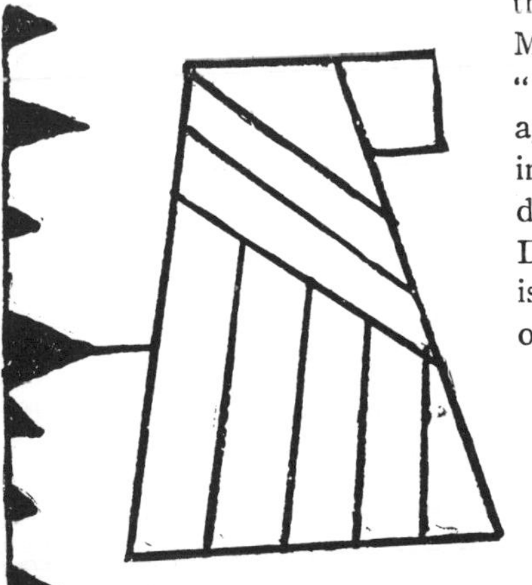

OCTOBER 19th.

It is curious, as I have already remarked, how in the early days of the Church personal quarrels and a desire for revenge, used the popular prejudice the laws and the antipathy to the Christian religion as a cloak beneath which any one of the Christian Faith could be punished. Ptolemy, Lucius and another companion in their martyrdom whom the Church remembers to-day furnishes another instance of the truth of this remark. Ptolemy was a zealous Christian at Rome and through his earnest endeavours and pleadings with a Roman matron he had succeeded in converting her and she openly proclaimed her belief. Her husband was deeply angered and vowed vengeance not only upon her but also on Ptolemy. Under a Roman law the matron at last secured a legal separation from the man who had so wantonly abused her. This was the signal for the Roman to use his best efforts to secure vengeance against Ptolemy. Appearing before Antoninus (Marcus-Aurel a Consul of Rome, who died A. D. 202) a known opponent of Christianity he lodged his complaint and it was sent to Urbicius, the prefect. Here the Roman accused Ptolemy of being a Christian, a crime that needed only the confession of the faithful man to secure for him condemnation to death. It was then that

Lucius another Roman Christian came upon the scene and protested against the injustice of the decree and Urbicius demanded of him: "Art thou too a Christian?" The reply: "I am!" was enough; Lucius was condemned to suffer with Ptolemy. Still a third noble man rose to protest and declared his faith, a man whose name has never been known though he like the other two suffered at the same time, the same death, on October 19, 166 and is honoured, according to Roman Martyrology: "At Rome with the other faithful worthies."

I can but briefly speak of St. Frideswide, Patroness of Oxford whose father, Didon was Prince of Oxford and the neighbouring territory during the early years of the VIII. century and who as a Christian Prince in 750 founded a nunnery in honour of St. Mary which he committed to the care of his daughter Firdeswide as its Abbess. She had not been without a romance in her life. Before she had become an Abbess her beauty, virtues and rank had captivated a Mercian prince named Algar who had tried in vain to secure her hand, since her resolution to live a religious life had been taken in early life. Even when she had entered the nunnery he pursued her and laid a plot to carry her off by force as her legend tells of her escape by hiding for a long time in a hog-stye and how the prince was mysteriously struck with blindness during his search for her; but he repented and after the earnest prayers of the saint his sight was miraculously restored. Later St. Frideswide built for herself a cell and oratory near Thornbury to which she retired living in holy sanctity until her death about 790.

OCTOBER 20th.

The Church to-day honours a saint from out of Pagan Persia. Euginius called by the Orientals Abus and the Chaldaens Avus (both meaning Our Father) was a disciple of St. Anthony, and one of the earliest missionaries into the far East. He established a large monastery near Nisibis from whence he sent out his emissaries through Syria and among the Persians and Saracens.

Among the converts thus made was one disciple of Abus named Barsabias who with some companions suffered under the first persecution of the Christians in Persia begun by Sapor or Chahpour II. and Sassanide, King (died 380) thus he is among the earliest martyrs in that country and therefore remembered on this day by the Church. With his ten monks Barsabias was preaching against the religion of the Magians and teaching that of Christ when they were apprehended loaded with chains and brought before the Governor at Astahara — a city near the famous ruins Persepolis — where after a mere farce of an examination was had, a death sentence was pronounced. This was in 342 and is especially interesting as being the inception of those relentless persecutions of Christians in that region and which was to continue for centuries.

St. Zenobius, Bishop of Florence and patron of that city, is also honoured this day at Florence, although his name appears in Roman Martyrology on May 25th.

OCTOBER 21st

Is the festival of St. Ursula and her virgin companions. Few tourists who ever visited Cologne have failed to listen to her legend, as they gazed at the gruesome row of skulls ranged around her chapel in the cathedral the remnant of the original eleven thousand virgins. There are a score of versions of this legend almost any of which would fill many pages, but probably the best that may be read is that given in Mrs. Jameson's "Sacred and Legendary Art," and known as the Cologne version.

It is impossible to condense any one of these legends within reasonable space and I shall not attempt it but only mention a few bald facts — if any of these legends has a right to credence — as told.

First Ursula was the daughter of a king of Brittany, and her beauty was hardly less than angelic while her mind was a perfect storehouse it was said of wisdom and a knowledge of every event from the days of Adam in the Garden until her own time. But rank, wealth, beauty and accomplishments were all secondary to her love of Christ. Naturally she was early sought in marriage and Prince Conon a pagan and the only son of King Agrippinus of England was among those who desired to win her. Thinking by onerous terms to escape any marriage she demanded that she should have ten virgins of the noblest blood of the kingdom for her ladies, that each of these should have a thousand virgins to attend them and she herself should have another thousand maidens, and lastly that she should have a respite of three years in which "to honour her virginity." The report of the ambassadors only made Prince Conon more eager and all she demanded was granted. The virgins were therefore gathered and sent to Britain. The prince was also so anxious to see this marvel of beauty and wisdom that he too came. Then Ursula had a revelation, that before her marriage she must make a pilgrimage to Rome with her virgins. At Cologne she had a vision that foretold that on her return she and her virgins would suffer martyrdom at that place. Prince Conon followed her to Rome where he was baptized by Cyriacus, receiving the name Ethereus. Leaving out all the details which led up to the event, St. Ursula and her virgins as well as Ethereus, her betrothed were while on their homeward journey, and in fulfillment of Ursula's vision slain by the pagan Huns at Cologne.

The Ursuline Order named in honour of this virgin was founded by Bishop Angela of Bresica in 1537. It was approved by Paul III. in 1544 and declared a religious order under the rule of St. Austin by Gregory III. in 1572.

OCTOBER 22d.

In the festival of SS. Nunelo and Alodia, Spanish Virgins and Martyrs whom the Church honours this day we are again reminded of how widely personal ambition or a desire for revenge lay back of and were often the indirect cause of not a few Christian martyrs. In this case nearly two centuries intervened between the original cause and these sufferers. But to tell it would be to recount pages of Spanish history and tell how in revenge for the vile outrages of Roderic the Gothic king had put on a sister of Count Julian, he had first brought the Moors and Saracens into Spain who later had possessed themselves of Mount Calpie which became the world famed Gibraltar, and so trace that wonderful conflict which continued long after the two virgins with which we have to do, had sealed with their blood, their faith as Christians in a town which through this conflict came under the control of the Saracens.

The father of these sisters was a Mohammedan; but like many others of his day had married a Christian wife and the children had been brought up in the faith of their mother. Had they as they came to mature age been less lax in their views they could have escaped their terrible fate. But their beauty won for them the undesired attention of many Saracen lovers for whom they were called upon to renounce their religion or suffer. Then was enacted that often repeated story of persecution on one side and a firm refusal to yield on the other. It involved a pretty romance that I can make no record of here, beyond its hard unjust conclusion whereby when their lovers backed by all the persuasions of the king's officers and endless promises of wealth and honour, these virgins chose for themselves death rather than the loss of their faith in Christ, and so, without a tremor, they went to their execution on October 22d in 851.

OCTOBER 23d.

Under the persecutions which Julian the Apostate instituted there was hardly a nobler example of Christian heroism and faith than that displayed by St. Theodoret whom the Church remembers on this day.

Julian the uncle of the emperor had been made "Count or Governor of the East"; a district which embraced the city of Antioch in which dwelt so large a number of Christians as well also, a large contingent of Arians. Among the Orthodox, (or as I have before explained Catholic) priests then living at Antioch, was a zealous priest who had during the reign of Constantine been active in destroying idols and in building churches over the relics of martyrs. To this faithful man's hands had been committed the care of the sacred vessels used by the church in its various ordinances and ritual. The intrinsic value of these had been greatly exaggerated but when Julian (the Governor) heard that a vast store of gold and silver vessels were in the hands of the Christians he resolved to confiscate them and as a first step ordered the clergy to be banished from Antioch. The priest Theodoret refused to obey this mandate and he was brought bound before Julian who accused him of having "thrown down the statues of the gods" during the previous night. Then began a series of tortures akin to those of the so-called Spanish Inquisition such as the "bastinado," the "stretching of the body," and similar acts. But I cannot bring myself to transcribe all the acts this fiend Julian ordered to be inflicted on this faithful man until in his impotent rage he commanded he should be beheaded.

Julian secured the treasures of the Church but unsatisfied yet he profaned and defiled them to crown his atrocities. Nemesis or more truly God's vengeance quickly punished Julian but this story my readers may find in any Roman history. This story of St. Theodoret is only an incident in Julian's life. It occurred in 362.

OCTOBER 24th.

St. Proclus, Archbishop of Constantinople, whose name appears in the Kalendar of to-day was one of the marked characters of his generation and his influence very widespread. He had from his ordination as Deacon been famous as a pulpit orator and had been chosen as the Archbishop of Cyzicus the metropolis of the Hellespont but the people refused to acknowledge the jurisdiction of the Bishop of Constantinople who had appointed him and for this declined to receive Proclus who returned to his native city but daily gaining in reputation for wisdom, until in 434 when he was promoted to the high honour of Archbishop of Constantinople.

Perhaps the most noted of the many writings which have kept the name of St. Proclus in memory are those he addressed to the Armenians in 436 when the Armenian Bishops came to consult with Proclus about the doctrine and writings of Theodorus then gaining ground among the Armenians.

The year 447 is yet notable for the earthquakes which befell many parts of Egypt including Constantinople from whence the people fled in consternation; even the Emperor Theodosius and his court being among these, but everywhere the figure of St. Proclus is named in his arduous efforts to comfort his scattered flock and it was through this incessant labour that death overtook him on October 24, in 447. In addition to Roman Martyrology St. Proclus' name appears in the Greek Menologues and in the Muscovite Kalendar for this day.

In the Ordo for this day in the United States, I notice an office in honour of the Feast of St. Raphael, Archangel.

OCTOBER 25th.

St. Crispin's Day is one of the most famous of the Saint Days not only in England, but in many parts of Europe.

St. Crispin and his brother Crispianian were natives of Rome and having become converts to Christianity traveled northwards into France to propagate the faith. They fixed their residence at Soissons where they preached to the people during the day and at night earned their subsistence by the making of shoes. In this they followed the example of the Apostle Paul, who worked at his craft of tent-making and suffered himself to be a burden to no man. They furnished the poor with shoes it is said at a very low price and their legend adds that an angel supplied them with leather. In the persecution under Emperor Maximian they suffered martyrdom and according to a Kentish tradition their relics after being cast into the sea were washed ashore at

Romney Marsh. In medieval art the two brothers are represented as two men at work in a shoemaker's shop and the emblem for the day in the Clog Almanacs is a pair of sandals or feet shod with them.

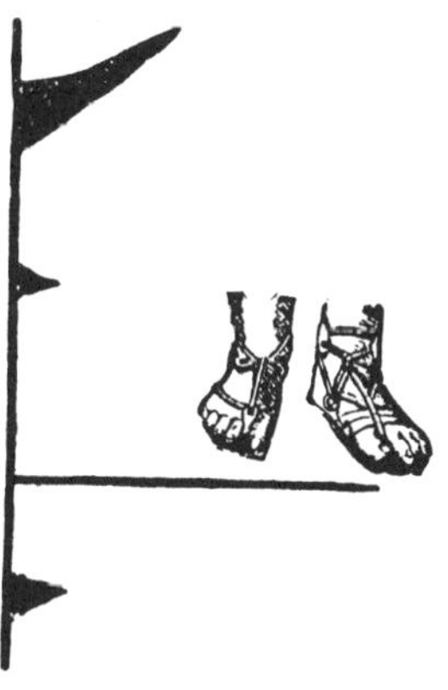

From time immemorial Crispin and Crispianian have been regarded as the patron-saints of shoemakers who used to observe and still in many places yet celebrate their day with great festivity and rejoicings. One special ceremony used to be a grand procession of the brethren of the craft with banners and music whilst various characters representing King Crispin and his court were sustained by different members.

OCTOBER 26th.

In the Roman Church this day is sacred to the memory of St. Evaristus who in the year 102 succeeded St. Anacletus as the head of the Christian Church in Rome and governed its affairs for nine years. In Pontifical records this pope is honoured with the title of Martyr, but beyond such trials as every Christian endured during the reign of Trajan there seems to be no record of a cruel death and he was buried: "near to St. Peter's tomb on the Vatican," the chronicles record. It was Evaristus who first divided Rome into separate parishes and assigned to each its especial priests and also named seven deacons to attend upon the Bishop. Some writers have ascribed to him the creation of the rank of Cardinal; but of this I cannot speak with any degree of certainty. Pope Evaristus died in 112.

OCTOBER 27th.

This day the name of St. Frumentius, the Apostle of Ethiopia is held in honour by the Church in Abyssinia.

During the reign of Constantine the Great, a scholar named Metrodosus had traveled into Farther Persia called by the ancients Ethiopia. Although he had been despoiled of many valuables by Sapor II. or Chahpour he brought home many rich treasures, diamonds and precious stones. This had inspired "Meropius, a philosopher of Tyre," (as chronicles call him) with an ambition to secure like treasures; he therefore planned for himself a similar expedition. On this, Meropius took with him his two nephews who were then only lads. The ship which Meropius had chartered for his voyage put into a small port to secure provisions when the barbarians attacked them and slew all except the two boys whom the prince took as his slaves. The lads seem to have in some way won the heart of the barbarian for they received only kindness at his hands and upon his death-bed he gave them their liberty. The Queen also who during the childhood of her son governed the land entreated them to remain with her and aid her in the government for by that time they were men. They consented and did so remain until the young prince assumed the government. Then the younger of the two erstwhile slaves returned direct to Tyre but Frumentius the elder who had never during all those years of his captivity failed to wish for the conversion of these heathens went first to Alexandria, where he sought out St. Athanasius to whom he related his story and expressed a hope that the Archbishop would send some one to Axuma as a missionary. A synod of Bishops was called who after long and careful consideration selected Frumentius himself as the proper person; whereupon he was duly ordained Bishop of Ethiopia. How truly and faithfully he fulfilled this new and arduous duty is too long a story to repeat here. But it is one of those records of early missionary work the Church justly prides itself upon. The Bishop continued his earnest work with apparently great success until about the year 405 when the "Supreme Pastor called him to his recompense." The Latin Church has ever honoured St. Frumentius on October 27th while the Greek Church commemorates him on November 30th. The Abyssinians adding to his name the title of the "Apostle of the Country of the Axumites."

OCTOBER 28th.

In passing it is not out of place to mention that this is the anniversary of the birth in 1467 of Desiderius Erasmus, who despite Luther's sarcasm was an influential factor in bringing about the great Reformation of which Luther was the exponent. Erasmus died on July 12, 1536.

In all Christian Churches this day is set apart for the honour of SS. Simon Zelotus (the Zelot) and Jude (Thaddaeus, or Lebbeaus) whose names have for ages been connected. Yet even in ecclesiastical biographies there is so much uncertainty, contradiction and confusion in regard to these Apostles that one hesitates as to what should be said. According to one tradition these were the same persons of whom St. Matthew speaks as brethren or kinsmen of our Saviour. But in quick succession another tradition tells us this could not be so; for according to this last they were two brothers who were among the shepherds to whom the angel revealed the birth of Christ. The only point wherein all agree seemingly is, that these Apostles preached the Gospel together in Syria and Mesopotamia. But whether they suffered martyrdom together or not is again a mooted point. One tradition claiming that both were put to death in Persia; St. Simon being sawn asunder with a timber saw and St. Jude killed by a halbert. Thus in some of the illustrations of the Apostles, St. Simon bears a saw as his attribute and St. Jude a halbert.

ST. SIMON. From Roodscreen Fritton Church, Norfolk.

ST. JUDE. From Roodscreen Fritton Church, Norfolk.

One tradition of St. Simon says that he came to England and was there crucified by the ancient Britons. In Greek art, St. Simon is represented as suffering martyrdom on a cross and so much like those of our Saviour, that but for the superscription "O CIMON" (the last O, being the Greek omega) they cannot

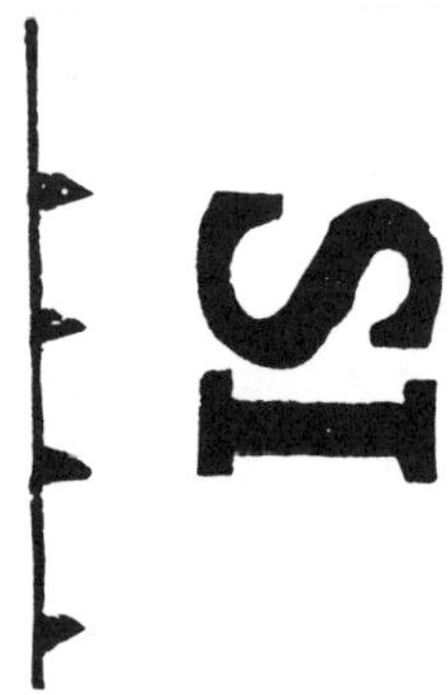

be distinguished. In Greek art also singularly St. Jude and St. Thaddaeus are shown as two distinct persons; though we know St. Jude was called both Thaddaeus and Lebbaeus and the gospels show was a kinsman of Christ. (See Matt. xiii., 55.) In some of the Runic Clog Kalendars SS. Simon and Jude's day is marked by a ship to represent their occupation as fishermen. The more common ones being like our illustration. To conclude this list of contradictions, I have before me another illustration of the martyrdom of St. Jude showing him being shot to death with arrows as if to add to the confusion already mentioned.

Even the careful painstaking Dr. Butler, finds it necessary to qualify his words by saying: "If this Apostle preached in Egypt, etc.," in his remarks on St. Simon. Thus showing how limited the knowledge of our best authorities is in regard to these Apostles.

OCTOBER 29th.

In St. Narcissus the venerable Bishop of Jerusalem whom the Church honours on this day we have if in no other respect a most remarkable instance of longevity. Born toward the close of the first century he was almost four-score years of age when he was placed at the head of the Church in Jerusalem as its Thirtieth Bishop. In 195 we find him with Theophilis, Bishop of Cæsarea, jointly presiding at the council of the Bishop of Palestine held in Cæsarea convened to consider that vexed question which so long troubled the Church as to the proper time for observing Easter.

Despite the reverence the holy Bishop was held in by good men of his day it is evident he had his enemies even "in his own household" because of his severity and strictness in observing the obligations imposed upon all Christians by the laws of the Church and by them was driven into exile for several years. But in the end he returned and supported by his faithful flock aided by a Coadjutor St. Alexander in his extreme old age once more ministered to his people until as I read in the Roman Martyrology for this day: "The blessed Narcissus, Bishop of Jerusalem, distinguished by his holiness patience and faith went to God at the age of one hundred and sixteen years."

OCTOBER 30th.

The Church holds a festival this day for St. Asterius, one of the early Fathers of the Church who wrote about A. D. 400 and whose works even yet are held in reverence for their wisdom and vigour. But they are more especially interesting to us from his mention of the keeping of the festivals of the Resurrection and Epiphany (or "of lights," as he calls it) as well as of Christmas. Another most interesting point is his sermon (still preserved) decrying against the pagan custom of going from door to door to "wish each other a Happy New Year." Showing how ancient that custom is, Asterius' objection being not the joyous wish but the wild riotous conduct of those who engaged in the act.

Few of us I fancy realise the obligation antiquarians and scholars owe to the Roman Church, for the preservation of ancient manuscripts like these sermons of St. Asterius which throw such a flood of light on those early customs in the old world ; filling out many gaps where profane history is silent.

OCTOBER 31st.

It is also the Vigil of All Saints and for which, both in the Anglican and Roman Churches, especial offices are ordained.

HALLOWE'EN.

There is perhaps no night in the year, which the popular imagination has stamped with a more peculiar character than the evening of the 31st of October, known as All Hallow's Eve, or Hallowe'en. It is clearly a relic of pagan times, for there is nothing in the church observance of the ensuing day of All Saints to have originated such extraordinary notions as are connected with this celebrated festival, or such remarkable practices as those by which it is distinguished.

The leading idea respecting Hallowe'en is that it is the time of all others when supernatural influences prevail. It is the night set apart for a universal walking abroad of spirits, both of the visible and invisible world; for one of the special characteristics attributed to this mystic evening is the faculty conferred on the immaterial principle in humanity to detach itself from its corporeal tenement and wander abroad through the realms of space.

A good sized volume would hardly suffice to record the superstitions which even yet to some degree hover round this evening and the variety of games which have become inseparably connected with it. Burn's Hallowe'en gives some of them and is well worth the reading again.

St. Quintin, the saint which is held in especial reverence this day is another of those noble examples which the history of the early Church furnish so many; and prove how earnest were those men who then professed the Christian faith. Descended from a Roman senatorial family he was a soldier by profession and already held high rank in the army when he became convinced of the truth of Christianity.

No sooner had he done this, than casting aside his worldly ambitions and a life of ease, he entered the service of his Divine Master, and attended by a single friend St. Lucian they took up the arduous life of missionaries, which then seemed to inspire the best and noblest men who abjured the Roman gods and professed the Christian faith; the same spirit which had scattered Christ's disciples to the "ends of the earth." Thus they went into Gaul in the end during 287, in the early years of the joint reign of Maximian Herculeus and Dioclesian to receive their crown of martyrdom; and win for themselves crowns of glory in another world.

NOVEMBER

This month was anciently styled the " Wint Monat " or Wind Month or Blot-Monath, Blood-Month, from the custom of slaughtering the cattle during this month for use during the winter for food; and also from ancient pagan sacrifices held in this month during which " blood offerings " to their deities formed part of the ceremony.

NOVEMBER 1st.

ALL SAINTS DAY.

This festival takes its origin from the conversion in the seventh century of the Pantheon at Rome into a Christian place of worship, and its dedication by Pope Boniface IV. to the Virgin and all the martyrs. The anniversary of this event was at first celebrated on the 1st of May, but the day was subsequently altered to the 1st of November which was thenceforth, under the designation of the " Feast of All Saints," set apart as a general commemoration in their honour. The festival has been retained by the Anglican church.

As early as the IV. century the Greeks kept a festival on the first Sunday after Pentecost in honour of " All Martyrs and Saints." There is still preserved in the archives of the Roman Church a sermon preached by St. Chrysostom (died September 14 A. D. 407) upon one of these anniversaries.

The feast was introduced into the Western Church by Pope Boniface IV. after the dedication of the ancient temple of the Pantheon as a Christian church under the name of " Sta Maria ad Martyrs," in 608. The temple having been made over to him by the Emperor Phocas, the feast was held on May 13th. About 731 Gregory III. constructed a chapel in St. Peter's Church in honour of " All Saints," since which time the " Feast of All Saints " or " All Saints' Day " as it is popularly known, has been kept by the Church on November 1st. After the Reformation this festival was one of those the Reformers retained, and in doing so they retained as well the day fixed by Gregory III. as the one on which to celebrate it. In 834, Pope Gregory IV. at the request of Louis " the Mild," extended the festival to the " Universal Church."

I can to-day name only one of the several saints whose names appear in the Kalendar, that of St. Cæsarius.

At Terracina among the pagan rites on certain occasions held in honour of Apollo, the tutelar deity of the city, it was the custom of some young man to offer himself as a voluntary sacrifice to the god. After having been for weeks pampered, carried and honoured by the citizens, decked with the richest apparel and most glittering ornaments, on the specified day the young devotee, immediately after the ceremonies of sacrifice to the god would rush from the temple and running at full speed through a crowd of eager spectators who lined each side of the way to a high precipice he would plunge into the sea, and be forever lost beneath its waves. According to pagan belief this act secured for the voluntary victim such favour from the hands of the gods in the next world, as could be no otherwise secured.

Cæsarius was a Christian deacon lately come from Africa where in A. D. 300 he happened to witness this vain, impious act, and regardless of Dioclesian's lately promulgated decree, dared to deprecate the act as useless. Two of the priests of Apollo overheard his words and hardly had they fallen from his lips, when he was seized, bound and dragged before the governor and accused, only of course to be condemned. The deacon did not deny his words but gave testimony to his faith in Christ and was taken from the presence of the governor, tied in a sack and cast from the same precipice where Apollo's voluntary victim had made his sacrifice.

NOVEMBER 2d.

ALL SOULS' DAY.

This is a festival peculiar to the Roman Church and is celebrated on behalf of the souls in purgatory, for whose release the prayers of the faithful are offered and masses performed in the churches from altars decked in black and with every insignia of mourning.

In explanation Dr. Butler says: "By purgatory, no more is meant by Catholics than a middle state of souls, namely of purgation from sin by temporary chastisement for a punishment of some sin and inflicted after death, which is not eternal. As to the place, manner or kind of these sufferings, nothing has been defined by the church. * * *"

This festival was first introduced by St. Odilo, the abbot of Cluni, who, to quote verbatim from Roman Martyrology, "was the first to prescribe that the commemoration of all the faithful departed should be made in his monasteries on the next day after the Feast of All Saints. This rite was afterward received and approved by the universal church."

Odilo de Mercoeur was the sixth abbot of Cluni and born in 962, dying in 1049, and his festival occurs on January 1st. This especial festival of All Souls was instituted in the early part of the XI. century but its observance soon was esteemed of such importance that in event of its falling on Sunday it was directed that it should not be postponed as in the case of some ceremonials, until Monday; "that the departed might suffer no detriment from the lack of the prayers of the church of the faithful."

On this day the Church pays honour to the memory of St. Victorinus, a father whom St. Jerom termed "one of the pillars of the church." He was a professor of oratory in Greece and is noted in Grecian annals of A. D. 290. It was as a writer and commentator on the Scriptures that he most excelled, though as Bishop of Pettan in Upper Pannonia, now in Styria, his eloquence bore wonderful fruit. Like many another he could not escape the far-reaching decrees of Dioclesian, and won his crown of glory in 304.

NOVEMBER 3d

Is sacred to St. Hubert, patron of huntsmen and of the chase. His is one of those interesting legends constantly met with as we read the lives of the saints of the Church, showing the mysterious working of Providence in turning many lives by some slight incident. Young, gay, rich and very handsome, no noble at the court of Theodebert III., King of Austrasia, was more courted or led a wilder life. In passing I notice this king is called Theodore by Dr. Butler and others. There was no king by that name in Austrasia, and the two names evidently have been confounded. Theodebert's father, Theodebert II., died in 612, and Theodebert III. was, though but a child, named his successor.

It was when Theodebert's court was at its height that Hubert of Aquitaine first appeared and made hunting in the forest of Ardennes so fashionable. There was no day too sacred for Hubert to refrain from his favourite sport and no remonstrance potent enough to keep him from indulging in it. Thus it was that in the early gloaming of an holy day in the forest of Ardennes, a young white stag stood before him. Its first horns were just sprouting and devoid of branches: but either from the shadows of the branches, or in his fancy, Hubert thought he saw a cross between them. The legend as told claims it was an actual cross. Be that as it may, the effect was the same to set his thoughts on the teachings he had neglected so long. His life quickly was a changed one. At first he sought out a band of brigands who infested the forest and some of whom he had met in his wanderings, and told them his story and won some of them over to seek a better life. At length Hubert went to the venerable St. Lambert, Bishop of Maestricht and patron of Leige, with whom he studied and by whom he was ordained. In 681 the holy prelate was murdered. Already Hubert had been advanced to the administration of the diocese as assistant of St. Lambert, and on his death he became the Bishop of Leige, as the see had been transferred thither. St. Hubert administered his holy office until May 30, 727, when he died. He was buried in the Church of St. Peter in Leige. His clog symbol is as in illustration a stag, sometimes with a cross between its horns.

NOVEMBER 4th.

"St. Charles Borromeo, the model of pastors and the reformer of ecclesiastical discipline in these degenerated ages," is the manner in which Dr. Butler opens the narrative of the life of one of the saints the Church remembers on this day. The story is too long an one to repeat in detail, yet most difficult to condense. He was the second son of Gilbert Borromeo, count of Arona, and Margaret of Medicis, a sister of John Angelus, afterward Pope Pius IV., while the Borromeo family was among the most ancient of the long list of which Lombardy can boast. From infancy he was destined for the church yet when a child of only 12 years of age, an uncle Julius Caesar Borromeo, resigned to him the rich revenues of the Benedictine monastery of SS. Gratinian and Felin, uncontrolled by anyone older and wiser to guide him. He studied Latin and "humanity" at Milan and civil and canon law at the University of Pavia during which time in 1558 when 20 years old, his father died, but he quickly returned from home and took his degree in 1559 and in 1561 his uncle, Pius IV., created him a cardinal. Enough one might think between his great wealth and rank to turn the head of an ordinary young man.

His uncle had been raised to the pontificate in 1559 and early in the next year named his nephew as the head of the council, and another uncle added the benefices of another abbey or priory which he controlled, to the young priest's income. The record of his life shows that all this wealth, honour and power had no influence upon his simple mode of living. Of his executive abilities and the promptness with which he disposed of the vast number of ecclesiastical affairs that came under his care, everyone speaks in the highest terms; but it was as a reformer of ecclesiastical abuses he was most noted. For this purpose he established the noble college of the Borromeos at Pavia, and sent missionaries into every part of his diocese to see that his people were cared for. Naturally he won the hatred of a class of priests who had used the Church revenues for their own indulgences, and one attempted to kill him as he was celebrating evening service.

It seemed as if the world had combined to spoil him by heaping wealth and honours on him, for King Philip II. settled an annual pension on him of 9,000 crowns and gave him the principality of Osia, but none of all these favours ever changed his simple life or led him to vary from the one great object set before him. As became his rank, he gave feasts of which he personally never partook. He died at Milan on the 4th of November, 1584. His last words were "Ecce Venio" (Behold I come).

NOVEMBER 5th

Is the festival of St. Bertille, Abbess of Chelles which was refounded by St. Bathildes, wife of Clovis II., and was about four leagues from Paris. This nunnery is chiefly remarkable for the number of noted females, of royal and noble birth that from time to time were gathered within its protecting walls, both of French and of foreign lineage. Among them we read the names of Hereswith, the Queen of East Angles, who became a nun at Chelles in 646, and also of Queen Bathildes who retired here in 665 after the close of her regency and Clotaire III. ascended his throne.

St. Bertille was herself from one of the noblest families in

Soissons in the reign of Dagobert I. and had been educated at Jouarre, a great double monastery at Brie, the nuns of which were under the famed St. Thilchildes; who selected St. Bertille at the request of Queen Bathildes as the first Abbess of the refounded nunnery about 646, and over which she ruled forty-six years until her death in 692.

NOVEMBER 6th

Is kept in honour of St. Leonard by both the Anglican and Roman Churches. He was a nobleman of high rank at the Court of Clovis I. where he was converted by St. Remigius who later instructed him in divinity.

Leonard had been a favourite with the king and still retained much of his old influence though he had after his conversion spent far less time at court than of old, his greatest pleasure now being to go from prison to prison in Paris striving to comfort the prisoners, learning from them their stories and providing for their wants. Not a few of those he thus met he found either were unjustly held or had by their long imprisonment been amply punished for their offences as the lax laws and indifferent judges often left such persons imprisoned for years awaiting even accusation. Such were the cases Leonard took in charge and as he discovered the truth brought them to the notice of Clovis and thus many were set at liberty. It was for this we find in the Clog Almanacs the symbol of a rude hammer is given him, or sometimes a broken chain. After a time Leonard decided in spite of the entreaties of the king to enter the monastery of Micy in Orleans, where he took on the religious habit and discipline, and devoted himself to study and reflection. Later he became a hermit, building for himself a cell and oratory near Limoges. After a period of retirement and devotion, though still leading his hermit life he began to instruct the neighbouring peasantry, thus filling up the measure of his years with good works until his death in 559. He had received the order of deacon but declined further advancement and so is usually represented in art in a deacon's dress and the broken chains of prisoners. He has ever been held in high honour by the English church as evidenced by the dedication of about one hundred and fifty churches to his name.

ST. LEONARD.
From Stained Glass, Sandringham Church, Norfolk.

NOVEMBER 7th.

The Roman Church this day honours another of those early missionaries who forgetful of themselves went forth to fulfil Christ's injunction, in the person of St. Willibrord who was born in the kingdom of Northumberland in 638 or about that date. The story of St. Willibrord in certain ways resembles that already told of others except that he was in some respects a man of far greater accomplishments. Before he was seven years of age he had been placed in the then celebrated monastery of Rippon, in Britain, which was still under the control of St. Wilfrid, its founder, a man of great learning and one who had the rare gift of inspiring his pupils with ambitions of the highest and noblest character. As I have before said, the Irish monastic schools were at that day hardly second to those upon the continent and drew to them the best class of students. Thus it was that when twenty years of age Willibrord went to Ireland where he joined St. Egbert and others and spent many years there in the study of the sacred sciences. It was not until he was thirty years old that he was ordained a priest. In the meantime one of Willibrord's early companions who had come from Rippon with him had gone from Ireland to Friesland as a missionary and after two years had returned. His other friend, St. Egbert, had also wished to go to Friesland, but for good reasons had not done so. Still this Friesland mission was one of such importance that Willibrord was inspired by a desire to undertake himself the arduous task, and at last in 699 he obtained permission to go to Lower Germany, or Friesland. It had long before been a missionary field, but the good work of the early workers had been nearly overcome by pagan priests when he reached there with his companions, and under the protection of Pepin of Herstel (or Pepin the Big), Duke of Friesland began their work which was ultimately to become so successful. I must not tell this long and interesting story for it is the history of the Early Church in Lower Germany. His monastery at Utrecht and the schools he built thus prepared the way for the good St. Boniface thirty years later; all under difficulties few, save men of such energy as Willibrord, could have overcome. Literally worn out with his labours his peaceful end came at extreme old age. The chronicles are greatly at variance on the point as to just when he died. If we accept Dr. Butler's dates—viz., birth about 638 and death in 738, he was a centenarian. All concur in his having reached great age and in testifying to his earnest, self-sacrificing labours and the wonderful ability which he at all times displayed in the management of his ecclesiastical duties, and of the love he inspired among his people and contemporary ecclesiasts.

NOVEMBER 8th.

By a coincidence, another Northumberland saint follows St. Willibrord in the Kalendar of those whom the Roman Church so justly honours, in the name of St. Willehad, Bishop of Bremen and the Apostle of Saxony, and whose mission evidently was inspired by the wonderful success of SS. Willibrord and Boniface in Friesland and Germany; for his first effort in 772 was in Friesland at a place called Docknow in West Friesland. His stay here was very brief. Crossing the Issel he made his way through the country now called Ober-Inel, not without a narrow escape of his life at the hands of infidels at a village called Humark. But a Providence seemed to watch over him and he continued his journey to

Wigmore where Bremen now stands and was the first Christian missionary to cross the Elbe. The Saxons had at that time spread themselves from the Oder to the Rhine and the Germanic ocean; thus occupying the greater part of the provinces of Northern Germany; and though divided into several cantons or tribes, they were in case of general war under one commander. It was here that St. Willehad preached until the great Saxon rebellion against Charlemagne broke out in 782 instigated by Whitikind, a Westphalian Saxon, who had been in rebellion in 777 and escaping had fled to Denmark. But we must not mix history, interesting as it is, with our story. During the three years of active warfare Willehad spent his time in retirement at the tomb of St. Willibrord engaged in transcribing the epistles of St. Paul and other sacred literature.

With the close of hostilities the Duke Whitikind was baptized, and with restored peace St. Willehad resumed his missionary work and upon July 15, 787, was ordained Bishop of Saxony fixing his see at Bremen, the city seemingly having about this time been founded and his cathedral church, we are told, was built of wood, but his successor rebuilt it of stone. St. Willehad lived but a short time after the completion of his church, his legend telling us that he died in a Friesland village in 789.

NOVEMBER 9th.

THE DEDICATION OF ST. JOHN LATERAN.

It would be difficult to find a more remarkable group of buildings than those which surround the "Piazza di San Giovanni," in Rome, in the center of which stands the Obelisk of the Lateran; the oldest object in all that wonderful city of antiquities, it having been — according to the translators of the hieroglyphics it bears — originally raised in memory of the Pharaoh Thothmes IV. in the year 1740 B. C. It was brought from the Temple of the Sun in Heliopolis, to Alexandria by Constantine, and later to Rome where it was used together with the obelisk now standing in the

Piazza del Popolo, to ornament the Circus Maximus. By order of Sixtus V. it was transferred in 1588 to its present site. Facing this venerable obelisk are the Baptistery and Basilica of the Lateran. The remaining edifices I must not take space here to notice. The Baptistery of the Lateran — sometimes called "St. Giovanni, in Fonte"— was built by Sixtus III. (430–40), though only portions of the original structure now remain. The Lateran derives its name from its having been the residence of a rich patrician, Plautius Lateranus, whose estates Nero confiscated and who was put to death for participating in the conspiracy of Piso. It became an imperial residence and Maximianus gave a portion of it to his daughter, Fausta, the second wife of Constantine. When Constantine the Great, by his victory over Maxentius in 312, became master of Italy and Africa, Christians everywhere began to erect sumptuous churches — checked in the East for a time in 319 by the persecutions — and among them Constantine built a church sometimes called "Constantinian Basilica," but now universally termed St. John Lateran. It was given to Pope Melchiades in 312 by Constantine who had laboured upon it with his own hands. It was consecrated on November 9, 324. The Lateran church is styled the heart, the mother and the mistress of all churches as an inscription on its walls imports: "Sacrosancta Lateranensis Ecclesia, Omnium Urbis et Orbis Ecclesianum Mater et Caput." The chapter of the Lateran takes precedence even over St. Peter's who once contested this, but by the bull of Gregory IX. and Pius V. the right of the Lateran was confirmed and therefore every newly elected Pope comes here for coronation. The story of the old Basilica is full of interest, and is told in many of the Roman guidebooks so fully I must not repeat it here. The consecration of a church edifice with the Roman Church is a very solemn observance and the rites and prayers are very strictly prescribed, hence the anniversary of this, the acknowledged Mother of Churches, is regarded as no ordinary festival.

NOVEMBER 10th.

St. Justus, Archbishop of Canterbury, whose name appears in the Kalendars of both the Anglican and Roman Church this day was a Roman by birth and a monk of St. Gregory's monastery; but his learning and virtues had won for him a very great reputation both in Rome and elsewhere. Therefore when St. Austin begged for some one to be sent to aid him in preaching in England Justus was selected as the man above all his brethren most fitted for the position. He arrived in England in 601 but his wonderful talent and the success that followed his work was so marked that in 604 he was created Bishop of the important see of Rochester, and for twenty years ministered to his people, winning not alone their love but adding many souls to the number of the faithful. In 624, on the death of St. Mellitus, Justus was raised to the Archbishopric of Canterbury, but filled it only during three years when, to quote Dr. Butler's quaint and most appropriate expression: "He went to receive his reward from the hands of the Prince of Pastors on the 10th of November in 627," leaving a name so pure and a memory so sweet that to quote again from a Church of England prelate: "We keep green his memory both because of the love we bear him and for the example he left us by his earnest holy life."

NOVEMBER 11th.

MARTINMAS

Is without doubt one of the most favourite festivals of both the English and Roman Churches in England; and the story of St. Martin is one of the noblest and truest that it will be my privilege to tell, even abridged as it must be.

St Martin, the son of a Roman military tribune, was born at Sabaria in Hungary about 316. From his earliest infancy he was remarkable for mildness of disposition; yet he was obliged to become a soldier, a profession most uncongenial to his natural character. After several years' service he retired into solitude from whence he was withdrawn, by being elected Bishop of Tours in the year 374. The zeal and piety he displayed in this office were most exemplary. He converted the whole of his diocese to Christianity, overthrowing the ancient pagan temples and erecting churches in their stead. From the great success of his pious endeavours Martin has been styled the Apostle of the Gauls; and being the first confessor to whom the Latin Church offered public prayers, he is distinguished as the father of that church. In remembrance of his original profession, he is also frequently denominated the Soldier Saint.

The true story of St. Martin's life is in itself a romance while the legends and fables told of him would fill a volume.

While a soldier he won the love of everyone with whom he came in contact for his true whole-hearted benevolence. The winter of 332 was one of unusual severity in Amiens where Martin was then stationed. Marching with his company one bitter day Martin saw a man scantily clothed shivering with the cold. Many already had passed but none had tried to succour him. Martin's impecuniosity was proverbial in the army, not from his extravagance but from his never failing generosity. But this day he surprised even those who knew him best. Having neither food nor money for the poor stranger Martin took the cloak from his shoulders and with the sharp blade of his sword divided it in half — laying one part over the shivering pauper and covering his own exposed person with the rest. The act was quickly done and so wholly unostentatiously that few saw it. Later he bore without a word the witty jibes of his fellows over his abbreviated garment. This much is literally true. His legend tells us that that night he had a vision in which he saw Jesus Christ wearing the half of the divided cloak, and saying to his angel host: "Martin, the catechumen hath clothed Me in this garment."

The name then given to this cloak was "chape" and according to Collin de Planey, the English words "chapel" and "chaplain" are both derived from it.

While I might fill pages with legends of St. Martin, I will limit myself to one, which may be termed a palindrome. St. Martin was enroute for Rome, journeying on foot. Satan, ever on watch, took occasion to taunt him on his not having a conveyance more suitable to his dignity as a bishop. On the instant St. Martin touched his Satanic Majesty and he was transformed into a mule upon whose back St. Martin rode. Whenever the transformed demon grew lazy or tired the saint would spur him on at full speed until the devil defeated and worn out exclaimed :

> " Signa te Signa : temere me tangis et angis :
> Roma tibi subito motibus ibit amor."

In English—" Cross, cross thyself : thou plaguest and vexest me without necessity ; for, owing to my exertions, thou wilt soon reach Rome, the object of thy wishes." The singularity of this distich consists in its being palindromical — that is, the same, whether read backwards or forwards. Angis, the last word of the first line, when read backwards, forming signa, and the other words admitting of being reversed in a similar manner.

St. Martin, at the time of his vision above spoken of, was yet unbaptized ; but very soon thereafter the sacred rite was performed, and when 40 years of age he left the military taking holy vows and for many years leading a hermit's life until in 371 he was named as Bishop of Tours. His life was ever one of those examples of Christian virtue that makes him one of the best loved both in the English and Roman Churches of almost any in the entire Kalendars. In art he is presented in the full robes of a Bishop with a naked beggar at his feet, the illustration given above being one of several of a similar design on Clog Almanacs.

NOVEMBER 12th

The Church remembers St. Martin, Pope and Martyr, who died in 655. He was a man who early in life became renowned for his learning, as was evidenced when Pope Theodorus sent him — while yet but a deacon — to Constantinople in the quality of "Apocrisiarius," or nuncio. Pope Theodorus died in July, 649, and in October of that year Martin was elected to the pontifical chair. The enmity of the Emperor Constans to Martin was well known but ineffective for when the time came for election he was chosen without a dissenting voice. In June, 653 the exarch of the Emperor arrived in Rome with orders to make charges against the Pope of concealing arms in his palace but none were found. Despite this, on the 18th of the same month the Pope, who had been sick in the Lateran, was seized and carried in a boat down the Tiber and thence to the island of Nixos where he was kept under guard for a year and in September, 654, carried on to Constantinople, and in December condemned to die. First he was stripped of his clothing save a tunic, an iron collar was put on his neck and thus he was dragged from the palace through the city to his prison where he was confined until in May, 655, when for some reason he was sent to Taurica Chersonesus, a pagan country where at that time a famine prevailed through which he suffered great privations, but happily on September 16th of that year death released the sufferer. The Latin Church selected November 12th for his festival, the Greeks naming April 13th and also Sepember 16 and 20th for his honour, while the Muscovites hold their festival for him on April 14th.

NOVEMBER 13th.

The list of canonized saints of the Roman Church has by no means been confined to their priesthood or the holy women from their nunneries. Thus to-day commemorates the name of St. Homobonus, a merchant, who was happily thus named. A man whose life story is a model for every young man — nay, and old men, too, if he has prospered in business — to follow. An earnest, hard-working Christian who was not "slothful in business;" on the other hand, a shrewd, far-seeing man but one whose honest gains were not hoarded for self-gratification or the accumulation of wealth. A man who provided liberally for his own household but who held himself responsible as an almoner of the Giver of all good gifts for the use of the wealth entrusted him. I cannot, of course, follow in detail the beautiful story of his "secret" charity; not content with paying "tithe of mint and anise and cummin" he did not omit weightier matters and beyond doubt he reaped his just reward when at matins in the very act of joining in the Gloria in Excelsis his summons came. In 1198 Pope Innocent III. canonized this just man.

Both the English and Roman Martyrologies name this day for St. Britius, or St. Brice, the successor of St. Martin of Tours in that famous bishopric.

This day is also named for one of the youngest saints in the entire Kalendar of the Church, St. Stanislas Kostka, son of John Kostka, a senator of Poland, and Margaret Kirska, sister of the Palatine of Muscovia in 1550. His is one of those stories sometimes met with of a pure young life which even from infancy was untainted by sin in any form and an inborn desire to do good to others that was only and continually coupled with a desire to give his life and service to the Society of Jesus. This last wish was violently opposed by his father and therefore he left his home secretly in 1567 and at length succeeded in reaching Rome and becoming a disciple of St. Francis Borgia, then general of the order. But his life was soon cut short for he died in August, 1568 when but seventeen years and nine months old. The sanctity of his short life was so marked that in 1604 Pope Clement VIII. was lead to beatify him — that is, to "declare him happy." He was canonized by Benedict XIII. in 1727.

NOVEMBER 14th

Is the festival of St. Laurence, Archbishop of Dublin. He was a son of Maurice O'Tool, a rich and powerful Prince in Leinster. His experiences in life began young for he was only ten years of age when his father was compelled to deliver his son to Dermond

MacMerchad, King of Leinster, as a "hostage." This man seems to have been a brutal fellow, and the sufferings of the poor child were horrible. At last O'Tool heard of them and the legend as it runs says "he obliged King MacMerchad to place the child in the care of the Bishop at Glendaloch."

But how he was able to coerce the King is not apparent, still it is evident the father must have been a man of more than ordinary power to control thus the acts of a king. Glendaloch was in County Wicklow and its Bishop was also Abbot of the monastery. Here Laurence remained receiving his education and ordination and ultimately, upon the death of the good prelate who had stood by him for those fifteen years, the young man found himself Abbot of the monastery and but for the canon of the Church regarding age, would have been then raised to the episcopate. When five years later Gregory, Archbishop of Dublin, died, so well established had Laurence's reputation both for learning and executive ability become, that he was chosen by a unanimous vote as the successor to this metropolitan see despite the fact that he was barely thirty years of age and just within the limit of canonical law. The manner in which Laurence conducted his see fully justified his having been chosen while yet so young.

In 1179 when Pope Alexander III. summoned the third general council of Lateran "for the reformation of manners and extinguishing of heretical errors" Archbishop Laurence was one of the delegates and made himself so valuable in many ways that the Pope named him "Legate of the Holy See in the Kingdom of Ireland." When Henry II. of England was offended at Doderic the Irish monarch, Laurence attempted to mediate, but he was refused by the King who soon set out for Normandy. But Laurence was a man who seemed to know no such word as "fail" and in due time followed Henry into France and renewed his efforts for peace, and the King was so won by both his logic, loyalty and piety that he at length yielded to the wishes of Laurence. It was the last victory of the noble prelate for at the monastery of Eu, on the confines of Normandy, when enroute for home the worthy saint sickened and died November 14th 1180. Pope Honorius issued the bull of his canonization in 1226.

NOVEMBER 15th

Is the festival of an English saint recognized by both the Anglican and Roman Churches, St. Malo or Mallou, the first Bishop of Aleth in Brittany. Though born in England he was educated in Ireland, as was the case of most men who attained any note for learning during the VI. century. His great ability was early recognized by everyone and he might have had preferment in the church in his own country but there arose some political difficulty just at the time that induced him to leave his native land and seek a refuge in Bretagne where he settled as a companion of a holy recluse near the city of Aleth. His name had preceded him and in 541 when the city was erected into a bishopric, he was chosen as its first Bishop, and later the city itself came to be called after his name. He died in 565.

NOVEMBER 16th.

St. Edmund, Archbishop of Canterbury, whom the English and Roman Church both honour to-day presents a rare combination of characteristics. Possessed of an intense desire for the attainment of knowledge with the facilities which were granted him, he became a very learned man. Coupled with this was an equally great love for religion and devotion to sacred thoughts. The two naturally led him to seek retirement and seclusion from the world but when circumstances called him to the front he laid aside his personal wishes and threw himself into the work laid out for him by his superiors.

As a child he had first been placed in the monastic schools at Evesham, from thence going to Oxford and lastly to Paris where for a time he taught in the schools, but later returned to his native land and from 1219 to 1226 was a professor of logic in the, even then, famous University of Oxford. A canonry at Salisbury being offered, he accepted it but had been there only a short time when a mandate from the Pope directed him to go forth and "preach the crusade against the Saracens," which he did with such vigour that his influence was felt far and near.

The see of Canterbury had long been vacant when Gregory IX. selected Edmund to fill it, and Henry III. most gladly confirmed the nomination and he was consecrated to his high office on April 2d in 1234. The exactions laid upon the clergy by Henry III. fill many pages in the life of Edmund and caused him endless trials and conflicts we may not enter upon here, but they ultimately compelled him to flee to France for safety where he died near Provins in Champagne on November 16th in 1242.

St. Margaret, Queen of Scotland, whose name appears this day in the Kalendar of the English church was one of those characters of sterling virtue to whom all creeds alike pay a respectful homage. Even if we pass the eulogy paid her by her confessor, Turgot, as too flattering, enough remains of true history for us to understand why Scotchmen revere her memory. She was a niece of Edward the Confessor and Edmund Ironside. Her youth was spent in exile under the guardianship of the King of Sweden, and it was through being wrecked on the Scottish coast Margaret came to meet King Malcolm, which resulted in their marriage. Her charity to the poor was unbounded and her kindness to English prisoners captured by the King won for her the veneration of the English. It was through her influence that the observance of the Sabbath, which had at that time become much neglected in Scotland, was again restored. Her last days were full of adversity borne with exemplary resignation. The Roman Church observes her festival on June 10th but in the Kalendar of the English church it appears on this day.

NOVEMBER 17th

Is the festival of St. Hugh, Bishop of Lincoln, and the builder of the Cathedral in this quaint, historic English town. The original church had been founded by William II. surnamed Ruber the Red—sometimes improperly termed "Rupert or Rufus"—at some period prior to 1100; but the Cathedral was this church rebuilt during the reign of Henry II. (1154-1189), the first building having been wrecked by an earthquake.

The early life of St. Hugh until he was nineteen was spent in Burgundy where he was born, but in 1159 he entered the monastery at Chartreuse where he was educated and duly ordained. In 1181 Henry II., who had founded the first Carthusian monastery in England at Witham in Somersetshire, sent for St. Hugh to become its abbot. Despite the fact that St. Hugh had not hesitated to criticise severely the King for certain acts, Henry held him in such high esteem that in 1186 he named him Bishop of Lincoln and lent him all the aid in his power, added to royal gifts of money to reconstruct the old church which had been begun by Remigius as early as 1086. As a result of St. Hugh's wonderful taste and knowledge of architecture, the beautiful Cathedral as it stands to-day, saving York-Minster, is the finest specimen of pure Gothic architecture to be found in England. No end of legends are still told in Lincoln of St. Hugh during the building of the Cathedral, of how, with his own hands he carried material for the workmen and even laid some of its stones. St. Hugh died on November 17, 1200, and so greatly was he revered that King John (who came to the throne in 1199) and King William, assisted by many of their nobles, three archbishops, fourteen bishops and more than one hundred abbots, carried his body to the tomb where it rested in a silver shrine.

ST. HUGH.
From S. Mary's Tower, Oxford.

NOVEMBER 18th

Is honoured by especial Offices and Masses in the Roman Church as the day of the dedication of the Vatican Churches of SS. Peter and Paul, the second patriarchal church at Rome and in which rest the bodies of those sainted men. It is impossible to recount the story of the Vatican here and a garbled one is quite out of place; but none can doubt the fitness of observing with solemn rites the anniversary of this historic and venerable church.

St. Hild or Hilda is one of the several saints, named in the Kalendar for remembrance on this day. With royal blood in her veins and all that it implied in those old days she, for the love she bore her Great Master, voluntarily laid aside earthly honours and left the court of King Edwin, her uncle, and took the habit of a humble nun. Her piety and holy life led S. Aiden to secure her appointment as abbess of (to quote a quaint phrase often used) a "numerous" monastery at Heartea, now Hartlepool in the bishopric of Durham. In passing it may be added this nunnery was in the "Isle of Stags," and was founded by "Hein," the first nun ever known in the kingdom of Northumberland. After some years spent here Hilda founded another great, double monastery—i. e., for monks and nuns, in separate buildings—on the bay of Lighthouse afterward called Prestby (from the great number of priests assembled and living there), and at present Whitebay in Yorkshire. Both of these were destroyed by the Danes, and no vestige is left of them.

ST. HILDA.

The wonderful wisdom of St. Hilda not alone in spiritual but in temporal affairs won for her so great a reputation that kings from far and near came to seek from her advice and counsel. To quote again from the chronicle of the period: "In the year of the

Incarnation of Our Lord 680, on the 17th of November, the Abbess Hilda * * * died and was carried into Paradise by Angels, as was beheld in a vision by one of her own nuns; then at a distance on the same night." The nun who saw this was later known as "St. Bees."

Those who desire to know more of this saintly woman may read a fuller account of her interesting life in S. Baring Gould's "Virgin Saints and Martyrs."

NOVEMBER 19th

Is the festival of St. Elizabeth of Hungary, daughter of the valiant, Christian King, Alexander II. who was born in 1207. And thereby hangs another of those old world, old-time tales; when children were betrothed by their parents while yet in their cradles. Such was the fate of Elizabeth when Herman the Landgrave of Thuringia and Hesse planned with King Alexander to marry her to his son Lewis, a child of her own age. It thus came that when Elizabeth was but four years of age she was sent from her home to the court of the Landgrave to be brought up and educated. Accompanied by twelve maidens from her father's household, "a silver cradle and a rich wardrobe," she reached the castle of Wartberg at Eisenach; and on the next day amid imposing ceremonies the babies were betrothed and laid side by side in the cradle. From thence on for several years the two were never separated and grew to love each other intensely. Despite the fact that little or no attention was paid to religion or religious ceremonies in the household of the Landgrave, our little saint never slighted her duties, being taught them by an unusually learned and pious priest, one Conrad of Marpurg. The charity which was one of her marked characteristics in life, early showed itself and in Herman she had a true friend; but upon his death, and when Lewis (or Louis as he is sometimes called) became Landgrave great opposition arose against the marriage; but Lewis proved true to the love of his childhood and the two were married when they were twenty years old and their life was one of perfect content. I will not recount her endless acts of kindness to the poor or the wondrous miracles her legend tells of; but I must make room to record how in the famine in Thuringia and during the plague which followed it she not only gave her jewels for the benefit of the sick but clothed them in her own royal garments; and how — to his credit it should be recorded — when the state officials complained of her having depleted the treasury by her gifts, her husband not only kissed, thanked and blessed her, but bade his Ministers to: "Let her do as she will."

The next year, 1227 Lewis set forth for the Crusade in Palestine but died in Calabria in the arms of the Patriarch of Jerusalem, on September 11th.

Then it was the hitherto suppressed hatred toward the loving, generous Landgravine broke forth and the jealousy of Henry the brother of Lewis, which during his lifetime he had not dared to show, was vented on the devoted widow and mother of his children whom he drove from her castle. In her poverty she supported herself and children by spinning wool.

When the Knights of the Holy Crusade returned they compelled Henry to take a different course until Elizabeth's son, Herman, came to his majority and to give her as her dower the city of Marpurg. But in the meantime she had drunk of the very dregs of sorrow. A brief three years later this saintly woman followed her loved and loving husband and died on November 19, 1231.

Many pictures remain of St. Elizabeth, the most noted being that painted by Murillo for the church of Castad, at Seville.

NOVEMBER 20th.

St. Edmund, King of the East-Angles, whose festival is held to-day, reached his throne when his cousin, Offe, resigned it to spend the remainder of his days in penance at Rome. Edmund was then but fifteen years of age but a boy of unusual qualities and most persistent in his pursuit of learning, as well as devout and religious. His reign for fifteen years was one of unusual peace for his subjects, until the invasion of the Danes, under Hengar and Hausa (or Hubba, as some write it) in 870. Of these bloody raids by the Danes so many and full accounts have been written in every English history no description need be repeated. They all were alikc in their bloody, heartless fury. In this one King Edmund and his court were made captives and, had they consented to abjure their Christian faith and adopt the religious rites of the pagan Danes their lives might have been saved. St. Edmund refused and after scourging he was tied to a tree and shot to death with arrows. The Clog symbol above is intended to represent a quiver of arrows. His legend tells how after his death, his head was thrown among briars and bushes, and that the Danes in departing from the scene of their butchery were lost and constantly misled by the head calling out "Here!" "Here!" and that the head was at last discovered by means of a pillar of light which stood over it and illuminated the space and that when found a wolf was standing guard over it. St. Edmund was buried at a place now called St. Edmundsbury and the arms of the town are the "three crowns of the East-Angles, and has for its crest a wolf, holding the King's head between its paws." St. Edmund has always held a high place in the Kalendar of the English church as well as in that of the Roman Church.

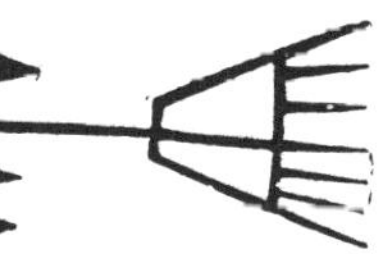

ST. EDMUND.
From a Painting on a Roodscreen in Norfolk.

NOVEMBER 21st.

THE PRESENTATION OF THE BLESSED VIRGIN

Is one of the most impressive festivals of the Roman Church. It had its origin from an ancient Jewish rite first mentioned in Holy Writ in the history of Samuel, and one so universally followed from that day. How early the festival was first introduced into the Christian Church is not known, but the most ancient of the Greek menologies extant mention the entrance of the Virgin into the Temple, and it was a Feast celebrated by the Greeks long before it was adopted by the Latin Church. The one central thought always being the consecration of herself (the Holy Virgin) to God.

Many legends are extant of the act itself but far too often they are confounded with the act of the presentation of the Christ-child himself at the Temple. That Mary lived a retired life is plainly true and some even claim the espousals were at first simply a "betrothal" instead of a marriage. In certain places this espousal has an especial office on January 22d, the date also assigned by some for the marriage of the Virgin.

ST. CECILIA.
From a print by Marcantonio.

NOVEMBER 22d

Is devoted to St. Cecilia, a virgin martyr.

This saint was a Roman lady of good family and having been educated as a Christian was desirous of devoting herself to heaven by her life of celibacy. Compelled, by her parents to wed a young nobleman named Valerian, she succeeded in converting both her husband and his brother to Christianity and afterwards shared with them the honours of martyrdom. Accounts differ as to the death which she suffered, some asserting that she was boiled in a cauldron, and others that she was left for days to expire gradually after being half decapitated. The legend states that the executioner, after striking one blow found himself unable to complete his task.

St. Cecilia is regarded as the patroness of church music and of music generally; but the reason for her holding this office is not very satisfactorily explained. Dr. Butler says that it was from her assiduity in singing the divine praises, the effect of which she often heightened by the aid of an instrument. She is generally represented singing and playing on some musical instrument, or listening to the performance of an angelic visitant. This last circumstance is derived from an ancient legend which relates that an angel was so enraptured with her harmonious strains as to quit the abodes of bliss to visit the saint. Dryden thus alludes to the incident in his ode for St. Cecilia's Day:

At last divine Cecilia came,
Inventress of the vocal frame;
The sweet enthusiast from her sacred store,
Enlarg'd the former narrow bounds,
And added length to solemn sounds.

St. Cecilia is generally represented playing on the organ or harp, or with organ-pipes in her hand. In the Church of St. Cecilia in Trastevere at Rome (rebuilt on the site of a church founded in the IX. century), she is represented as a recumbent figure, with the face downwards and a deep wound on the back of her neck, evidently alluding to the legend which says that the executioner being unable to behead her, left her half dead to linger three days. She is sometimes represented as being boiled in a cauldron and occasionally carries a sword in one hand and an instrument of music in the other.

NOVEMBER 23d.

St. Clement, the third Pope of the Church of Rome, is this day honoured both by the Roman and English Churches.

Clement was a Roman by birth but of Jewish extraction. He was converted to the Christian faith by St. Paul and it is claimed with much reason, that he is the person alluded to in the Philippians iv. 3; since it is well known that Clement was a constant attendant of both St. Peter and St. Paul in their labours, and upon the death of St. Cletus in A. D. 91 he was made Bishop or Pope of Rome and according to the Liberian Kalender sat in the Apostolic chair for "nine years and eleven months." It was through his teaching that Domitilla, the daughter of the Emperor Domitian, became a Christian and through her influence Clement secured immunity where others suffered. But when Trajan, who governed Rome during the absence of the emperor, instituted his persecution Clement was banished to the island quarries worked by convicts; a punishment but little less terrible than death by torture. There was no water for these miserable creatures and Clement in prayer begged for their deliverance. As he opened his eyes he saw a lamb standing on a hill and went thither where he digged a well and found a spring of clear fresh water. It was for this act his legends say, he was condemned to death. This was accomplished by tying him to an anchor and afterward cast into the sea. His legend continues that when Christians prayed "the waters of the sea were driven back and a ruined temple was disclosed in which his body still fast to the anchor was found," and still more marvelously it adds that for many years on the anniversary of St. Clement's death the water each year receded and remained so for three days. For this reason in art St. Clement is always, as in our illustration represented with an anchor.

ST. CLEMENT.
From the Lubeck Passionale.

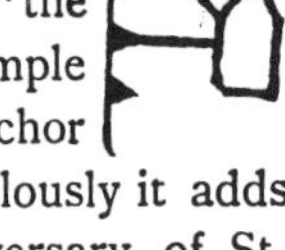

In Clog Almanacs his symbol is sometimes a water bottle. Plot in describing a "Clog Alamanak" said, "that a pot is marked against the 23d of November for the feast of St. Clement, from an ancient custom which doubtless took its rise from some tradition of the above mentioned miracle of going about on that night to beg drink to make merry with." Herewith also I give another from an English Clog but it, like many of them, seems to have a secret or Runic meaning.

Many miracles are credited to St. Clement both before and after his death, but I must omit mention of them.

NOVEMBER 24th.

St. John of the Cross whose festival the Church keeps this day, was by birth a Spaniard from Old Castile; who took upon himself the habit of the Carmelites, when twenty-one years of age entering the monastery at Medina. When St. Teresa set about her work of reforming the Carmelite Order the reputation of the Medina monk had reached her ears and she sought him out. His humility and the purity of his life won her admiration and she chose him as one of her chief assistants in establishing the Order of Our Lady of Carmel; and on Advent Sunday in 1568 John entered the poor little house in the village of Dunville, from which was evolved the "Barefooted Carmelite Friars," whose institution was approved by Pope Pius V. and in 1580 confirmed by Gregory VIII. The austerities of this order I have already commented on; but John added if possible, even greater trials for himself, and his life was indeed a series of crosses. The old Carmelite Friars did not take kindly to St. Teresa's reformations and found in John the victim whom they sought, and in their chapter condemned him to imprisonment. After many months his release came and with it a series of preferments, until in 1588 he became Vicar-Provincial of Andalusia and first definitor of the Order. In 1591 he found himself again in disfavour with the Order when its chapter met at Madrid, and he retired in disgrace to the solitude of a small convent in the mountains of Sierra Morena; where he composed several works that have made his name famous and where he passed his last hours. St. John was canonized by Benedict XIII. in 1726, and his office in the Roman Breviary was fixed for this day.

NOVEMBER 25th.

St. Catharine, who is honoured alike by the Anglican and Roman Churches on this day, was the daughter of Cortis (a half-brother of Constantine), King of Egypt.

Among the earlier saints of the Romish Kalendar St. Catharine holds an exalted position both from rank and intellectual abilities. She was one of the most distinguished ladies of Alexandria in the beginning of the fourth century. From a child she was noted for her acquirements in learning and philosophy and while still very young she became a convert to the Christian faith. During the persecution instituted by the Emperor Maximinus II., St. Catharine assuming the office of an advocate of Christianity, displayed such cogency of argument and powers of eloquence as to silence thoroughly her pagan adversaries. Maximinus, troubled with this success, assembled together the most learned philosophers in Alexandria to confute the saint; but they were both vanquished in debate and converted to a belief in the Christian doctrines. The enraged tyrant thereupon commanded them to be put to death by burning, but for St. Catharine he reserved a more cruel punishment. She was placed in a machine composed of four wheels connected together and armed with sharp spikes, so that as they revolved the victim might be torn to pieces. A miracle prevented the completion of this project. When the executioners were binding Catharine to the wheels a flash of lightning descended from the skies, severed the cords with which she was tied and shattered the engine to pieces, causing the death both of the executioners and numbers of the bystanders. Maximinus still bent on her destruction, ordered her to be carried beyond the walls of the city where she was first scourged and then beheaded. The legend proceeds to say that after her death her body was carried by angels over the Red Sea to the summit

ST. CATHARINE.
From Stained Glass,
West Wickham
Church, Kent.

of Mount Sinai. The celebrated convent of St. Catharine is situated in a valley on the slope of that mountain and was founded by the Emperor Justinian in the sixth century, and contains in its church a marble sarcophagus, in which the relics of St. Catharine are deposited. Of these the skeleton of the hand covered with rings and jewels is exhibited to pilgrims and visitors.

In art St. Catharine bears a sword, indicative of the mode of her death, but even thus, as seen in our illustration, the wheel, symbolic of the suffering intended for her, is often introduced. In the Clog Almanacs the wheel always appears.

The legend of St. Catharine of Alexandria is by no means an ancient one — as these saintly legends run — for even among the Greeks it cannot be traced back beyond the eighth century, for it is first told in the Greek menology of the Emperor Basil in the ninth century. It apparently had its birth among the monks of Mount Sinai and was brought from the east by the Crusaders of the eleventh century who told it in gratitude for the protection this "Invitissimo Ervina" was credited with giving protection to the Christian Warriors in the Holy Land. In the fifteenth century an attempt was made to remove St. Catharine from the Kalendar by certain prelates of France and Germany, but she has not only retained her place in Roman Martyrology but as well in the English Reformed Church, and probably, next to Mary Magdalene is to-day the most popular among the female saints in both the Kalendars.

St. Catharine of Alexandria must not be confounded with St. Catharine of Siena, a saint of the fourteenth century, whose festival is held April 30th.

NOVEMBER 26th.

Among others of the saints the Church pays honour to on this day is St. Conrad, Bishop of Constance, whose name has more especial interest to my English readers, as he was connected by blood with the illustrious house of the Guelphs, whose pedigree is derived from Clodion, King of the Franks, and Wittekind the Great (first Duke of Saxony), and consequently from Woden, the chief god, and thus of the stock of the principal royal families of the Saxons who founded the Heptarchy in England. The name Guelph, or Guelf, was only taken during the reign of Charlemagne, when the family were simply "Counts of Altroff," now called Weingarten, in Suabia, and not to be confounded with the Altroff near Nuremberg in Franconia, nor with the capital of Uri in Switzerland. But I have digressed too far already, and I must not follow this interesting genealogy of our saint, from Conrad Rudolph, the second Count of Altroff, the founder of the house of Guelph, to our St. Conrad.

From childhood Conrad had displayed his desire for a religious life and the temptations and ambitions of worldly rank and power had no influence over him, and from the time he entered the monastery his biographer tells how "everyone approached him with awe, veneration, mixed with confidence and affection inspired by his tender charity and humility." He was rapidly promoted from the time of his ordination as a priest until in 934 he was named as Bishop of Constance to fill a vacancy which happened in that year. From his wealth he richly endowed the church at Constance as well as providing for the poor of his flock. For forty-two years he filled this sacred office, dying in 976 full of years and good works.

Thus with this day we complete the list of the Feasts, Fasts and Festivals of the Christian Church and mention of most of the holy men, whom both the Roman and Reformed Churches have honoured; though to keep within required limits I have been compelled to leave unmentioned not a few I would gladly have spoken of.

In concluding this series of articles I should not be doing justice if I failed to acknowledge the great obligations I am under to more than one of the reverend gentlemen connected with St. Bernard's Seminary for not alone placing at my service many rare and valuable books from the rich library of the Seminary, but far more than this ; their kindly suggestions as to where among these books I would find the information I desired and without which I many times would have been sadly at a loss for definite data.

It has been an ever-increasing debt, and one I cannot repay, made all the greater by the gentle, kindly hearts behind which constantly were ready to aid and advise me.

I also desire to acknowledge the references I have in many cases made to such valuable books as :

" Die Attribute der Hallinger Hanover, 1843 ;" " Conybeare and Housons ;" " Catholic Dictionary of Addis and Arnold ;" " Kirchenlexikon ; " " The Golden Legend," printed by Wynkin de Worde from the Latin of Jacobus de Viragine, and re-printed by T. Fisher Unwin with a preface by S. Baring-Gould and an introduction by John Ashton. " The Catalogus Sanctorum et Gestorum," etc. (1538). " The Lives of the Saints," by Dr. Alban Butler, and many other works I have tried to name as I quoted from them.

A Chronological List

OF THE

BISHOPS AND POPES

of the Christian Church from the death of St. Peter.

A. D.	
65	St. Peter.
65– 76	" Linus.
76– 89	" Cletus.
89–100	" Clement.
100–109	" Anacletus.
109–109	" Evaristus.
109–119	" Alexander.
119–128	" Sixtus I.
128–139	" Tilesphorus.
139–142	" Hyginus.
142–157	" Pius I.
157–168	" Anicetus.
168–176	" Soter.
176–192	" Eleutherius.
192–202	" Victor.
202–218	" Zephyrinus.
218–223	" Calistus.
223–230	" Urban.
230–235	" Pontian.
235–236	" Anterus.
236–250	" Fabianus.
251–252	" Cornelius.
252–253	" Lucius.

A. D.	
253–257	St. Stephen.
257–258	" Sixtus II.
259–269	" Dionysius.
269–275	" Felix.
275–283	" Eutychian.
283–296	" Caius.
296–304	" Marcellinus.
308–310	" Marcellus.
310–310	" Eusebius.
311–314	" Melchiades.
314–335	" Sylvester.
336–336	" Mark.
337–352	" Julius.
352–366	Liberius.
366–384	St. Damasus.
385–398	" Sericius.
399–402	" Anastasius.
402–417	" Innocent I.
417–418	" Zozimus.
418–422	" Boniface.
422–432	" Celestine.
432–440	" Sixtus III.
440–461	" Leo "The Great."

A. D.
461–468 St. Hilary.
468–483 " Simplicius.
483–492 " Felix II.* (or III?)
492–496 " Gelasius.
496–498 " Anastasius.
498–514 Symmachus.
514–523 Hormisdas.
523–526 St. John I.
526–529 Felix III.* (or IV.)
529–531 Boniface II.
532–535 John II.
535–536 Agapetus.
536–538 St. Sylverius.
538–555 Vigilius.
555–559 Pelagius I.
559–572 John III.
573–577 Benedict I.
577–590 Pelagius II.
590–604 St. Gregory "the Great."
604–605 Sabinian.
606–606 Boniface III.
607–614 Boniface IV.
614–617 Deusdedit or Adeodutus.
617–625 Boniface V.
626–638 Honorius I.
640–640 Severinus.
640–642 John IV.
642–649 Theodorus.
649–655 St. Martin.
655–658 Eugenius I.
658–672 Vitalian.
672–676 Adeodatus.

A. D.
676–679 Domnus.
679–682 St. Agatho.
682–683 " Leo II.
684–685 Benedict II.
685–686 John V.
686–687 Conon.
687–701 Sergius.
701–705 John VI.
705–707 John VII.
708–708 Sisinnius.
708–715 Constantine.
715–731 St. Gregory II.
731–741 Gregory III.
741–752 St. Zachery.
752–752 Stephen II. (four days)
752–757 Stephen III.
757–767 Paul I.
768–772 Stephen IV.
772–795 Adrian.
795–816 Leo III.
816–817 Stephen V.
817–824 Paschal.
824–827 Eugenius II.
827–827 Valentine.
828–844 Gregory IV.
844–847 Sergius II.
847–855 St. Leo IV.
855–858 Benedict III.
858–867 Nicholas I.
867–872 Adrian II.
872–882 John VIII.
882–884 Marin or Martin II.
884–885 Adrian III.
885–891 Stephen VI.

---

* See Dr. Alban Butler's "Lives of the Saints."

A. D.
891–896 Formosus.
896–897 Stephen VII.
897–898 Romanus.
898–898 Theodorus II.
898–900 John IX.
900–903 Benedict IV.
903–905 Leo V.
905–911 Sergius III.
911–913 Anastasius III.
913–914 Lando.
914–928 John X.
928–929 Leo VI.
929–931 Stephen VIII.
931–936 John XI.
936–939 Leo VII.
939–943 Stephen IX.
943–946 Martin III.
946–956 Agapetus II.
956–964 John XII.
964–964 Leo VIII.
964–965 Benedict V.
965–972 John XIII.
972–974 Benedict VI.
974–975 Domnus II.
976–984 Benedict VII.
984–985 John XIV.
986–996 John XV.*
996–999 Gregory V.
999–1003 Sylvester II.
1003–1003 John XVII.
1004–1009 John XVIII.
1009–1012 Sergius IV.
1012–1024 Benedict VIII.
1024–1033 John XIX.

A. D.
1033–1044 Benedict IX.
1045–1046 Gregory VI.
1046–1047 Clement II.
1048–1048 Damasus II.
1049–1054 St. Leo IX.
1055–1057 Victor II.
1057–1058 Stephen X.
1058–1061 Nicholas II.
1061–1073 Alexander II.
1073–1085 St. Gregory VII.
1086–1087 Victor III.
1087–1099 Urban II.
1099–1118 Paschal II.
1118–1119 Gelasius II.
1119–1124 Calixtus II.
1124–1130 Honorius II.
1130–1143 Innocent II.
1143–1144 Celestine II.
1144–1145 Lucius II.
1145–1153 Eugenius III.
1153–1154 Anastasius IV.
1154–1159 Adrian IV.
1159–1181 Alexander III.
1181–1185 Lucius III.
1185–1187 Urban III.
1187–1187 Gregory VIII.
1187–1191 Clement III.
1191–1198 Celestine III.
1198–1216 Innocent III.
1216–1227 Honorius III.
1227–1241 Gregory IX.
1241–1241 Celestine IV.
1243–1254 Innocent IV.
1254–1261 Alexander IV.

* John XVI., appears as an antipope 997–8, when he died.

A. D.
1261–1265 Urban IV.
1265–1268 Clement IV.
1271–1276 Gregory X.
1276–1276 Innocent V.
1276–1276 Adrian V.
1276–1277 John XX. or XXI.*
1277–1280 Nicholas III.
1281–1285 Martin IV.
1285–1287 Honorius IV.
1288–1292 Nicholas IV.
1294-1294 St. Peter Celestine V.
1294–1303 Boniface VIII.

The following Popes sat at Avignon.
1303–1304 Benedict XI.
1305–1314 Clement V.
1316–1334 John XXII.
1334–1342 Benedict XII.
1342–1352 Clement VI.
1352–1362 Innocent VI.
1362–1370 Urban V.
1370–1378 Gregory XI.

The following Popes sat at Rome while others sat at Avignon.
1378–1389 Urban VI.
1389– Boniface IX.

Contemporary Popes at Avignon

A. D.
1378–1394 Clement VII.
1394–1398 Benedict XII.
Who was chosen by the French and Spaniards.

In 1413 Benedict XIII. was restored, but deposed in 1417 when Clement VIII. was elected but not acknowledged.
1389–1404 Boniface IX. At Rome.
1404–1406 Innocent VII.
1406 Gregory XII.
1409 Gregory XII.
Deposed.
1409–1410 Alexander V.
1410 John XXIII.
1415 John XXIII.
Deposed.
1417–1431 Martin V.
1431–1447 Eugenius IV.
1447–1455 Nicholas V.
1455–1458 Calixtus III.
1458–1464 Pius II.
1464–1471 Paul II.
1471–1484 Sixtus IV.
1484–1492 Innocent VIII.
1492–1503 Alexander VI.
1503–1503 Pius III.
1503–1513 Julius II.
1513–1521 Leo X.
1522–1523 Adrian VI.
1523–1534 Clement VII.
1534–1549 Paul III.

* St. John XVI. as Antipope makes the succeeding numbers certain.

A. D.
1550-1555 Julius III.
1555-1555 Marcellus II.
1555-1559 Paul IV.
1559-1565 Pius IV.
1566-1572 St. Pius V.
1572-1585 Gregory XIII.
1585-1590 Sixtus V.
1590-1590 Urban VII.
1590-1591 Gregory XIV.
1591-1591 Innocent IX.
1592-1605 Clement VIII.
1605-1605 Leo XI.
1605-1621 Paul V.
1621-1623 Gregory XV.
1623-1644 Urban VIII.
1644-1655 Innocent X.
1655-1667 Alexander VII.
1667-1669 Clement IX.
1670-1676 Clement X.

A. D.
1676-1689 Innocent XI.
1689-1691 Alexander VIII.
1691-1700 Innocent XII.
1700-1721 Clement XI.
1721-1724 Innocent XIII.
1724-1730 Benedict XIII.
1730-1740 Clement XII.
1740-1758 Benedict XIV.
1758-1769 Clement XIII.
1769-1774 Clement XIV.
1775-1779 Pius VI.
1800-1823 Pius VII.
1823-1829 Leo XII.
1829-1830 Pius VIII.
1831-1846 Gregory XVI.
1846-1878 Pius IX.
1878-1903 Leo XIII.
1903 Pius X.

In the earlier days, the head or chief ruler of the Christian Church was termed Bishop.

The name Pope (Latin Papa, or Father) was, according to the Catholic dictionary: "given at first as a title of respect to ecclesiastics generally, and among the Greeks is to-day given *all* priests and was thus used as late as the Middle Ages by inferior clerics. In the West it seems very early to have become the spiritual title of Bishops. Even as late as the VI. century the title of Pope was given to all Metropolitans in the West. Gradually, however, the title was limited to the Bishops of Rome and we find a synod of Pavia in 998 rebuked an Archbishop of Milan, for calling himself Pope."

Gregory VII. at a Roman council in the year 1073 formally prohibited the use or assumption of this title by any other than Roman Bishops.

Alphabetical Index

OF

CANONIZED SAINTS AND OTHERS.

Letters indicate, A. Abbot; Ab. Archbishop; B. Bishop; C. Confessor*; H. Hermit or Anchorit; M. Martyr; R. Recluse; V. Virgin; V. A. Virgin Abbess.

The date indicates the day which the Roman Church has selected as their saint-day, or the day on which they are honoured.

A.

St. Aaron, A. June 21.
" Aaron, M. July 1.
" Abbam, A. Oct. 27.
" Abdon, M. July 30.
" Abraamius, B. M. Feby 5.
" Abraham, H. March 15.
" Abrogastus, B. C. July 2.
" Acepsimas, A. March 14.
St. Adalard, A. Jan. 2.
" Adalbert, B. M. April 23.
" Adamnan, A. Sept. 23.
" Adelbert, C. June 25.
" Adjustre, Sept. 30.
" Ado, B. C. Dec. 16.
" Adhelm, M. May 25.
" Adrian, M. Sept. 8.

---

* CONFESSOR—From the Dictionary of Addis and Arnold, I take the following: "Confessor. A name used from the earliest times for persons who *confessed* the Christian faith under persecution, thus exposing themselves to danger and suffering, but who did *not* undergo martyrdom. For a time the martyrs were the only saints who received special and public honour after death from the Church and Martyrs only (with the Blessed Virgin and the Apostles) are mentioned in the Canon of the Roman Mass, though the Cumbrosian Canon has the names of other saints also. But at the beginning of the IV. century public honours were also given to persons of heroic sanctity even if they had not been martyred. Thus St. Anthony, as St. Jerom tells us, directed that his body after death should be concealed, because he did not wish "Martyrium" enacted in his honour. Thus the name Confessor got the technical meaning which it now has in the Missal and Breviary—*i. e.*—it was applied to all male saints who did not fall under some special class, such as martyr, apostle, evangelist, etc. St. Martin, Bishop of Tours, who died in 397, was the first or among the very earliest of the Confessors that the church honoured with "an office and feast." In the office on Good Friday, the word "Confessor," means "singer" because in the Scriptures "confessing" to God—is used for singing his praises.

St. Adrian of Scotland, B. M. March 4.
" Adrian of Palestine, M. March 5.
" Adrian, A. Jan. 9.
" Adulph, M. June 17.
" Aëlred, A. Jan. 12.
" Æmilianus, M. Dec. 6.
" Ængus, B. C. March 11.
" Afra, M. Aug. 5.
" Agape, M. April 3.
" Agapetus, M. Aug. 18.
" Agapetus, Pope, C. Sept. 20.
" Agapius, M. Aug. 19.
" Agatha, V. M. Feb. 5.
" Agatho, Pope, Jan. 10.
" Agilbert, M. Jan. 25.
" Agilus, A. Aug. 30.
" Agnes, V. M. Jan. 21 and Jan. 28.
" Agnes of Monte Pulciano, V. A. April 20.
" Agoard, M. June 25.
" Agricola, M. Nov. 4.
" Agulus, B. C. Feb. 7.
" Aibert, B. April 7.
" Aicard, A. C. Sept. 15.
" Aid, A. April 11.
" Aidan of Mayo, B. Oct. 20.
" Aidan of Lindisfarne, B. C. Aug. 31.
" Aithilahas, M. March 24.
" Ajutre, R. C. April 30.
" Alban, Protomartyr of Britain, June 22.
Blessed Albert, Patriarch of Jerusalem, April 8.

St. Albeus, B. C. Sept. 12.
" Albinus, B. March 1.
" Alcmund, M. March 19.
" Alchmund, B. C. Sept. 7.
" Aldegondes, V. A. Jan. 30.
" Alden, (see Maidoc).
" Aldehelm, B. May 25.
" Aldric, B. C. Jan. 27.
" Alexander of Cæsarea, M. March 28.
" Alexander, B. of Jerusalem, M. March 18.
" Alexander, B. of Alexandria, C. Feb. 26.
" Alexander, Pope, M. May 3.
" Alice, or Adelaide of Cologne, V. A. Feb. 5.
" Alice or Adelaide, Empress of Germany, Dec. 16.
" Alipius, B. C. August 15.
" Almachus, M. Jan. 1.
" Aloysius Gonzaga, C. June 21.
" Alphæus, M. Nov. 18.
" Alphonsus Turibius, M. March 23.
" Alphonsus Liguori, Aug. 2.
" Alto, A. Sept. 5.
" Amand, B. C. June 18.
" Amandus, B. C. Feb. 6.
" Amator, B. C. May 1.
" Amatus of Sion, B. C. Sept. 13.
" Amatus of Loraine, A. Sept. 13.
" Ambrose, B. C. Dec. 7.
" Ambrose, B. of Milan, Apr. 4.

St. Ammon, H. Oct. 4.
" Amphilochius, B. C. Nov. 23.
" Anacletus, Pope, M. July 13.
" Anastasia, M. Dec. 25.
" Anastasia "the Elder," Dec. 24.
" Anastasius, M. Jan. 22.
" Anastasius "the Sinaite," Apl. 21.
" Anastasius, Patriarch, April 21.
" Anastasius "the Younger," B. M. April 21.
" Anastasius, Pope, C. April 27.
" Andeolus, M. May 1.
" Andrew Corsini, B. C. Feb. 4.
" Andrew of Crete, M. Oct. 17.
" Andrew Avellino, C. Nov. 10.
" Andrew, Apostle, Nov. 30.
" Angelus, M. May 5.
" Anian, B. C. Nov. 17.
" Anianus, B. April 25.
" Anicetus, Pope, M. April 17.
" Anysia, M. Dec. 30.
" Anne, Mother of the B. V. Mary, July 26.
" Anno, B. C. Dec. 4.
" Ansbert, B. C. Feb. 9.
" Anscharius, B. C. Feb. 3.
" Anselm, B. C. March 18.
" Anstrudis, V. A. Oct. 17.
" Anterus, Pope, Jan. 3.
" Anthelm, B. C. June 26.

St. Anthimus, B. M. April 27.
" Anthony of Padua, C. June 13.
" Anthony, M. April 14.
" Antipas, M. April 11.
" Antoninus, B. C. May 10.
" Antony (or Anthony), A. Jan. 17.
" Anthony Cauleas, B. C. Feb. 12.
" Aper, B. C. Sept. 15.
" Aphraates, H. April 7.
" Apian, M. April 2.
" Apollinaris, B. Jan. 8.
" Apollinaris, B. M. July 23.
" Apollinaris Sidonius, B. C. Aug. 23.
" Apollo, A. Jan. 25.
" Apollonia, V. M. Feb. 9.
" Apollonius in Egypt, M. March 8.
" Apollonius "the Apologist," M. April 18.
" Arbogastus, B. C. July 21.
" Arcadius, M. July 12.
" Archinimus, M. March 29.
" Armogastes, M. March 29.
" Arnoul of Soissons, B. C. Aug. 15.
" Arnoul, B. C. July 18.
" Arsenius, H. July 19.
" Artemius, M. Oct. 20.
" Augustine of England, B. C. May 26.
" Augustine of Hippo, Aug. 28.
" Aulanus, M. April 28.

St. Aunaire, B. Sept. 25.
" Aurea, V. A. Oct. 4.
" Aurelian, B. C. June 16.
" Austremonius, C. Nov. 1.
" Auxentius, H. Feb. 14.
" Azades, M. April 22.

B.

St. Babolen, A. June 26.
" Babylas, B. M. Jan. 24.
" Bademus, A. M. April 10.
" Bain, B. June 20.
" Baldrede, B. C. March 6.
" Barachius, M. March 29.
" Baradat, Solitary, Feb. 22.
" Barbara, V. M. Dec. 4.
" Barbasceminus, M. Jan. 14.
" Barbatus, B. C. Feb. 19.
" Barhadbesciabas, M. July 21.
" Barlaam, M. Nov. 19.
" Barnabas, Apostle, June 11.
" Barr, B. C. Sept. 25.
" Barsabias, M. Oct. 20.
" Barsanuphius, H. Feb. 6.
" Barsimæus, B. M. Jan. 30.
" Bartholomew of Dunelin, C. June 24.
" Bartholomew, Apostle, Aug. 24.
" Basil of Ancyra, M. March 22.
" Basil the Great, B. C. June 14.
" Basilides, Quirinus, etc., M. M. June 12.
" Basiliscus, M. May 22.
" Basilissa, M. April 15.

St. Bathildes, Queen of France, Jan. 30.
" Bavo, H. Oct. 1.
" Bauhus, M. Oct. 7.
" Beanus, B. Dec. 16.
" Becan, A. April 5.
" Becket (Thomas à), M. Dec. 29.
" Bede, C. May 27.
" Bega, V. Sept. 6.
" Begga, A. Dec. 17.
" Benedict Biscop, A. M. Jan. 12.
" Benedict of Anian, A. Feb. 12.
" Benedict, Patriarch of Western Monks, March 21.
" Benedict II., Pope, C. May 7.
" Benedict XI., Pope, C. July 7.
" Benezet, C. April 14.
" Benignus, M. Nov. 1.
" Benignus of Ireland, B. Nov. 9.
" Benjamin, M. March 31.
" Bernard of Menthon, C. June 15.
" Bernard of Clairvaux, A. Aug. 20.
" Bernard Ptolemy, C. Aug. 21.
" Bernardin of Sienna, C. May 20.
" Bernward, B. C. Nov. 20.
" Bertha, A. July 4.
" Bertille, A. Nov. 5.

St. Bertin, A. Sept. 5.
" Bertran, B. July 3.
" Bettelin, H. C. Sept. 9.
" Beuno, A. April 21.
" Bibiana, V. M. Dec. 2.
" Birinus, B. C. Dec. 3.
" Blaan, B. Aug. 10.
" Blaithmaic, A. Jan. 19.
" Blase, B. M. Feb. 3.
" Bobo, C. May 22.
" Boisil, C. Feb. 23.
" Bolcan, A. July 4.
" Bona, V. A. April 24.
" Bonasus, M. April 21.
" Bonaventure, B. C. July 14.
" Boniface, M (under Dioclesian), May 14.
" Boniface of Scotland, B. C. March 14.
" Boniface of Mentz, Apostle of Germany, June 5.
" Boniface of Magdeburg, Apostle of Russia, June 19.
" Boniface I., Pope, C. Oct. 25.
" Bonitus, B. Jan. 15.
" Bonosius, M. Aug. 21.
" Botulph, A. June 17.
" Braulio, B. C. March 26.
" Breaca, V. June 4.
" Brice, B. C. Nov. 13.
" Bridget or Bride, Patroness of Ireland, Feb. 1.
" Bridget of Sweden, Widow. Oct. 8.
" Brieuc, B. C. May 1.
" Brinstan, B. Nov. 4.
St. Brithwald, B. Jan. 9.
" Briocus of Wales, M. May 1.
" Bronacha, V. A. April 2.
" Bruno of Segni, B. C. July 18.
" Bruno, C. Oct. 6.
" Brynoth, B. C. May 9.
" Burckard, B. C. Oct. 14.
" Buriana, June 4.
Dr. Butler (Alban), Author. May 15.

C.

St. Cadoc or Cadroc, A. Jan. 24.
" Cadroe, C. March 6.
" Cæsarius, C. Feb. 25.
" Cæsarius, B. C. Aug. 27.
" Cæsarius, M. Nov. 1.
Poet Cædmon, Feb. 11.
St. Caius, Pope, Aug. 20.
" Cajetan, C. Aug. 7.
" Calais, A. July 1.
" Calixtus, Pope, M. Oct. 14.
" Callinicus, M. Jan. 28.
" Camillus de Lellis, C. July 14.
" Cammin, A. March 25.
" Canicus or Kenny, A. Oct. 11.
" Cantianus, M. May 31.
" Cantius, M. May 31.
" Canut, Jan. 7.
" Canutus, King, M. Jan. 19.
" Caradoc, H. April 13.
" Caraunus, M. May 28.
" Carpus, B. M. April 14.

St. Casimir "the Good", Earl of Flanders, C. Mar. 4.
" Cassian, M. Aug. 13.
" Castus, M. May 22.
" Cataldus, B. May 10.
" Cathan, B. C. May 17.
" Catharine of Alexandria, V. M. Nov. 25.
" Catharine of Bologna, V. Mar. 9.
" Catharine of Genoa, Widow, Sept. 14.
" Catharine of Sienna, V. April 30.
" Catharine of Sweden, V. Mar. 22.
" Catharine of Ricci, V. Feb. 13.
" Ceadda, B. M. Mar. 2.
" Cecilia or Cecily, V. M. Nov. 22.
" Cecilius, C. June 3.
" Cedd, B. Jan. 7.
" Celestine, Pope, C. April 6.
" Celsus, B. April 6.
" Ceolfrid, A. Sept. 25.
" Ceslas, C. July 20.
Chair of St. Peter, Antioch, Feb. 22.
Chair of St. Peter, Rome. Jan. 18.
Blessed Charlemagne, E. Jan. 28.
St. Charles "the Good", M. Mar. 2.
" Charles Borromeo, B. C. Nov. 4.
St. Charles V. of Rome, Aug. 11.
" Chef, A. Oct. 29.
" Chelidonius, M. Mar. 3.
" Chillen or Kilian, C. Nov. 13.
" Christina, V. M. July 24.
" Christopher, M. July 25.
" Chrodegang, B. C. Mar. 6.
" Chromatius, C. Aug. 11.
" Chronan, A. April 28.
" Chuniald, Priest, Sept. 24.
" Chrysanthus, M. Oct. 25.
" Chrysogonus, M. Nov. 24.
" Cianan, B. C. Nov. 24.
" Ciman, M. Dec. 12.
" Clare, V. A. Aug. 12.
(Founder of Order of Poor Clares).
St. Clare of Monte Falio, V. Aug. 18.
" Clarus, M. Nov. 4.
" Claud, B. M. June 6.
" Claudius, M. Aug. 23.
" Clement I., Pope, M. Nov. 23.
" Clement of Alexandria, B. C. Dec. 4.
" Clement, B. M. Jan. 23.
" Cletus, M. April 26.
" Clotildis, Queen of France, June 3.
" Clou, B. C. June 8.
" Cloud, C. Sept. 7.
" Coëmgen, B. C. June 3.
Blessed Collette, V. M. Mar. 6.
St. Colman, B. C. June 7.
" Colman Elo, A. C. Sept. 26.
" Colman, M. Oct. 13.

St. Colman, A. Dec. 12.
" Columba, Apostle of Picts, A. June 9.
" Columba, V. M. Sept. 17.
" Columba, V. M. Dec. 31.
" Columba, A. Dec. 12.
" Columban, A. C. Nov. 22.
" Comgall, A. May 10.
" Comgall, A. July 27.
" Conall, A. May 22.
" Concordius, M. July 2.
" Conon, B. Jan. 26.
" Conon and Son, MM. May 29.
" Conrad, B. C. Nov. 26.
" Conran, B. C. Feb. 14.
" Constant, C. Nov. 13.
Blessed Constantine, King of Scotland, M. April 2.
St. Constantine (supposed to have been a king in Britain), Mar. 14.
" Constantine, one of the Seven Sleepers, July 27.
" Corbinian, B. C. Sept. 8.
" Corentin, B. C. Dec. 12.
" Cormac, B. C. Sept. 14.
" Cormac, A. Dec. 12.
" Cornelius, Pope, M. Sept. 16.
" Cosmas, M. Sept. 27.
" Crispin, M. Oct. 25.
" Crispinian, M. Oct. 25.
" Crispina, M. Dec. 5.
SS. Crowned Brothers, MM. Nov. 8.
St. Cucufas, M. July 25.
St. Cumin, B. Aug. 19.
" Cunegunda, Empress, Mar. 3.
" Cuthbert, B. C. March 30.
" Cuthbert, Translation of Relics, Sept. 4.
" Cuthburge, Q. Aug. 31.
" Cuthman, Founder of the Order of Trinitarians, Feb. 8.
" Cybar, R. July 1.
" Cyprian, B. M. Sept. 16.
" Cyprian, M. Sept. 26.
" Cyriacus, M. Aug. 8.
" Cyrian of Carthage, M. Sept. 16.
" Cyril, Patriarch of Alexandria, Jan. 28.
" Cyril, Ab. of Jerusalem. Mar. 18.
" Cyril, M. May 20.
" Cyril, M. C. Dec. 22.
" Cyrus, M. Jan. 31.

D.

St. Dabius, C. July 22.
" Damasus, Pope, C. Dec. 11.
" Damhnade, V. June 13.
" Damian, M. Sept. 27.
" Daniel, M. Feb. 21.
" Daniel, B. C. Nov. 23.
" Daniel, the Stylite, C. Dec. 11.
" Daria, M. Oct. 25.
" Datira, M. Dec. 6.
" Daterus, M. Feb. 11.

St. David, of Wales, B. March 1.
" David, Patron of Muscovy, July 24.
" Declan, B. July 24.
" Deicolus, A. Jan. 18.
" Delphine, M. Sept. 27.
" Dennis, see Dionysius.
" Desiderius, B. M. May 23.
" Deusdedit, C. Aug. 10.
" Didacus, C. Nov. 13.
" Didymus, M. April 28.
" Die, or Dio, B. June 19.
SS. Dionysia and Dativa, MM. Dec. 6.
St. Dionysius, the Areopagite, B. M. Oct. 3.
" Dionysius of Alexandria, B. Nov. 17.
" Dionysius of Corinth, B. M. April 8.
" Dionysius, or Dennis of Paris, M. Oct. 9.
" Dionysius, Pope, C. Dec. 26.
" Dionysius, One of the Seven Sleepers, July 27.
" Disen, B. C. Sept. 8.
" Docmail, C. June 14.
" Dominic, Founder of the Order of Friar Preachers, Aug. 4.
" Dominic Loricatus, C. Oct. 14.
" Domninus, M. Oct. 9.
" Donatian, B. C. Oct. 14.
" Donatus, B. C. Oct. 22.
" Donatus, B. M. Aug. 7.
St. Dorotheus, of Tyre, M. June 6.
" Dorothy, V. M. Feb. 6.
" Dositheus, Monk, Feb. 23.
" Dotto, A. April 9.
" Droctrovius, A. March 10.
" Drostan, A. July 11.
" Druon, B. April 16.
" Dubricius, B. C. Nov. 14.
" Dumhade, A. May 25.
" Dunstan, B. C. May 19.
" Duthak, B. C. March 8.
" Dympna, V. M. May 15.

E.

St. Eadbert, B. C. May 6.
" Eadburge, A. Dec. 12.
" Eanswide, V. A. Sept. 12.
" Ebba, M. April 2.
" Ebba or Abba of Coldingham, V. A. Aug. 25.
" Ecrigan, King of Scotland. April 21.
" Edana, V. July 5.
" Edburge, V. Dec. 21.
" Edelburga, V. July 7.
" Edelwald, C. March 23.
" Editha, V. Sept. 16.
" Edmund, King of England, M. Nov. 20.
" Edmund, B. C. Nov. 16.
" Edward, King of England, M. March 18.
" Edward, King, Translation of Relics of the Confessor, June 20.

St. Edward "the Confessor," King, Oct. 3.
" Edwin, King of Northumbria, Oct. 4.
" Egwin, B. Jan. 11.
" Eingan, C. April 21.
" Elesbaan, King of Ethiopia, C. Oct. 27.
" Eleutherius, B. M. Feb. 20.
" Eleutherius, Pope, M. May 26.
" Elias, M. Feb. 16.
" Elier, H. M. July 16.
" Eligius, B. C. Dec. 1.
" Elizabeth of Hungary, Widow, Nov. 19.
" Elizabeth, Queen of Portugal, July 8.
" Elizabeth of Sconauge, V. A. June 18.
" Elizian, M. Sept. 27.
" Elphege, B. M. April 19.
" Elphege "the Bald," B. April 19.
" Elzear, M. Sept. 27.
" Emerentiana, V. M. Jan. 23.
" Emiliana, V. M. Dec. 24.
" Emmeran, B. M. Sept. 22.
" Enna, A. March 21.
" Ennodius, B. C. July 17.
" Enric, Nov. 4.
" Ephrem, Deacon, C. July 9.
" Epimachus, M. Dec. 12.
" Epiphanius of Pavia, B. Jan. 21.
" Epiphanius of Salamis, B. May 12.

St. Epipodius, M. April 22.
" Equitius, A. Aug. 11.
" Erasmus of Antioch, B. M. Nov. 25.
" Erasmus, B. M. June 2.
" Erhard, A. C. Feb. 9.
" Eric, King of Sweden, M. May 18.
" Erlulph, B. M. Feb. 10.
" Eskill, B. M. June 12.
" Ethbin, A. Oct. 19.
" Ethelbert, King of Anglia, M. May 20.
" Ethelbert, first Christian king in Britain, C. Feb. 24.
" Ethelburge of Barking, V. A. Oct. 11.
" Etheldreda or Audry, V. A. June 23.
" Etheldreda or Audry, of Ely, V. A. Oct. 17.
" Etheldritha, V. Aug. 2.
" Ethelwold, B. C. Aug. 1.
" Eubulus, March 1.
" Eucherius, B. C. Feb. 20.
" Eucherius, B. C. Nov. 16.
" Eugendus, A. Jan. 1.
" Eugenia, V. M. Dec. 25.
" Eugenius, B. C. July 13.
" Eugenius, of Ireland, B. Aug. 23.
" Eugenius of Paris, M. Nov. 15.
" Eulalia, V. M. Dec. 10.
" Eulogius, M. March 11.

St. Eulogius, Patriarch of Alexandria, B. C. Sept. 13.
" Eunan, B. Sept. 7.
" Euphemia, V. M. Sept. 16.
" Euphrasia, V. March 13.
" Euplius, M. Aug. 12.
" Eusebius, M. at Gaza, Sept. 8.
" Eusebius, B. M. June 21.
" Eusebius, A. Jan. 23.
" Eusebius, M. at Rome, Aug. 14.
" Eusebius, C. Aug. 14.
" Eusebius, Pope, C. Sept. 26.
" Eustachius, M. Sept. 20.
" Eustasius, A. March 29.
" Eustathius, B. C. July 16.
" Eustochium, V. Sept. 28.
" Eustochius, B. Sept. 19.
" Euthymius, A. Jan. 20.
" Eutropius, M. Jan. 12.
" Evaristus, Pope, M. Oct. 26.
" Everildis, V. July 9.
" Evertius, B. C. Sept. 7.
" Evroul, A. Dec. 20.
" Ewalds (The Two) MM. Oct 3.
" Exuperius, B. Sept. 28.

F.

St. Fabian, Pope, M. Jan. 20.
" Faine, see Fanchea.
" Faith of Rome, V. M. Aug. 1.
" Faith of Gaul, V. M. Oct. 6.
" Fanchea, V. Jan. 1.
" Fara, V. A. Dec. 7.
" Faro, B. C. Oct. 28.
St Faustinus, M. July 29.
" Faustus, M. Oct. 13.
" Fechin, A. Jan. 20.
" Fedlemid, B. C. Aug. 9.
" Felan, A. Jan. 9.
" Felicitas, M. March 7.
" Felix of Nola, Priest, Jan. 14.
" Felix, B. C. Aug. 9.
" Felix of Cantalicio, C. May 21.
" Felix I, Pope, M. May 30.
" Felix, Pope, M. July 29.
" Felix of Nantes, B. C. July 7.
" Felix of Carthage, M. Sept. 10.
" Felix of Dunwich, M. Mar. 8.
" Felix of Thiabura, B. M. Oct. 24.
" Felix of Valois, C. Nov. 20.
" Ferdinand III., King of Castile and C. May 30.
" Ferreol, M. Sept. 18.
" Ferreolus, M. June 16.
" Ferrutius, M. June 16.
" Fiachna, C. April 29.
" Fiaker, H. C. Aug. 30.
" Fidelis of Sigmaringen, M. April 24.
" Fidharleus, A. Oct. 1.
" Finan of Lindisfarne, C. April 7.
" Finbar, A. July 4.
" Finian "the Leper" Mar. 16.

St. Finian, B. C. Sept. 10.
" Finian, A. Oct. 21.
" Finian, B. C. Dec. 12.
" Fintan, A. Feb. 17.
" Fintan, A. Oct. 21.
" Flavia Domitilla, V. M. May 12.
" Flavian, B. M. Feb. 17.
" Flora, V. M. Nov. 24.
" Florence (An Irish Saint) A. Dec. 15.
" Flour, B. C. Nov. 3.
" Foilan, M. Oct. 31.
" Forty Martyrs of Sebaste, March 10.
" Four Crowned Brothers, M. Nov. 8.
" Francis of Assisium, C. Oct. 4.
" Francis Borgia, C. Oct. 10.
" Francis di Girolamo, May 11.
" Francis of Paula, C. April 2.
" Francis of Sales, B. C. Jan. 29.
" Francis Solano, C. July 24.
" Francis, Stigmas of, Oct. 4.
" Francis Xavier, C. Dec. 3.
" Frances, Widow, March 9.
" Frederick of Utrecht, B. M. July 18.
SS. Friar Minors, The Five, M M. July 6.
" Friar Minors, The Seven, MM. Oct. 13.
St. Frideswide, Patroness of Oxford, V. Oct. 19.
" Fridian, B. C. March 18.
" Fridolin, C. March 6.
SS. Fructuosus, B. and others, MM. Jan. 21.
St. Fructuosus, B. C. April 16.
" Frumentius, B. C. Oct. 27.
" Fulgentius, B. C. Jan. 1.
" Fursey, A. and an Irish King Jan 16.
" Fuscian, M. Dec. 11.

G.

St. Gal, B. July 1.
" Galdin, B. C. April 18.
" Galdus, B. Jan. 31.
" Gall, A. Oct. 16.
" Galla, Widow, Oct. 5.
" Galmier, C. Feb. 27.
" Gamaliel, C. Aug. 3.
" Gatian, B. C. Dec. 18.
" Gaucher, A. April 9.
" Gaudentius of Brescia, B. C. Oct. 25.
" Gelasinus, M. Aug. 26.
" Gelasius, Pope, C. Nov. 21.
" Genebrard, M. May 15.
" Genesius, B. C. June 3.
" Genesius, M. Aug. 26.
" Genesius, of Arles, M. Aug. 26.
" Genevieve, V. Jan. 3.
" George, Patron of England, M. April 23.
" Gerald, B. March 13.
" Gerald, A. April 5.

St. Gerald, Count of Aurillac, C. Oct. 13.
" Gerard of Tours, B. C. Apr. 23.
" Gerard of Chonad, B. M. Sept. 24.
" Gerard, A. Oct. 3.
" Gerimonia, Sept. 7.
" German, M. Feb. 21.
" Germanus, Patriarch of Constantinople, B. May 12.
" Germanus, B. C. May 28.
" Germanus of Auxerre, B. C. July 26.
" Germanus of Capua, B. C. Oct. 30.
" Germer, A. Sept. 24.
" Gertrude, V. A. Nov. 15.
" Gervasius, M. June 19.
" Gery, B. C. Aug. 11.
SS. Getulius and others, MM. June 10.
St. Gilasinus, M. Aug. 26.
" Gilbert, A. Feb. 4.
" Gilbert, B. April 1.
" Gildard, B. C. June 6.
" Gildas "the Wise," A. Jan. 29.
" Gildas, "the Albanian," C. Jan. 29.
" Giles, A. Sept. 1.
" Glastian of Scotland, B. Jan. 23.
" Goar, C. July 6.
" Gobain, M. June 20.
" Godard, B. C. May 4
St. Godeschalc, Prince of the Western Vandals, M. June 7.
" Godfrey of Amiens, B. Nov. 8.
" Godric, H. May 21.
" Gontran, King of Burgundy, C. Mar. 28.
" Gregory, B. Jan. 4.
" Gregory II. Pope, C. Feb. 13.
" Gregory X. Pope, C. Feb. 16.
" Gregory of Nyssa, B. C. Mar. 9.
" Gregory "the Great" Pope, C. Mar. 12.
" Gregory Nazianzen, B. C. May 9.
" Gregory VII. Pope, C. May. 25.
Blessed Gregory, B. C. June 15.
St. Gregory of Ulnith, A. C. Aug. 25.
" Gregory, Apostle of Armenia, B. C. Sept. 30.
" Gregory Thaumaturgus, B. C. Nov. 17.
" Gregory of Tours, B. C. Nov. 17.
" Gregory, M. Dec. 24.
" Grimbald, A. July 8.
" Grimonia, V. A. C. Sept. 7.
" Gudula, V. Jan. 8.
" Gudwall, A. Oct. 9.
" Gummar, C. Oct. 11.
" Gundleus, C. Mar. 29.
" Gunthiern, A. July 9.
" Guthlake, H. April 11.

St. Guy, C. March 31.
" Guy, C. Sept. 12.
" Gybrian, Priest, C. May 8.

H.

" St. Harold VI. of Denmark, King, M. Nov. 1.
" Hedda, B. C. July 7.
" Hedwiges, Widow, Oct. 17.
" Hegesippus, C. April 7.
" Helen, M. July 31.
" Helen, Empress, Aug. 18.
" Hemma, Widow, June 29.
" Henry, H. Jan. 16.
" Henry of England, Blessed, B. M. Jan. 19.
" Henry of Treviso, C. June 10.
" Henry II., Emperor of Germany, July 15.
Blessed Herman Joseph, C. April 7.
St. Hermas, C. May 9.
" Hermenegild, M. April 13.
" Hermes, M. Aug. 28.
" Hidulphus, B. July 11.
" Hilarion, A. Oct. 21.
" Hilary, B. Jan. 14.
" Hilary of Arles, B. C. May 5.
" Hilda, A. Nov. 18.
" Hildegardis of Monte St. Disibode, V. A. Sept. 17.
" Hippolytus, M. Aug. 13.
" Hippolytus, Early Author, B. M. Aug. 22.
" Homobonus, C. Nov. 13.
St. Honoratus, B. Jan. 16.
" Honoratus, B. C. May 16.
" Honorius, B. C. Sept. 30.
" Hope of Rome, M. Aug. 1.
" Hormisdas, M. Aug. 8.
" Hospitius, R. Oct. 15.
" Hubert of Liege, B. C. Nov. 3.
" Hugh of Lincoln, M. Aug. 27.
" Hugh, B. C. April 1.
" Hugh of Cluni, A. C. Aug. 29.
" Hugh of Lincoln, B. C. Nov. 17.
" Humbert, B. M. Nov. 20.
" Hyacinth, C. Aug. 16.
" Hyacinthus, M. Sept. 11.
" Hyginus, Pope, M. Jan. 11.

I.

St. Ibar, B. April 23.
" Ida, Widow, Sept. 4.
" Idaberga, V. June 20.
" Idus, B. July 14.
" Ignatius, B. M. Feb. 1.
" Ignatius Loyola, C. July 31.
" Ignatius, Patriarch of Constantinople, Oct. 23.
" Ildephonsus, B. Jan. 23.
" Illidius, B. C. June 5.
" Iltutus, A. Nov. 6.
" Innocent I., Pope, C. July 28.
" Irchard, B. C. Aug. 24.
" Irenæus of Sirmium, B. M. March 24.

St. Irenæus, B. M. June 28.
" Isaac, B. M. Nov. 30.
" Isabel, V. Aug. 31.
" Ischyrion, M. Dec. 22.
" Isaias, M. Jan. 14.
" Isidore, Hospitaler of Alexandria, Priest, Jan. 15.
" Isidore of Scete, H. Jan. 15.
" Isidore of Pelusium, Monk, Feb. 4.
" Isidore, Patron of Madrid, C. May 10.
" Isidore of Seville, B. April 4.
" Ita, V. Jan. 15.
" Ivia, B. April 25.

J.

St. James of Sclavonia, C. April 20.
" James, M. April 30.
" James, "the Less" Apostle, May 1.
" James, "Major," Apostle, July 25.
" James of Nisibis, B. C. July 11.
" James (Intercisus) M. Nov. 27.
" James La Marca of Ancona, C. Nov. 28.
" Jane, or Joan of Valois, Queen of France, Feb. 4.
" Jane Frances de Chantal, Widow, Abbess, Aug. 21.

St. Januarius and others, B. M. M. Sept. 19.
" Januarius of Cordova, M. Oct. 13.
" Jariat, B. C. Dec. 26.
" Jeremy, Cæsarea, M. Feb. 16.
" Jerom Æmiliani, C. July 20.
" Jerom, Priest, Doctor of the Church, C. Sept. 30.
" Joachim, C. April 16.
" Jonas, M. March 29.
" Joannicius, A. Nov. 4.
" Joavan, B. C. March 2.
" Jodoc, C. Dec. 13.
" John, "the Almoner" Patriarch, Jan. 23.
" John Calybite, R. Jan. 15.
" John Chrysostom, B. C. Jan. 27.
" John of Rheomay, A. Jan. 28.
" John of Matha, C. Feb. 8.
" John Joseph of the Cross, March 5.
" John of God, C. March 8.
" John of Egypt, B. March 27.
" John Climacus, A. Mar. 30.
" John at Latin gate, May 6.
" John Damascen, C. May 6.
" John of Beverley, B. C. May 7.
" John "the Silent." B. C. May 13.
" John Nepomucen, M. May 16.
" John of Prado, M. May 24.

St. John, Pope, M. May 27.
" John of Sahagun, C. June 12.
" John Francis Regis, C. June 16.
" John of Rome, M. June 26.
" John of Moutier, Priest, C. June 27.
" John, one of the "Seven Sleepers," July 27.
" John Gualbert, A. July 12.
" John Columbini, C. July 31.
" John the Baptist, Nativity of, June 24.
" John the Baptist, Decollation of, Aug. 29.
" John "the Dwarf," R. Sept. 15.
" John of Bridlington, C. Oct. 10.
" John Capistran, C. Oct. 23.
" John Lateran, Dedication of the Church, Nov. 9.
" John of the Cross, C. Nov. 24.
Blessed John Marinoul, C. Dec. 13.
St. John, Apostle, Evangelist, Dec. 27.
SS. Jonas and others, MM. March 29.
St. Joseph of Leonissa, C. Feb. 4.
" Joseph of Arimathea, Mar. 17.
" Joseph, Husband of the Virgin Mary, Mar. 19.
St. Joseph Barsabas, C. July 20.
" Joseph Calasanctius, C. Aug. 27.
" Joseph of Cupertino, C. Sept. 18.
" Jude, Apostle, Oct. 28.
" Julia, V. M. May 23.
" Julian, M. Jan. 9.
" Julian of Manns, B. Jan. 27.
" Julian of Palestine, M. Feb. 17.
" Julian of Toledo, B. C. Mar. 8.
" Julian of Cilicia, M. Mar. 16.
" Julian, H. July 6.
" Julian Sabas, H. Oct. 18.
" Julian, M. Aug. 28.
" Juliana, V. M. Feb. 16.
" Juliana Falconieri, V. June 19.
" Julitta, M. July 30.
" Julius, Pope, C. April 12.
" Julius, M. May 27.
SS. Julius and Aaron, MM. July 1.
" Justa and Rufina, MM. July 20.
St. Justin, M. June 1.
" Justin, M. Oct. 18.
" Justina, V. M. Oct. 7.
" Justinian, H. M. Aug. 23.
" Justus, B. C. Sept. 2.
SS. Justus and Pastor, MM. Aug. 6.
St. Justus, B. C. Nov. 10.
SS. Juventin and Maximin, MM. Jan. 25.

K.

St. Kebius B. April 25.
" Kenelm, King of Mercia, M. Dec. 13.
" Kenney, A. Oct. 11.
" Kennocha, V. March 13.
" Kentigern, B. Jan. 13.
" Kentigerna, Widow, Jan. 7.
" Keyna, V. Oct. 8.
" Kiaran, B. C, March 5.
" Kiaran, A. Sept. 9.
SS. Kilian, Colman and others MM. July 8.
St. Kings, V. July 24.
" Kinnia, V. Feb. 1.
SS. Kyneburge, Kyneswide etc. MM. March 6.

L.

St. Ladislas, King of Hungary, C. June 27.
" Lamalisse, C. March 2.
" Lambert, B. M. Sept. 17.
" Landelin, A. June 15.
" Landry, B. C. June 10.
" Largus, M. Aug. 8.
" Laserian, B. April 18.
" Laurence of Canterbury, B. Feb. 2.
" Laurence the Spaniard, M, Aug. 10.
" Laurence Justinian, B. C. Sept. 5.
" Laurence of Dublin, B. C. Nov. 14.
" Lea, Widow, March 22.
St. Leander, B. C. Feb. 27.
" Lebwin, C. Nov. 12.
" Leo, M. Feb. 18.
" Leo the Great, Pope, April 11.
" Leo IX., Pope, C. April 19.
" Leo II., Pope, C. June 28.
" Leo IV., Pope, C. July 17.
" Leocadia, V. M. Dec. 9.
" Leocritia, M. March 15.
" Leodegarius, B. M. Oct. 2.
" Leonard, H. Nov. 6.
" Leonides, M. April 22.
" Leonorus, B. July 1.
" Leopold, Marquis of Margams, Austria, C. Nov. 15.
" Lethard, B. C. Feb. 24.
" Leucius, M. (245) Jan. 28.
" Leufredus, A. June 21.
" Lewine, V. M. July 24.
" Lewis, B. C. Aug. 19.
" Lewis, King of France (see Louis).
" Liberatus, M. Aug. 17.
" Liborius, B. C. July 23.
" Licinius, B. C. Feb. 13.
" Lidwina, V. April 14.
" Lifard, A. June 3.
" Limneus, M. Feb. 22.
" Linus, Pope, M. Sept. 23.
" Lioba, V. A. Sept. 28.
" Livin, B. M. Nov. 12.
" Lo, B. Sept. 21.
" Loman, B. C. Feb. 17.
" Lomer, A. Jan. 19.

St. Louis, King of France, C. Aug. 25.
" Luanus, A. Aug. 4.
" Lucia, M. Sept. 16.
" Lucian, Priest, Jan. 7.
" Lucian of Beauvais, M. Jan. 8.
" Lucian of Nicomedia, M. Oct. 26.
" Lucius, Pope, M. Mar. 4.
" Lucius, M. (166) Oct. 19.
" Lucius, an early king of Britain, C. Sept. 19.
" Lucy, V. Sept. 19.
" Lucy, V. M. Dec. 13.
" Ludger, B. March 26.
" Luican, C. July 27.
" Luke, Evangelist, Oct. 18.
" Lullus, B. C. Oct. 16.
" Lupicinius, M. Feb. 28.
" Lupus of Troyes, B. C. July 24.
" Lupus of Sens, Archb. Sept. 1.

M.

" Macarius of Alexandria, H. Jan. 2.
" Macarius "the Elder," Jan. 16.
" Maccai, A. April 11.
" Mac-cartin, B. C. Aug. 15.
" Macedonius, A. Jan. 24.
SS. Machabees, "the Seven," MM. Aug. 1.
St. Mackessoge, B. C. Mar. 10.
" Macrina, V. July 19.

St. Macull, C. April 25.
" Maculindus, B. Sept. 16.
" Madelberte, V. A. Sept. 7.
" Maden, C. May 17.
" Magloire, B. C. Oct. 24.
" Magnisius. B. Sept. 3.
" Maguil, May 30.
" Maharsapor, M. Nov. 27.
" Maidoc, (also called Alden), B. Jan. 31.
" Maieul, A. May 11.
" Main, A. Jan. 15.
" Majoricus, M. Dec. 6.
" Malchus of Cæsarea, M. March 28.
" Malchus, one of the Seven Sleepers, July 27.
" Malachy, B. C. Nov. 3.
" Malo, B. November 15.
" Malrubius, A. April 21.
" Malrubius, B. M. August 27.
" Mamas, M. August 17.
" Mammertus, B. C. May 11.
" Mammolin, M. October 16.
" Mans or Magnus of Orkney, B. M. April 16.
" Mansuet, B. Sept. 3.
" Marcella, Widow, Jan. 31.
" Marcellina, V. July 17.
" Marcellinus, M. June 2.
" Marcellus, Pope, M. Jan. 16.
" Marcellus, M. Sept. 4.
" Marcellus, M. Oct. 7.
" Marcellus, M. Oct. 30.
" Marcellus, B. C. Nov. 1.
" Marcellus, A. Dec. 29.
" Marcian, Priest, Jan. 10.

St. Marcian, M. Oct. 4.
" Marcian, H. C. Nov. 2.
" Marciana, V. A. Jan. 9.
" Marcou, A. May 1.
" Marcus, M. June 18.
" Marcus, M. Oct. 4.
Blessed Margaret, Princess of Hungary, V. Jan. 28.
St. Margaret, Queen of Scotland, June 10.
" Margaret of England (XII. century), V. Feb. 3.
" Margaret of Cortona, Penitent, Feb. 22.
" Margaret of Antioch, V. M. July 20.
" Margaret, V. M. Sept. 2.
" Marina, V. June 18.
" Marinus, M. March 3.
" Maris, M. Jan. 19.
" Marius, A. Jan. 27.
" Mark of Arethusa, Syria, B. C. March 29.
" Mark, Evangelist, April 25.
" Mark, Pope, C. Oct. 7.
" Mark of Jerusalem, B. C. Oct. 22.
" Marnan, B. C. March 2.
" Maro, A. Feb. 14.
" Martha, V. July 29.
" Martial, B. June 30.
" Martin of Tours, B. C. Nov. 11.
" Martin, Pope, M. Nov. 12.
" Martina, V. M. Jan. 30.
" Martinian, one of the Seven Sleepers, July 27.
St. Martinanus, H. Feb. 13.
SS. Martyrs for the Holy Scriptures, Jan. 2.
Martyrs of Japan, Feb. 5.
Martyrs of Alexandria (in the pestilence) Feb. 28.
Martyrs Forty, of Sebaste, Mar. 10.
Martyrs of Alexandria in 303, March 17.
Martyrs of Hadiab, April 6,
Martyrs of Massylitan, April 9.
Martyrs, Roman Captives, April 9.
Martyrs of Saragossa, April 16.
Martyrs of Rome, under Nero, June 24.
Martyrs of Gorcum, July 9.
Martyrs, Seven Brothers, July 10.
Martyrs, Seven Sleepers, July 27.
Martyrs of Utica, Aug. 24.
Martyrs, Twelve Brothers, Sept. 1.
Martyrs of Triers, Oct. 4.
Martyrs, Seven, of Samosata, Dec. 9.
Martyrs, Ten, of Crete, Dec. 23.
St. Maruthas, B. C. Dec. 4.
Mary, B. V. Purification of, Feb. 2.
Mary, B. V. Annunciation of, March 25.
Mary, B. V. Visitation of, July 2.
Mary, B. V. ad Nives, Aug. 5.

Mary, B. V. Assumption of, Aug. 15.
Mary, B. V. Nativity of, Sept. 8.
Mary, B. V. Presentation of, Nov. 21.
Mary, B. V. Conception of, Dec. 8.
St. Mary of Egypt, April 9.
" Mary of Pazzi, V. May 23.
" Mary, niece of St. Abraham, Penitent, March 15.
" Mary of Oignies, June 23.
" Mary Magdalen "the Sinner," July 22.
" Mary, M. Nov. 1.
" Mary of Cordova, V. M. Nov. 24.
" Matthew, Apostle, Sept. 21.
" Matthias, Apostle, Feb. 24.
" Mathurin, C. Nov. 9.
" Maud, Queen of Germany, March 14.
" Maura, V. Sept. 21.
" Maurice, M. Sept. 22.
" Maurilius, B. C. Sept. 13.
" Mauront, A. May 5.
" Maurus, A. Jan. 15.
" Maw, C. May 17.
" Maxentia, V. M. Nov. 21.
" Maxentius, A. June 26.
" Maximian, one of the Seven Sleepers, M. July 27.
" Maximilian, M. March 12.
" Maximinus, B. C. May 29.
" Maximinus, B. C. June 8.
" Maximus, M. April 30.
St. Maximus of Normandy, M. May 25.
" Maximus, B. C. June 25.
" Maximus of Riez, B. C. Nov. 27.
" Maximus, C. Dec. 30.
" Mechtildes, V. A. April 10.
" Medard, B. C. June 8.
" Mel, Feb. 6.
" Meen, A. June 21.
" Melania "the Younger," Dec. 31.
" Melanius, B. C. Jan. 6.
" Melchiades, Pope, Dec. 10.
" Meleusippus, M. Jan. 17.
" Melito, B. C. April 1.
" Mellitus, B. C. April 24.
" Mello, B. C. Oct. 22.
" Memmius, B. Aug. 5.
" Meneve, A. July 22.
" Mennas, M. Nov. 11.
" Merriadec, B. C. June 7.
" Merri, A. Aug. 29.
" Methodius, Patriarch of Constantinople, C. June 14.
" Methodius of Tyre, B. M. Sept. 18.
" Methodius, C. Dec. 22.
" Michael, Apparition of, May 8.
" Michael, Dedication of, Sept. 29.
" Milburge of Shropshire, V. A. Feb. 23.
" Mildred, V. A. Feb. 20.
" Milgithe, V. Jan. 17.
" Milles, B. M. Nov. 10.

St. Mitrius, M. Nov. 13.
" Mochoemoc, A. Mar. 13.
" Mochteus, B. C. Aug. 19.
" Mochua or Cronan of Bella, Ireland, A. Jan. 1.
" Modan, A. Feb. 4.
" Modomnoc, B. C. Feb. 13.
" Modwena, V. July 5.
" Molingus, B. C. June 17.
" Moloc, B. C. June 25.
" Monan, M. March 1.
" Monegondes, R. July 2.
" Monica, Widow, May 4.
" Moninna, V. July 6.
" Monon, M. Oct. 18.
" Montanus, M. Feb. 24.
" Mummolin, B. C. Oct. 16.
" Munde, A. April 15.
" Mungo, see Kentigern.
" Muredack, B. Aug. 12.

N.

St. Nabor, M. July 12.
" Narcissus, M. Oct. 29.
" Nathalan, B. C. Jan. 8.
" Nathy, Priest, Aug. 9.
" Nazarius, M. July 28.
" Nemesianus, M. Sept. 10.
" Nemesion, M. Dec. 19.
" Nennius, A. Jan. 17.
" Nennus of Aran, A. June 14.
" Nenoc, V. June 4.
" Neot, H. C. Oct. 28.
" Nereus, M. May 12.
" Nestabulus of Gaza, M. Sept. 8.
" Nestor of Gaza, M. Sept. 8.
St. Nestor, B. M. Feb. 27.
" Nicander, M. June 17.
" Nicasius, B. M. Dec. 14.
" Nicephorus, M. Feb. 9.
" Nicephorus, Patriarch of Constantinople, C. Mar. 13.
" Nicetas, A. April 3.
" Nicetas, M. Sept. 15.
" Nicetius, B. C. April 2.
" Nicetius, B. C. Dec. 5.
" Nicholas of Lincopen, B. C. May 9.
" Nicholas of Tolentino, C. Sept. 10.
" Nicholas, B. C. Dec. 6.
" Nicodemus, Aug. 3.
" Nicomedes, M. Sept. 15.
" Nicon, C. Nov. 26.
" Nilammon, H. Jan. 6.
" Nilus "the Younger," A. Sept. 26.
" Nilus, H. C. Nov. 12.
" Nincon, Jan. 4.
" Ninian, B. C. Sept. 16.
" Nissen, A. July 25.
" Norbert, B. C. June 6.
" Nunilo, V. M. Oct. 22.
" Nympha, V. M. Nov. 10.

O.

St. Odilo or Olon, A. Jan. 1.
" Odo, B. C. July 4.
" Odo, A. C. Nov. 18.
" Odrian, B. May 8.
" Odulph, C. July 18.

St. Oduvald or Odwald, A. C. May 26.
" Olaus, King of Norway, M. July 29.
" Olmypias, Widow, Dec. 17.
" Omer, B. C. Dec. 9.
" Onesimus, disciple of St. Paul, Feb. 16.
" Onuphrius, H. June 12.
" Oportuna, V. A. April 22.
" Optatus, B. C. June 4.
" Osith, V. Oct. 7.
" Osmanna, V. Sept. 9.
" Osmund, B. C. Dec. 4.
" Oswald, B. Feb. 29.
" Oswald, King of Northumbria, M. Aug. 5.
" Oswin, King of Deira, M. Aug. 20.
" Othilia, V. A. Dec. 13.
" Otho, B. C. July 2.
" Oudoceus, B. July 2.
" Ouen, B. C. Aug. 24.

P.

St. Pachomius, A. May 14.
" Pacian, B. C. March 9.
" Pacificus of San Severino, Sept. 24.
" Palladius, B. C. July 6.
" Pambo of Nitria, A. Sept. 6.
" Pammachus, C. Aug. 30.
" Pamphilus, M. June 1.
" Pancras, M. May 12.
" Pantænus, Father of the Church, July 7.
" Pantaleon, M. July 27.

St. Paphnutius, B. C. Sept. 11.
" Papoul, M. Nov. 3.
" Paregorius, M (at Patara) Feb. 18.
" Paschal, Baylon, C. May 17.
" Paschasius Radbert, A. C. April 26.
" Pastor, M. Aug. 6.
" Paternus, B. C. April 15.
" Patiens, B. C. Sept. 11.
" Patrick, Apostle of Ireland, B. C. March 17.
" Patricius, B. M. April 28.
" Paul, the first Hermit, Jan. 15.
" Paul and 36 Companions in Egypt, MM. Jan. 18.
" Paul of Verdun, B. C. Feb. 8.
" Paul "the Simple," H. Mar. 7.
" Paul of Leon, B. C. Mar. 12.
" Paul of Narbonne, B. C. Mar. 22.
" Paul of Constantinople, B. M. June 7.
" Paul, M. (at Rome, A. D. 362) June 26.
" Paul, Apostle, June 30.
" Paul, Conversion of, Jan. 25.
" Paul, H. Dec. 20.
" Paul of Gaza, M. July 25.
" Paula, Widow, Jan. 26.
" Paulinus, Patriarch, Jan. 28.
" Paulinus of Nola, B. C. June 22.

St. Paulinus of York, B. C. Oct. 10.
" Pega, V. Jan. 8.
" Pelagia, V. M. June 9.
" Pelagia, Penitent, Oct. 8.
" Peleus, M. Sept. 19.
" Pellegrina, B. Aug. 1.
Blessed Pepin of Landon, C. Feb. 21.
St. Perpetua, M. Mar. 7.
" Perpetuus, B. C. April 8.
" Peter of Pisa, Founder of Hermits of St. Jerom, June 1.
" Peter Balsam, M. Jan. 3.
" Peter of St. Austin's, A. Jan. 6.
" Peter of Sebaste, B. C. Jan. 9.
" Peter Nolasco, C. Jan. 31.
" Peter Damian, B. Feb. 23.
" Peter Gonzales, C. April 15.
" Peter, M. (1252), April 29.
" Peter of Tarentaise, B. May 8.
" Peter Regalati, C. May 13.
" Peter, M. (250), May 15.
" Peter Celestine, Pope, C. May 19.
" Peter, M. (about 304), June 2.
" Peter, Prince of the Apostles, June 29.
" Peter of Luxemburg, B. C. July 5.
" Peter of Alcantara, C. Oct. 19.
St. Peter of Alexandria, B. M. Nov. 26.
" Peter Chrysologus, B. C. Dec. 4.
" Peter Paschal, B. M. Dec. 6.
" Peter ad Vincula, Aug. 1.
SS. Peter and Paul, Dedication of their churches at Rome, Nov. 18.
St. Petroc, A. June 4.
" Petronilla, V. May 31.
" Petronius, B. C. Oct. 4.
" Phæbadius, B. C. April 25.
" Philastrius, B. C. July 18.
" Phileas, B. M. Feb. 4.
" Philibert, A. Aug. 22.
" Philomen, Nov. 22.
" Philoromus, M. Feb. 4.
" Philip, Apostle, May 1.
" Philip Neri, C. May 26.
" Philip "the Deacon," June 6.
" Philip Beniti, C. Aug. 23.
" Philip of Heraclea, B. M. Oct. 22.
" Philogonius, B. C. Dec. 20.
" Phocas, M. July 3.
" Piat, M. Oct. 1.
" Pionius, M. Feb. 1.
" Pius I., Pope, M. July 11.
" Pius V., Pope, M. May 5.
" Placidus, A. M. Oct. 5.
" Plato, A. April 4.
" Plechelm, B. C. July 15.
" Plutarch, M. June 28.
" Pœmen, A. Aug. 27.
" Pollio, M. April 28.

St. Polycarp of Smyrna, B. M. Jan. 26.
" Polyeuctus, M. Feb. 13.
" Pontian, Pope, M. Nov. 19.
" Pontius, M. May 14.
" Poppo, A. Jan. 25.
" Porphyrius, B. C. Feb. 26.
" Postidius, B. C. May 17.
" Potamiana, M. June 28.
" Potamon, B. M. May 18.
" Pothinus of Lyons, M. June 2.
Martyrs of Pontus, Feb. 5.
St. Praxedes, V. July 21.
" Pretextatus, B. C. Feb. 24.
" Primus, M. June 9.
" Prior, H. June 17
" Prisca, V. M. Jan. 18.
" Priscus, M. Mar. 28.
" Prix, B. M. Jan. 25.
" Probus, M. Oct. 11.
" Processus, M. July 2.
" Proclus, B. C. Oct. 24.
" Procopius, M. July 8.
" Projectus, B. M. Jan. 25.
" Prosdecimus, B. M. Nov. 7.
" Prosper of Acquitain, C. June 25.
" Protasius, M. June 19.
" Proterius, B. M. Feb. 28.
" Protus, M. Sept 11.
" Prudentius, B. C. April 6.
" Psalmod, H. Mar. 8.
" Psalmodius, H. June 14.
" Ptolemy, M. Oct. 19.
" Publius, B. M. Jan. 21.
St. Publius, A. (near Zeugma, in Syria), Jan. 25.
" Prudentiana, V. May 19.
" Pulcheria, V. Sept. 10.

Q.

St. Quadratus, B. C. May 26.
" Quintin, M. Oct. 31.
" Quiricus, M. June 16.
" Quirinus, B. M. June 4.

R.

St. Radbod, B. C. Nov. 29.
" Radegundes, Queen of France, Aug 13.
Blessed Raingarda, " the Venerable Widow, June 26.
St. Ralph, B. C. June 21.
" Randaut, M. Feb. 21.
" Raymund of Pennafort, C. Jan. 23.
" Raymund Nonnatus, C. Aug. 31.
" Regina, V. M. Sept. 7.
" Regobert, M. June 4.
" Regulus, B. Mar. 30.
" Remaclus, B. C. Sept. 3.
" Rembert, B. C. Feb. 4.
" Remigius, B. C. Oct. 1.
" Respicius, M. Nov. 10.
" Restituta, V. M. May 17.
" Richard, King of West Saxony, C. Feb. 7.
" Richard, B. C. April 3.
" Richard, B. C. June 9.
" Richard of Andria, B. C. Aug. 21.

St. Richarius or Riquier, A, April 26.
" Rictrudes, A. May 12.
" Rigobert, B. Jan. 4.
Blessed Robert of Arbrissal, C. Feb. 23.
Blessed Robert of Chaise Dieu, A. April 24.
St. Robert, A. April 29.
" Robert of Newminster, A. June 7.
" Rock or Roch, C. Aug. 16.
Blessed Roger, A. Feb. 13.
St. Roger, C. Mar. 5.
" Romanus, Patron of Muscovy, A. Feb. 28.
" Romanus, M. July 24.
" Romanus (Roman Soldier), M. Aug. 9.
" Romanus of Rouen, B. C. Oct. 23.
" Romanus of Palestine, M. Nov. 18.
" Romaric, A. Dec. 8.
" Romuald, A. Feb. 7.
" Rosa of Viterbo, V. Mar. 8.
" Rosalia, V. Sept. 4.
" Rose of Lima, V. Aug. 30.
" Rouin, A. Sept. 7.
" Ruadham, one of the Twelve Apostles of Ireland, B. April 15.
" Ruffin, M. July 24.
" Rufina, V. A. July 10.
" Rufina, V. M. (under Dioclesian), July 20.
" Rufinus, M. June 14.
St. Rufus, H. April [illegible].
" Rufus, M. Dec. 18.
" Rumold, Patron of Mechlin, B. M. July 1.
" Rumon, B. C. Jan. 4.
" Rumwald, C. Nov. 3.
" Rupert or Robert of Saltzburg, B. C. Mar. 27.
" Rusticus, B. Sept. 24.

S.

St. Sabas, M. April 12.
" Sabas, A. Dec. 5.
" Sabina, M. Aug. 29.
" Sabinianus, M. Jan. 29.
" Sabinus, B. M. Dec. 30.
" Sadoth, B. M. Feb. 20.
Saints, All, Nov. 1.
St. Salvius, B. Jan. 11.
" Salvius, B. Sept. 10.
" Sampson, B. C. July 28.
" Samthana, V. A. Dec. 19.
" Sapor, B. M. Nov. 30.
" Saturninus, B. M. Nov. 29.
" Saturninus, M. Feb. 11.
" Saturninus, M. Nov. 29.
" Saturus, M. Mar. 29.
" Scholastica, V. Feb. 10.
" Sebastian, M. Jan. 20.
" Sebbi or Sebba, King of Essex, C. Aug. 29.
" Secundin of Meath, Ireland, B. Nov. 27.
" Secunola, M. (II. century), July 10.
" Senan, B. C. Mar. 8.
" Sennen, M. July 30.

St. Sequanus, A. Sept. 19.
" Serapion, M. Jan. 31.
" Serapion "the Sindonite," Mar. 21.
" Serapion "the Scholastic," A. March 21.
" Serapion, B. C. Mar. 21.
" Serenus, M. Feb. 23.
" Serf, B. April 20.
" Sergius, M. Oct. 7.
" Servatius, B. May 13.
" Servulus, C. Dec. 23.
" Severianus, B. M. Feb. 21.
" Severin, B. C. Oct. 23.
" Severin or Surin, B. Oct. 23.
" Severinus, A. Jan. 8.
" Severinus, A. Feb. 11.
" Sexburg, A. July 6.
" Sidronius, M. Sept. 8.
" Sigebert II., King of Austrasia, C. Feb. 1.
" Sigefride, B. Feb. 15.
" Sigismund, King of Burgundy, M. May 1.
" Silave, B. C. May 17.
" Silverius, Pope, M. June 20.
" Silvin, B. C. Feb. 17.
" Simeon Stylites, C. Jan. 5.
" Simeon, B. M. Feb. 18.
" Simeon of Ctesiphon, B. M. April 17.
" Simeon, July 1.
" Simeon Stylites "the Younger," Sept. 3.
" Simon, an Infant, M. Mar. 24.
" Simon Stock, C. May 16.
St. Simon, Apostle, May 28.
" Simplicius, Pope, C. Mar. 2.
" Simplicius, M. July 29.
" Sina, Deacon, M. Nov. 10.
" Sindulphus, Priest, Oct. 20.
" Siran, A. Dec. 4.
" Sisinnius, M. May 29.
" Sisoes, H. July 4.
" Sixtus I., Pope, M. April 6.
" Sixtus III., Pope, Mar. 28.
" Smaragdus, M. Aug. 8.
" Socrates of Britain, M. Sept. 17.
" Sola, H. Dec. 3.
" Sophia, V. M. April 30.
" Sophronius, B. C. Mar. 11.
" Soter, Pope, M. April 22.
" Soteris, V. M. Feb. 10.
Souls, All, Nov. 2.
St. Speratus, M. July 17.
" Speusippus, M. Jan. 17.
" Spiridion, B. C. Dec. 14.
" Stanislas, B. M. May 7.
" Stanislas Kostka, C. Nov. 13.
" Stephen of Grandmont, A. Feb. 8.
" Stephen, A. Feb. 13.
" Stephen of Citeaux, A. C. April 17.
" Stephen, Pope, M. Aug. 2.
" Stephen, King of Hungary, C. Sept. 2.
" Stephen of Britain, M. Sept. 17.
" Stephen "the Younger," M. Nov. 28.

St. Stephen, Proto-martyr, Dec. 26.
" Stephen, "Invention of his Relics," Aug. 3
" Sulpicius, Pious, B. C. Jan. 17.
" Sulpicius le Débonnaire, B. Jan. 17.
" Sulpicius Severus, Jan. 29.
" Sulpicius, B. Jan. 29.
" Suranus, A. M. Jan. 24.
" Susanna, V. M. Aug. 11.
" Swidbert "the Ancient," B. C. Mar. 1.
" Swithin, B. C. July 15.
" Syagrius, B. C. Aug. 27.
" Sylvester Gozzolini, A. Nov. 26.
" Sylvester, Pope, C. Dec. 31.
" Symmachus, Pope C. July 19.
" Symphorian, M. Aug. 22.
" Symphorosa and her Seven Sons, MM. July 18.
" Syncletica, V. Jan 5.
" Syra, V. June 8.

T.

St. Tanco, B. M. Feb. 16.
" Tarachus, M. Oct. 11.
" Tarasius, Patriarch of Constantinople, C. Feb. 23.
" Tecla, V. A. Oct. 15.
" Telesphorus VII., Pope, M. Jan. 5.
" Teresa, V. Oct. 15.
" Ternan, B. C. June 12.
St. Tertius, M. Dec. 6.
" Thaïs, "the Penitent," Oct. 8.
" Thalassius, M. C. Feb. 22.
" Thalilæus, R. C. Feb. 27.
" Thea, M. July 25.
" Thecla, V. M. Sept. 23.
" Theliau, B. C. Feb. 9.
" Theobald, C. July 1.
" Theobald, A. July 8.
" Theodora, a Greek Saint, Empress, Feb. 11.
" Theodora, V. M. April 28.
" Theodore, B. C. Sept. 19.
" Theodoret, M. Oct. 23.
" Theodorus (Stratilates), M. Feb. 7.
" Theodorus, B. C. April 22.
" Theodorus (Tyro), M. Nov. 9.
" Theodorus "the Studite," A. Nov. 22.
" Theodorus Grapt, C. Dec. 27.
" Theodorus of Tabenna, A. Dec. 28.
" Theodosia of Cæsarea, V. M. April 2.
" Theodosius, Cenobiarch, Jan. 11.
" Theodota, M. Sept. 29.
" Theodotus, M. May 18.
" Theodulus, M. Feb. 17.
" Theonas, B. C. Aug. 23.
" Theophanes, A. C. Mar. 13.
" Theophilus, B. C. Dec. 6.
" Thierri, A. July 1.

St. Thillo, R. Jan. 7.
" Thomas of Aquino, D. C. March 7.
" Thomas of Alexandria, Archb. Aug. 23.
" Thomas of Villanova, B. C. Sept. 18.
" Thomas of Hereford, B. C. Oct. 2.
" Thomas, Apostle, Dec. 21.
" Thomas à Becket, see Becket.
Thomas à Kempis, Nov. 10.
St. Thrasilla, M. Dec. 24.
" Thyrsus, M. Jan. 28.
" Tibba, M. (VII. century) March 6.
" Tibertius, M. Aug. 11.
" Tiburtius, M. April 14.
" Tigernach, B. C. April 5.
" Tilberht, B. C. Sept. 7.
" Timothy, disciple of St. Paul, B. M. Jan. 24.
" Timothy of Cæsarea, M. Aug. 19.
" Timothy of Antioch, M. Aug. 22.
" Titus, B. Jan. 4.
" Tochumra, V. June 11.
" Totnan, M. July 8.
" Tresain, C. Feb. 7.
" Tron, C. Nov. 23.
" Trypho, M. Nov. 10.
" Turiaf, B. July 13.
" Turibius, B. April 16.
" Turninus, C. July 17.
" Tygrius, M. Jan. 12.
St. Tyrannio, M. Feb. 20.

U.

St. Ubaldus, B. May 16.
" Ulfrid, B. M. Jan. 18.
" Ulmar, A. July 20.
" Ulpian, M. April 3.
" Ulrick, R. Feb. 20.
" Ulrick, B. C. July 4.
" Ultan, B. Sept. 4.
" Urban, Pope, M. May 25.
" Ursmar, B. April 19.
" Ursula, M. Oct. 21.

V.

St. Valentine, Priest, M. Feb. 14.
" Valentina, V. M. July 25.
" Valerian, M. April 14.
" Valerian of Lyons, M. Sept. 4.
" Valery, A. Dec. 12.
" Vandrille, A. July 22.
" Vaneng, C. Jan. 9.
" Vanne, B. C. Nov. 9.
" Vauge or Vaught, H. June 15.
" Vedast, B. C. Feb. 6.
" Venantius, M. May 18.
" Venerand, M. (in Normandy), May 25.
" Verda, V. M. Feb. 21.
" Veronica of Milan, V. Jan. 13.
" Veronica Giuliani, V. July 9.
*** Vettius Epagatus, M. June 2.

St. Victor of Arcis, H. C. Feb. 26.
" Victor, M. April 12.
" Vietor, M. (early) May 8.
" Victor of Marseilles, M. July 21.
" Victor, Pope, M. July 28.
" Victoria, V. M. Dec. 23.
" Victorian, M. Mar. 23.
" Victoricus, M. Dec. 11.
" Victorinus, M. Feb. 25.
" Victorinus, B. M. Nov. 2.
" Vigilius, B. M. June 26.
" Vimin, B. C. Jan. 21.
" Vincent or Vivian, M. Jan. 22.
" Vincent Ferrer, C. April 5.
" Vincent of Lerins, C. May 24.
" Vincent, M. June 9.
" Vincent de Paul, C. July 19.
" Virgil, B. C. Nov. 27.
" Vitalis, M. April 28.
" Vitalis, M. Nov. 4.
" Vitus, B. C. Feb. 5.
" Vitus, M. June 15.
" Vulgan, C. Nov. 2.
" Vulsin, B. C. Jan. 8.

W.

St. Walburge, V. A. Feb. 25.
" Walstan, C. May 30.
" Walter, A. May 8.
" Walter, A. June 4.
" Walthen, A. C. Aug. 3.
" Waltrude, Widow, April 9.
" Wasnulf, C. Oct. 1.
St. Wenceslas, Duke of Bohemia, M. Sept. 28.
" Wenefride, V. M. Nov. 3.
" Wereburge, V. A. Feb. 3.
" Werenfrid, C. Nov. 7.
" Wigbert, A. C. Aug. 13.
" Wilfrid of York, B. C. Oct. 12.
" Willehad, B. C. Nov. 8.
" William, B. C. Jan. 10.
" William of Maleval, H. Feb. 10.
" William of Norwich, M. Mar. 24.
" William of Eskille, A. C. April 6.
" William, B. C. June 8.
" William of Monte Vergine, June 25.
" William of Brieuc, B. C. July 29.
" William of Roschild, B. C. Sept. 2.
" Willibald, B. C. July 7.
" Willibrord, B. C. Nov. 7.
" Winebald, A. Dec. 18.
" Winoc, A. Nov. 6.
" Winwaloe, A. Mar. 3.
" Wiro, B. May 8.
" Wistan, M. June 1.
" Witen, see Guy.
" Withburge, V. July 8.
" Wolfgang, B. Oct. 31.
" Wulfhad, M. July 24.
" Wulfhilde, V. A. Dec. 9.
" Wulfran, B. Mar. 20.
" Wulstan, B. C. Jan. 19.

X.

St. Xistus, see Sixtus I.

Y.

Blessed Yvo of Chartres, B. C. May 20.

St. Yvo, C. (1353), May 22.

Z.

St. Zachary, Pope, C. Mar. 15.

" Zachæus, M. (under Dioclesian), Nov. 18.

St. Zeno, B. C. April 12.

" Zeno, M. (at Gaza), Sept. 8.

" Zenobius, B. C. Oct. 20.

" Zenobius, M. Feb. 20.

" Zephyrinus, Pope, M. Aug. 26.

" Zita, V. April 27.

" Zoticus, B. M. July 21.

" Zozimus of Syracuse, B. Mar. 30.

" Zozimus, M. (116). Dec. 18.

Readers must not think this list comprises *all* of the Canonized Saints, for it does not. There are many others, this list naming only the more noted ones.

GENERAL INDEX

N

P